Raising the World

SARA FIELDSTON

Raising the World

Child Welfare in the American Century

HARVARD UNIVERSITY PRESS
Cambridge, Massachusetts, and London, England   2015

Library of Congress Cataloging-in-Publication Data

Fieldston, Sara, 1983–
   Raising the world : child welfare in the American century / Sara Fieldston.
     pages cm
   Includes bibliographical references and index.
   ISBN 978-0-674-36809-5 (alk. paper)
  1. Child welfare—United States—History—20th century. 2. Child rearing—
United States—History—20th century. I. Title.
   HV881.F52   2015
   362.7—dc23   2014028417

To my mother and grandmother,
Nina Woldin and Gloria Fondiller

Contents

Author's Note

THIS BOOK draws frequently on letters exchanged between foreign children and their American friends. Only a tiny fraction of such letters has been preserved in the papers of organizations or recopied in internal letters or publicity materials. Those that did survive are likely not representative; they had often been singled out because they were perceived as extraordinary. On occasion, letters from children overseas can be found in individuals' personal papers. These notes, in their ordinariness, likely reflect the majority of letters that passed between foster parents and their children: gifts are acknowledged and gratitude expressed; school progress is reported; the passage of seasons and the celebration of holidays are noted. This mundane correspondence reflects a remarkable fact: for thousands of children around the world, writing a letter to a stranger in the United States was a regular obligation, sometimes one that persisted until adulthood.

Letters to American foster parents and friends provide valuable insight into the lives of children, whose perspectives are often overlooked by historians. But they are slippery sources. Written as a mandatory part of larger programs of material aid, it is difficult to discern which letters express "genuine" sentiment and which reflect what letter writers thought recipients might want to hear. Any given letter might have been written by a child independently, might have been the product of coercion, or might have even been penned by an adult. Child sponsorship agencies enlisted caretakers to compose letters on behalf of children too young to write, a fact usually but not always indicated in the letters themselves. Voluntary workers sometimes copied portions of children's letters into reports or publicity materials, and it is impossible to know if they did so faithfully. In addition, children wrote letters in their native languages, and agency staff translated them into English. Nevertheless, reading carefully and keeping these limitations in mind, it is still possible to use letters to glean insights into what children said and felt—and into what children and adults alike thought they had to say.

A note on language: Prior to the 1960s, child sponsorship programs were commonly referred to as "adoption" programs. Unless indicated, references to "adoption" refer to child sponsorship, not legal adoption. Likewise, the terms "foster parents" and "sponsors" refer to people who chose to participate in child sponsorship programs. In the case of children and foster parents not already in the public record, only first names have been used.

Raising the World

Prologue

Tales of Love and Global Power

IN 1968, a twelve-year-old Korean girl, Soon Ok, penned a letter to Casey Miller, an American woman she had never met:

> Although you are far from here, I feel like you are living with me in my mind all the time. . . . I know the fact that your love for me is so deep and wide that it is beyond description. I cannot think out a way by means of which I might do something to reciprocate your love at present. I just think it will be good enough to make you pleased with me if I try to study industriously and to be a fine citizen who can serve our country and help needy people with love.[1]

Soon Ok had been abandoned as an infant on the streets of Pusan amid the social upheaval that followed the Korean War.[2] Miller, a writer and an editor, was one of scores of Americans who responded to calls from U.S. voluntary agencies to act as so-called foster parents to children overseas, a fictive relationship of kin cultivated through the exchange of letters, parcels, and, ideally, love. Through child sponsorship programs, American foster parents committed to support from afar a particular foreign child for a certain period of time.

Miller exchanged letters with a series of international foster children for more than thirty years. The first was Nadine, a little French girl, whom she began sponsoring in 1951. When Nadine reached adulthood, Miller began sponsoring Soon Ok in Korea. She then served as a foster parent to Mei Ying, a Chinese refugee girl in Hong Kong. Finally, Miller sponsored Edith, a youngster in Buenaventura, Colombia. Through the years, Miller was privy to an intimate portrait of foreign childhoods. She heard about pets, favorite games, holiday celebrations, and academic successes and frustrations. She also received letters that were more difficult to read: stories of the death of loved ones, the hardships of poverty, and the loneliness of being without biological kin. Miller supported each of her foreign foster children until they reached adulthood or no longer required her assistance. She continued to correspond with some of the youngsters even after their official sponsorship programs had ended.

During the three decades following World War II, American voluntary agencies initiated a panoply of programs designed to improve the lives of foreign youngsters. Groups including the American Friends Service Committee, the American Jewish Joint Distribution Committee, Christian Children's Fund, Foster Parents' Plan, Save the Children Federation, and the Unitarian Service Committee established programs to assist both orphans and poor children living with their families. Child sponsorships, which collected funds from an individual American donor to provide for a particular youngster's care and schooling, were the public face of overseas child welfare. Heeding voluntary agencies' calls for foster parents, Americans such as Miller sponsored tens of thousands of children around the world during the latter half of the twentieth century.

While sponsorships were the most publicized and visible element of American overseas child welfare, they were but one component of voluntary groups' programs for children abroad. American agencies also supported orphanages, redesigning homes already in existence and constructing new buildings that reflected the latest theories of institutional care. They set up nursery schools, where young children could engage in stimulating activities. They helped children and their families obtain education and vocational training. And they educated foreign parents, teachers, and social workers in "modern" childcare theories, stressing the importance of play and the primacy of children's psychological health.

These child welfare programs were humanitarian gestures with the aim of relieving human suffering. They were also political projects. American child welfare efforts publicly displayed the United States' concern for the social welfare of all peoples. They showcased values—love of family, protection for the vulnerable, and concern for individual growth and expression—widely considered by American commentators to epitomize the democratic way of life. Programs for children generated goodwill, connecting the world's youngest citizens to the United States through bonds of personal friendship. Most importantly, overseas child welfare projects served as a form of social engineering. When Soon Ok described Miller's love as inspiring her to be a good citizen, she articulated, perhaps unknowingly, one of the core goals of American child welfare programs overseas. Voluntary workers from the United States looked to child rearing as a means of molding a new generation that would promote political freedom and stimulate economic development. Individual transformations would be the engine of global change, and political and economic revolutions would emerge from the personal drama of human development.

Ideas about child rearing, personality development, and the family shaped Americans' understanding of their role—and the role of the United States—within the postwar world. The United States emerged from World War II with unprecedented military, economic, and cultural power, a global dominance that fueled an outpouring of aid to the perceived less fortunate overseas. The U.S. government spearheaded programs such as the Marshall Plan, which offered aid to Europe, and the Point IV program, which extended aid to the developing world. These programs channeled billions of dollars abroad in the name of helping suffering people—and as a means of preventing the spread of communism. But the years between 1945 and 1949 also saw the birth of nearly two hundred new private voluntary organizations working overseas, the majority based in the United States. With the support of the American public, U.S. voluntary agencies offered succor to foreign populations in the form of food packages, clothing, and medicines.[3]

As foreign aid workers initiated programs of relief and rehabilitation, child welfare experts popularized new understandings of human development, some of which emerged from children's experiences during the war. These theories cast childhood as a critical period of personality formation and described the family as essential to the development of healthy people and to the creation of good democratic citizens. Children raised with love, stability, and individualized attention would grow into strong members of the free world; those maturing in the absence of these familial comforts would become adults susceptible to the lures of totalitarian leaders. Child welfare programs, then, were at once a means of helping the vulnerable and a way to reshape the postwar world in the image of the United States.

Fueled by the twin goals of saving children and uplifting nations, American humanitarianism expanded in tandem with U.S. global hegemony during the latter half of the twentieth century. American voluntary agencies' child welfare programs aimed to win the "hearts and minds" of the world's youngest citizens. They also sought to mold children with the personal characteristics, such as emotional stability and independent thought, seen as bolstering democratic regimes. Child welfare efforts invited Americans to support and participate in the United States' expansionist postwar foreign policy even as the ostensibly private nature of child rearing and the family cloaked these programs' political ambitions in the mantle of love and benevolence. When Christian Children's Fund (CCF), the largest child sponsorship agency in the postwar United States, boasted that "the sun never sets on the orphanages of CCF," the agency conveyed both the breadth of its far-flung child welfare projects and its own quasi-imperial ambitions. Sponsorship programs provided Americans with a seemingly intimate connection to foreign lands, forging international relationships that were sometimes rich and emotionally textured. At the same time, they naturalized the United States' role as global parent charged with bringing up a family of nations.

At the forefront of American child welfare efforts overseas was a cadre of experts devoted to improving the care of children across the globe. While some served short stints abroad, many spent the majority of their careers outside of the United States. Evelyn Peters started working for the American Jewish Joint Distribution Committee (JDC) in 1956, when she was thirty-three years old. A native of Milwaukee who had taught child development and early education courses at the University of California, Berkeley, Peters's first posting was Iran, where she trained the local staffs of the JDC's day nurseries. Peters's work with the JDC took her to Morocco, Tunisia, and across Europe, where she established early childhood education programs. In 1967, Peters helped author a handbook for child-care workers in developing countries that remained in use for decades to come. By 2001, when she passed away, Peters had served as the JDC's country director in Tunisia, Algeria, and India.[4]

Like Peters, Helen Tieszen, an educator with degrees in child development and early childhood education from the University of Minnesota, spent the majority of her career overseas. Tieszen arrived in war-ravaged Korea in 1955, where she conducted training courses for orphanage workers. She spent the majority of the next four decades in the country, teaching courses on child care and development. Tieszen remained involved in Korean child welfare even after her retirement, serving as the editor of a Korean journal of child studies until 2009.[5]

Americans across the country supported the work of child-care professionals such as Tieszen and Peters. By writing letters to children, sending gifts, and contributing toward the establishment of orphanages and schools, ordinary Americans taught themselves and their counterparts around the world to view the United States as the world's guardian and provider. And they came to understand foreign diplomacy as a responsibility that extended well beyond official government channels.[6] "The close of the war found the United States of America the Number 1 power in the world. With this power comes responsibility for world affairs far beyond any ever assumed heretofore by our country. This compels our interest in other countries and their peoples if we are to fulfill the obligation we have to them and ourselves," argued Omer Carmichael, superintendent of the Louisville, Kentucky public schools, explaining the decision to make efforts to assist children overseas an integral part of the school system's curriculum in 1948.[7] Child-care experts working abroad, together with Americans across the country, expanded America's global reach even as they suggested that the United States was extending only the sheltering hands of friendship.

*   *   *

America's role in transnational adoption is well known. During the latter half of the twentieth century, American families legally adopted thousands of children from abroad. In the process, they reshaped contemporary understandings of kinship and spurred a robust dialogue about the intersection between the ostensibly private realm of the family and global inequalities of power. American efforts to assist children in their lands of origin, however, have received far less attention.[8] Many American voluntary workers who established programs for children overseas saw their efforts as complementing transnational adoption: not all needy foreign children could find new homes in the United States. But if the stated objective of transnational adoption was to improve the lives of individual youngsters (and to satisfy the American demand for adoptable children), the goals of child sponsorship and other programs for children residing overseas were often far loftier. American voluntary agencies sought to mold children and, through them, to remake nations. These efforts helped shape the way a generation of Americans understood the power of child rearing and the place of the United States within the world community.

By linking personal and national development, American child welfare workers crafted a role for themselves—and for thousands of ordinary Americans—in U.S. foreign affairs. American voluntary agencies endowed women's traditional child-rearing duties with global significance and gave foreign mothers and child-care workers an expanded part to play in national reconstruction and development. At the same time, international child welfare projects opened the lives of children and their caretakers, particularly mothers, to increased scrutiny and control. And while many voluntary workers believed that foreign governments should expand their social welfare responsibilities, their emphasis on individual psychology cast international development as a personal, familial project, rather than the responsibility of the state.

Suffering foreign children have long served as icons of need, striking symbols of the shameful gap between the First World and the Third. And destitute youngsters have lured more than American money overseas: the trope of saving women and children has often been used to justify American military interventions in foreign lands. The image of the suffering child—helpless, in pain, and alone—is a central component of what the historian Laura Briggs refers to as "the visual iconography of rescue," a powerful symbol that structures the way Americans understand their country's relationship with the rest of the world.[9] But behind the image of the suffering child was a shadow image—that of the foreign child as political actor. American agencies solicited funds for children because they were understood to be helpless and innocent. But they also focused on children because they were perceived to be malleable. Given the proper upbringing, many American workers argued, youngsters were the most promising agents to guide their countries into a free and prosperous future. Maturing under the wrong influence, children had the potential to upend the global order.

The perceived connections between child rearing and national development were present in the United States from the country's very beginning. In the decades following the American Revolution, a cultural discourse elevated mothers as the shapers of future citizens. But the political significance of child rearing—and the perceived malleability of youngsters—sometimes justified programs that removed children from the influence of their parents altogether. During the nineteenth century, "orphan trains" transported children, some of whom were not truly orphans, from urban slums to new families out West. Schools for Native American children separated young-sters from their families, sometimes by force, as a means of encouraging their assimilation into mainstream society.[10]

In the hands of foreign missionaries, the connections between child rearing and the social order writ large went global. Some saw saving children as a means of uplifting and "civilizing" entire populations. One missionary, writing in 1888, described young people as "the leaven . . . [which] shall leaven the whole mass." By the early twentieth century, missionaries were joined by humanitarian workers offering succor to populations displaced by war and other crises. During World War I, American agencies extended aid to children in war-torn Europe. Other foreign conflicts, particularly the Spanish Civil War (1936–1939) and the Second Sino-Japanese War (1937–1945), cat-alyzed American aid to children overseas, some of it administered for the first time through programs of child sponsorship.[11]

Efforts to help children in war-torn or developing countries were not con-fined to Americans. Canada, Great Britain, and many other countries es-tablished international child welfare programs during the twentieth century. In fact, Great Britain's Save the Children Fund pioneered the sponsorship system in the 1920s. Save the Children Fund, and the eponymous organi-zations it inspired in Commonwealth nations including Canada and Aus-tralia, continued to use child sponsorship as a fund-raising tool into the post–World War II era. But the emphasis on familial affection and friendship so integral to American child welfare organizations was not shared to the same extent by their international peers. Newsletters published by the Com-monwealth Save the Children Funds during the postwar years rarely mention the sponsorship system explicitly. By contrast, Save the Children Federation, the American offshoot, regularly published newsletters replete with stories about foster parents and their adopted youngsters. While international friendship projects enjoyed support across the globe, only in the United States did voluntary groups tie international child welfare so inextricably to the rhetoric of love and mutual affection. In situating the United States at the head of an affectionate family of nations, American humanitarian organizations offered their supporters a way of understanding the newly ascendant world power's place—and their own position—on a transformed global stage.[12]

The United Nations also entered the field of international child welfare. The United Nations Children's Fund (UNICEF) established welfare programs around the world beginning in 1946, many of which focused on improving child and maternal health. The UN also passed the Declaration of the Rights of the Child in 1959 and the Convention on the Rights of the Child in 1989, enshrining children's status as vulnerable beings worthy of special rights and protections.[13]

Yet the idea that children's vulnerability made them worthy of special treatment was actually a relatively new one in the post–World War II era. Prior to the late nineteenth century, even as reformers and child-care experts connected the fate of children to the fate of nations, children were accorded few special rights; for many, childhood was a time for work, not for learning or play. As the nineteenth century waned, however, declining rates of child labor and infant mortality helped transform children from economically valuable to economically "worthless" but emotionally "priceless" beings. Western thinkers began to understand childhood as a biologically and psychologically distinct phase of life properly isolated from the troubles and productive labor of the adult world. Building on these ideas, psychologists and other child welfare experts developed a comprehensive understanding of children's basic welfare that considered both physical and emotional needs. While this understanding of childhood enjoyed varying levels of acceptance among parents and other caregivers, the idea that children had distinct needs—and the notion that some of these needs were psychological in nature—had by the mid-twentieth century gained widespread credence among American child care professionals.[14]

American child welfare workers made it their mission to spread this understanding of childhood around the world.[15] Children's presumed innocence and helplessness added impetus to American efforts to save them. It also rendered child welfare efforts morally unimpeachable: children, unlike their elders, were by nature blameless victims. American child welfare programs thus sought to mold political subjects even as the perceived universality and vulnerability of childhood made them appear private, altruistic, and apolitical.

Postwar culture, as historians such as Elaine Tyler May have demonstrated, positioned the nuclear family as a haven of security in a threatening world. But the ideal of the family was just as apt to encourage Americans to set their sights across the ocean as it was to narrow their focus to the confines of the home. It was just as likely to provide expanded professional opportunities for female social workers and educators as it was to discourage the employment of women in the public sphere. For many Americans, the family served not only as a retreat from the anxiety and uncertainty of the Cold War world but also as a means of reshaping that world. Indeed, the United States' well-known strategy of containment took place alongside a less-studied effort to fight communism by uniting the free world through the bonds of love and friendship.[16]

During the 1950s and 1960s, the United States undertook a number of ambitious projects with the goal of "modernizing" the developing world. Guided by a series of beliefs often referred to as modernization theory, government officials and private voluntary workers alike dammed rivers, built roads, and introduced new ways of growing crops and breeding cattle. American development experts also sought to change the way local people thought about both themselves and their environment, promoting, in the words of David Ekbladh, the "modernization of mind."[17]

Historians of modernization have scrutinized American-led development efforts across the globe and carefully charted the ideas and assumptions that supported them. But they have said little about the role of women and children within the modernization project. This perhaps should not be surprising: the vast majority of the government officials and social scientists involved in overseas development during the 1950s and 1960s looked to men in developing countries as the primary agents of modernization. When John Kenneth Galbraith, writing about India in 1957, contrasted the "world of the women's quarter, of the extended family" to "the world of the Second Five-Year Plan and government files and public service," he conjured vividly not only the dichotomy of traditionalism and modernity but also the opposition of female and male, of the private sphere of the family and the public universe of government planning. As Catherine V. Scott has argued, becoming modern involved moving from the backward-looking, female-centered household to the forward-looking, male-dominated public sphere.[18]

But in fact, women were central to the modernization project. Many of the American voluntary agencies active in overseas development work looked to projects on behalf of children and their female caretakers as the key to promoting social and economic progress overseas. And a good number of the social workers, educators, and other voluntary personnel employed by these agencies were women. These American voluntary workers situated the private sphere not as a relic of traditionalism but as an active and fertile site for interventions aimed at shaping a generation psychologically equipped to launch the developing world into the future. They looked to methods of child rearing as a means of imbuing foreign citizens with the personality traits they understood as conducive to national progress. Development projects were not the exclusive domain of government officials and technocrats; they involved a larger and more diverse cast than historians have recognized.

* * *

Even as American voluntary groups united around the goals of stimulating international development and promoting democracy, they pursued divergent approaches to assisting children overseas. Christian Children's Fund, the most politically conservative of the groups under consideration, focused on supporting children in institutions. Foster Parents' Plan supported some children in orphanages but devoted the bulk of its work to helping children living with their families. Save the Children Federation, meanwhile, assisted only children living at home. The American Friends Service Committee, the American Jewish Joint Distribution Committee, and the Unitarian Service Committee—organizations on the more liberal end of the political spectrum—reached children through schools, day nurseries, and neighborhood centers. Many other American groups, including the International Friendship League, the Girl Scouts, the World Jewish Congress, and the American-Korean Foundation, joined these organizations in their attempts to build international friendships and improve the lives of children overseas.

These groups participated in two distinct but overlapping projects. First, they attempted to improve on and professionalize the care of children around the world, providing foreign social workers, child-care workers, teachers, and parents with training in the latest theories of child psychology and methods of child rearing. Second, they sought to forge international friendships that bound the United States to its allies overseas with ties of love and kinship—as well as with gifts and material aid. International friendships supported American efforts to improve foreign child care, as they were seen as providing youngsters with the emotional security and individualized attention necessary for their healthy psychological development. And programs to improve child care were seen as bolstering international friendship, as American social workers and child-care experts worked alongside their foreign counterparts to impart the "latest" child welfare knowledge.

In the decades following World War II, many American programs on be-half of foreign children evolved from programs of assistance to individual youngsters to efforts designed to uplift whole families and communities. They shifted from providing relief to war-torn areas to establishing long-term de-velopment projects with the goal of addressing deeply entrenched problems such as poverty and hunger. American agencies also followed shifting inter-national currents, setting up programs in areas of the world perceived to be of importance to U.S. foreign relations. But the permanence of the institu-tions they established, coupled with some groups' commitment to assisting children until they reached maturity, meant that many groups were only somewhat nimble in following geopolitical shifts. For example, programs for children in southern European countries such as Greece and Italy, established in the 1940s, continued for decades, even as memories of such events as the Greek Civil War faded into memory. Likewise, the surge of American in-terest in East Asia in the wake of the Communist revolution in China and the Korean War led to the establishment of many child welfare programs in the region during the 1950s. Many of these programs still existed well into the 1970s, even as the center of gravity for Cold War concerns shifted away from East Asia. Moreover, while geopolitics provided a guide for geo-graphic expansion, so too did the particular interests of voluntary groups themselves. The JDC, for example, worked only in areas with sizable Jewish communities.

At the heart of American child welfare agencies' efforts overseas was the belief that child rearing was a means of effectuating larger political changes. Voluntary workers and the Americans who supported their work remained united in this belief, even as they sometimes disagreed regarding the vision of the world they sought to create. Enlisting the science of human develop-ment in the service of remaking the world, voluntary agencies helped forge a new role for the United States on the global stage. American efforts on behalf of foreign children bolstered U.S. power even as they recast it as humanitarianism—and even as they ultimately revealed its limits and internal tensions. The world's children were at once humanity's most vulnerable members and the seeds of a new global order.

CHAPTER ONE

Manufacturing the Citizens of the World

THROUGHOUT THE SPRING OF 1944, as Allied troops prepared for the D-Day assault on Normandy, a group of Americans gathered to plot their own attack on Nazism. Inside the walls of Columbia University's College of Physicians and Surgeons, psychologists, anthropologists, sociologists, and educators planned for the reformation of Germany after the war. Much attention had been given to Germany's military, political, and economic institutions, the scholars noted. But to truly erase Hitler's legacy required something more—it required a change in German people themselves. Nazism grew out of an aggressiveness deeply rooted in the German character, a personality trait passed down from generation to generation. Eradicating fascism, then, required disrupting the process of cultural transmission. To accomplish this would demand intervention in the rearing of children. The scholars recommended training German parents in new methods of child care. They suggested establishing preschools and extracurricular programs for German youngsters. As military leaders aimed their weapons and tanks at the beaches of France, conference participants set their sights on nurseries, schools, and orphanages in Germany and across the war-ravaged world.[1]

The scholars who convened at Columbia University were no strangers to the significance of childhood. Anthropologist Margaret Mead's studies of child rearing and adolescence in New Guinea and Samoa had made her a household name during the late 1920s and 1930s. Behavioral scientist Lawrence K. Frank was the former director of the child development program at the Rockefeller Foundation and was involved in the founding of *Parents'* magazine. Marion E. Kenworthy, a psychiatrist who specialized in the field of children's mental health, had worked with American voluntary groups to assist European refugee children during the early war years. Pediatrician Frank Spooner Churchill had recently authored a proposal urging the U.S. government to prioritize child guidance clinics as it established reconstruction agencies in postwar Europe. Psychologist Erik Erikson, who would soon publish his groundbreaking book on developmental psychology, *Childhood and Society*, was also involved in the planning of the Germany after the War conference, though he was unable to attend in person.[2]

Driving these scholars' interest in children was the conviction that human difference was rooted in culture rather than blood. These individuals rejected the claims of eugenicists who understood personal characteristics as governed by heredity. An individual's personality was not predetermined at birth, they argued, but bore the indelible stamp of early childhood experiences. This belief invited, in the words of historian Joanne Meyerowitz, "a biopolitics of child rearing."[3] Anxieties over who gave birth to children were replaced by concerns regarding how and by whom children were reared. It was those who molded the malleable matter of childhood who ultimately determined the nature of adult personality—and, by extension, the shape of nations.

During the Second World War, intellectuals and child-care experts on both sides of the Atlantic developed and popularized new theories regarding the needs of children and the connection between methods of child care, the family, and the larger social order. These theories reshaped best practices for child care in the United States, placing a new emphasis on emotional health and tying children's well-being to the family, particularly to mothers. They also profoundly influenced the American social workers, psychologists, and educators who would travel abroad in the years directly following the war. American relief workers who journeyed to war-torn Europe and Japan located the roots of both democracy and totalitarianism in the experiences of early childhood. They looked to the family, to social work, and to child-rearing practices as a means of reforming society at large.

But even as child-care experts extolled the family as the key both to youngsters' healthy development and to the rehabilitation of the postwar world, they also fretted over the harmful influence of parents unschooled in "modern" precepts of child rearing. If parents were responsible for forging strong democratic citizens, they also had the power to create the next generation of fascists. As the primary institution responsible for shaping young minds, the family emerged from the war more loved—and more mistrusted—than ever.

THE EXPERTS' ADVICE

American understandings of the family's influence on children changed over time. During the opening decades of the twentieth century, the influential eugenics movement asserted that parents bequeathed a bevy of immutable physical and mental characteristics to their children. To "have really good children," explained David Starr Jordan, a leading eugenicist and the chancellor of Stanford University in 1914, "the parents must be of good stock themselves. Bad fruit is borne mainly by bad trees, and the inheritance of badness springs from inherent tendencies." Eugenicists aimed to encourage those of "good stock" to procreate and discourage those likely to bear "bad fruit" from doing so. But not all early twentieth-century thinkers saw children of questionable parentage as helpless prisoners of their heredity. Reformers who set up day nurseries to care for poor and immigrant children did so in the belief that they could instill in these malleable youngsters better habits, values, and personality traits than those learned at home. Children would serve as emissaries carrying new patterns of thought and behavior back to their parents.[4]

During the interwar years, this notion of childhood's plasticity gained ground on eugenicists' convictions about the importance of heredity. John Watson, a behavioral psychologist whose advice manuals for parents propelled his rise to prominence in the 1920s, famously claimed that he could take any infant at random and mold him into a doctor, an artist, or a thief, regardless of his background. As Watson understood it, children were blank slates, and parents, particularly mothers, had the ability to determine their personalities. But precisely because they wielded this great power, parents' interactions with their young ones were to be strictly circumscribed. In order to ensure that children's nascent characters developed properly, Watson and his fellow behaviorists prescribed rigid schedules of care and feeding. Watson warned that showing children too much affection would spoil them and render them emotionally unprepared to function in the world. Calling excessive mother love dangerous, he instructed mothers to greet children with a handshake rather than a kiss. Watson fantasized about rotating babies among different mothers or nurses so that they did not grow too attached to a single caregiver.[5]

As Watson and other experts promoted an approach to child rearing that paid little heed to children's psychological well-being, another group of specialists focused primarily on children's emotional health. For the psychiatrists, psychologists, and social workers who constituted the new "child guidance" movement, psychological security was the key to children's healthy development, and parents were essential to providing this security. In their view, childhood misbehavior stemmed from emotional disturbances, and parents and educators ought to prevent those disturbances. "We can no longer get the satisfaction of blaming the child; we must stop and think what made him misbehave," asserted educational psychologist Caroline Zachry in 1934. Through clinics established across the country, and through the child-focused, experiential programs of progressive education championed by John Dewey and his colleagues, the ideas promoted by the child guidance movement gained a wide audience by the 1940s and 1950s.[6]

Behaviorists like Watson and proponents of the child guidance movement like Zachry differed in their basic philosophies of child care. But they shared a belief in children's inherent malleability. This belief reflected a larger intellectual shift within the social sciences. Beginning in the late 1920s, an influential group of scholars associated with the "culture-and-personality" school began to dismantle biological theories. Casting aside eugenics, they described adult personality as the product of cultural conditioning during childhood. Scholars associated with the culture-and-personality school, among them Margaret Mead and Lawrence K. Frank, wove together anthropology, psychiatry, and psychoanalytic theory to argue that cultural-specific child-rearing patterns were responsible for all varieties of human difference.[7]

The implications of this new understanding of human difference were not lost on governments: if personality was malleable, then transforming individuals offered a route to reforming society at large. As the twentieth century progressed, governments sought to marshal the social sciences to further their own political agendas. From war making to social welfare projects, nations projected their transformative ambitions, in the words of Greg Eghigian, Andreas Killen, and Christine Leuenberger, "not only *on*to society but also *in*to individuals."[8] When the United States entered World War II, the government called on psychologists and other social scientists to examine recruits, treat injured servicemen, and conduct research on propaganda and public opinion. U.S. government officials also relied on studies of "national character" conducted by culture-and-personality scholars who scrutinized early childhood experiences in an effort to understand the psychological and cultural underpinnings of adult group behavior. For example, anthropologist Geoffrey Gorer argued that Russians' alleged rage originated in the practice of swaddling infants and that the supposed compulsiveness of the Japanese was a product of strict routines of toilet training. The United States Children's Bureau solicited information from anthropologists, including Gorer, Margaret Mead, and Ruth Benedict, regarding European child-rearing practices and the "psychological and cultural factors" to take into consideration when planning programs of postwar relief and reconstruction. Culture-and-personality scholars sometimes took issue with one another's conclusions. In particular, some scholars dismissed Gorer's focus on infancy as "diaper-ology," insisting that personality formation continued well into childhood and beyond. Others criticized the very notion of "national character" as homogenizing, a critique that would gain momentum during the early 1950s. But the culture-and-personality school's basic premise—that human differences were not innate but stemmed from cultural conditioning, particularly during the formative years—was widely accepted by midcentury.[9]

As culture-and-personality scholars looked to methods of child rearing to explain individual and national differences, American ideas about how to rear children were themselves changing. By the 1940s and 1950s, the child guidance movement's emphasis on children's psychological health had eclipsed the behaviorists' focus on habit formation. Child welfare professionals now promoted a more "natural" and "child-centered" approach that took as its main goal the satisfaction of children's emotional needs.[10] This approach was bolstered by a new body of literature on child growth and development stimulated by World War II. City evacuations, parents' service in the military and war industries, and the persecution of Jews and other ethnic groups fractured European families and deprived great numbers of children of parental care. War nurseries and other group homes served as "living laboratories" for psychologists interested in studying the effects of children's separation from their parents.

The Hampstead Nurseries in England, under the direction of Anna Freud and Dorothy Burlingham, were at the epicenter of this research. Austrian-born Freud had studied psychoanalysis with her father, Sigmund Freud; Burlingham, an American, had moved to Vienna in 1925 to study psychoanalysis at the Vienna Institute. Joined by many of their colleagues, Freud and Burlingham left Vienna following the Nazi invasion in 1938 and resettled in England. With financial support from an American voluntary agency, Foster Parents' Plan for War Children (PLAN), Freud and Burlingham established the Hampstead Nurseries in 1940. The Nurseries comprised three children's homes, two in London and one in Essex, which provided care to children of all nationalities who had become parentless due to the war, either temporarily or permanently.[11]

Freud and Burlingham's observations of their young wards formed the basis of several influential works on children's personality development and on the effects of maternal deprivation. Infants and young children in the residential nursery, Freud and Burlingham noted, developed at a different rate than that of their peers who were raised in families. Infants in the nursery enjoyed some developmental advantages with regard to weight gain and motor skill development. But intellectually and emotionally, the psychologists argued, motherless infants' growth was seriously stunted. Young children without mothers had difficulty forming habits such as toilet training, exhibited delays in speech, and—most significantly—had trouble forging lasting emotional bonds. Drawing on psychoanalytic theory, Freud and Burlingham argued that humans modeled all intimate relationships on the loving relationship first experienced with their mothers. Young children for whom these maternal bonds were broken or nonexistent would grow into adulthood emotionally stunted, unable to form meaningful interpersonal connections. Just as malnutrition during the formative years led to lasting physical ailments, the psychologists maintained, lack of maternal love during the first few years of childhood would result in persistent psychological deformities.[12]

Freud and Burlingham acknowledged that parental separation was often unavoidable and that, particularly during wartime, children's institutions filled an important need. To combat the doleful effects of maternal deprivation, the psychologists suggested that infants and young children in residential nurseries be assigned to an artificial family of three to five children under the care of a single child-care worker. This individual would serve as a "mother substitute," providing the emotional stability and personal attachment that babies and young children needed to grow into healthy adults. Freud and Burlingham believed that fathers, in addition to mothers, played a role in their children's emotional development; but they assumed that mothers would be young children's primary caretakers, and they described maternal bonds as more crucial to a child's development than paternal ones.[13]

Psychologists on both sides of the Atlantic echoed and elaborated on Freud and Burlingham's findings on the deleterious effects of maternal deprivation. In 1948, the World Health Organization commissioned British psychologist and psychoanalyst John Bowlby to write a report on the mental state of Europe's displaced children. Bowlby's study, published in 1951 as *Maternal Care and Mental Health,* drew on meetings he conducted with child-care workers in the United States, Britain, and several countries in continental Europe. Like Freud and Burlingham, Bowlby described maternal love as essential to children's healthy development. Infants and young children separated from their mothers, he argued, were likely to suffer deep psychological scars from which they might never recover. Bowlby's influential work put emotional maladjustment on par with physical disease and rendered deprived children not only pitiable but also potentially threatening to society. "Deprived children, whether in their own homes or out of them, are the source of social infection as real and serious as are carriers of diphtheria and typhoid," Bowlby warned. While some experts criticized Bowlby's ideas as overstated, his theories received widespread publicity in the United States and helped bolster an already growing focus on children's psychological well-being and the importance of motherhood.[14]

The new emphasis on children's emotional health was epitomized in Benjamin Spock's best-selling advice manual *The Common Sense Book of Baby and Child Care,* published in the United States in 1946. Spock, a pediatrician who was connected to the culture-and-personality school through his friendship with Margaret Mead (he cared for her daughter, Mary Catherine), encouraged mothers to abandon strict schedules of eating and sleeping. Instead, he urged them to focus on responding to their babies' emotional needs. "Every baby needs to be smiled at, talked to, played with, fondled—gently and lovingly—just as much as he needs vitamins and calories, and the baby who doesn't get any loving will grow up cold and unresponsive," Spock told parents. Spock described a warm, steady, and attentive caretaker—a mother, he unquestioningly assumed—as essential to children's development, particularly during the first three years of life.[15]

Spock and the army of lesser-known child-care experts and social workers who echoed his advice owed a heavy debt to psychoanalytic theory, though they generally downplayed Freudian ideas about sexuality in favor of an emphasis on interpersonal relationships. Developed in Vienna, psychoanalytic theory's popularity in the United States during the 1940s was bolstered by the influx of German and Austrian psychoanalysts, psychologists, and social workers who arrived on American shores seeking refuge from Hitler. Spock and his peers neatly repackaged imported ideas as distinctly American. Indeed, many child-care professionals understood their child-rearing philosophy as epitomizing the United States' democratic ideals. Their advice to parents reinforced a democratic sense of respect for young ones' individual needs and desires—even as it bound mothers ever more tightly to their roles as caregivers. By the time the U.S. Department of State broadcast portions of Spock's book to French radio listeners in 1949 as part of an effort to portray "a full and fair picture of American life, culture and customs," caring for children the "American way" had become a badge of national identity. Grounded in the family, in respect for children's individuality, and in a focus on youngsters' emotional security, "American-style" child rearing was an emblem of the democratic way of life.[16]

THE DEMOCRATIC FAMILY

Even before World War II, some American commentators had cast the family as a key pillar of democracy. The 1940 White House Conference on Children in a Democracy drew U.S. government officials, social workers, and other helping professionals from across the country. Conference participants concluded that since children's first environment was the home, the family could serve as "a school for democratic life"—a training ground for future citizens. The family took on added importance as America entered the war, as a means of safeguarding American democracy during a period of social instability.[17] In the aftermath of the conflict, the notion of the democratic family shifted from a defensive to an offensive one. No longer merely a means of preserving American society, the family now provided a method by which to shape foreign peoples.

As Americans prepared to rebuild the shattered world in the years following the war, psychologists, social workers, and educators looked to child-rearing methods and the family as a means of remaking foreign societies. "Education for citizenship in a democratic society must begin as education for

citizenship in a democratic family. Therefore, we have special concern about
what happens now, in Germany, to families, children and youth," concluded
the Conference of Consultants on Services to Children in Germany, convened by Katharine Lenroot, chief of the U.S. Children's Bureau, in September 1949. Conference attendees—among them psychologists, representatives from private voluntary organizations, and members of the Children's
Bureau and other U.S. federal agencies—described modern psychological
understandings of child growth and development as key to undermining authoritarian attitudes within the family and, by extension, within German
society at large. Participants noted an urgent need to "replace the outmoded
psychology which now supports German education with dynamic concepts
acceptable to reputable scientists in more advanced Western cultures" and
stressed the importance of assisting German parents and child-care practitioners in making their relationships with children "more creative and less
authoritarian."[18]

These sentiments were echoed a year later at a conference convened by
the Josiah Macy Jr. Foundation with the cooperation of the U.S. Children's
Bureau, the National Institute of Mental Health, and the U.S. Department
of State. The conference, the first in a series of three, took place in Princeton,
New Jersey. Most of the participants were American, although there were
several Europeans, including four Germans, in attendance. While the conference focused broadly on health and human relations in Germany, many
of the problems and suggestions that attendees discussed centered on children and the family. After all, noted psychiatrist Frank Fremont-Smith, a
Germany after the War conference participant and medical director of the
Macy Foundation, "both the organization and structure of society and culture flows [sic] from the parent-child relationship."[19] Conference attendees
recommended programs of parent education to reshape the German family
along more egalitarian lines and to make parents better aware of their children's emotional needs. They also noted the imperative need to train German
psychologists, social workers, and child-care professionals in the precepts of
modern psychology. Delegates recommended strengthening child guidance
clinics; supporting the publication of a journal dealing with newer aspects
of psychiatry, such as child development and interpersonal relations; and
bringing German psychologists and social workers to the United States for
training. Programs directed at the family and those professions charged with
its well-being were crucial, the conference report noted:

In the contemporary world, authoritarianism within the family circle is intimately connected with authoritarianism in political, economic, and social life. It is, therefore, exceedingly desirable that the processes of social change should take place simultaneously both inside and outside the family, so that they may lead as directly and promptly as possible from the one area to the other.[20]

If the family could serve as a training ground for democracy, however, it could also nurture totalitarianism. In the 1940s and 1950s, a number of scholars grappling with the existence of prejudice and the rise of totalitarian regimes in Europe found an explanation for these phenomena in the experiences of early childhood. American psychiatrist Bertram Schaffner's widely read 1948 book *Father Land,* which boasted an introduction by Margaret Mead, explained the rise of Nazism by examining the relationship between German parents and their children. "What makes the study of the German family so crucial," Schaffner wrote, "is the remarkable parallel between the rules that govern it and the credos of national, political life. The parallelism and similarity cannot be merely coincidental." Schaffner's ideas were not entirely new: the connections he drew between the family and politics writ large echoed earlier writings by psychoanalysts such as Erich Fromm and Wilhelm Reich, though Schaffner never explicitly acknowledged their influence on his work. What made Schaffner's book unique was his use of recently collected empirical data to substantiate his claims. Schaffner had served alongside psychiatrist David Levy, one of the participants in the Germany after the War conference, at the screening center established by the U.S. Military Government in Germany. In this capacity, he had conducted personal interviews with German citizens, which he drew on in his book. Schaffner's interactions with Germans led him to conclude that the roots of Hitler's ascendance lay in the structure of the German family. Conditioned from a young age to unquestioningly obey their authoritarian fathers, it was only a small step for Germans to transfer their allegiance to a brutal leader who demanded citizens' absolute loyalty. Schaffner insisted that efforts to eradicate Nazism in German public life would succeed only if accompanied by changes in the private relationships between husbands, wives, and children.[21]

Scholars made similar observations about Japan. Anthropologist Ruth Benedict had been commissioned by the U.S. government's Office of War Information to write a study of Japanese cultural patterns during the war. The result of her research (which Benedict conducted from afar by studying

Japanese cultural productions and interviewing Japanese Americans, as she was unable to travel to wartime Japan) was the 1946 book *The Chrysanthemum and the Sword: Patterns of Japanese Culture.* In the book, Benedict described patterns of child rearing as reinforcing the Japanese focus on hierarchy: "While the mother still carries the baby strapped to her back she will push his head down with her hand, and his first lessons as a toddler are to observe respect behavior to his father or older brother. . . . It is important in trying to understand [the Japanese people's] demand for hierarchy in the wider fields of government and economic life to recognize how thoroughly the habit is learned in the bosom of the family."[22]

Connections between the family and the larger social order also found voice in the influential book *The Authoritarian Personality,* published in 1950. Authored by a group of American and European émigré social scientists—Theodor W. Adorno, a sociologist and philosopher; Else Frenkel-Brunswik, a psychologist affiliated with the Berkeley Institute of Child Welfare; Daniel J. Levinson, a psychologist; and Nevitt Sanford, a psychologist and psychoanalyst—the book was part of a several-volume study on the origins of prejudice sponsored by the American Jewish Committee. *The Authoritarian Personality* connected the repression of young children within the family to the development of totalitarian modes of government. Prejudiced adults, the authors argued, were more often than not the products of parents who practiced "a relatively harsh and more threatening type of home discipline."[23] Unable to voice their fears and frustrations at home, these children repressed their emotions until they finally erupted in adulthood— often in the form of displaced hatred directed against marginalized groups, such as the Jews. Like Schaffner, Adorno and his colleagues found the roots of totalitarian regimes planted firmly in the soil of the family circle. The wrong kind of parenting, the authors argued, could facilitate the rise of a dictatorship and rouse the world to war.

With the decline of biological explanations for human difference, the formative years of personality development during childhood took on a new-found importance. Many Americans were enthusiastic about the potential of child rearing as a tool for transforming the world. "It seems to me that this is potentially one of the greatest scientific discoveries of modern times, not only to mental hygienists, but to every citizen of the world," one anthropologist noted in 1949. "*The single most important thing in human cultural behavior is literally and specifically the way we bring up our children. And the single most important thing ultimately in the politics of the world is the kind of human being,* temperamentally, that we manufacture."[24] But who should be responsible for "manufacturing" the future citizens of the world? While Freud and Burlingham enumerated the dangers that threatened children without parents, Adorno and his peers argued that perils lurked within the family as well. The family was at once the wellspring of children's emotional health and the root of dreadful personality disturbances that threatened the social order.

The scholars at the Germany after the War conference were not unaware of these tensions. Even as they recommended schooling and extracurricular activities as a means of countering the pernicious German home environment, they recognized that efforts to remove children from their parents' influence brought up thorny questions regarding the appropriate limits of American intervention overseas. "What legitimate responsibility have all peoples for all children? Where is the limit beyond which it is legitimate to go, in influencing the development of children in other cultures?" queried an appendix of the conference report likely penned by Margaret Mead. If democratic tenets discouraged meddling in other nations' affairs, to what extent could or should American experts intervene in the intimate practice of child rearing? The conference report left these questions unanswered.[25] The tension between the desire to mold children by reforming their families and the impulse to remove children from the influence of their parents would confound American child welfare workers overseas for many years to come.

But it would not dim Americans' enthusiasm for child rearing as a tool for reshaping the world in the aftermath of the war. A report summarizing the conclusions of the Germany after the War conference circulated widely among U.S. government agencies and private organizations, where it was frequently received with enthusiasm.[26] Shortly after the conflict drew to a close, child-care experts employed by both the American government and private voluntary groups embarked for Europe and Japan. Their mission was to improve the welfare of children in these war-torn areas. At stake was not only the fate of families but also the future of nations.

AMERICAN CHILD-CARE EXPERTS OVERSEAS

To American observers, uprooted children in Europe and Japan embodied both the physical destruction and the moral chaos that plagued the postwar world. Journalists and relief workers who traveled abroad in the months and years following the war documented a generation suffering from malnutrition, disease, and homelessness. But in keeping with the recent trends in American child welfare, they also paid close attention to youngsters' emotional and psychological ills. Children had been forced to lie, cheat, and steal in order to survive; they had been placed in anxiety-provoking shelters and hiding places; they had been ripped from their parents and tormented under conditions too dreadful to contemplate. "Modern psychology stresses the fateful and lasting effect of the impact of such events on children during the formative years," noted the Unitarian Service Committee (USC), one of the American agencies that sent a sizable team of relief workers overseas in the years following the war. "These early experiences will not fade from the memories of children who have never seen harmonious family life, who have known nothing of childhood in a normal world."[27]

Relief workers found that children, from Jewish orphans to former Nazi youth, often eluded traditional methods of mass relief and rehabilitation. "The child's approach to and outlook on life and the world at large, has been distorted in such a way, that mere feeding and a return to relative comfort cannot make normal human beings out of them," wrote D. N. Schnabel, the director of a home for mentally disturbed children in France run by the USC. Ernst Papanek, an Austrian-born child psychologist and educator who immigrated to the United States in 1940, argued that children's mental maladies represented a more grievous problem than did their physical ailments. Pediatrician Frank Spooner Churchill implored the U.S. Children's Bureau to construct child guidance clinics across postwar Europe, in order to treat children before their psychological scars became permanent.[28]

A generation of psychologically unstable youngsters, many observers fretted, was fueling an alarming increase in the rate of juvenile delinquency—a term that incorporated both minor offenses, such as stealing food, and more serious ones, such as assaulting Allied soldiers or engaging in prostitution—in all war-devastated countries. In Germany, authorities apprehended troublemakers as young as eight years of age. In several German regions in 1948, 12 percent of all youngsters between the ages of fourteen and seventeen appeared before the youth court as delinquents. Juvenile delinquency in Japan more than doubled in the year following the war. Observers described gangs of fearless child smugglers, thieves, and even murderers. For many child welfare experts, juvenile delinquency had both economic and psychological roots. "Homelessness is in itself a factor in delinquency, not only because of the temptations which are involved in it, but also because emotional deprivation often makes a thief of a child," argued Dorothy Macardle, who wrote a book on the "children of Europe." Relief workers agreed that children's psychological problems, if left untreated, imperiled youngsters' healthy growth and development—and threatened to derail the recovery of their countries. Emotionally unstable children also menaced other lands. "The recent advances in the physical sciences that are forcing the whole world into one community make it imperative—now more than ever—that the citizens of the world be healthy-minded, good men and women," argued social worker Melvin A. Glasser.[29]

In the aftermath of the conflict, the U.S. government and private relief organizations alike turned to social workers, psychologists, and other trained personnel to observe the state of child welfare in war-devastated countries and to make recommendations for improving the care of youngsters. Dozens of such professionals, many of whom were women, traveled overseas in the years following the war. Some served very brief stints overseas, primarily making observations and putting forth proposals; others served abroad for longer periods of time, putting welfare programs into place. Generally well-versed in new theories of human development and in the importance of childhood emotional health, the child-care teams dispatched to continental Europe and to Japan were consistently dismayed by the dearth of trained social workers and by local child-care professionals' apparent unfamiliarity with psychological theories of child development.

In both the United States and Europe, social work was generally considered women's work, an understanding reflected in the lower wages and prestige accorded to social workers as compared to their peers in related male-dominated fields. However, even before the war wreaked havoc on its infrastructure, European social work also differed substantially in training and in practice from its American counterpart. Beginning in the years following World War I, American social work training became heavily influenced by psychiatry and psychoanalysis, an emphasis that only increased during World War II. In Europe, by contrast, social workers generally lacked psychiatric training; the discipline had historically focused on meeting concrete material needs rather than emotional ones. European schools of social work had a younger student body than did American ones, had lower educational requirements for admission, and provided less comprehensive training in the social sciences. The divergent emphases of American and European social work were emblematic of larger differences in attitudes toward social welfare, including the welfare of children. In Japan, social work was not recognized as a profession; public welfare duties had traditionally been the domain of volunteer workers.[30]

In Europe, American workers encountered child welfare practices that appeared to them to be dangerously outdated. In Germany, the Nazi regime had forbidden the practice of social work and thus isolated the country from developments in the science of child psychology. Moreover, many psychologists and psychoanalysts had fled Germany after Hitler's rise. As a result, American workers contended, German child-care standards resembled the U.S. standards of nearly fifteen or twenty years prior. "It is one of those strange quirks of history that in Germany, one of the birthplaces of modern psychology, its findings seem to be little known or utilized," noted Edrita G. Fried and Marjorie Fiske Lissance, psychologists who studied youth in the American Zone in Germany.[31]

In 1949, the U.S. Army sent a team of child-care professionals to assess the state of maternal and child health and welfare in Germany. The U.S. Mission on Maternal and Child Health and Welfare toured the American Zone, met with doctors and child-care workers, and visited children's institutions. In their report, the experts described Germans as largely oblivious to the precepts of childhood mental health. "There seemed to be only a limited awareness on the part of German youth welfare authorities of the dynamic need of a child for security and affection from within his own home and of the serious and destructive consequences if this need is not met adequately," Gunnar Dybwad, one of the child welfare experts on the team, contended. Germans took a "mechanical, stale approach to the problems of children" and allowed youngsters to languish, deprived of the emotional support they needed.[32]

Other visiting experts in Germany had similar experiences. German-born social worker Gisela Konopka spent three months in Germany as a welfare consultant to the Public Health and Welfare Branch of the U.S. High Commissioner for Germany in 1950. Like many of her American colleagues, Konopka was surprised by the failure of German welfare workers to recognize children's psychological issues. In a report, Konopka described a visit she paid to a German institution for boys that was home to an unusually large number of bed wetters. "When I said that these were perhaps boys with night-fears and whether anybody had found out about their anxieties, I got the answer, 'oh, they are just deep sleepers,'" Konopka recounted. "I think that is just an example of the frightening ignorance in this area."[33]

American social workers were particularly troubled by the biological orientation of German child welfare, an emphasis that John Bowlby described as "reminiscent of Calvinist predestination." By the 1940s, eugenics had largely fallen out of favor in the United States, particularly due to its association with Nazism. But Germans continued to blame problems like juvenile delinquency on children's inborn depravity and thought it useless to devote educational resources to children born to families with a history of criminal behavior, American child-care workers reported. "Criminality on the part of an uncle seems to the German social worker of greater significance than the quality of the emotional ties between child and parents," Dybwad complained. An uncompromising emphasis on heredity led German social workers to overlook the significance of children's emotions and interpersonal relationships— and threatened to create a generation of psychological misfits.[34]

American workers sometimes blamed Germany's slow acceptance of the principles of mental hygiene on the authoritarian nature of the country's institutions. Psychological theories and methods of treatment, these workers argued, respected the needs of each individual and thereby challenged the rigid hierarchical structures that characterized both the German family and the German system of social services. "The majority of German homes are still perpetuating the same authoritarian patterns of family relationships in which the parents themselves were reared," contended a child psychologist who spent three months educating German parents at the request of the U.S. Army. In the authoritarian, father-dominated German family, Dybwad argued, "attention is not focused on [the child's] own growth process but rather on his submission to authority."[35]

American workers accused German social workers, like German parents, of resorting to discipline rather than trying to understand the root of children's problems. In German social workers' reports on juvenile delinquents "one finds such comments as that the child needs 'firm handling,' but rarely any reference to kindness or reassurance," noted Herschel Alt, an American child welfare specialist who traveled to Germany in 1948 as an adviser to the U.S. Military Government. American observers described German social service agencies themselves as harboring authoritarian tendencies, jealously guarding their own cases and refusing to work with one another. Collaboration, American experts insisted, went against the very nature of German society: "the German language has no word which corresponds to the American term 'community.'"[36]

If German methods of child care and social welfare embodied the essence of German authoritarianism, American social work represented the country's democratic culture. Social workers often described the democratic character of American social work as most clearly expressed in America's unique contribution to social welfare: the casework method. Centered on the relationship between the social worker and her individual client, casework represented, in the words of German émigré social worker Hertha Kraus, the "union of psychoanalytical concepts and democratic procedure." Caseworkers offered personal, emotional support to clients, responding to their individual needs and problems and encouraging them to draw on their own inner strengths to achieve personal adjustment and emotional security. "Social casework," Kraus noted in an introduction to a book on American casework methods she compiled for publication in Germany in 1949, "can make the tenets of democratic living a deeply personal experience."[37]

Casework also embodied the psychiatric and emotional emphasis of American social work. The casework method was emblematic of the shifting focus of social work in the United States during the first half of the twentieth century, as social workers moved from providing material relief to assisting individuals with issues of personal emotional adjustment. Indeed, caseworkers' primary focus was on the fears, insecurities, and resentments that hindered individual growth and personal happiness. Caseworkers often described emotional security as intensely personal, divorced in large measure from the greater social order. Many individuals still suffered from problems of personal adjustment "even after the gratification of material needs through social legislation," argued Jan F. de Jongh, a Dutch social worker who spent 1949 studying in the United States. "Emotional security does *not* necessarily follow as an automatic result from provisions for the security of employment, income, home, health, education, and leisure time, or from provisions for religious expression," Kraus agreed.[38] In elevating emotional security into a class by itself, social workers like de Jongh and Kraus implied that the road to democracy lay not in Europe's extensive system of government-provided social welfare—a model from which the United States had borrowed liberally in decades past—but in the intimate, private relationships between parents and children, caseworkers and their clients.

In Japan, as in Germany, American child welfare experts saw their work as deeply intertwined with efforts to promote democracy. The war left vast numbers of Japanese children—according to one report, over 120,000—

orphaned or homeless. Many of these youngsters lived in railroad stations or in the ruins of buildings, scraping together a living by shining shoes, selling newspapers, recycling used cigarette butts, picking pockets, or begging. The Japanese government's only organized response to this army of street children was to round them onto trucks and cart them to detention centers, where they often met with harsh discipline and physical abuse.[39]

In 1947, General Douglas MacArthur, supreme commander for the Allied powers, asked Edward J. Flanagan, a Roman Catholic priest and founder of the famous Boys Town orphanage in Nebraska, to survey child welfare problems in Japan and in Korea, which had recently obtained its independence after more than three decades of Japanese rule. Flanagan's orphanage was well known for its democratic ethos: youngsters of different races and religions lived together peacefully, and the boys elected their own mayor and other leaders from among their ranks. Flanagan was also famous for his faith in children's malleability, expressed in his credo, "there is no such thing as a bad boy." Flanagan visited schools and children's homes in both countries. He gave lectures on child welfare and met with social workers, government officials, educators, and the emperor and empress of Japan. Flanagan also attended a Japanese professional baseball game. His suggestion that the small boys congregating near the gates be admitted for free resulted in an onrush of seven thousand eager youngsters and led to the establishment of an annual Flanagan Day, on which children were invited to attend a baseball game free of charge.[40]

Baseball aside, Flanagan was not encouraged by what he saw. Institutionalized children in both Japan and Korea were often cared for by individuals with no training, youngsters had little opportunity for recreation, and some children were forced to perform labor for hours a day under the guise of receiving vocational training. Flanagan recommended "less regimentation in child care" and urged that orphanages be made "more attractive, home-like, where love, care, and guidance predominate." He argued that children's homes, if run properly, could play an important role in the effort to strengthen democracy in the Asian countries. Flanagan also made a case for the importance of religious—namely, Christian—instruction, noting during a press conference upon his return to the United States that Japanese "paganism" did little to motivate citizens to care for homeless children. "The Japan of tomorrow," Flanagan contended, "will be determined by the manner in which its children are cared for today."[41]

In many ways, Americans' impressions of Japanese child care closely resembled their assessments of German child rearing. To American welfare workers, Japanese parents and child-care workers showed little concern for children's individual rights and appeared ignorant regarding the precepts of children's personality development. Americans complained of a lack of public consciousness surrounding social welfare, epitomized in Japan, as it had been in Germany, by the absence of "an equivalent for the English word 'community.'" But if the German family was authoritarian, the Japanese family was clannish and potentially exploitative. The close-knit Japanese family system traditionally provided for its own needy members, American observers noted. But families in Japan cared little about children not related to them by blood, resulting in a nearly complete absence of public concern for the well-being of the country's thousands of orphans. Moreover, American social workers complained, Japanese families showed no respect for the rights and desires of their individual members, ignoring the best interests of children if they clashed with the best interests of the family group. The perceived disregard for children's rights led to the perpetuation of practices such as child labor and even child prostitution, which continued even though they were officially illegal.[42]

Emilie Baca Putnam, an American social worker who served as a welfare adviser with the U.S. Military Government in Japan, analogized the position of children within the Japanese family to that of feudal subjects. The suppression of children's rights within the family "is the end result of the process whereby the rights of the individual were overridden by his obligations to the household, the household to the family, the family to the daimyo (feudal lord), the daimyo to the shogun (supreme military commander), and the shogun to the emperor," she contended. The care of Japan's children both inside and outside of the family, Putnam argued, was in great need of reform.[43] It was to this task that American child welfare workers quickly turned.

In the years following World War II, scholars' understandings about the connections between child rearing and society made their way from the pages of reports and books into the agendas of relief workers and postwar planners on the ground. The decline of eugenics and the growth of new psychological theories of child development cast human nature as infinitely malleable, at least during childhood. To many Americans, interventions into child-rearing practices had the potential to reshape nations and to change the course of world history. The U.S. Mission on Maternal and Child Health and Welfare explained:

> Through the contributions of modern psychology and dynamic psychiatry and results of research in the development of the child, we now have proof that human behavior is modifiable. Previously held traditional views with regard to the inevitability of group conflict and war, on the grounds that they were inherent in 'human nature' are now shown to be without valid foundation. As a result of our new knowledge has come an understanding of how much human beings are the product of their upbringing. The periods of infancy, of childhood and of adolescence are the periods in which personality is molded.[44]

This new understanding of child development offered hope that the horrors of the Second World War might never be repeated. It endowed mothers, childcare workers, and ordinary families with newfound significance and responsibility. And it placed children and those who cared for them on the front lines of American interventions overseas.

CHAPTER TWO

Reading Dr. Spock in Postwar Europe and Japan

ON MARCH 16, 1948, Alice Pollard, a woman living in Hanover, New Hampshire, wrote a letter to William L. Clayton, one of the architects of the Marshall Plan. In her missive—which she hoped Clayton would not find "presumptuous"—Pollard shared her vision for a new model of European aid. The United States' programs of relief and rehabilitation were neglecting to harness the "human forces" so important to winning a lasting peace, Pollard argued. She had designed a remedy: a volunteer peacetime army of American women trained in the psychological care of children. These women would be deployed to neighborhood centers and welfare agencies across Germany and, perhaps eventually, all over Europe, where they would care for youngsters and educate local mothers in the best methods of child rearing. "We now have a body of knowledge tested by experience which shows us how the life of an adult may be cripple[d] or well directed, depending upon the treatment he received in the early years of life," Pollard asserted. American women could help in the essential task of rearing a psychologically sound generation that valued peace.[1]

Pollard was a Wellesley College graduate with no foreign policy credentials; her connection to Clayton was through her friendship with his niece. Nonetheless, her proposal, which she promoted widely, was well received both inside and outside of government. Margaret Mead offered encouragement.

Clayton wrote that he "like[d]" her approach. The proposal generated a series of meetings with members of United States federal agencies, including the Children's Bureau and the Department of State, and voluntary organizations, such as the American Friends Service Committee. Pollard's idea never became part of the Marshall Plan, as she had hoped.[2] But the notion that methods of child rearing had bearing on the realm of international relations would continue to influence the work that American voluntary organizations performed overseas in the years immediately following the war.

Influenced by new currents in the social sciences and by contemporary child-care wisdom, the American social workers and educators active in the U.S. reconstruction effort sought to debunk biological explanations for children's behavior. Instead, they promoted new understandings of human difference that rooted personality in culture. In both Europe and Japan, American overseas workers established neighborhood centers. They built orphanages and redesigned older ones. They also created training programs and schools of social work to impart to their foreign counterparts the importance of providing children with a sense of familial belonging and emotional security.

A good number of the social workers and educators who traveled overseas were women; for many of them, service abroad opened up new professional opportunities. In postwar Europe, in particular, a diminished network of state-provided social services and a dearth of trained personnel allowed a largely female network of American social welfare workers to exert its influence abroad at a time when its domestic stature was ebbing. American relief and rehabilitation organizations endowed the work traditionally performed by women with international significance. Their understanding of child rearing as a tool for social engineering promoted a new vision of foreign relations in which women, children, and families were key players. But grounding postwar reconstruction in methods of child care also elevated individual emotional adjustment over broad measures of economic security. And it justified far-reaching interventions into the lives of youngsters and their caretakers.

MODERNIZING EUROPEAN CHILD CARE

In the years following the war, the U.S. government and private voluntary groups initiated a number of efforts aimed at modernizing European child care. Government-sponsored programs focused largely on Germany, which the United States occupied during the decade following the war. The Office of the U.S. High Commissioner for Germany—the entity responsible for the U.S. occupation beginning in 1949—provided financial support for child guidance clinics, sent visiting experts to gather information on child welfare and to train parents and child-care practitioners, and sponsored exchange programs that brought German social workers to the United States for training. The U.S. Army was also responsible for a comprehensive program of recreational activities for German youth. Under the supervision of American GIs, German boys (and some girls) played sports, participated in youth clubs, and, U.S. officials hoped, absorbed some democratic values in the process.[3]

American voluntary groups also sent sizable teams to Europe, where they supported orphanages, set up training programs for foreign parents and child-care workers, and constructed neighborhood centers to provide social services to families. One of the more elaborate programs was the Unitarian Service Committee's Education and Child Care Institute, which met in German cities each summer from 1949 to 1953. Founded in 1940, the USC led a number of humanitarian efforts, including medical missions, in postwar Europe. It conducted its institute in conjunction with the Arbeiterwohlfahrt, a liberal German social work agency that survived twelve years of Nazi suppression.[4] The Education and Child Care Institute provided German social workers, teachers, and other child-care professionals from Berlin and the three Western zones of Germany with training in modern child psychology and state-of-the-art American methods of child care.

Katharine Taylor—former director of the Shady Hill School, a private progressive school near Boston—served as director of the institute, which employed female social workers drawn from the USC staff and a rotating cast of outside consultants, including Bertram Schaffner, Gunnar Dybwad, and psychologist Otto Klineberg. Aiming to "influence the basic attitudes of the Germans along democratic lines," American experts shared living accommodations with their German colleagues and imparted to them the myriad developments in child care and psychology from which they had been isolated during the Nazi years. Although the ideas they shared reflected contemporary child-care wisdom in the United States, USC social workers described their lessons as reflecting the universal principles of child psychology. "The psychological needs of childre[n] are the same everywhere—in a middle class American family with its automobile, or in a homeless German family which had taken shelter in a bunker in a destroyed city," one USC team member asserted. USC social workers urged their German counterparts to look for the emotional roots of difficult behavior in children and to "work at the source of these problems rather than merely to discipline the behavior."[5]

A typical day at one of the three-week-long sessions might include talks on the developmental phases and needs of children; skits by American experts demonstrating the differences between "authoritarian leadership, laissez-faire leadership, and the leader in the role of the 'enabler' "; and an afternoon session in the art studio, during which German participants were encouraged to express themselves freely through painting and modeling with clay. Institute leaders encouraged German social workers and teachers to experience democratic social relations firsthand. USC staff members attempted to avoid lecturing at students and relied instead on the discussion method, a manner of teaching with which Germans were wholly unfamiliar, in order to elicit meaningful conversations among participants and to foster a spirit of egalitarianism. In total, close to three hundred German social workers and teachers participated in the institute, some for several summers in a row. During the fall and winter, Katharine Taylor and USC social worker Marianne Welter paid visits to German participants in their hometowns, where they talked to parents, teachers, and social workers about human development, child care, and the casework method. Between the institute and visits to various towns, the USC estimated that its program reached a total of eight hundred German professionals.[6]

The USC described its Education and Child Care Institute as supporting larger, official efforts at German reconstruction. The U.S. government had made great strides in the reconstruction of the German economy and in the development of democratic political structures, the organization noted. "Such economic and political structures must, however, be undergirded by human beings whose basic attitudes toward themselves and others include respect for the dignity and worth of the individual as such without regard to his position in a hierarchy," the USC argued. The U.S. government recognized the importance of the USC's programs. When USC associate director Howard Brooks visited Washington, D.C., reported Katharine Taylor, he found that "the State Department seemed well aware of our Institute and that the Children's Bureau is using it as a model for what ought to happen all over Germany." High Commissioner for Germany John McCloy praised the USC's

Education and Child Care Institute as "highly successful" and as one of the "most intensive" reorientation activities in the field.[7] A cadre of social workers, parents, and children trained in democratic social relations, the USC and the U.S. government agreed, would be a powerful force in German society for preventing the rise of another dictator.

The American Friends Service Committee (AFSC) also looked to interventions in child care as a means of restructuring German society. "The children of Germany," the organization noted, "are probably the most important raw material out of which a regenerated Germany can be built."[8] Founded in 1917, the AFSC was an American voluntary agency with a long history of involvement in European child welfare efforts. During the early war years, the organization was instrumental in facilitating the emigration of hundreds of European Jewish children, many of whom would likely have perished at the hands of the Nazis. The AFSC also ran large-scale child feeding programs, which nourished many youngsters throughout the continent. In the years following the war, the organization sought not only to provide for children's physical care but also to safeguard their psychological well-being. In Wuppertal, AFSC social workers supported their German colleagues' efforts to establish a child guidance clinic, providing the clinic with American materials on methods of group work and play therapy. AFSC workers organized day-care programs for children and planned parent education meetings for their mothers. They also hosted speakers who gave well-attended lectures on child psychology and development. In Berlin, the organization ran a neighborhood center that hosted monthly meetings in which American, British, French, and German social workers discussed social welfare problems and shared effective solutions.[9]

The social workers of another voluntary agency, the American Jewish Joint Distribution Committee, were also deeply concerned with improving the care of children in Europe. Like the USC and the AFSC, the JDC saw modern methods of social work and child care as key to the rehabilitation of society. The JDC, however, was concerned specifically with the welfare of the Jewish community. Founded in 1914 and headquartered in New York, the JDC was the largest Jewish relief organization working in postwar Europe. It worked on behalf of Jews of all denominations, operating in Europe in large part through local Jewish welfare agencies. The JDC considered child-care work "an A1 priority"; in 1948, the organization estimated that its assistance reached more than 75 percent of the Jewish children in postwar Europe.[10]

The JDC fed, clothed, and housed children across the European continent. But JDC officials were also concerned about children's psychological well-being. Like many of their American colleagues, JDC officials decried the dearth of trained social workers and the absence of mental health facilities in Europe. In many of the orphanages the organization supported in France, children exhibited behavioral problems. But French agencies lacked the resources to provide appropriate psychiatric care. "Practically all of the children who receive any kind of service from any of the agencies we subvention have had a history of separation from, and loss of one or both parents, concealment, falsification, fear, and anxiety, all of which are factors strongly predisposing to more or less emotional difficulties in childhood, adolescence, and adult life," noted a JDC worker. To address the unmet need for psychiatric assistance, the JDC worked to set up a children's mental hygiene service. The service focused on preventing children's mental ills and on extending psychological assistance to a broad swath of children, including those who did not exhibit overt behavioral problems. Unable to find a trained psychiatric social worker—"this category," the JDC noted, "is practically unknown in France"—the organization recruited American personnel.[11]

But the JDC was not satisfied with relying on American experts to facilitate its programs overseas. In 1949, the organization established the Paul Baerwald School of Social Work in a chateau in Versailles, France. Staffed by a team of six American instructors, the school was designed to train a cadre of Jewish social workers for service in the Jewish communities of Europe and North Africa and in the newly established state of Israel. Described as "the first American-type social work school in Europe," the school instructed a largely female student body in casework methods and in modern psychological theories of human growth and development. All students were required to complete a course in "psychological concepts underlying social service," and students choosing a focus in child care and institutional management completed further courses in child psychology.[12]

Philip Klein, a professor at the Columbia University School of Social Work who served as the Paul Baerwald School's director of research, argued for the relevance of American-style social work methods overseas. In contrast to European systems of social insurance, pensions, and industrial welfare services, Klein explained, American social work centered on individual adjustment and on "techniques for making the services offered to individuals and families effective and efficient." Trained in American-style social work, graduates of the Paul Baerwald School would be equipped to offer the Jewish communities in Europe and elsewhere the personalized services of which they were in need. In 1951, the school expanded its scope and offered short-term courses in American social service techniques in Belgium, France, Germany, Switzerland, Tunisia, and Morocco.[13] The Paul Baerwald School relocated to Israel in 1958, where it continues today as part of Hebrew University.

The JDC's insistence on the importance of trained social workers in rebuilding the Jewish community extended beyond the Paul Baerwald School. "With rare exception," the JDC noted, the local organizations it supported were "staffed with social workers having no training or understanding of the most simple concepts of sound social work practice." But the JDC held the members of these European organizations to the same professional standards as Paul Baerwald School graduates. Indeed, continued funding often depended on local social welfare agencies' willingness to conform to the JDC's standards of professional social work practice. For example, the JDC cut funding to two French social work agencies because, the organization explained, "after continued work with them toward developing sounder social work practice, we arrived at the conclusion that the individuals responsible for the existence of these organizations could not be helped to move beyond their 'Lady Bountiful' attitude toward child care."[14] The JDC's emphasis on modern social work techniques rendered unprofessional female charitable work outdated and ineffectual.

Like the child-care workers encountered by the JDC, Europeans were not universally receptive to American methods of social work and psychologically oriented programs of child care. While some parents and child-care practitioners sought out American-led training programs as a means to better assist their children or to further their careers, others adapted new methods reluctantly or only in part. Still others rejected American offers of assistance altogether. As a generation of American mothers discovered, psychologically oriented methods of child rearing required intensive emotional labor. For some European child-care practitioners, this labor was a means to professional advancement or personal satisfaction. To others, it represented a burden they were unable or unwilling to shoulder.

For example, the AFSC consistently complained of low turnout at the mothers' groups it conducted in the German cities of Cologne and Darmstadt. One particularly ill-attended meeting in April 1951 drew only one mother. German mothers made use of the organization's child-care programs, but most had little time or inclination to discuss methods of child rearing. Even participants in the USC's Education and Child Care Institute—a self-selected group of professionals interested in learning from their American colleagues—displayed some resistance to new theories and methods of child rearing. When psychologist Otto Klineberg challenged biological theories of character development at the 1950 Education and Child Care Institute in Berlin, for example, a number of German social workers defended their reliance on heredity. Experiencing a challenge to their basic worldview was "very painful for most of the participants," acknowledged Helen Fogg, director of the USC's child and youth projects.[15]

The USC ran homes for uprooted and orphaned children in several countries, including Germany, France, Belgium, and Czechoslovakia, and the organization attempted to train local staffs in modern methods of child care. But orphanage workers were often particularly unwilling pupils. If instances of aggressive behavior, stealing, or bed wetting occurred too frequently, "'the whole liberal-soft-democratic-American approach' is questioned and temporarily rejected. It was so much easier when one could quickly dish out a slap (Ohrfeige) or two or three and be done with it," USC social worker Marianne Welter noted with regard to her local colleagues at a German children's home.[16]

Orphanage workers' intransigence was evident at the Hana Benesova Children's Home, located outside of Prague. A joint project of the British and American Unitarian Service Committees in coordination with the Czechoslovakian Ministry of Labor and Social Welfare, the Hana Benesova Children's Home was established in 1947 to serve as a model children's institution. The British and American committees each sent one professional child-care worker to aid the Czech personnel. But after several months of operation, the American child-care worker and her colleagues in the United States were disappointed by their inability to direct the methods of child care in the home. The Czech directors were strict disciplinarians who did nothing, according to the Americans, to build loving bonds with the children. The woman in charge of child care was known to hit her young charges. Frustrated, the American child-care worker gave her Czech colleagues a book of psychological case studies, hoping it would "open their eyes a little to a different way of handling children." Ernst Papanek, child psychologist and USC consultant, contemplated altering the USC's contract with the

Czechoslovakian government to allow for a greater presence of trained American child-care workers in the home.[17]

For the staff of the Hana Benesova home, as for other local child-care workers and mothers, new methods of caring for children were an unwelcome intrusion into their lives. Other Europeans had more deep-seated objections to American methods. To some European social workers, casework and its emphasis on emotional and personal relationships appeared out of place in the context of postwar poverty and social upheaval. A number of European social work professionals studying in the United States took issue with the individualized nature of American social services and with the fact that these services were available only to a relatively small percentage of the population. These services, they told their American hosts, would fit uneasily into European societies, which had a tradition of universal, state-supported social welfare programs. Indeed, American casework was to some Europeans "a rather unsatisfactory substitute for important links missing in the social security network," observed Hertha Kraus. Some European social workers rejected the American emphasis on individual emotional security and upheld a European tradition of social services that addressed material needs and were available to all.[18]

Even those Europeans who embraced casework training found that large caseloads, local agencies' lack of resources, and the dismissive attitudes of colleagues made it difficult to put their training into practice. In letters written to their former professors, Paul Baerwald School graduates who went to work in Israel noted that the overwhelming social needs in the fledgling state often made the practice of casework impossible. Alumnus Peter Melvyn described a skeptical Israeli colleague who tried to get a fellow Paul Baerwald School graduate to admit that "all this 'casework' we learned was really pretty useless for the work here." But even with too many clients to deliver individualized casework treatment, Melvyn reported, his peers found that the "basic attitude" they acquired through casework training was useful to them in their work.[19]

American experts also sometimes found individuals who were eager to adopt their recommendations but who fundamentally misunderstood modern psychological concepts. In one German town, citizens' well-meaning but ill-informed attempt at democratic social relations involved proposing a plebiscite on whether children could be beaten in school. One American psychologist noted that German parents expressed great interest in psychology but often "interpreted the American idea as meaning a swing from authoritarianism to complete lawlessness."[20] American agencies could impart new methods of social work and child care, but they generally had little control over the ways in which their students put their training into practice.

Moreover, some clients were not receptive to new methods of treatment. Most children were not in the position to reject assistance or to attempt to direct the manner in which it was given, and one can assume that the vast majority of children appreciated bans on practices like corporal punishment. But traces of resistance to the emotional invasiveness of psychologically oriented social work can be discerned among older children. For instance, a boy assisted by the European-Jewish Children's Aid, an American voluntary agency, dismissed his social worker's attempts to get him to discuss his feelings with the Yiddish word *narrishkeiten*—"foolish nonsense"—and the organization acknowledged that its attempts to encourage young clients to explore their inner conflicts were sometimes rebuffed. Casework "is a service the client is not asking for," the European-Jewish Children's Aid noted.[21]

But new theories and methods of child care found an eager audience among some European mothers and child-care workers. American overseas workers often fielded requests from local colleagues for information on American child guidance, psychology, and group work methods. They also noted the popularity of books on child development among their European peers. In Europe, noted one American worker, "Dr. Benjamin M. Spock's *The Common Sense Book of Baby and Child Care* is coming to be a classic." Although the AFSC's classes for German parents generally yielded only a small turnout of mothers, those who did attend were eager to discuss their child-rearing dilemmas. Likewise, lectures on child psychology and development often drew large German audiences. A U.S. government-sponsored exchange program that sent German social welfare workers for training in the United States elicited a large number of applicants, many expressing sentiments similar to those of German social worker Liesel Miltenberger, who wrote, "Having found out, that our social-work wants improving and having read that the methods of working in USA are different from ours and might be better, I hope to improve my work by comparing the different ways of working. I want to know of American social-work as much as possible."[22]

American-style methods of child care also found their way into the German system of public welfare. In 1953, the Federal Republic of Germany (FRG) amended its national child welfare law to provide for the establishment of an extensive network of *Erziehungsberatungsstellen*, or child guidance stations. Modeled on child guidance institutions in the United States and Great Britain, Germany's network included clinics, schools, children's homes, day-care centers, and recreational facilities that offered psychological and therapeutic services to youngsters and their families. By 1957, the FRG boasted 320 *Erziehungsberatungsstellen*, almost half of which were fully supported by public welfare agencies. A good number of the children and families who used the child guidance stations were referred to them by the courts or other authorities, but many parents also took the initiative to seek out their services. At a typical station, about a quarter of the caseload had been referred by parents themselves. The stations' promotion of psychological understandings of human development signaled a powerful break from the past and a rebuke to the biological theories espoused by the Nazi regime. Their emphasis on preventive care, as opposed to more punitive methods of correctional education, supported a vision of a new Germany committed to democratic values and individual rights.[23] While American child-care methods made uneven inroads within individual German families (and, it must be noted, within individual American families as well), the institutionalization of American child welfare methods was one measure of the success of U.S.-led efforts to reform German society.

CHILD WELFARE IN JAPAN

American voluntary groups and the U.S. government also spearheaded programs to improve child-care methods in Japan. As part of the effort to transform Japan from an authoritarian state into a functioning democracy, American occupying forces overhauled the country's child welfare legislation and infrastructure. American voluntary organizations supported orphanages, established neighborhood centers, and aimed to bring modern methods of child care to the country.

One voluntary group concerned with the care of Japan's children was China's Children Fund (CCF), based in Richmond, Virginia. Founded in 1938 to assist Chinese children uprooted by the Second Sino-Japanese War, CCF began supporting homes for Japanese orphans in 1948. CCF was the brainchild of J. Calvitt Clarke, a Presbyterian minister with extensive experience in foreign relief work, and his wife, Helen. The organization used a novel method of assisting children, matching foreign youngsters with foster parents in the United States who committed not only to a series of monthly donations but also to a regular exchange of letters with their foster children. CCF mandated Bible teaching in all of the orphanages it supported, and it funded only Protestant institutions. While CCF's proselytizing aims set it apart from its counterparts such as the USC and the AFSC, the methods of child rearing its workers embraced were not unique. CCF officials sought to provide orphaned children with a sense of love and belonging. They also worked to train Japanese workers in new child-care methods. Frustrated by their inability to locate professionally trained child-care workers in Japan, CCF officials would eventually establish Clarke Junior College (later renamed Izumi Junior College), Japan's first school dedicated to the training of child-care and orphanage workers.[24]

In order to locate suitable institutions to support, CCF tapped into a network of American missionaries whose presence in Japan predated the war. One of the institutions to which the organization extended aid was the Jiai No Mura, one in a series of children's homes located outside Kumamoto that had been established by an American Lutheran missionary, Maud Powlas. The homes sought to provide orphaned, abandoned, and "problem" children with the warmth and familial love American workers insisted they needed to grow into good citizens. The children in Powlas's homes received education and agricultural training. "But the real thing that has transformed them," asserted CCF, "is a 'mother's' love." Esther Barnhart, an American Lutheran missionary, conducted training courses on child psychology and general welfare work for the workers at each of the homes. Child-care workers at Powlas's homes impressed their peers by taking in and rehabilitating boys and girls previously classified as delinquents. CCF described the loving care children received at the Jiai No Mura as helping to build a more peaceful, democratic Japan—and as staving off less desirable forms of government that threatened to plague the country in the war's immediate aftermath. "Here," the organization proclaimed, "[children] will not fall under the blight of Communism or Fedualism [sic]. . . . Here we believe they will learn the ways of peace and learn to accept and love the Saviour who died for them."[25]

CCF's articulation of the connection between child rearing and democracy differed from the egalitarian, liberal vision promoted by its peers in postwar Europe. In contrast with the USC, the AFSC, and the JDC, CCF promoted a conservative vision of the family closely tied to Christian ideals. CCF's conflation of democratic, familial, and Christian values showcased an early articulation of what historian Arissa Oh has termed "Christian Americanism," a Cold War amalgamation of vaguely Christian values and ideals, such as love of family, considered to be uniquely American.[26] But even as CCF emphasized the religious significance of its work, it added its voice to the chorus of scholars and child-care experts who linked child development with the structure of government and with the social order writ large.

CCF's fusion of Christian and democratic values was shared by General Douglas MacArthur, who directed the American occupation of Japan. MacArthur welcomed missionaries to Japan while almost completely barring American educators without a connection to the church, and he argued that Christianity offered the Japanese "a sure and stable foundation on which to build a democratic nation." MacArthur also shared CCF's desire to improve child welfare in Japan. In the years following the war, the U.S. occupying forces employed a cadre of American social workers tasked with overhauling Japan's system of social welfare. In Japan, unlike in the United States, primary responsibility for social welfare rested with the national government, and American advisers worked to write child welfare improvements into federal law. In 1947, acting on advice from American welfare officials, the Japanese government passed a comprehensive Child Welfare Law intended to "modernize" the care of children. The new law charged the state with responsibility for the well-being of all children, not just those suffering due to poverty or homelessness. It established child welfare centers in each of Japan's forty-seven prefectures to provide psychological guidance to families and placement services to orphans. The law also established national and prefectural child welfare boards to study and advise on the needs of children, provided for the employment of professional child welfare workers across the country, established Japan's first system of foster care, offered maternal and child health-care services at no cost to those unable to pay, and put in place legal safeguards to prevent the exploitation of children's labor.[27]

Although Japanese officials were responsible for implementing the provisions of the Child Welfare Law, American military officials and social workers closely monitored their enforcement. Frustrated by the public's seemingly sluggish use of the new child welfare facilities and consultation services, U.S. officials spearheaded efforts to publicize information on good child-rearing practices and to instill in Japanese citizens a sense of public responsibility for the welfare of all children. An occupation official noted in 1949, "The extent to which we can mold public opinion to the need of an adequate Child

Welfare Program and the power we exercise in having the Japanese Government accept this full responsibility . . . will measure the progress of the Occupation in implanting the full meaning of democracy in the minds and hearts of Japan's young—where it can reflect itself in the years ahead."[28]

American military officials enlisted Japanese welfare agencies and media outlets to distribute information on child care and psychology, and they encouraged information centers run by the U.S. Military Government's Civil Information and Education Division to publicly display books on child development. As they had in Germany, American workers tried to replace biological theories of child development with new ideas centering on children's inherent malleability. "A child is not delinquent because of inherited 'bad blood,'" U.S. Civil Information officers noted in a compilation of background material to be promulgated to the Japanese public. "He is generally a normal child reacting normally to an unwholesome social situation." An exhibit prepared by occupation officials explained to Japanese parents the importance of treating children with warmth and understanding: "Bad children do not come from happy homes. A child must receive a great deal of love and affection." The Japanese Welfare Ministry worked to put into circulation similar ideas. Under the banner "Let's respect children's human rights," the ministry publicized the country's new network of child guidance, foster care, and health services. A poster prepared by the ministry depicted a father hitting a child next to an image of a youngster smoking a cigarette. "No juvenile delinquents come from cheerful homes. It is important to raise children with love," the poster explained.[29] Occupation officials hoped that new methods of child rearing would not only reduce the scourge of juvenile delinquency but also help transform Japan into a democratic country, where respect for individual rights was paramount.

Like their counterparts in Europe, American welfare workers in Japan aimed to cultivate a cadre of professionally trained social workers and child-care workers. American welfare workers associated with the occupation helped establish social work training programs, including Japan's first four-year college of social work, and worked with Japanese government officials and social workers to plan training courses for child-care workers. Alice K. Carroll, a social worker trained at the University of Pittsburgh, supervised the staff of child guidance centers and wrote a manual for child welfare workers that was published by Japan's newly formed Children's Bureau. Although her manual incorporated elements of psychoanalytic theory and provided instructions on the practice of social casework, Carroll insisted that psychological theories must be tailored to local conditions. Her textbook would assume an important place in the training of Japanese child welfare workers for years to come.[30]

American missionary Maud Powlas was pleased with the Japanese government's assumption of responsibility for child welfare. She credited the U.S. Army's efforts to publicize new child-rearing ideals, especially in the form of films, with changing the way Japanese teachers interacted with the orphaned children under her care. But Powlas noted that new democratic ideals had the potential to tear at the fabric of society. "Under this new democracy," Powlas recalled later, "all the old coercion had been lifted. Police authority had been curtailed, teachers had been given a 'no-whipping' command, parents were told by American 'experts' to give their children more freedom. The result of this sudden release from all authority was bedlam."[31]

The "release from all authority" was not universal. As they had in Europe, American methods of child rearing generated mixed reactions among Japanese parents and child-care professionals. Japanese families were initially slow to use child guidance clinics and other new child welfare services. The notion that "bad children do not come from happy homes" placed the blame for children's misbehavior squarely on the shoulders of parents, an implication that no doubt sat uneasily with some mothers and fathers. Many parents and child-care practitioners, trained to measure children's development in terms of conformity or obedience, had difficulty assimilating new psychological understandings of child growth.

Several years after the American occupation of Japan ended, Tsuyako Shimada, a professor of personality development, noted that new child-rearing ideals had made only limited headway among Japanese families. "Despite the fact that one can find some democratic family groups, especially in the larger cities and among those with better educations, the attitudes of most family members to each other are still based on the feudalistic family system, which defines the status and roles of its members," Shimada reported. Japanese social workers also actively debated the merits of casework, another perceived democratizing influence. Some took issue with the use of casework in the context of public welfare, resenting the implication that postwar poverty was rooted in individual emotional problems. Others—particularly those in the field of child welfare—began using the casework method. During the

1950s and 1960s, a growing number of private family guidance clinics offered casework services to parents and children.[32]

The American occupation left behind a comprehensive network of services for children in Japan. But occupation officials ultimately promulgated competing understandings of social welfare. On the one hand, they espoused a vision of comprehensive government-provided social services available to all. On the other, they promoted casework and related therapeutic methods that grounded societal woes in the problems of individuals, casting Japan's rehabilitation in personal and psychological terms.[33]

WOMEN, SOCIAL WORK, AND CHILD WELFARE

In the United States, social workers' efforts at professionalization and their heavy reliance on psychiatry during the decades following World War I led to a professional identity crisis by the 1940s. A mostly female contingent of social workers found itself perched uncomfortably on the lowest rung of the professional ladder, below the largely male ranks of psychologists and psychiatrists. Social work had eschewed sisterly benevolence in favor of scientific professionalism, only to fight a losing battle for prestige with male helping professionals.[34]

For American social workers practicing abroad in the years after World War II, however, the professional landscape was different. The war had disrupted the training of many would-be European social workers, psychologists, and psychiatrists, and it forced many who had such training to flee the continent. Moreover, European social work had never embraced psychiatry to the same extent as its American counterpart. In Japan, social work had not been recognized as a profession prior to the postwar years. A resulting dearth of psychiatrists, psychologists, and social workers in both Europe and Japan opened the door for American social workers, many of whom were women, to rise to positions of influence that might have been more difficult to attain in the United States.

Overseas work offered expanded opportunities for other American female professionals as well. From the late nineteenth century until the 1930s, a network of female social reformers working in private institutions such as settlement houses and in the federal Children's Bureau developed maternal and child welfare programs that became key components of the American welfare state. By the 1940s, historians have argued, due in part to its own success, this female network had largely deteriorated. But women associated with the Children's Bureau network maintained leadership positions with regard to child welfare abroad during the postwar years. Both the U.S. government and private organizations and individuals looked to the Children's Bureau to serve as a clearinghouse for information on all aspects of child welfare overseas. Female leaders within the Children's Bureau advocated for the recruitment of women for postwar child welfare work abroad. In a letter to Philip Jessup, chief of the Division of Personnel and Training in the Office of Foreign Relief and Rehabilitation Operations, Children's Bureau associate chief Martha Eliot emphasized "the great importance of giving preference to women" with regard to relief positions "whose duties will relate primarily to children and women." Children's Bureau leaders corresponded with social welfare experts both at home and abroad in efforts to identify professionals who might be interested in assisting the United States in its international rehabilitation work after the war. They recommended welfare workers, the majority of whom were women, to their colleagues in the Office of Foreign Relief and Rehabilitation Operations, and they directed aspiring overseas workers to private agencies seeking personnel.[35] The network of female child welfare professionals thus sustained itself internationally even as it lost influence with regard to domestic child welfare.

The international arena also gave female social welfare experts an opportunity to revive an old institution: the settlement house. Late nineteenth-century female reformers, inspired by the British settlement house movement, had established settlements in impoverished neighborhoods in cities across the United States. These centers offered immigrants and other urban residents an array of social services, such as day care, English classes, and recreational activities. As the twentieth century progressed, the U.S. government—inspired in part by Germany's comprehensive network of state-provided social services—assumed many of the functions once provided by the settlement home. But in the years following World War II, Germany's program of government welfare was in disarray. The social settlement, often called the "neighborhood home," could again serve as an important focal point for community services. "In a devastated and war-torn community where many of the normal city-wide functional services may have deteriorated or are unable to operate for other reasons, the neighborhood approach may again be the best solution," insisted social worker Hertha Kraus. Neighborhood homes also played a central role in Alice Pollard's proposal for U.S. aid to Europe. Pollard envisioned the construction of neighborhood centers all over Germany, which would host American women trained in child welfare and provide a variety of educational and welfare services to children and their mothers.[36]

During a talk at the USC's Education and Child Care Institute, its director, Katharine Taylor, likened the social upheaval and the influx of refugees in postwar Germany to the conditions in turn-of-the-century cities in the United States that precipitated the settlement house movement. In both situations, Taylor noted, the settlement house could assist people with problems of individual adjustment and serve as a training ground for community leadership. A number of women working in the field of social welfare overseas had prior experience serving in social settlements in the United States. Taylor spent her childhood at the Chicago Commons, a settlement house in Chicago founded by her father, Graham Taylor. Her sister Lea Demarest Taylor, a resident of the Chicago Commons and president of the National Federation of Settlements and Neighborhood Centers, also participated in the USC's Education and Child Care Institute in Germany. Several other members of the USC's overseas child-care team also had previous experience working in social settlements in the United States.[37]

The USC would draw on these women's expertise as it worked to give its child-care and education program a permanent home in Germany. In 1951, with the aid of a grant from the Ford Foundation, the organization established a neighborhood home in the German city of Bremen. The USC established the center in collaboration with the city, which donated the land on which it was built, and the Arbeiterwohlfahrt, the German social work agency. Billed by its promoters as a social settlement in the American tradition, the home was staffed by American and German experts in child care, education, and social work. The Bremen center was designed to fulfill Americans' vision of a Germany free of authoritarian tendencies: it would serve as a demonstration center for democratic group work, provide parent education and training for education and social work students, and stimulate interagency cooperation and community initiative.[38] The USC would maintain an active role in the neighborhood center until 1958, when its German partners assumed full responsibility for the home.

The AFSC also consolidated many of its programs during the postwar years in a series of neighborhood homes it established in German and Japanese cities. The AFSC's neighborhood homes in Germany were the brainchild of

German-born social worker Hertha Kraus, whose efforts to modernize social welfare in her home country extended well beyond her book on American casework methods. The former director of the public welfare department of Cologne, Kraus immigrated to the United States after the rise of Hitler. She worked on public welfare issues for the U.S. government as part of the Social Security Board and served as associate professor of social economy at Bryn Mawr College. Kraus had started settlement houses in German cities after the First World War, and in 1943 she submitted a proposal to the AFSC calling for the creation of neighborhood centers in Germany after the conclusion of the war. These centers would serve as the hub of AFSC programs, providing social services to German citizens, training social workers and child-care professionals, and aiding in promoting democratic social relations.[39]

The U.S. Military Government gave the AFSC permission to build the neighborhood centers in early 1947; between 1947 and 1952, the AFSC constructed centers in eight German cities. These centers sponsored children's programs, recreational activities, English classes, a sewing room, and a shoe repair shop. But while they provided many services that would have been at home in a turn-of-the-century settlement, both the USC's and the AFSC's neighborhood homes reflected the psychiatric and professionalizing emphasis of mid-twentieth-century social work. Neighborhood homes in various German cities hosted gatherings of social workers and invited social work trainees to gain experience working in their children's programs. Several homes hosted speakers and classes for parents on child care and psychology. The AFSC's neighborhood center in Wuppertal was home to the only child guidance clinic in the city.[40]

During the early twentieth century, the social welfare activities of American social settlements had served as a model for cities, as public agencies assumed responsibility for a variety of social services. While American-run neighborhood homes were the occasional beneficiaries of public funds or grants from the U.S. and German governments, they were largely supported by private funds. This model of private welfare was jarring to some Germans who were accustomed to a tradition of state-provided social services. For example, American worker Rose Albert Porter encountered local resistance when she tried to raise private funds for the AFSC's neighborhood home in Wuppertal. A group of businessmen approached for donations "explained very carefully to the American worker that in Germany the State has always taken care of the 'underprivileged,'" Porter related. "However, when it was pointed out to them that one could hardly call living in the bunker care, and that the problem was evidently so big that the State was having difficulty even beginning to meet it, they were ready to listen," she noted. The AFSC did not oppose public welfare. On the contrary, organization officials hoped that the AFSC's neighborhood centers would bolster public welfare services in Germany and that city welfare departments would eventually assume responsibility for the centers.[41] Nonetheless, the disintegration of state-run social services in Germany after the war provided a new opportunity for American women such as Porter to craft private welfare programs and to assume positions of leadership within neighborhood settlement homes.

Following the success of its neighborhood centers in Germany, the AFSC established three neighborhood centers in Japan. One center was located in Mito, a city that had been nearly completely destroyed during the war. The additional two centers were located in Tokyo, one in a housing project and one in a government camp for repatriated and displaced persons. The centers boasted such facilities as sewing rooms, libraries, and public meeting spaces, but child care occupied an important place as well. Each of the neighborhood centers housed either a day nursery or a kindergarten—one of the centers in Tokyo offered the only nursery in the city caring for two- to four-year-olds—as well as recreational activities for youngsters, such as folk games and dances, puppet making, and sports. The neighborhood centers also held meetings for mothers during which child-care methods were discussed. Local people associated with the neighborhood centers described them as helping to build a cooperative community that valued peace.[42]

In Germany, Japan, and elsewhere, American social workers and child-care experts found expanded professional opportunities. So, too, did some local women. In Japan, a predominantly male cadre of untrained voluntary workers had traditionally assumed responsibility for social welfare activities. The drive to professionalize the social work profession that began during the postwar years opened up new opportunities for Japanese women, who studied social work in newly created university programs in increasing numbers. By early 1948, more than six hundred professionally trained child-care workers, most of whom were women, had fanned out across the country to help run the network of child welfare services created under the Child Welfare Law. Shizue Yoshimi, a Japanese social worker trained at the New York School of Social Work, served as head of the Child Care Section of the newly created Children's Bureau, giving her the distinction of being the first woman to hold a position of high responsibility within the Japanese government. Although the field of social welfare as a whole remained male dominated, the professionalization of the fields of social welfare and child care in Japan expanded some women's professional horizons.[43]

In Europe, where social welfare work was already a predominantly female field, training in American methods of social work and child care no doubt opened the door for increased professional opportunities for some women. American organizations likely provided some foreign families with a welcome new model for relationships between husbands, wives, and children. But while some European women embraced new methods of child care, others resented the intrusion into their private and professional lives and resisted the increased emotional labor that these methods required.

American commentators stressed the importance of empowering women within the context of the allegedly authoritarian German family. But while American workers encouraged German women to step out of the shadow of the authoritarian father, they expected women to assert themselves primarily as mothers. In the traditional German family, noted writer Harriet Eager Davis in an article in *Parents'* magazine, "mothers might express natural love when alone with their children, but the moment father appeared, they dropped submissively into an inferior role . . . acquiescing in everything [their] husband[s] did, even if it was cruel or unjust and against the child's best welfare." Davis contrasted this role with the new woman a German wife might become: "a mother so vital and protective that she can defend her child even against her own husband if necessary."[44] It was as self-confident, assertive mothers that German women could make a lasting contribution to the world, rearing a generation of psychologically sound children who eschewed their authoritarian heritage and actively promoted peace.

Davis's comments can be read not only as an indictment of German mothers but also as a defense of their American counterparts. During the 1940s, a chorus of commentators stoked American fears about the doleful effects of domineering and overprotective mothers. Authors such as Philip Wylie, who published a scathing critique of American mothers in 1942 titled *Generation of Vipers,* accused American mothers of smothering their children and rearing weak, effeminate sons who were ill equipped to lead the country.[45] But if powerful mothers posed a threat to the social order, Davis implied, one need only look to Germany to witness the cataclysmic consequences of submissive motherhood.

Although American organizations assumed that girls should sew while boys performed carpentry projects, they did not advocate divergent routines of care for boys and girls; an awareness of children's universal psychological needs largely overshadowed gender differences. A USC consultant described the promotion of childhood gender equality as a distinctly American value. "I would be in favor of making even the dining room jobs rotate among boys and girls, not to let the boys grow up in the European manner where a man is supposed to be too 'good' for house and kitchen work," the consultant argued in a memorandum on the organization's home for adolescents in Verden, Germany. "If they migrate to other countries later on, they had better get rid of those old-fashioned European ideas now."[46] But American concern with developing a new generation of responsible leaders ultimately dictated different roles for girls and boys. Male children would presumably grow up to be political leaders, while female children, equipped with the latest psychological knowledge, would eventually inherit the responsibility for molding a new generation.

Through efforts to reform foreign child-care practices, American voluntary agencies cast political endeavors—rebuilding Europe and Japan, preventing the rise of future totalitarian leaders—as personal problems whose resolutions could be found in the lives of children and their caretakers. This understanding reflects a larger cultural shift within the postwar United States: the growth of a therapeutic approach that offered, in the words of historian Elaine Tyler May, "private and personal solutions to social problems."[47] Postwar society and culture positioned the private joys of home and family, rather than organized action in the public sphere, as remedies for social ills.

American social workers and educators marginalized the European state-run social welfare system that had served as a model for the U.S. welfare state in earlier decades, even as many owed their careers to an American state that was rapidly extending its reach overseas. They promoted personalized services that guaranteed emotional, rather than material, security, and charged the family, rather than the state, with the responsibility for providing it. But to child psychologists and postwar planners alike, emotional security—especially that of children—had a significance that reverberated beyond the confines of the home. Children's plasticity meant that child rearing offered a method for reshaping the postwar world. From the orphanages and nurseries of Europe and Japan would emerge a new generation that valued tolerance and peace.

CHAPTER THREE

Building International Friendship in an Orphan Age

ON TUESDAY, FEBRUARY 10, 1948, the boys of Cub Scout Pack 232 had an important appointment: a meeting at the U.S. Department of State. Neatly attired in blue and gold uniforms, the nine- through eleven-year-olds from Bethesda, Maryland, met with Secretary of State George Marshall and told him about their plan to "adopt" eight needy European boys for a year, providing gifts and funds for their support. The boys' "Junior Marshall Plan" delighted its namesake. Their project, Marshall assured the youngsters, "is of great international importance in establishing relations of friendship and good will and trust that are so important to our Government, to our people and to the world and to peace." The boys' plan, the secretary of state noted, was a powerful symbol of Americans' broadened understanding of the world and of the increased prominence of the United States within the international community. "In the short period of my lifetime, we are now recognized everywhere as being the most powerful nation in the world and being the acknowledged leader in the world," Marshall told the children. "At their age," he marveled later, "my world extended about 6 miles."[1]

The Bethesda Cub Scouts' project was not unique. During the years immediately following World War II, many American organizations established international child sponsorship or "adoption" programs similar to the one described by Pack 232. These programs sought to forge friendships and fictive families that stretched across oceans, connecting American citizens with youngsters around the world. Sponsorship involved virtual, not legal, adoption: American foster parents or friends committed to correspond with—and, generally, support financially—a particular child for a certain period of time.

Many Americans looked to child sponsorship programs as a means of building "one world"—a way of expressing allegiance to a global, rather than a national, community.[2] They described relationships cultivated across the globe, particularly those involving impressionable children, as forging the bonds of international kinship that would prevent another world war. Like the Marshall Plan itself, however, the sponsorship programs established in the aftermath of the war reflected both the United States' growing sense of responsibility to the world community and the country's self-interested concern for its image abroad. As Marshall's comments to the Cub Scouts suggest, international friendship programs were inextricably tied to the United States' new global stature. They showcased the United States' position as a world leader even as they suggested that private citizens were better equipped than government to rehabilitate the world and to forge the connections that would bind people together in peace.

Like the efforts to impart new child-rearing techniques that were unfolding at the same time, child sponsorship programs relied on and popularized new understandings of human development. International friendship programs called on ordinary Americans to provide foreign children with the emotional security necessary to their healthy development. But the agencies that ran such programs also broadened and reshaped psychological theories in order to apply them to their work with children overseas. Maternal deprivation became familial deprivation; the plasticity of early childhood became the plasticity of childhood and adolescence more broadly. Instead of relying on parents or trained child-care workers, sponsorship programs gave ordinary citizens the opportunity to rehabilitate the war's youngest victims. They made average families in the United States and abroad key players in international affairs.

A NEW FORM OF ADOPTION

Child sponsorship programs were part of a proliferation of international friendship projects that sprang up in American communities large and small in the years following the Second World War. Some efforts involved the adoption of whole communities. For example, residents of Brooklyn, New York,

adopted the city of Breukelen, Holland, showering their Dutch counterparts with nearly fifteen tons of relief goods and more than four thousand
letters. Firemen in Los Angeles adopted firemen in Calais, France. Citizens in Albany, New York, sent packages to a town in Holland where many
local war veterans had seen action during the war, and the two cities com-
menced a weeks-long chess match via airmail. By 1948, more than two hundred towns across the United States had adopted communities in France,
Holland, Italy, Luxembourg, and Germany. In late 1945, several American
voluntary agencies joined together to form CARE (Cooperative for American Remittances to Europe; later, Cooperative for Assistance and Relief Everywhere), an organization through which Americans could send food and
gift packages to their counterparts in Europe. One million food parcels were
sent to individual European families through the organization in 1946 alone.[3]

A number of American voluntary organizations spearheaded and helped
coordinate these adoption programs. But many observers described international friendship projects as organic and spontaneous expressions of Americans' desire to connect with and assist their neighbors across the globe in
the aftermath of a devastating and divisive war. "It may seem too simple for
this complex age, but a new grass roots kind of internationalism is spanning
the Atlantic, without official red tape, legislative oratory or diplomatic jab-
berwocky," noted one journalist in 1948.[4]

International friendship programs were not an entirely new phenomenon
in the post–World War II period. During the interwar years, some Americans had called on children to build bridges of friendship with their counterparts overseas as a means of securing world peace. Churches had organized a number of projects, including an international doll exchange, to
promote friendship between children around the world. Some American
schools had revised their curricula to emphasize internationalism, and more
than five thousand American schoolchildren had penned letters to youngsters overseas. In 1927, the Girl Scouts established the Juliette Low World
Friendship Fund, which sent American girls abroad to meet fellow Girl
Scouts.[5] World War II interrupted some of these international friendship efforts, but the United States' mobilization for the war gave further impetus
to the idea that individual actions had wider political resonance. During the
war, the U.S. government and American voluntary groups called on citizens
young and old to plant victory gardens, buy war bonds, and collect scrap

materials. These individual activities, American leaders insisted, were an invaluable component of the United States' war effort.

After World War II, the number of international friendship efforts expanded exponentially. Advances in communication and transportation made it easier for Americans to send letters and packages around the world. In addition, as Marshall noted, the war had expanded many Americans' sense of the world and their place within it. Wartime service had sent thousands of American men, and some women, abroad for the first time, and the conflict had also brought those on the home front into closer contact with events and peoples across the globe.

Among postwar international friendship programs, those aimed at children predominated. Needy children pulled heartstrings, and American groups could cast youngsters, even those of aggressor nations, in the role of innocent victims more easily than they could their parents. In addition, new understandings of child development emphasized the importance of the formative years in determining adult personality. "How would it make you feel to know that one boy who might have grown into a rabble-rouser will be loyal to democratic principles because of your friendship to him?" the Unitarian Service Committee asked supporters in 1946. As youngsters were understood to harbor no inherent national, racial, or religious prejudices, they were seen to be the consummate ambassadors of goodwill. "European adults face the future with misgivings and hatred, while children face it with love and a desire to share toys," noted Edna Blue, executive chairman of the American sponsorship agency Foster Parents' Plan for War Children.[6]

Children's impressionability also had darker implications. Children growing up without adequate food, clothing—or kindness—were likely to mature into adults susceptible to the empty promises of a future dictator. "Will such adults take their stand with the democratic way of life—the American Way—and be willing to risk their lives to support it—because they have found it the best? Or will these citizens tomorrow follow the first new Superman who puts guns in their hands and promises them the comforts they have never had?" the USC asked supporters in 1947. "Only by supplying these helpless children—with whom our children must build the future—with material and spiritual help can our western civilization and our democratic way of life be saved," insisted a Philadelphia-based "Project to Establish Understanding between American and European Youth." The war's youngest victims, these and many other organizations insisted, would determine the fate of the postwar world.[7]

Americans hoping to make friends with children overseas could choose from a variety of programs. Informal correspondence and gift-exchange schemes matched a foreign child or group of children with a friend or group of friends in the United States. These international friendship programs involved the exchange of letters and sometimes material aid, and they often involved groups of schoolchildren or troops of Girl and Boy Scouts. The largest organization in this category was the Boston-based International Friendship League, founded in 1936 by Edna MacDonough. MacDonough had initiated an international pen-pal program while she was a student at Wellesley College in response to a Danish visiting professor's complaints about young Americans' isolation. Operating on a shoestring budget, MacDonough rented a tiny office and reached out to ministries of education around the world to request the names of schoolchildren who might be interested in participating. When Massachusetts House Speaker Christian Herter heard about MacDonough's project, he worked with her to establish the International Friendship League. Although it focused on young people, not all participants were children; most pen pals were between the ages of nine and twenty-five.[8] Herter would later serve as the governor of Massachusetts and as secretary of state under President Dwight D. Eisenhower. His political influence would bring the International Friendship League to the attention of the U.S. federal government.

In contrast to international correspondence and pen-pal schemes, more formal child sponsorship programs asked Americans to act as foster parents to a needy child at a cost ranging from $96 to $365 annually. Child sponsorship agencies sometimes invited potential foster parents to select the gender and nationality of their sponsored child. After committing to support a child for a year (generally in the form of monthly payments), foster parents would often receive a photograph of the child and a case history that detailed his or her personal characteristics, history, and current living situation. Child sponsorship programs typically channeled donations, letters, and parcels through a central office, where they were read, translated, and coordinated by agency staff. Although standards varied, most child sponsorship programs involved children under eighteen years of age. While informal correspondence programs often used the language of international friendship, child sponsorship programs explicitly invoked familial language and imagery. Indeed, child sponsorship programs were often referred to as adoption programs.

First pioneered by U.S. voluntary agencies during the 1930s, child sponsorship programs expanded rapidly during the years following World War II, spurred in part by the challenge of caring for huge numbers of war orphans. Along with the China's Children Fund, the most prominent American child sponsorship agencies were Foster Parents' Plan for War Children (PLAN) and Save the Children Federation (SCF). Founded in 1937 in Britain by journalist John Langdon-Davies and refugee worker Eric Muggeridge, PLAN first solicited foster parents to support children orphaned by the Spanish Civil War. The organization soon moved its headquarters to the United States and extended support to children affected by World War II. PLAN maintained a stated commitment to political neutrality and supported children without regard to creed. SCF, an offshoot of the British Save the Children Fund, began assisting children in Appalachia in 1932. The organization turned its attention abroad during the Second World War. Like PLAN, SCF was nonsectarian.[9]

These agencies were joined by numerous smaller groups, many with religious or national identities. Rescue Children, founded in 1946 by a group of orthodox Jewish men in New York, matched European Jewish children with American sponsors. Likewise, the World Jewish Congress (WJC), an international federation of Jewish communities and organizations headquartered in New York, recruited Jewish families in the United States to act as correspondents or foster parents to Jewish children abroad. Groups such as the American Friends of Czechoslovakia and American Relief to Italy matched children in those countries with friends in the United States. In addition, several of the voluntary agencies that worked to improve the care of children overseas during the post–World War II years—the American Friends Service Committee, the American Jewish Joint Distribution Committee, and the Unitarian Service Committee—also ran international friendship programs that connected Americans with foreign schoolchildren.

Americans' material contributions through programs of child sponsorship made a significant difference to the lives of many foreign children, some of whom lacked even the basic necessities of survival. Child sponsorship was also an effective fund-raising tool, as it guaranteed a steady stream of monthly contributions, a portion of which was used for overhead expenses. CCF's

J. Calvitt Clarke noted in a letter to a colleague that the sponsorship system "stabilizes one's income better than any other method of raising money." But many sponsorship organizations argued that material donations represented more than just physical assistance. In discussions of relief to European young-sters, foreign voluntary organizations cloaked material aid in the mantle of emotion, insisting that donations served to fortify needy recipients psycho-logically as much—or more—than they did physically. This understanding of foreign assistance mirrored U.S. policymakers' understanding of the psy-chological benefits of American aid to Europe. American diplomat George Kennan reflected on Marshall Plan assistance in a 1953 interview: "The psy-chological success at the outset was so amazing that we felt the psycholog-ical effect was four-fifths accomplished before the first supplies arrived."[10]

Aid to children served a particular psychological purpose: it provided the emotional security that experts such as Anna Freud insisted children needed in order to grow into well-adjusted adults. "YOU can give them what food and medicine alone can never give. These forsaken children need *a sense of belonging*. They must feel that they belong to someone who loves them and cares for them," asserted Rescue Children. The American Friends of Czech-oslovakia agreed: "Each American package is a godsend to them. Yet even more important is the moral support of their sponsors. These orphans long and wait for the letters from their American 'aunts' and 'uncles' who have filled, at least, part of the emptiness left in their hearts." Beneficiaries over-seas often described American aid in similar terms. War orphans needed more than material aid to develop the strength of character needed to be-come healthy adults, argued a child-care worker at a Polish orphanage in a letter to her institution's American benefactors. "They need the sympathy and love of the wide world, and this atmosphere is created through your let-ters and parcels. They are dear to us not for their material value but because they are sent by loving hands and careful thought," the orphanage worker asserted.[11]

To their proponents, international friendship programs often reinforced psychologists' lessons about the significance of children's emotional well-being. Edna Blue recounted a chilling anecdote about how PLAN had come to recognize the emotional importance of letters to children: "It was only after we had been informed that a Czech boy 12 years old hung himself with his necktie and left this note, 'I thought I had friends—but I haven't. The other boys got letters from America but I didn't.' "[12] Catherine Varchaver, a

Russian-born social worker trained at Columbia University who led the WJC's Child Care Division, expressed similar sentiments:

> We were deeply convinced that the first need of these children, after the war and occupation ceased, would be the need of "belonging," the need of love and affection. . . . If, before the end of the war, our projects were founded on a guess, the first letters of children which reached us directly or through the American correspondents early in the Fall and Winter of 1945–46, proved that we have not been mistaken.[13]

According to a study conducted by the WJC, 20 percent of the children involved in its Correspondents' Service actually preferred letters to packages. Another 76 percent of children mentioned their need for material items only after being coaxed by their American friends, the study found. Only 3 to 4 percent of children asked for goods "in a way that might be disagreeable."[14]

Many American voluntary officials celebrated individualized adoptions as providing uprooted children with the sense of kinship, belonging, and emotional solidarity that current child-rearing wisdom described as essential to healthy development. "Does not the present day psychology give us enough knowledge to understand that insecurity and unhappiness in childhood creates instability in adult life?" Varchaver queried. She described her agency's Correspondents' Service as a therapeutic program for children that complemented the efforts of Europe's few trained social workers. For a displaced European child, Varchaver argued, corresponding with an American "constitutes a kind of psychological shock therapy giving him new incentive to live and act again as he feels that 'there is someone in the world who takes a personal interest in him.'" In an article published in a professional social work journal, Varchaver described European children's deep need for affection and gave a name to the principle upon which the WJC based its Correspondents' Service: "rehabilitation through personal contact." PLAN also insisted that personal relationships between European children and their foster parents were key to the children's psychological rehabilitation. "Material help is not enough to heal these children of their scars of war and resulting maladjustments," the organization argued.[15]

Youngsters' emotional health, many argued, was intimately connected with the fate of the postwar world. Psychologically maladjusted children made poor democratic citizens. A democracy required strong, competent, responsible people, explained child psychologist Mary Langmuir; the time to build these strengths was in childhood. Meeting the emotional needs of children, Langmuir contended, was "the only foundation on which a democracy can be built and preserved." Katharine Lenroot, chief of the U.S. Children's Bureau, agreed. "Concerted effort on the part of those responsible for children must be given to the establishment of permanent human ties, or we cannot develop in these orphans of the war the love of freedom and the principles of democracy," Lenroot argued in 1946. She urged her fellow child welfare professionals to focus their attention not only on the war's young victims but also on the offspring of the United States' former enemies.[16]

Indeed, while Americans looked to international friendship programs to heal the emotional wounds of war orphans, they also looked to them as a means of reforming and reeducating children in Germany. When the *Saturday Evening Post* published an article describing a gang of streetwise German teenagers living in a bombed-out house and surviving by stealing food and other necessities, Anna Caples of the American Association for a Democratic Germany suggested that personal letters might help to reform the toughened youngsters. "Maybe your young people would be interested in writing to Dieter in Cologne, the gang leader described in the 'Saturday Evening Post' article," Caples wrote to psychologist Ernst Papanek, who ran an international friendship organization. "If he gets some offers of friendship and understanding from children in other countries he might turn into a constructive citizen and not a hardened criminal as the author of the 'Saturday Evening Post' article seems to expect." The AFSC described German youngsters as eager to cultivate relationships with friends in the United States. "From all over Germany, the American Friends Service Committee receives letters, especially from young people, asking simply that someone write to them, and day after day our workers report a deep hunger for friendship on the part of German youth," the organization reported. AFSC officials argued that international friendships could offer German schoolchildren a practical lesson in democracy and in the American value of individual dignity. Even General Lucius Clay worked to recruit American sponsors for German children after retiring from his position as military governor, lauding the work performed by sponsorship organizations as a "contribution to future world peace."[17]

But not all voluntary agencies were convinced that sponsorship programs were in foreign children's best interest. JDC officials were uncomfortable with adoption programs because individual packages and letters escaped agency oversight. This made it difficult for the JDC to accurately assess a child's needs and to adjust the nature of the assistance provided as these needs changed over time. Moreover, the JDC condemned adoptions as violating the basic social service principles of fairness and equitable distribution, as some children would inevitably be matched with foster parents or friends with more resources and enthusiasm than others, while others would be left without any international relationships at all.[18] JDC officials were convinced that relief was best administered under the auspices of a centralized organization committed to objective social work principles, not by ordinary Americans via the long-distance post.

The JDC's position brought it into conflict with another Jewish organization, the WJC. The WJC's attempt to enlist the assistance of the JDC in administering its Correspondents' Service in 1948 resulted in a heated exchange of letters between the WJC's Catherine Varchaver and JDC official Henrietta Buchman. Buchman charged that the WJC's Correspondents' Service and other adoption programs were governed by "luck and chance factors" that the organization could never adequately control and that such programs were bound to "fall short of meeting the fundamental needs of the children." Varchaver responded that "luck and chance" factors inevitably played a role in determining the nature of children's relationships, as some European youngsters had blood relatives in the United States while others were without kin. Moreover, she insisted, the JDC's understanding of children's "fundamental needs" was flawed. "Am I to understand that the 'fundamental needs' of children consist exclusively of their physical needs, which, by the way, are also not completely met by the existing relief agencies?" Varchaver wrote. "It is my opinion that the fundamental needs of the children include not only their physical, but even more their emotional needs. . . . This service provides ample opportunity to meet the emotional needs of the children."[19]

Varchaver's comments reveal the extent to which emotional security had by midcentury assumed a prominent position as one of the "fundamental needs" of childhood. Indeed, few of the JDC's fellow voluntary agencies saw a conflict between individualized sponsorship programs and the sound precepts of social work that Americans sought to share with their European peers. And, given the popularity of these adoption programs among the American public, even the JDC relented: the organization ran a "school adoption" program that matched European and American schools, and its European director, Joseph Schwartz, condoned children's adoption programs that involved only the exchange of letters, not material aid.[20]

The connections between international friendship programs and children's emotional health were strengthened by some of the programs' associations with prominent psychologists and child welfare experts. PLAN provided financial support to Anna Freud and Dorothy Burlingham's famous Hampstead Nurseries during World War II and for several years thereafter. Although Freud and Burlingham never publicly equated child sponsorship with emotional rehabilitation, the connections between sponsorship and modern child psychology were bolstered by the psychoanalysts' close relationship with the organization (during the war years, Freud and Burlingham penned monthly reports on the nurseries to send to PLAN supporters in the United States). Psychologist Ernst Papanek founded an organization called American Youth for World Youth (AYWY) following the conclusion of World War II. Initially affiliated with the USC, AYWY facilitated the exchange of correspondence and material aid between children and young people in the United States and around the world. AYWY's executive chairman was prominent progressive educator William Heard Kilpatrick, and its advisory board included child welfare luminaries such as Katharine Lenroot and Martha Eliot (until time constraints led her to resign). Many of the organizations committed to promoting children's psychological health—the USC, the AFSC, the JDC—also ran or supported correspondence programs during the immediate postwar years. Child sponsorship programs reaffirmed the focus on the individual that was at the heart of American social work. Unlike mass relief projects, international friendship programs required a certain level of knowledge about each individual being assisted. This requirement often turned untrained child-care workers into de facto caseworkers, enlisted to compile case histories that related to American sponsors the identities and experiences of foreign youngsters.

Proponents of these adoption and correspondence programs worked in concert with the child guidance movement and psychologically oriented child-rearing experts such as Benjamin Spock to disseminate to the American public current theories regarding the psychological importance of the family and the detrimental effects of children's unmet emotional needs. But voluntary agencies also reworked the tenets of child development expounded by psychoanalysts such as Anna Freud and John Bowlby. American organizations depicted a larger window for emotional damage than psychoanalysts generally recognized, but they also described this damage as potentially less en-during than many experts appreciated. For example, Freud and Burlingham enumerated the detrimental physical and psychological effects of maternal deprivation on young children. The effects of paternal separation, the psy-choanalysts argued, were less severe than those associated with separation from mothers.[21] Voluntary organizations working with children, however, spoke not of maternal deprivation but of familial deprivation more generally. Moreover, while psychoanalysts saw maternal separation as most deleterious to infants and very young children, voluntary workers described separation from family as potentially damaging to youngsters of any age, even to ado-lescents. And while psychoanalysts saw the damaging effects of childhood deprivation as permanently imprinted on a child's psyche, voluntary agen-cies generally portrayed such damage as largely reversible, with the appro-priate intervention.

American workers portrayed family bonds—even artificial, long-distance ones—as capable of healing children's psychological scars and providing them with firm emotional grounding. While child psychiatrists elevated maternal care, voluntary groups implied that anyone, male or female, young or old, could fill the role of emotional provider. American organizations attempted to recruit both men and women to serve as foster parents. PLAN, for ex-ample, described itself as offering "a mother's love, a father's strength and a brother's hand." An orphan needs the "strong hand of a grown brother who takes this little, little one, who hasn't any way of getting by, and lifts him over the rough going," declared New York City mayor William O'Dwyer, who adopted a Jewish war orphan through Rescue Children, in an appeal that appeared to be aimed specifically at men.[22] Psychologists described the presence of a warm, steady caretaker as essential to children's emotional health. American agencies stretched this theory to its breaking point, maintaining that foster parents need not even meet their adopted children in person. A steady stream of letters and packages, American workers insisted, could cement a child's sense of emotional security.

Voluntary organizations' reinterpretation of psychological theories stemmed in part from a desire to reach as many children and donors as pos-sible: a larger body of damaged youngsters, along with an expanded pool of people capable of assisting them, served the purposes of groups wishing to expand their overseas programs. But sponsorship organizations' faith in the ability of foster parents to reshape the lives of foreign youngsters was also rooted in a sense of confidence and optimism generated by new theories about children's malleability. Many culture-and-personality scholars embraced child rearing as a tool for social engineering; indeed, one scholar called the discovery of the transformative power of child rearing "potentially one of the greatest scientific discoveries of modern times."[23] But Margaret Mead and her fellow theorists also generally acknowledged that enacting cultural change was rarely a direct or an immediate process. Sponsorship groups absorbed the culture-and-personality school's theories and enthusiasm but not its caveats. Bending new theories to meet their own needs, voluntary groups insisted that long-distance parenting could enhance children's psychological well-being and help mold a generation that differed drastically from the one that preceded it.

LONG-DISTANCE FAMILIES

Virtual adoption programs allowed Americans to directly assist foreign youngsters without bringing these children to the United States. In the years following the war, American offers to legally adopt European children far exceeded the number of youngsters available. Several pieces of postwar legislation facilitated the immigration of unaccompanied children to the United States. But by September 1951, only a small number of Europe's parentless youngsters—about 2,500—had immigrated to the United States under this legislation. This figure included many older teenagers who were unlikely candidates for adoption by American families. The majority of European countries did not wish to relinquish their orphans. Of eleven European governments polled by American officials, only three indicated interest in sending youngsters to the United States for adoption. American adoptions of European children were further impeded by social workers' adherence to the practice of religious matching. American agencies' refusal to place children with families outside of their religious faith hindered American families' efforts to legally adopt European children. The practice of religious matching made adoption particularly difficult for Jewish families. There were far more American Jewish families wishing to adopt a child than there were Jewish children available for adoption, both in the United States and abroad. In Europe, many Jewish children who had survived the war were no longer of adoptable age; among those children young enough to benefit from adoption, many were taken in by relatives or chose to immigrate to Israel instead of to America.[24]

Through child sponsorship programs, Americans could cultivate a personal relationship with a war orphan at a time when legally adopting such a child was difficult, if not impossible, for many families. But these programs ultimately represented a different impulse than did legal adoption. Legally adopting a war orphan involved incorporating that child into the American social body. Sponsoring a child overseas, however, served as a means of rehabilitating not only that youngster but also his or her country. "It has always been our feeling that children should be brought up in their own countries," noted Edna Blue. "Surely every devastated country in Europe will need its children."[25] Sponsorship endowed the act of child rearing with expansive political significance even as it presented sponsors with a pared-down version of parenthood that need not extend beyond the monthly post.

With a vast ocean between them, children and foster parents united through sponsorship and correspondence programs could avoid the problems that frequently plagued actual families. Liberated from the conflicts of day-to-day family life, these relationships of fictive kin promised the emotional benefits of kinship without its attendant hazards. Perhaps it is not surprising, then, that many European children sought to cultivate intimate relationships with American foster parents. For Jewish children, many of whom had seen all of their relatives perish at the hands of the Nazis, connections forged with Americans helped stave off loneliness and provided the assurance that someone cared about them as individuals. Children like Robert, who had lost both of his parents during the war, sought out a fictive family in an effort to reestablish the personal bonds that the Nazis had severed. The boy addressed a note to the WJC from the children's home where he was residing:

> As I have no family anymore, I would like very much to start a correspondence with a Jewish family who would understand what I suffered during these horrible years, and I will show myself grateful for the affection that they will give me. Therefore I am addressing you, to meet my new family.[26]

French youngster Charles likewise expressed gratitude for his new, long-distance kin. "It is very good to have a mother," he wrote to his foster mother in New York. "I have lost mine and now that I have no mother I feel how much I miss her in everything." Even young adults appreciated the affectionate bonds of fictive kinship. "You cannot imagine my happiness when I get a letter from you," twenty-three-year-old Yichak of Italy wrote to Anna of Brooklyn, New York. "It is like getting a letter from my own parents." Children often expressed gratitude for the emotional security and friendship that foster parents provided. Tamara and Natan, residents of the Otwock Children's Home in Poland, informed their American friends: "We are very pleased when your packages arrive. Not because they bring us cloth[e]s, but because they are greetings from you, because they tell us that you remember us and we feel much less lonely."[27]

Of course, not all children saw their American foster parents as a source of love and emotional security. Some youngsters saw overseas parents as a source for much-desired material goods. European children's conceptions of Americans as wealthy benefactors were shaped by their interactions with U.S. servicemen as well as by the popular media. American soldiers commonly treated local children to candy, chewing gum, and Christmas parties. Many American movies, popular among European youth, reinforced the notion that the United States was a land of plenty. European children "think of America (as I'm afraid much of Europe does) as a fairyland with Hershey chocolate bars and Wrigley chewing gum trees lining every road," an American relief worker reported in 1946. Children asked their foster parents for a variety of items: clothing, shoes, dolls, and typewriters. Some, such as eleven-year-old Jacob, were quite specific. "Since long I dream to have my own football boots," the Belgian orphan informed his foster parent, carefully noting his shoe size.[28]

Packages from America were a source of delight for children. A child in Brussels described to her American "godmother" the reception her package had received: "when the postman brought it my little brother delivered it to me with an Indian dance, and when the package was opened, the three of us [the writer and her foster brothers] started dancing in Indian fashion so that my aunt was quite amazed when she found us a[t] it. You can hardly imagine what pleasure you have given to me."[29] One Japanese girl wrote to her American friends: "For the splendid Western clothes I received the other day thanks very much. I was so happy I couldn't sleep." Packages sent by American youngsters in the Junior Red Cross elicited a similar reaction among children, a Norwegian schoolteacher attested:

> The children unpacked the boxes with trembling hands and as the wonderful gifts were coming to light, the joy was tremendous. I was quite afraid that the kids would get hysteric. The children cried and laughed. They clapped

their hands and they jumped and embraced each other, they ran to and fro to show and to look.

The mood of ecstasy was broken only when the children attempted to eat the unfamiliar gift of marbles.[30]

But gratitude for American plenitude could slip into resentment for the material advantages enjoyed by those in the United States. "We are glad that you live well and you don't know our bad life in this country," Zsusi, a Hungarian girl, grudgingly informed her foster parent. "I have neither clothing nor shoes, and I have not eaten chocolate for five years." Tony, an Italian youngster, wrote in a letter to the United States, "When we had to go to the air-raid shelters, maybe you were enjoying yourselves; even during the school hours we had to run to the shelter."[31] American largesse cemented the bonds of friendship between foster parents and foreign children, but it also made startlingly clear the disparities in the standards of living of donor and recipient. This was particularly true in programs that matched foreign children with peers in the United States. While differences in wealth or class were naturalized to a certain extent in the child-foster parent relationship—parents, after all, traditionally provided for the needs of their offspring—socioeconomic disparities between youngsters themselves often stood out in sharp relief.

These disparities hindered the development of the AFSC's school affiliation program, which facilitated the exchange of correspondence and material aid between American and European schoolchildren. "The American children in their naïvety write the things that normal American children of middle-class families would write—of their big schools with gymnasiums and auditoriums where they have movies, of riding in cars and playing with bicycles and electric trains," noted Dorothy Barrus, an AFSC representative stationed in Italy. Such topics failed to establish common ground with impoverished Italian children. Similarly, students at a French school were hesitant to respond to letters from their overseas friends due to an awareness of the vast social differences that divided them from their American peers. The children were afraid their letters "may seem colorless and without attraction to your young girls," explained the French director in a letter to the head of her school's Richmond, Virginia, affiliate.[32]

Correspondence from abroad could also make American children feel ill at ease. For example, students in an American second-grade class found it difficult to relate to their classmates in Europe. "It was hard for the children to realize that there were boys and girls who wanted soap more than toys," their teacher reported. Thirteen-year-old Jeanette wrote to her pen pal in New York City about the day the Germans shot her father and burned her home before her eyes.[33] Stories such as Jeanette's gave American children an intimate view of the atrocities of war, but they also drove home uncomfortable distinctions between European children, who had lived in a war zone, and youngsters in the United States, who had experienced the conflict at a much greater remove.

Alfred E. Stearns, headmaster of Phillips Andover Academy and chairman of the AFSC's Overseas Schools Committee, noted the vital importance of instructing American pupils "to construct their letters [so] that feelings on the other side of the water may not be hurt and social and financial differences be minimized." But Stearns doubted that relationships between children of vastly different social backgrounds could prove enduring. A number of the European children participating in the program "would be termed peasants in their own country, and much as they would need and profit by contacts with our American boys and girls, it is difficult for me to believe that these contacts would be continued in later years," Stearns contended.[34] Socioeconomic differences hindered the development of international friendships and stymied American organizations' efforts to cultivate enduring peer relationships that crossed national lines.

Still, international friendship programs allowed Americans to craft relationships that not only reached across national boundaries but also crossed the lines of religion and race. For example, the leftist Jewish Labor Committee (JLC), an organization founded in 1934 in New York by Jewish trade union leaders as a vehicle for opposing Nazism, organized a child sponsorship program during the postwar years. The JLC supported the children of Jewish partisans, writers, and labor leaders who had been victimized by the Nazis, as well as children whose parents had died fighting fascism and children of non-Jews who had perished trying to assist Jews. In keeping with the JLC's liberal politics, the organization's program encouraged labor unions to adopt children across religious and racial lines as a means of fighting racism and promoting democratic values. Through the JLC, Italian workers adopted a Jewish orphan and Jewish workers sponsored a Christian child whose father had been killed during an anti-fascist uprising. "Often the membership of the unions and shops 'adopting' the children is of mixed origin, such as Italians,

Mexicans, Negroes, etc. The participation of workers of all religions, races and nationalities in this program is a significant force for democratic ideals and against anti-Semitism in the shops and unions," the JLC asserted.[35]

While sponsorship and correspondence programs expressed participants' tolerance and their sense of responsibility to the world community, however, they just as often reinforced social categories as they eroded them. The JLC's call for adoption across racial and religious lines, for example, was also a call for class solidarity. Groups such as the American Friends of Czechoslovakia, which offered adoptions of Czech children, likely appealed largely to a constituency of the same national background. Many of the sponsorship and correspondence programs initiated in the immediate postwar years were spearheaded by Jewish organizations, which appealed to American Jews to take part in the rehabilitation of the European Jewish community in the wake of the Holocaust. Some people even looked to international friendship programs as a means of solidifying American Jews' religious identity. "I am sure that the meeting of minds across the sea is something which would go far toward making Jewish boys and girls here living in a peaceful, happy, and liberal environment realize that they are Jews in a very real sense," noted a student hoping to interest his peers in corresponding with young Holocaust survivors in Europe. International friendship programs reinforced a version of what Benedict Anderson has called "long-distance nationalism"—a sense of national pride and solidarity among the members of a community in exile.[36] By providing a venue through which Americans could give aid to children of their own national or religious heritage, child sponsorship programs strengthened the affective ties between U.S. citizens and their conationalists and coreligionists across the globe.

With the exception of CCF, which assisted children in six Asian countries, most of the agencies that ran sponsorship and international friendship programs in the immediate postwar years worked primarily in Europe. By 1948, for example, the AFSC's school affiliation service had only one affiliated school in Japan but had 117 in France, 62 in Germany, 15 in Holland, 8 in Italy, and 2 in Poland.[37] Ties of kinship and cultural affinity bound American families to their counterparts in Europe. Meanwhile, U.S. immigration laws stifled Asian immigration to America, and the Japanese American population within the United States was comparatively small and marginalized. Influenced by the virulent racialized hatred directed at the Japanese during the war, many Americans no doubt hesitated to reach out to Japanese youngsters in the war's immediate aftermath. Expressing solidarity with the children of Japan was politically problematic for Americans of Japanese descent, many of whom had spent the duration of the war in internment camps as suspected potential traitors. International friendship programs were shaped by U.S. demographics and by logistical realities, such as the ability to translate letters. But they were also influenced by shared understandings of which children counted as victims and as friends. During the immediate postwar years, Americans were far more eager to extend support and friendship to children in Europe—even those in Germany and Italy—than they were to reach out to children in Japan and elsewhere in Asia.

Furthermore, Americans generally viewed their participation in international friendship and adoption programs as a means of assisting war victims and contributing to international affairs, not as a means of assisting the foreign poor. The British Save the Children Fund, for example, noted that its American subscribers preferred to help children who had been affected directly by the war, such as victims of air raids and children whose fathers were serving with the armed forces, rather than assist poor foreign children more generally. The fund assigned its many cases of needy children who had been affected only indirectly by the war to its British subscribers. Likewise, PLAN catered to donors' desire to assist young war victims. The organization's English director, Judy Mason, cut down a list of potential children to be sponsored in London's East End, she wrote to Edna Blue, "as although they were all poor, they were not suffering from the effect of war and I knew they would not help at all."[38]

"MORE POWERFUL THAN THE ATOMIC BOMB"

One of the most public displays of international friendship after the war was the first annual celebration of the World Christmas and Chanukah Festivals, a Europe-wide event organized by American voluntary organizations. Held on December 18, 1945, the festivals brought together thousands of children in war-ravaged capital cities. In London, children congregated at the Mansion House. In Prague, youngsters replaced the German tanks that had recently occupied the Old Town Square. In Brussels, Copenhagen, and Athens, children gathered at city halls. In Paris, four thousand children attended a celebration at the Gaumont Palace, where they heard speeches from dignitaries, including General Charles de Gaulle. In twelve cities across the European continent, more than 200,000 children who had lost parents in concentration camps or in the resistance movement received gift packages donated by American children. Marked with the name and address of its American donor, each package was not only a token of holiday cheer but also an invitation to build an ongoing friendship with a child across the Atlantic. One organizer described the festivals as "uniting millions in love and friendship like members of one family around the globe."[39]

The World Education Service Council and the World Festivals for Friendship, the American voluntary agencies that organized the World Christmas and Chanukah Festivals, were among the plethora of American organizations devoted to building peace through international friendship. The World Education Service Council was founded in 1944 by a group of American and European émigré educators and led by Reinhold Schairer, a German-born educator who had fled the Nazi regime. The World Festivals for Friendship, founded the following year, was an associated group established by Schairer's wife, Gerda, a Danish-born social worker. Both Reinhold and Gerda Schairer had been active in educational reconstruction and international friendship efforts during the war. Reinhold Schairer had also been a participant in the Germany after the War conference. In putting together the World Christmas and Chanukah Festivals, their organizations were assisted by dozens of American voluntary groups across the country, whose members held collection drives, wrapped gift packages, and sent them to warehouses in New York, where they awaited their trans-Atlantic voyage. The gifts were shipped overseas on "unity boats," so called because they marked a united Christian-Jewish effort to brighten the holidays of children overseas. The World Christmas and Chanukah Festivals would be celebrated in mid-December each year for several years to come, expanding both in size and in breadth. By 1947, about half a million gifts collected by Americans had been distributed to children in fifteen countries; by 1948, the figure had reached nearly a million.[40]

The festivals were an occasion for Europe's children, some of whom had never received a holiday gift, to partake in the joy of the season. But they also carried subtle (and not-so-subtle) political messages. In focusing, at least initially, on children who had lost parents in concentration camps or in the resistance movement, they created a hierarchy of worthiness for aid that privileged children who had been victimized or whose parents had espoused the "proper" politics. Moreover, like most international friendship programs, the festivals favored European youngsters: while eight crates of gifts were earmarked for China in 1945, the vast majority were sent to Europe. Poland, for example, received forty-nine crates of gifts; France received forty-two; the Netherlands received thirty-eight; and even Russia received ten crates (none were sent to Germany in 1945, likely due in part to military restrictions). And although the festivals were touted as an opportunity to cement the bonds of worldwide friendship, they did more to support America's friendship with Europe—and, indeed, to showcase the generosity of the United States—than to unite the world as a whole. At the Paris celebration, for example, organizers played the Marseillaise and the Star-Spangled Banner, attendees heard speeches on Franco-American friendship, and American soldiers donned Santa Claus suits and distributed the gift packages. Children attending the festivals across Europe also heard a radio program broadcast from New York City's Carnegie Hall. The World Education Service Council asked American children to pledge to give "one present a year to one child overseas."[41] The festivals and the activities surrounding them situated consumer goods as a chief medium of international communication and friendship. They trained American children and their peers abroad to see the United States as the preeminent global benefactor.

On the one hand, the World Christmas and Chanukah Festivals—and child sponsorship and other international friendship programs more generally—were part of a brief postwar moment in which new forms of worldwide interaction and cooperation appeared both desirable and politically viable. These programs reflected a widely shared optimism regarding the power of international activism and friendship in forestalling another global crisis and in creating "one world" united in peace. On the other hand, however, international friendship programs suggest that the immediate postwar period was not a fleeting interlude of international cooperation snuffed out by the impending Cold War but the first chapter of the Cold War itself. In supporting a vision of the United States as the undisputed global leader—as Secretary of State Marshall stated in his speech to the Cub Scouts, "the most powerful nation in the world"—the international friendship programs of the late 1940s subtly assisted in laying the groundwork for a divided world order in which America was hegemonic.

Among the architects of this postwar order was the atomic bomb. Many observers noted that the bomb had completely shattered the distinction between the home front and the battle zone, making every citizen—man and woman, adult and child—a central player in world affairs. In the atomic age, Alice Pollard noted in her proposal to Marshall Plan designer William

Clayton, "no government on earth can offer protection in a secure, paternalistic way to its people. . . . We who make up the population of the world,
in our feelings are like orphans; we cannot look to our governments for authority or protection. . . . Ours is in essence an orphan age."[42] The inability
of states to protect their citizens made international relations the concern,
and the responsibility, of each and every person.

Some people saw relationships cultivated across the Atlantic, particularly
those involving impressionable children, as a means of supporting official
efforts of postwar rehabilitation and reconciliation. Eleanor Roosevelt, for
example, praised international friendship efforts as "the best background for
successful operation of the United Nations or the Marshall Plan." Roosevelt
sponsored several European children through PLAN during World War II,
taking time out of her official duties as First Lady to pay them a personal
visit. A Marshall Plan administrator in Italy noted that the work of the American voluntary agencies engaged in sponsorship work "supplements, and to
some degree, complements the activities of our Mission here."[43]

Others viewed government-sponsored rehabilitation efforts with more
skepticism, casting child sponsorship programs as one response to a world
in which citizens were charged with guaranteeing their own safety and survival. "It is becoming clear," Lawrence K. Frank asserted in 1948, "that the
task of maintaining peace and good-will on earth rests with the parents and
teachers of our future citizens." CCF described child sponsorship as a form
of security appropriate for an atomic age. "The days for building a Chinese
wall or a Maginot Line are past. The only walls that will stand are the sheltering walls of friendship. Such walls are not built around a single country
but enclose one world," the organization argued in 1948. Some foreign participants described international friendship programs in similar terms. "We
all believe that your way of making friends in other countries is a very important step towards the One World we all want," a girls' school in Vienna
wrote to its American correspondents.[44]

The atomic bomb was evidence of the unprecedented destructive capa-
bilities made possible by modern science. But, some insisted, modern science also offered a means by which to counter the bomb's terrifying power.
The atomic bomb was, after all, created by humans. And new theories of
child development suggested that nothing about human nature—not aggression, not insecurity, not authoritarianism—was preordained. "If it is the nature of human nature to be thus malleable, then, in the face of this fact, the

atomic bomb, which is only a creature of man, itself recedes into secondary importance," explained culture-and-personality theorist Weston LaBarre. Adoption and international friendship programs were a means by which all Americans could assist in molding peace-loving citizens who would never contemplate using the bomb, let alone create an even more powerful one. The real draftsmen of the postwar order would be those who crafted humans, not those who created weapons. "Together," opined Harriet Eager Davis, writing in *Parents'* magazine, "we parents and children must find the ways to keep the human heart and the human head more powerful than the atomic bomb."[45]

Voluntary groups elevated private citizens over the government in mitigating the threats of the atomic age. But their efforts were in many ways made possible by the American state's newly expansive global reach. U.S. government officials around the world recognized the political significance of correspondence and sponsorship programs and often lent their support to them. U.S. Army officials in Germany facilitated the exchange of letters between German and American children, helped coordinate affiliations between German and American schools, and on occasion even matched individual German children with pen pals in the United States. "Here the personal relationships can be established which make possible the transmission of dynamic ideas," argued Lois E. Wells, an official with the Public Welfare Branch of the U.S. Military Government. "Here the groundwork for 'one world' begins." The U.S. government used Voice of America broadcasts to recruit foreign youngsters to serve as pen pals to American children. By 1953, American embassies had received such a large quantity of requests for foreign correspondents from both the United States and abroad that the Department of State established guidelines to deal with the influx. Each embassy received a list of private organizations to whom potential pen pals (both children and adults) could be referred. State Department officials refused to provide funding to friendship organizations, believing that government involvement would undermine the value of letters and taint them as propaganda. But it did attempt to steer some groups, most notably the International Friendship League, toward private foundations that might be willing to fund their operations.[46]

The U.S. government also supported private efforts in a more abstract sense: state-sponsored programs such as the Marshall Plan helped teach Americans that their own fate was inextricably connected with that of Europe and the world at large, a lesson that encouraged American participation in international friendship projects. Despite their ambivalence toward government-sponsored programs, proponents of private efforts provided veiled acknowledgments of the state's continued significance even in the so-called orphan age: Alice Pollard was writing to the U.S. government even as she argued for its waning relevance in the realm of international security. Moreover, the government itself joined private groups in their mistrust of state-sponsored friendship efforts, concerned that such programs could appear to be propaganda. International friendship programs extended the power of the American state even as they questioned its efficacy in building a more peaceful and secure world order.

For their part, foreign participants in pen-pal and sponsorship programs often made little distinction between their American friends and the U.S. government at large. Gifts from the United States were at once expressions of private goodwill and evidence of American global power, a fact not lost on many recipients. "I thank all the American people for all what they have done for the liberation of our country and what they do for the whole world now and especially for Holland," wrote a Dutch child in a letter to his American friends. A twelve-year-old French boy told his sponsor, "I was in Lyons at the time of the liberation and had the great pleasure to acclaim the American army and even to kiss one of your soldiers; we were so happy to be liberated. I would like to thank you again and please allow me to send you a big hug." A Belgian headmaster also associated his students' American sponsors with U.S. soldiers: "I just distributed a few packages (Christmas presents from the United States) which were sent to me from Brussels. My little pupils were very happy and hailed the United States of America. (That reminded me of September 1944 and of your soldiers, our liberators)."[47] Conflating ordinary American people with representations of American global power more broadly, these foreign participants erased the distinction between private expressions of friendship and public expressions of U.S. influence and authority.

International friendship programs allowed Americans to celebrate the United States' new global stature even as they lamented their government's inability to protect them in the atomic age. They allowed Americans to embrace an internationalist ethos even as they assisted youngsters of their own national and religious backgrounds—and even as they focused on their country's own image abroad. Merging the emotional security of children and the physical security of the postwar world, international friendship programs addressed the needs of war orphans and "orphaned" citizens alike.

CHAPTER FOUR

Raising Little Cold Warriors

ON DECEMBER 12, 1952, a woman's impassioned plea interrupted the last session of the International Study Conference on Child Welfare in Bombay, India. Organized by the Geneva-based International Union for Child Welfare, the conference had drawn participants from twenty-six countries, including the United States. Over the course of a week, delegates had discussed issues relating to child health, development, and education, and considered the role of child welfare in helping to raise the standard of living in underdeveloped areas. Participants had already voted to pass resolutions recognizing mankind's responsibility to children and affirming the importance of teaching youngsters the principles of cooperation. Then, a young Indian woman rushed onto the platform and argued powerfully for a final resolution. Describing peace as essential to the world's children, she urged the conference to pledge its cooperation with all groups involved in the movement to promote world peace.[1]

The woman's proposal alarmed American participants. It was, noted one observer, a "somewhat disguised way of providing for cooperation with international communist front organizations." The resolution "was so worded that it would commit the Conference to some new 'Stockholm peace petition,'" reported an American embassy official, referring to a nuclear disarmament measure suspected of communist backing. American delegate Evelyn Hersey successfully defused the situation by suggesting a broad resolution that eliminated references to cooperation with international groups. Her proposal for a general commitment to the promotion of world peace and human solidarity received the audience's enthusiastic approval.[2]

U.S. officials had anticipated communist attempts to influence the conference proceedings in Bombay. Secretary of State Dean Acheson and President Harry Truman urged American participation in the conference, seeing it—along with the Sixth International Conference of Social Work held in Madras the following week—as a prime opportunity to combat communist propaganda that described the United States as indifferent to social welfare. Although the Department of State did not generally send representatives to conferences organized by nongovernmental organizations, American officials agreed that the social welfare conferences in India were particularly significant meetings with "broad political implications." The American ambassador to India, Chester Bowles, underscored the importance of U.S. participation in a telegram to Washington: "Earnestly hope funds will be available . . . allow us do bang-up job these two conf. Last year Commies more effective than we this sort of project and it is essential we get on top and stay there in whole field social progress." The Department of State funded the participation of four American delegates associated with the Federal Security Agency. It held several meetings, including a five-day "indoctrination course" organized by the U.S. embassy in India, to brief all American conference participants on U.S. policy in South Asia and to prepare them to respond to criticisms from communists and communist sympathizers whom they might encounter. Rumors circulated of communist attempts to organize a rival conference in Bombay to run simultaneous to the child welfare conference, but no such conference ever materialized.[3]

The concerns surrounding the International Study Conference demonstrate the extent to which child welfare was becoming, by the early 1950s, a battlefield in the intensifying Cold War. In the years immediately following World War II, American agencies had promoted overseas child welfare projects as a means of creating international peace and goodwill. They saw their efforts as helping to shape a new generation of citizens who would eschew the prejudices and militarism of their forebears and forge a more secure world community. But the dawning of the Cold War rendered peace efforts suspect and lent further weight to the impulse—always present in American efforts on behalf of children abroad—to use child welfare as a means of burnishing America's image overseas. In a newly divided world, many

American organizations recast their international programs for children as a means of staving off communism in critical regions across the globe.

As one of the first child welfare conferences to be held in the East, the International Study Conference on Child Welfare represented the shifting epicenter of American humanitarian efforts overseas. With the Chinese Revolution in 1949 and the outbreak of the Korean War the following year, the Asian continent moved quickly to the forefront of American foreign policy. A rebounding European economy, along with a recognition of the strategic significance of what many referred to as "underdeveloped" regions, led American voluntary organizations to gradually phase out programs in Western Europe during the 1950s, replacing them with efforts devoted to helping children in southern Europe, Asia, and the Middle East. (Smaller agencies often ended their programs of aid altogether.) While a number of organizations, including the American Friends Service Committee and the International Friendship League, continued to run international friendship programs, the child sponsorship field in the United States was soon dominated by three large agencies: China's Children Fund, Foster Parents' Plan for War Children, and Save the Children Federation. All three directed their attention eastward.

As American organizations expanded across the globe during the 1950s, child welfare was at once an emblem of democracy and a tool wielded to reshape foreign societies. By assisting the youngest and most vulnerable members of nations overseas, American agencies showcased U.S. generosity and benevolence on a global stage. As private organizations, their efforts served as a testament to the superiority of American voluntarism and free enterprise. Intimate relationships between Americans and children overseas would curtail the spread of communism, binding together the citizens of the free world with ties that supported the United States' political alliances.

"OUR CHOSEN WEAPONS"

Some voluntary officials were quick to connect aid to children with growing Cold War strategic concerns. For example, SCF's Charles R. Joy penned a report on aid to Poland in 1947:

> It is very important that the Polish people should know that these things are the gift of the western democracy. Therefore, it will be worth any cost in time or trouble or money to label garments, and tag shoes, and stamp cartons and

cases. If the American flag could be used it would be wonderful. If the tags could be in Polish it would greatly help. But the word America, whether in English or Polish, should appear everywhere. After all we are fighting a battle for freedom and democracy ourselves, even though our chosen weapons are food and shoes and overcoats and kindness.[4]

Joy saw SCF as a central participant in the struggle against what he would later refer to as "the terrible menace of this evil thing in the world." Likewise, CCF's J. Calvitt Clarke saw his organization as a player in the global fight against communism. "If I want to injure Communism in China," he noted in 1950, "I know of no better way to fight it than to support the children in the orphanages of China's Children Fund because they have instilled in them a realization that America saved their lives."[5]

But Clarke's anticommunist crusade in China would not last very long. By late 1950, the political climate in China rendered American aid to Chinese children impossible. Verent Mills, who would soon assume the role of CCF's overseas director, sent home troubling reports about the thousands of children sponsored by Americans. In letters to CCF's Richmond headquarters, Mills documented the new Chinese government's efforts to indoctrinate youngsters. The Communist regime had forced the orphanages in Canton to take a vow to avoid all contact with Americans, he reported, making youngsters hoping to correspond with their foster parents fear for their lives. The orphanages had also participated in a government-mandated Down with America program, in which children chanted slogans and sat for examinations that tested their knowledge of party orthodoxy. Finally, the Chinese government froze CCF's assets and took over administration of the orphanages it supported. Both CCF and PLAN ended their programs in China in late 1950. PLAN had been caring for over six hundred children in China; CCF had been sponsoring over five thousand. It took Mills four months to comply with the new government's onerous exit visa requirements.[6]

Ousted from China, Clarke shifted his attention to other countries across the Asian continent. He changed his organization's name to Christian Children's Fund (also known by the acronym CCF) and established its new overseas headquarters in Hong Kong. From there, CCF prepared to continue the fight against communism. The organization housed, fed, and educated child refugees who had fled mainland China. In Korea, CCF would offer support to thousands of children orphaned or displaced by the Korean War.

In India, it established an orphanage that one admirer called "one of the most effective answers to Communism I observed in all Asia." By 1961, one of its employees would boast, "The work of the Christian Children's Fund has done more for America's prestige abroad than $10,000,000,000 in armament assistance!"[7]

As in China, political vicissitudes dictated the shuttering of programs in Eastern Europe. As the Cold War heated up, American agencies found their programs unwelcome in all countries behind the Iron Curtain. Helen Fogg, director of child and youth projects for the Unitarian Service Committee, visited Czechoslovakia following the Communist coup in 1948 to see if a training program for child-care workers in the organization's Hana Benesova Children's Home could be carried out under Communist rule. The project appeared unwelcome, and the organization ended its Czechoslovakian program that year. In 1949, the Bulgarian, Czechoslovakian, Hungarian, Polish, and Romanian governments informed a number of American agencies that their work was no longer necessary. In a 1950 letter to PLAN, the Czechoslovakian Ministry of Labor and Social Welfare credited the "altruistic help of the USSR" in helping the country provide for its own needy children. PLAN assured sponsors that their Czech, Polish, and Chinese foster children would never forget them. "Someday, somehow," the organization promised, "these children as future citizens of the world will help cement the peace."[8]

Just as international politics influenced the closing of American programs, agencies' strategies for expansion were guided in large part by geopolitical concerns. Voluntary organizations set up programs in Greece in the aftermath of its civil war (1946–1949). Hong Kong became a focal point for American aid in the years following the Chinese Revolution. With the outbreak of hostilities in Korea in 1950, American voluntary agencies flocked to the country. The 1950s also saw the initiation of programs aimed at assisting children in the newly independent countries of India, Pakistan, and Vietnam, along with the expansion of programs in Europe to help refugees fleeing the Soviet sphere. "It seems to me that the next strike on the part of the communists unless they should strike in Yugoslavia would be in Burma or particularly in Indo-China," Clarke predicted in 1951, as he initiated efforts to support an orphanage in Vietnam. Collecting donations from thousands of individuals, Clarke's organization expanded rapidly throughout the 1950s. By 1953, CCF supported 12,000 children in twenty-three countries; by 1961, it cared for 36,000 children in forty-eight countries.[9] Like the United States itself, American child welfare agencies' footprints spanned key areas of the globe.

CCF's work with children overseas furthered its missionary aims. All of the institutions supported by the organization gave children religious instruction and reared them in a Protestant environment. Many of the homes that CCF supported had been established or were run by Western missionaries. As religion was understood as anathema to communism, CCF's Christian identity became another weapon in the Cold War battle. Indeed, the organization's insistence on providing religious instruction raised the ire of Communist officials both in China and elsewhere around the world. "The Communist officials recognize Christianity as one of the forces most detrimental to their cause in Finland," reported a CCF worker who visited an orphanage in Lapland supported by the agency in 1954; "the Communists will do everything in their power to hinder [the institution's] operation." Religious ideology also supported CCF's efforts to spread "modern" child-care methods around the world: care for the vulnerable and respect for individual dignity were at the heart of both Christian philosophy and American social work. "Christian principles and good child care concepts," one CCF official opined, "are inextricably intertwined."[10] CCF's nearly seamless merging of religious ideals, democratic values, and child-care expertise helped to make it one of the largest international child welfare organizations in the United States.

PLAN also paid heed to U.S. strategic concerns in considering the countries in which it should initiate programs. In April 1956, the organization amended its charter, expanding its stated mission from working on behalf of children distressed as a result of war to that of caring for children rendered needy as a result of war, disaster, poverty, or other causes. The organization dropped the phrase "for War Children" from its name and changed its stated places of operation to "all countries and places in the entire world." Two months later, the agency considered countries to which it might expand. It weighed the merits of initiating programs in Austria and Vietnam, finally deciding on a short-term program geared at assisting refugees in Austria and a long-term program in Vietnam. Helping the children of refugees fleeing Iron Curtain countries "is a most popular cause today," Lenore Sorin, the organization's publicity director, acknowledged. But ultimately, she recommended, "Plan should be looking toward Asia which is now the critical area in world affairs."[11]

Geopolitical considerations occasionally took precedence over demonstrated need. In the aftermath of the Chinese Revolution, CCF wished to support children in Taiwan. The organization worked with Ruth Fisher, a missionary stationed in Taichung, in an attempt to organize an orphanage. But Fisher had trouble locating needy children to populate the home. "Our big problem is that we are starting an orphanage in a place that is really not in need and for this reason it will take some time," she informed CCF. "However we hope to soon have our fifty if possible, but it does not seem right to take children from good homes and put them in an institution just because they are orphans."[12]

Communist regimes' hostility toward American agencies hindered the agencies' ability to help needy children and sometimes meant the loss of institutions into which significant resources had been invested. But their rejection by Communist countries helped American organizations and their supporters understand their work as an extension of U.S. foreign policy. In 1959, shortly after President Dwight D. Eisenhower and Soviet Premier Nikita Khrushchev met in Washington, SCF published an article in its *World Reporter* titled " 'Friendship Fallout'—A Sponsorship Review." In the article, the organization explained the important role played by American foster parents in improving American foreign relations. "As 'Ambassadors of Goodwill,' sponsors quickly and easily find their way to a 'meeting at the summit' with the children and their families," the organization asserted. "More than 8,000 sponsorships means that more than 8,000 such 'meetings at the summit' are now in progress, and the number grows as more and more sponsors join the federation family." These intimate meetings never garnered the publicity accorded to the gatherings of heads of state. But, SCF contended,

> Their significance *is* communicated, durably and surely—sometimes in a village school when a child tells his classmates about his 'friend in America,' or when by lamplight in a peasant hut a mother reads to her eagerly listening neighbors the latest letter from 'our American friend.' Those are the times when, no matter what others may say and no matter how insistently they may say it, an image of America looms in their hearts and minds, warm, shining and beautiful.[13]

Transforming "fallout" from a fearsome aspect of nuclear destruction into a symbol of international amity, SCF cast its supporters as "Ambassadors of

Goodwill." If governments were unable to protect their citizens from the threats of the atomic age, then it fell to American families to forge the bonds of friendship that would unite and strengthen the free world.

Organizations such as SCF insisted that their work supported American Cold War objectives. But international friendship and anticommunism were not linked naturally or indisputably, and not all agencies wished to connect their work with official foreign policy concerns. The AFSC remained committed to placing people before politics. One of the popular arguments for assistance, particularly in Central Europe, was to build a bulwark against communism by offering aid to desperate people, AFSC executive secretary Clarence Pickett noted in 1948. He urged his organization to resist the temptation to appeal for funds on such a basis. "We offer our services to people because they are in need and because we feel called to help them," he insisted. Political outcomes, Pickett argued, must be left solely in the hands "of those whom we serve."[14]

PLAN also distanced itself from the fight against communism. PLAN official Fred Mason worried in a personal letter that "communism, radiating from Russia, intends to absorb the whole world." But he steadfastly refused to let his personal political ideals color his work with the nonpolitical organization. In a 1951 field report describing a trip to southern Italy, Mason scoffed at the suggestion that he avoid the town of Cerignola, which was known to be the home of many communists. "Well, of course, you know we don't have any truck with politics—children have no politics—and so, off we went," Mason recounted. He described meeting a "nice" family of "avowed communists" who let him take photographs of their small stone hut.[15]

Even among overseas welfare workers affiliated with the U.S. government, the commitment to anticommunism was hardly absolute. In 1950, the U.S. Children's Bureau sent Deborah Pentz, a child welfare expert, to India. Pentz's assignment was to assist the University of New Delhi in establishing a training course in family and child welfare work. She helped develop teaching materials that centered on Indian social problems and assisted local practitioners in adapting Western social work techniques to the needs and problems of their country. U.S. officials explicitly connected Pentz's work to foreign policy concerns, noting that social welfare measures were "needed to allay fears and check the discontent that often leads distressed people to lend a ready ear to communism." But Pentz herself was uncomfortable with the political implications of her work. "We say we are giving assistance to build a bul-wark against communism which we feel other nations feel is as great a threat to their way of life as we feel it is to ours," Pentz noted in a confiden-tial letter to her supervisor in 1953. "Leaving my personal convictions aside, I do not believe this assumption is a valid one and it injects into whatever we do the implication that we require adherence to our beliefs or help will be denied." Pentz described American overseas workers as reluctant to wield social welfare as a Cold War weapon. "I think social workers are well aware of the reaction to the 'or else' technique and deploring its effects have aban-doned it," she asserted. Pentz cautioned against the belief that India looked to the United States as a model for development: "I think we are mistaken when we think that India wants to emulate us. . . . If we assume that she should develop in our likeness the help we hope to offer will be rejected and we will be feared and despised."[16]

But even those overseas workers critical of the United States' anticom-munist campaign often found the Cold War intruding on their work, espe-cially as the 1950s progressed. In the United States, a rising tide of conser-vatism and anticommunist sentiment curtailed liberal activism. A number of organizations working for international peace, many of which were led by women, came under fire. Critics denounced peace as appeasement and internationalism as lack of patriotism. Some of the organizations that came under suspicion were called to testify before the House Un-American Ac-tivities Committee (HUAC), which attempted to uncover communist ac-tivities within the United States. Others engaged in self-censorship, hoping to avoid unwelcome scrutiny and accusations of disloyalty. Domestic anti-communism did not completely destroy groups advocating for peace and international understanding, but it did significantly narrow the limits of acceptable discourse and action.[17]

Organizations working with children were not exempt from the anticom-munist crusade. In late 1952, a prominent French rabbi accused the Amer-ican Jewish Joint Distribution Committee of aiding children's homes main-tained by communists in France. "Under the ruse of helping war orphans in homes supported by JDC, Red organizations in France induced masses of guileless Jews to join the Party," he contended. The accusations might not have been completely baseless: the JDC had in fact matched American spon-sors with communist schools in the past. But as Cold War tensions height-ened, such sponsorships were no longer politically viable. Aware of a rising tide of criticism, the organization cut aid to the allegedly communist homes. Ironically, communists in Hungary were at the same time denouncing the JDC as a capitalist tool aimed at destroying communism.[18]

Agencies that promoted international friendships could just as easily face accusations of national disloyalty as they could receive plaudits for supporting American foreign policy. The experiences of two organizations—the Girl Scouts and PLAN—shed light on the multiple and competing meanings ascribed to international friendship programs. The Girl Scouts' troubles began in 1954, when a conservative Florida newsman, Robert LeFevre, charged that the newest edition of the *Girl Scout Handbook* promoted "world citizenship" instead of national patriotism with its "International Friendship" and "World Neighbor" activities. Several months later, LeFevre's accusations reached an even wider audience when the Illinois department of the American Legion echoed his criticisms. The department passed a resolution calling on its members to discontinue support of the Girl Scouts until the organization provided "irrefutable proof to the American public that they have taken definite measures to eliminate these un-American influences from the Girl Scout handbook."[19]

National Girl Scout leadership privately dismissed the criticisms as ridiculous. One supporter quipped that critics' charges were based on a visit to a Girl Scout camp, where they witnessed "one girl driving a nail in a tent floor with a hammer and another girl cutting weeds with a sickle." The organization had prominent supporters who denounced its critics. In her daily column, Eleanor Roosevelt, a longtime proponent of international friendship programs, called the American Legion's resolution "ludicrous." "The Girl Scouts have always emphasized the value of getting to know young people in other areas of the world," Roosevelt noted. Cartoonist Herb Block mocked the Illinois department in a newspaper cartoon. "Stand fast, men—they're armed with marshmallows," proclaims one man in the cartoon as he and his fellow Legionnaires approach a Girl Scout campsite. The Girl Scouts recognized, however, that facing public accusations of communism was "no small matter." Worried about its reputation, the organization departed from its nonpolitical stance with a sharp response to critics titled "Girl Scouting: One Answer to Communism." The organization then carefully pruned its handbook of terms and phrases that might be subject to political misinterpretation.[20]

The public scrutiny to which the Girl Scouts were subject illustrates how international friendship had become, in the words of one journalist, "a dangerous idea."[21] Interest in forging human relationships that transcended national boundaries could be interpreted as a desire to erode these boundaries entirely, undermining national sovereignty and promoting a vision of "one world," which conservative critics now denounced as unpatriotic. Indeed, the term "one world" virtually disappeared from international child welfare organizations' literature by the 1950s. The broad conception of international citizenship articulated by many Americans in the years immediately following the Second World War increasingly came under assault as the 1950s progressed. As fear of communism in the United States increased, organizations wishing to promote friendship across national lines were required to tread carefully.

But while the Girl Scouts controversy demonstrates the extent to which "international friendship" had become a suspect term, it also highlights the substantial—though perhaps less vocal—contingent of citizens who remained committed to forging relationships that crossed national borders. The publication of the revised version of the *Girl Scout Handbook* in late 1954 initiated a new phase of criticism and controversy for the organization. Although Girl Scout leaders insisted that the changes made to the handbook were largely semantic and aimed at preventing further misinterpretation, many people responded critically to what seemed to be a concerted effort to place a reduced emphasis on international friendship. More than two-thirds of the letters received by the organization in the wake of the publication of the new handbook were critical. Parents and local troop leaders expressed disappointment in the Girl Scouts for appearing to bow to political pressure and for excising from the handbook the phrase "one world." "Even if our world is at present divided," asserted Ruth W. Clark, a Rhode Island woman, "we should still keep the idea of one world eventually." Charles S. Milligan, the father of a Massachusetts Girl Scout, agreed: "The time to promote world friendship is precisely when forces of organized ignorance would endeavor to promote hatred."[22]

PLAN, too, would find its commitment to political neutrality severely tested. In 1954, PLAN found itself under investigation by Greek intelligence officials, who were alarmed that the organization had extended support to the offspring of men and women who had served with the communist rebels during Greece's recent civil war. These children were undoubtedly needy: their families were poor, and many had lost a parent during the war. But Greek authorities were concerned that funds provided to these children were being channeled to relatives on the other side of the Iron Curtain or, even worse, being used for "communistic purposes" within Greece itself. PLAN agreed that support should be withdrawn from families who were in fact using American money to fund communism. But it was uncomfortable denying support to children solely on the basis of their parents' political views and preferred to deal with potential abuses of funds on an individual basis. Even as it reaffirmed its commitment to political neutrality, however, the organization was aware that public opinion in the United States ran strongly against communism. Organization officials struck from the children's case histories the details of their parents' political affiliation. Instead, they noted simply that the children had lost parents who fought in the civil war. In Greece, PLAN's director agreed to monitor the mothers of children whose rebel fathers had fled to the Soviet Union. In New York, officials at the organization's home office pledged to subject to special scrutiny the letters written by these children to their American foster parents. "It would have been ruinous for PLAN here if it got around that we were helping Communists," noted Gloria Matthews, who had succeeded Edna Blue as the organization's executive director in 1954.[23]

But PLAN's commitment to political neutrality would soon fall by the wayside. Accusations of communism would force the agency, as they had the Girl Scouts, to go on the offensive. In February 1957, Henry La Cossitt, who had written about PLAN's work in the past, published a story in *Parents' Magazine and Family Home Guide* that showcased the organization's accomplishments in Italy. La Cossitt whisked readers thirty miles east of Rome and transported them to Monteflavio, a small town of medieval stone houses, ancient olive trees, and narrow, steep streets. He introduced Elma Baccanelli Laurenzi, an American woman who had first come to Italy during World War II as a broadcaster for the U.S. Office of War Information and now served as the head of PLAN's Italian program. When Laurenzi first journeyed to Monteflavio in early 1956, La Cossitt wrote, there were only six overcoats in a town of 1,500 inhabitants. As Americans began "adopting" the town's children, empty stomachs were filled and cold feet warmed. But American aid infuriated the local Communist Party, which saw its own power being threatened. The town's children, cozy in their new American coats and intrigued by the stream of letters arriving from far-off places like Chicago and New York City, remained loyal to their American friends. When it came time to vote in the town elections, La Cossitt recounted, the youngsters took it upon themselves to assure a Communist defeat. Engaging in a series of humorous pranks, they succeeded in exposing the Communist Party's empty promises. Thanks to the efforts of the adopted children of American foster parents, the Christian Democrat flag waved from the top of Monteflavio's bell tower for the first time in a decade.[24]

Elma Baccanelli Laurenzi was unsettled by La Cossitt's lighthearted retelling of her work in Monteflavio. Writing to Lenore Sorin, PLAN's publicity director in New York, Laurenzi expressed surprise that the story would be published. She had shared the tale of the children's antics with her American colleagues without the intention or desire that it be used for publicity purposes. And she found it unfitting that the organization commemorate its twentieth anniversary with a story that focused on a political victory. Sorin defended her decision to publicize the Monteflavio tale. "While it is absolutely true that we are non-propaganda and non-political," Sorin wrote in a letter to Laurenzi, "every other agency's material has been stressing the political." PLAN had been faced with accusations of communism, Sorin noted, and the organization needed to refute these accusations. Furthermore, if PLAN refused to take a political stand, donors would shift their support to an organization that did. "We have to, in the end, take some position," Sorin insisted to Laurenzi. "Here in this country the lines are drawn very tightly regarding the communist situation." Sorin pushed the organization's nonpolitical stance to its limit. In a promotional letter, she described PLAN as a nonpolitical organization. "But, in viewing our work of the past, the present and the current world situation," she reflected, "it is evident that Plan, wherever it operates, becomes an important bulwark against Communism."[25]

Even the AFSC, which strove mightily to remain above the political fray, occasionally indulged in anticommunist rhetoric. In 1948, Clarence Pickett urged his fellow social welfare leaders to administer aid without regard to politics. In 1953, he penned an editorial in the *Nation* that connected U.S.-led international friendship and social welfare activities to national security concerns. In the piece, Pickett expressed his skepticism regarding the effectiveness of four years of American rearmament efforts in rendering the United States more secure. "It is true that Communists understand strength and can prepare to meet it. But can they compete with us if our central purpose is the welfare of all? The only real aid we can offer," Pickett argued, "is friendship and confidence." The same year, an AFSC official described a kindergarten run by the organization at a neighborhood center in Japan as helping to "diminish the effects of Communist propaganda prevalent in such depressed areas."[26]

Although several organizations working with children overseas faced accusations of communism, none were subject to official suspicion on the part of the U.S. government or called to testify before HUAC. For some organizations, the decision to align themselves with anticommunism may have spared them from negative scrutiny. Furthermore, unlike groups committed solely to promoting peace, organizations helping children overseas generally coupled international friendship efforts with gifts of material aid. This policy nicely mirrored U.S. official efforts, ranging from the Marshall Plan to the Food for Peace program, which sought to prevent the spread of communism through donations of funds and commodities to critical areas abroad.[27] Finally, organizations helping vulnerable children had a mission that was, despite the criticisms leveled against them, ultimately difficult to impeach.

"TRULY VOLUNTARY REPRESENTATIVES"

American organizations working with children overseas had become—eagerly or reluctantly—unofficial emissaries of U.S. foreign policy. But many voluntary officials continued to express ambivalence about the U.S. government's ability to effectively forge the bonds of international friendship on which the security of the postwar world depended. "The international good will and understanding that can result from the personal relationship inherent in the child sponsorship is infinitely greater than that which can arise from governmental or intergovernmental actions," argued SCF in 1953. American culture had always celebrated voluntarism and private initiative, but these ideas took on a new symbolic weight in the context of the struggle against the totalitarian state. To many, the robustness of voluntary initiatives in the United States signaled the superiority of American democracy and free markets. "It is worth noticing," noted former AFSC executive secretary Lewis M. Hoskins in 1960, "that while Communist nations may provide competent technicians in their official aid programs throughout the world, they have been unable to supply truly voluntary representatives."[28]

Many saw private agency programs as more effective than government-sponsored projects overseas. Richard P. Saunders, who assumed the presidency of SCF in 1952, liked to repeat a quote he attributed to John Foster Dulles: "the motives of governments are always suspect, and rightly so." Saunders contrasted government-provided foreign aid with the unimpeachable assistance offered by private agencies. "There can be no comparable suspicion of the motives of private citizens in a role in which the only returns for their contributions are better understanding, the satisfaction of helping little children, and the belief that the world of tomorrow may well be a better one," he argued. The USC's Helen Fogg also described voluntary agencies, representing "the spontaneous generosity" of the American people, as less suspicious and therefore more effective than U.S. government–sponsored initiatives overseas. "Voluntary agency personnel neither think of themselves as part of a cold war army nor are they so regarded as a rule in the host country," Fogg opined. Although the USC received U.S. government funding and logistical support in connection with at least two overseas programs involving children during the 1950s, it worked hard to maintain its identity as a voluntary agency and to distance itself from the government.[29]

Voluntary agencies agreed that private aid was more effective in winning hearts and minds than government-sponsored assistance. But the question of whether voluntary agencies' programs were intended to support—or to replace—official aid initiatives remained unanswered. In many ways, though, the goals and outlooks of private agencies and the U.S. government converged to such a degree during the 1950s that such questions became unnecessary. The notion of a state powerless to protect its citizens from atomic threats, articulated by some advocates of international friendship during the immediate postwar years, largely gave way to a more confident image of the United States on the global stage as the 1950s progressed. Friendships forged across national lines would bolster America's position as the unabashed leader of the free world. They would strengthen the country's international alliances even as their promoters insisted that their private nature placed them outside the realm of politics. Critiques of the government's effectiveness now centered on the tendency for official aid to be viewed as propaganda, not on the state's inability to protect its citizens from the dangers of the postwar world.

The U.S. government shared voluntary agencies' sentiments about the efficacy of private foreign aid. As such, it sometimes sought to conceal its own cooperation with voluntary groups. In 1958, for example, CCF received a U.S. government grant to help fund the construction of a hospital in Hong Kong to provide medical aid to Chinese political refugees and their children. The government requested that its involvement in the project remain confidential. CCF complied, referring to the government grant as a gift from an "anonymous donor."[30]

American government officials regarded private voluntary agencies' programs as an important component of official diplomatic efforts overseas. Government officials oversaw and coordinated the activities of private agencies working abroad through the Advisory Committee on Voluntary Foreign Aid (ACVFA). A successor to the World War II–era President's War Relief Control Board, the ACVFA was initially under the aegis of the Department of State. Later, it would become part of the Foreign Operations Administration and then the United States Agency for International Development (USAID). Membership in the ACVFA, which was not mandatory, entitled voluntary organizations to government-subsidized ocean freight for relief supplies, the ability to take advantage of agreements in certain countries providing for duty-free entry and free transportation of supplies, and the eligibility to receive U.S. surplus foods under P.L. 480, the Food for Peace program. Another "intangible but important benefit," the Foreign Operations Administration noted, "is the fact that registration indicates United States Government approval of the aims and purposes of that agency."[31]

President Eisenhower looked to private agencies and individuals to help counter communist propaganda. "If our American Ideology is eventually to win out in the great struggle being waged between the two opposing ways of life, it must have the active support of thousands of independent private groups and institutions and of millions of individual Americans," he argued in 1956. Government officials also relied on voluntary agencies to support U.S. operations overseas. Lucy Adams, chief of the U.S. government's Community Development Division in Korea, praised the contributions of private American organizations, which by 1958 had reached 2 million Koreans. Although the voluntary agency program was not under U.S. government jurisdiction, Adams told a gathering of voluntary officials, "the Government is happy to have a part in supporting [it] to some degree."[32]

The U.S. government's commitment to public-private cooperation found expression in President Eisenhower's People-to-People program, launched in 1956 as part of the United States Information Agency (USIA). The People-to-People program connected ordinary Americans with their counterparts overseas. The International Friendship League, the Boston-based international young people's pen-pal association, was a member of the People-to-People program; one of its founders, Christian Herter, would later serve as Eisenhower's secretary of state. While child sponsorships were not officially part of the People-to-People program, government officials recognized that they represented a similar impulse and offered praise for American foster parents.[33]

American agencies were proud of their country's tradition of voluntary action. But in many Eastern countries, American welfare workers were dismayed to find what they saw as a lack of public concern regarding social welfare, particularly the welfare of orphaned and abandoned children. "The concept of group action for the common good, as expressed in the multitude of voluntary activities and organizations in this country, is not comprehended nor even recognized in many countries," SCF contended. "The farther East one goes the more evident is this situation."[34] Many American workers blamed the dearth of voluntary charitable initiatives on the perceived clannishness of Eastern cultures. In crafting programs for children overseas, American workers looked to the structure and warm emotions of the family as a means of helping children grow into healthy adults. But at the same time, they sought to promote a new, more expansive concept of the family that extended beyond blood ties.

The close-knit family groups that characterized Eastern societies sheltered and sustained their own members. But those without a family, American workers contended, were left utterly adrift. "In a society where the individual derives status solely from his family position, it is sometimes difficult to get even a professional social worker to take a real interest in a child without family," noted Helen Tieszen, an American educator who worked in Korea in the aftermath of the war. Tieszen recounted an interaction between an American director of a school for orphan boys and an inquisitive Korean. "Why do you help the orphans?" the American director was asked. "They aren't good boys, otherwise they wouldn't be orphans." In Iran, a welfare worker related, local citizens did not understand American efforts to build a modern children's home. "They (orphans) come from the streets. It is not necessary to provide beds for them," the Iranians reportedly insisted. Children without families were often deprived of adequate care and education. As adults, they were severely handicapped in obtaining jobs and marriage partners. Even children who had been legally adopted into families, American workers noted, did not completely shed the stigma of having once been orphans. American voluntary workers in Asia and the Middle East saw Eastern progress stymied by citizens' deficient sense of social responsibility. Social welfare "must escape from the restricting confines of the family, the clan, the village and the province and develop into the wider concept of the broad public and national concern for social welfare," argued Ernest Nash, who directed CCF's Korean operation in the mid-1950s.[35]

To make matters worse, American workers lamented, many countries in Asia and the Middle East lacked not only voluntary agencies but also government-supported social welfare services. Between 1945 and 1955, forty-five countries around the world adopted new constitutions or constitutional amendments assigning basic social welfare responsibilities to the state. But the public social welfare networks in these countries were often fragmentary, suffering from a dearth of resources and trained personnel. American workers advised foreign governments on the drafting of child welfare laws and urged them to devote resources to children.[36] They sometimes described private agencies' programs as providing a model for social services that could eventually be assumed by the state.

The AFSC was particularly committed to developing social welfare projects for which foreign governments might at a later date assume responsibility. In Hong Kong, AFSC workers wanted to organize a program for refugees "that would give the government a handle in developing its own program." In 1960, the organization established a cooperative day nursery for the children of working mothers. This nursery allowed refugee women to work to support their families while their children were cared for in a safe, nurturing environment. The organization also offered vocational training courses for youth. The AFSC anticipated that its projects would be taken over by the Hong Kong Social Welfare Department once the country had managed to train a body of social workers capable of administering its programs. But AFSC workers found the Hong Kong government comfortable with the presence of foreign voluntary agencies and reluctant to assume responsibility for the AFSC's, or any other agency's, programs. The Social Welfare Department "could not envision any private agencies leaving, and saw even less likelihood of their being asked (or even wanting?) to take over anyone else's work," an AFSC worker reported.[37]

The AFSC encountered a similar situation in Acre, Israel, where it had opened a neighborhood center in 1950. The AFSC hoped that the municipal government would eventually assume responsibility for the center, but the government dragged its feet. Finally, in June 1960, the AFSC withdrew from the center. "We knew that as long as we continued to operate it, the municipality would not assume responsibility for it," noted an AFSC official. As the organization predicted, the Israeli municipal government took over administration of the center following the AFSC's departure, reopening it as a center for youth.[38]

While the AFSC saw its programs as a stopgap measure necessary until foreign governments could assume support of their communities' neediest members, CCF's J. Calvitt Clarke was somewhat less enthusiastic about the prospect of helping foreign governments extend their social welfare responsibilities. "I don't believe in a Welfare State," Clarke wrote in a letter to a colleague in Hong Kong. "I think we ought to do what we can to avoid making any contribution to Socialism." As Clarke's remarks suggest, Cold War politics could render suspect the encouragement of state-supported social welfare services. Moreover, countries with relatively weak systems of public welfare generally allowed foreign voluntary agencies greater latitude in developing their own programs for children. In Korea, where the government devoted comparatively few resources to child welfare, noted Ernest Nash, CCF was accorded a "chance for a greater degree of initiative." By contrast, in countries with well-established public aid programs, such as Japan, the organization was forced to conform to social welfare regulations and to mold its programs around those already provided by the state.[39]

Since many foreign governments had meager resources to devote to social welfare projects in any case, some overseas workers sought to stimulate the efforts of private citizens to meet public needs. By the late 1950s, efforts to uplift the countries of the East—now often referred to as the "developing world"—increasingly centered on programs of "community development." These programs focused on imparting knowledge and skills in addition to supplies and capital, with the goal of helping local people help themselves. The U.S. government and private voluntary agencies alike sponsored community development programs. So, too, did some foreign governments. Some voluntary workers argued that community development, or CD, was not really a new idea. "CD—as you will know—are the latest fashionable initials in social work circles for helping the people to help themselves, which of course is old hat," a PLAN official noted dismissively in 1957. But even if community development was not entirely novel, the approach did signal an increased interest in the value of group action—generally on the part of private citizens—to improve the common good.

The ideal of self-help also took on political connotations. American officials and foreign aid workers portrayed community development as a distinctly democratic means of meeting social welfare needs and encouraging
economic growth. "Community Development now stands forth as the democratic alternative to the Communist concept of the 'commune' or the 'collective farm' with their rigid state-controlled economy and social organization," argued Lucy Adams.[40]

SCF was on the forefront of the community development movement. By
the late 1950s, the organization was working with local citizens to encourage
"village self-help" projects in Korea, Greece, and Lebanon. SCF presented
its projects as evidence that personal liberties and free markets need not be
sacrificed to bring about better living conditions. "The work here [in Korea]
is especially significant in contrast to the changes taking place in neighboring
Red China where the cost of increased economic development is enslavement," the organization contended in 1959. Community development, SCF
asserted, "is democracy in action." Even when supported by government
funds, community development projects generally relied on local people to
articulate felt needs rather than establishing a central authority to dictate
development goals. And community development projects looked to the
family, rather than the state, as the primary agent of progress. "The creative
forces inherent in strong family relationships advance development," argued
SCF's program director, Glen Leet, in 1959. "Instead of hate as a motivating
force, we rely on the universal love for children."[41]

Community development in many ways functioned as social casework
writ large: development workers stood in for caseworkers and endeavored to
ignite the potential of whole communities rather than individuals. The community development worker, noted a survey of international social work
training published by the United Nations in 1958, served as a "catalytic agent"
who aimed to create confidence in the possibility of progress. "This concept
seems to be similar to that of the social worker as an 'enabler,' someone who
is able accurately to identify problems and resources for meeting them," the
survey noted.[42]

Just as supporters of child sponsorship programs saw their primary significance as emotional rather than material, proponents of community development often elevated the psychological benefits of self-help projects above
the roads and buildings they yielded. Community development "produces
its own end result in the form of experience and skill in the use of democratic processes," argued the International Cooperation Administration (ICA),

the government agency charged with administering U.S. economic and technical assistance overseas, in 1957. Proponents also described community development projects as instigating large-scale psychological changes. "The Village Self-Help Program of the Federation uniquely and effectively combines economic aid with psychological motivation—one to trigger a reversal of the downward economic cycle and the other to catalyze a change in the view of life itself," SCF asserted in 1960. This was particularly true for a community's youngest members. Self-help programs could "transform the entire emotional environment of the children affected," argued Richard Saunders in 1959.[43] American overseas workers saw community development projects as providing a model for social and economic progress that centered on voluntary action, on the family, and on the personal transformation of each of its members.

BUILDING A FAMILY OF NATIONS

In the context of the Cold War, the family became an emblem in the struggle against communism. Many American commentators saw the family as essential not only to children's healthy emotional development but also to the perpetuation of democracy. "As Lenin himself once said," a report in *Time* magazine noted, " 'Revolution is impossible as long as the family exists.' " Margaret Mead explained, "Right within the family, a child can learn the basic feeling for a democratic society—that every individual has dignity and matters, that what each person does is necessary, that what each person does is different and cannot so easily be done by someone else."[44] The family was a multivalent emblem that sat at the intersection of a number of ideals— individual rights, privacy, domesticity, religiosity—that were coming to the fore in the postwar United States. The familial ideal was capacious enough to appeal to American citizens across the political and cultural spectrum, uniting people whose views on other issues, such as the scope and nature of anticommunism, might otherwise be at odds.

American condemnations of communist regimes often used images of families torn asunder and children trained to blindly obey the state. In a 1953 article in the *Saturday Evening Post* titled "They're Afraid of Their Own Children," author Joseph Wechsberg introduced American readers to family life in the Soviet sphere, where children attending state-run nurseries and kindergartens were taught to spy on their parents. "Within less than five years, the communists in Czechoslovakia—and the story is more or less repeated in the other satellite countries behind the Iron Curtain—have succeeded in alienating the children from their own parents," Wechsberg wrote. In another article, he described a typical Czech family destroyed by their daughter's political indoctrination:

> It had all begun one day two years ago, when Bozena came home from school with red flags and pictures of Soviet leaders. Soon she discarded her dolls and talked only about politics. During the general election she canvassed the neighborhood, distributing communist leaflets. At night she would go out with her nine-year-old classmates and secretly paste communist emblems over the election posters of other parties.

By the time Bozena turned eleven, Wechsberg reported, her parents no longer discussed politics in her presence, terrified she would report them to school authorities. Indeed, reported the *Christian Science Monitor,* Communist officials across the Soviet sphere valorized Pavel Morozov, a Soviet child martyr who denounced his parents as enemies of the Communist state.[45]

American commentators regularly cited Communist state-run nurseries as an example of the state's unjust usurpation of parental rights. Propaganda materials released by the USIA described Soviet families in which mothers dropped off their children in nurseries on Monday morning and did not see them again until the end of the workweek on Saturday night. The role of nurseries in the lives of children in Communist countries was generally exaggerated: American social workers who visited the Soviet Union in 1956 found that the majority of Soviet children were in fact reared in their own homes, with only 12–15 percent of children under school age receiving outside care during the day. But state-run nurseries loomed large in the American imagination. William H. Wilbur, a high-ranking U.S. Army official who visited the Soviet Union in 1957, was appalled to witness babies cared for in public nurseries in which workers were forbidden to comfort them when they cried. "The family is man's only institution that develops sympathy, kindness, gentleness, patience, and affection. Communist leaders do not want Soviet citizens to develop these qualities," Wilbur contended.[46]

American descriptions of China also relied on the trope of broken families and children reared in collectivized environments. In a book titled *Children of China,* child development expert Margaret Wylie described the

Chinese government's efforts to erode family ties, projecting Chairman Mao as a substitute father figure. Wylie shared with her readers a chant intoned by Chinese children: "The Party is more intimate than our parents in bringing us up to maturity; firmly we follow the line of the Party and hasten to obey its commands." It was no wonder, Wylie noted, that children reared under these conditions informed on parents with divergent political views. Author Pearl S. Buck, who spent her childhood in China as the daughter of missionaries, decried the Chinese state for depriving children of the familial love so essential to their healthy growth. "What sort of men and women will they be?" she lamented. If Americans were unconvinced by the political and economic arguments against communism, stories of families torn apart served as a heartrending testament to the evils of Communist regimes. American condemnations of communist child-care practices also served to further dispel support for state-funded nurseries within the United States, painting all public provisions for child care with the brush of radicalism.[47]

From Bulgaria to Cuba, the American family and American methods of child rearing were an integral part of the U.S. government's Cold War information offensive. The USIA frequently used narratives that focused on the family and on child care as a means of drawing vivid distinctions between life in a democracy and life under Communist rule. In Bonn, West Germany, in 1955, for example, the USIA released 100,000 copies of a pamphlet titled *Building the Community through Family Life,* which followed the lives of several average families in Buffalo, New York. The pamphlet stressed the respect Americans accorded to the family—"one of the most strongly guarded institutions in our society"—and drew attention to American methods of child rearing. Children in the United States, the pamphlet explained, were given every opportunity to develop their individual skills and personalities. "Each child," the pamphlet noted, "is a precious part of society."[48]

American voluntary agencies engaged in child sponsorship elaborated on and reworked the connections among child development, the family, voluntarism, and democracy. They described their efforts to create affectionate kinship networks as a means of extending America's influence across the globe. "National forms and national governments are to an extent artificial and their structure changeable," noted CCF's Ernest Nash. Governments were thus poor conduits for enduring international friendships. But private voluntary agencies, Nash argued—particularly those that cared for children when their minds were most malleable—were uniquely capable of securing lasting friends for the United States:

> In our CCF homes thousands of Koreans, at the most impressionable ages of childhood and adolescence, are aware morning, noon and night, that their "fatherhood" and "motherhood," to which they owe their very lives, are being undertaken for them by Americans. This knowledge is fixed in their earliest consciousness. The certainty of this love of distant "parents" is thus ineradicable through the years.[49]

To Nash, the plasticity of childhood presented a political opportunity. Familial love merged seamlessly with diplomatic alliances; filial duties blurred with political obligations. The intimate sphere of the family and the gradual unfolding of children's personalities became the front lines of the American fight against communism.

As Christina Klein has argued, American leaders' commitment to the strategy of containment was complemented by a "logic of inclusion," an effort to welcome other members of the free world into a U.S.-headed family of nations. Not solely a masculine project, the struggle against communism also relied on an ideological framework centered on the family and domesticity. Love itself was a formidable weapon capable of remaking the world. In a book about the work of CCF, author Edmund Janss expressed skepticism that American armament assistance could repel communism in Asia: "The best investment, dollar-for-dollar, . . . will be the tangible love sent by Americans who 'adopt' Asia's babies."[50]

American agencies engaged in international friendship and sponsorship activities offered anecdotal evidence of their programs' success both in Europe and in Asia. In 1952, an American worker who visited an orphanage in France bearing letters from friends in the United States reported encountering cries of "Welcome to France, Vive les Yankees." When American foster mother Constance Capron Fucito traveled to Italy to visit her "adopted" son, she recounted in *Reader's Digest,* the villagers who welcomed her also extended their goodwill to her country and its leader: "Hooray for Aunt Connie," "Hooray for U.S.A.," "Hooray for President Ike," banners traversing the narrow streets of the village proclaimed. In Korea, CCF chronicled in its newsletter, children supported by Americans sung hymns inside a Salvation

Army center as American soldiers engaged in fighting outside. When the soldiers entered the building, the organization reported, the children eagerly pointed out the hiding places of Communist soldiers.[51]

Letters from foreign beneficiaries suggest that programs for children sometimes did generate goodwill toward the United States (at the very least, they trained recipients to express warm sentiments toward the country as a whole). "HURRAH FOR AMERICAN [*sic*] AND HER CHILDREN!" one Italian youngster wrote in a letter to his friends in the United States. Soon Ok, a little Korean girl supported through PLAN, was confused after seeing an American cops and robbers movie. "She seems to think that all Americans are good, honest and kind just like her Foster Parents," her nurse reported in a letter to her foster mother in the United States.[52]

Foreign participants in international friendship programs sometimes shared Americans' anticommunist agenda—or they appropriated anticommunist rhetoric as a means of garnering support. "Our poor Europe has a hard time to recover from the horrible war, followed by the silent clashes between the Orient and the West," wrote a schoolteacher in France in a letter to her American counterpart in 1948. "The naïve and delightful letters of your little pupils deny strongly a loud lying propaganda aimed by some foreigners against the noble United States." In 1956, CCF decided to withdraw its support of a Brazilian orphanage. An American missionary associated with the institution warned Clarke that his organization's departure would empower America's enemies. "I'm afraid the home will suffer—and I also fear that some leaders might use the opportunity to encourage ideas against the United States (for some are all too ready to seize any such opportunity)," she noted in a letter. When CCF decided to continue to fund the orphanage, the missionary thanked Clarke for bolstering the American cause. "By aiding in this project you are combatting [*sic*] Communism which says that all the U.S. cares about is exploiting the wealth of this nation," she told him. Anticommunist rhetoric even made its way into some children's letters. A Korean youngster wrote to his foster parents: "Due to Communist invasion I became a lonesome child. Thank you very much for aiding my helplessness. I tell you and promise that I will study hardest with the money you gave me and sometime become a strong member of a democratic country."[53]

Agencies working on behalf of children overseas championed a vision of the United States as a humanitarian global leader. They trained Americans to understand their country's interventions abroad as gestures of kindness rather than acts of empire. And they encouraged Americans to view the friend-ship of overseas beneficiaries as spontaneous and voluntary rather than ob-ligated or coerced. From a surgery that enabled a polio-stricken child to walk again to donations that allowed an impoverished family to trade cardboard bedding for a mattress, voluntary agencies cloaked American power in the mantle of benevolence.[54] By sending funds, writing letters, and in some cases traveling overseas themselves, foster parents from the United States partici-pated in the project of American expansionism. A military officer who had visited his foster children in Greece, Italy, and Colombia declared trium-phantly: "Last year Europe. This year South America. Next year—the World."[55]

But even as the power that adhered to American donors mirrored—and extended—the United States' growing global influence, the personal rela-tionships that developed between foster parents, their children, and some-times their children's families at times subtly undermined this hierarchy. These relationships did not transcend the global order that gave rise to them; they suggest, however, that on an individual level, Americans' acknowledged power and privilege sometimes gave way to perceptions of mutuality. One foster parent described herself as initially skeptical about the merits of child spon-sorship programs: "Was affection being traded for dollars, and if so, who would benefit?" But after visiting her four-year-old foster daughter and her family in Italy—she recounted in an article in *Good Housekeeping*—she had a change of heart. "What they feel toward me," she asserted, "is not grati-tude for a well-heeled benefactor, but affection for a friend." When Lena and Kenneth Knowles, an American couple, visited their foster son in Korea, they were shocked by the bareness of his small dirt-floored home and by the pov-erty of the refugee camp in which he and his family resided. But they were also deeply touched by feelings of warmth and mutual understanding. "The people smiled at us and we smiled back, and it was as if together we had built a bridge . . . on which we could meet and see into one another's hearts and understand one another," Kenneth Knowles recounted. An observer de-scribed a meeting between another American foster father and his Italian foster child: "One look, and [they] rushed into one another's arms, both talking at once, one in English, the other in Italian, and no interpretation was needed."[56]

In 1955, Letters Abroad, an international pen-pal agency that matched American children and adults with pen pals around the world, took a survey of its members. In response to a query about "the principal satisfactions" of international correspondence, 13 out of the 176 respondents selected "clearing up misunderstandings, making friends for U.S."; the most commonly selected responses were "knowledge of other countries" (41 votes), "better understanding of others" (39 votes), and "friendship" (24 votes). While some participants associated the program with a projection of American identity— "I seem to have re-established my friend's faith in Americans," one letter writer noted—many others described their involvement in more personal terms. A woman described her pleasure in sending her daughter's outgrown clothes to her pen-pal family overseas. A girl noted that her participation had taught her an important lesson: "I have learned that boys are the same everywhere."[57]

Child sponsorship attracted a wide range of individuals. The ranks of foster parents in the United States included senators and housewives, railroad workers and movie stars, high school clubs and groups of prison inmates. Letters from foster children hung on the bulletin board in the Maryland Penitentiary, were posted in a cabinet next to the school principal's office at P.S. 80 on New York City's Upper East Side, and were read aloud to the crew of the destroyer the USS *George E. Davis* at the 8 a.m. muster. Foster parents' letters to their children often conveyed expressions of friendship and sometimes employed familial language. "We all love you just as much as though you were a separate daughter to each of us. So now you have many kinds of 'Daddies,' some are big, some small," noted the lieutenant commodore of the USS *George E. Davis* in a letter to the crew's adopted Italian daughter.[58]

Some youngsters cherished the missives sent by their overseas foster parents. They waited anxiously for the monthly mail and reread the letters until the type was blurry and the paper ragged. Children often hung pictures of foster parents on their walls, placed them in frames on their tables, or adorned them with wreaths of flowers. Some children's letters to their foster parents conveyed warmth and deep affection. Shin Kil, a Korean youngster, wrote, "I have cried for my mother's warm arms often and though you are living in a far country across the ocean I am happy that you are my foster mother and father. I have not had the words mother and father on my lips for three years since they died." Van, a twelve-year-old Vietnamese boy, expressed similar sentiments: "This is the first time I write to you, a stranger, and call you Mother," he wrote in a 1957 letter. "It seems very funny, daring, bashful, but I rely on your understanding, even now I feel something sacred I lacked for a long time." Anna, a refugee child in West Germany, asserted, "A drop of Love is sometimes more precious than a whole sack of money!"[59]

Children's letters were a medium of communication rife with contradictions. Intimate expressions of love and friendship, they were as a rule never private. Agency staff always read and translated children's missives, and they frequently published excerpts in publicity materials, betraying the privacy of the foster parent-child bond even as they testified to its strength and profoundness. Letters penned by youngsters were mundane accounts of daily life: stories of school exams, summer vacations, and holiday celebrations. But they were also a valuable currency that provided youngsters with access to crucial material benefits from American sponsors.

At times, children's missives strayed from the expected script. In 1949, American foster parents who supported Chinese youngsters through PLAN began to learn firsthand about the Communist revolution. Beginning in July, dozens of letters reached American shores exalting the new Communist government and denouncing the Nationalists. "The people are all very happy about the liberation of Shanghai because the Liberation Army is very kind to the people. . . . Every one hates the shameless and mad reactionaries," Chung-lan reported. "I am sure that you must have read about the victory of the Chinese Communist Party from your papers. This victory will bear a splendid fruit in the hope cherished by the children of China," noted Lin-hui. One youngster told his American friends of his eagerness to join the Communist Youth Corps. Another child reported her classmates' delight in hearing childhood stories about Chairman Mao. Schoolchildren wrote letters describing dancing in a Liberation Army parade, exultant despite a downpour of rain that soaked them. Feng-ming, who had actually participated in the revolutionary struggle, wrote about her experience fighting alongside communist guerilla warriors in the hills and her keen disappointment in having to return to school after being diagnosed with a heart ailment. "Do you have communists in the States?" wondered Fu-kun. "Have you joined them?"[60] Expressing friendship toward American foster parents while parroting communist dogma, the children's letters no doubt vexed American voluntary workers and Chinese officials alike. Children's letters to their American foster parents reveal youngsters as political actors in their own right even as they point to the limits of children's independent political action.

As American foster parents forged fictive networks of international kin, they created virtual interracial families. Adoption across racial lines served as an advertisement for the United States' race blindness and a means of countering Soviet charges of American racism. Indeed, Americans responded enthusiastically to calls to adopt Asian children, though they preferred Korean children (members of a country defending itself valiantly against a communist attack) over Japanese youngsters (offspring of a recent enemy with a perceived rebounding economy). And although Americans were eager to adopt Asian children, sponsorship agencies largely excluded black children until the early- to mid-1960s. Racial concerns shaped American agencies' decisions to forgo work in Africa during the 1950s. CCF, one of the first organizations to include black youngsters among its ranks of sponsored children, found few Americans willing to sponsor "colored GI babies" in 1951. As late as 1967, PLAN officials noted that an advertisement featuring a black child elicited "markedly less response from the American public than a white child." Wary of racist attitudes in certain regions of the United States, PLAN assigned black children exclusively to sponsors in the North and West, as well as in Canada. The agency matched black children with sponsors in Southern states only if the sponsors specifically requested such a child.[61]

During the decades following World War II, child sponsorships took place against the backdrop of an increasing number of legal intercountry adoptions. Animated initially by the impulse to "rescue" mixed-race "GI babies" from a life of perceived social ostracism in Korea, Americans legally adopted over four thousand children—some "GI babies" and some not—in the aftermath of the Korean War. Between 1953 and 1962, American families legally adopted a total of approximately 15,000 children from overseas. A series of amendments to the U.S. immigration laws in the 1950s facilitated the adoption of foreign-born children by Americans; Congress would amend the Immigration and Nationality Act in 1961 to put in place permanent provisions for intercountry adoption.[62]

But not all American families could legally adopt a child, either abroad or at home. Single people, along with older couples, were generally prohibited from adopting children. Laws mandating that a child be of the same faith as his or her adoptive parents made adoption more difficult for many Catholics and Jews. For some people, sponsoring a child may have served as a means of creating a family when legal adoption was difficult or impossible. This was the case for Harvey G. Nash, a single, fifty-two-year-old linotype operator from Wisconsin. Nash told a reporter that his adoption of Lidia, a little Italian girl, "helped to ease the child hunger in my heart." A physician who sponsored a child in China told a similar story. She praised her "son" as the solution to her feelings of "frustrated motherhood" and recommended child sponsorship to "all the 'old maid' schoolteachers, editors, saleswomen, etc., that you can reach." A New Jersey woman who sponsored a child in Hong Kong noted that she was unable to legally adopt a child because she was older than the age limit of forty imposed by her state. Sponsorships could even kindle maternal feelings in those disinclined to motherhood, argued actress Tallulah Bankhead, who sponsored a youngster in Greece. "Few, if any, would care to go on record as saying I am the motherly type," Bankhead wrote in an article in *Cosmopolitan* magazine. But, she recounted, she took "very real pride" in the letters she received from her Greek foster daughter, Barbara, addressing her as "Darling Mother."[63]

Child sponsorships may have helped lay the groundwork for the surge of legal intercountry adoptions, as they enabled Americans to imagine themselves as the parents of children with a race and nationality different from their own. Couples sometimes asked to legally adopt children whom they had been sponsoring. But American agencies continued to see child sponsorships as representing a different impulse than legal adoptions. "I also would like to impress upon our representatives in Korea, Japan, Formosa, and elsewhere that each time a legal adoption occurs, this takes away from our general ability to give proper care to children overseas," J. Calvitt Clarke noted in 1954. A child brought to the United States gained a family and an increased standard of living. But transforming foreign children into American citizens—documented dramatically in newspaper articles with headlines such as "Korean Waif Becomes Real American Boy"—did little to uplift the lands of their births.[64] Sponsoring children overseas, meanwhile, served as a means of rebuilding nations and of shaping a generation of foreign youngsters.

Child sponsorship programs challenged American social hierarchies, but they also re-inscribed older ideas about racial and national differences. They redefined "family" to include fictive kinships forged across the boundaries of nation and race. Flouting the taboo on single parenthood, they invited unmarried men and women to create imagined families of their own making. But some children stood outside of these imagined families on account of their race. And sponsorship programs naturalized an imbalance of power between the United States and the rest of the world. While Americans both sent and received letters, funds flowed in only one direction—from the United

States to countries overseas. America was the undisputed head of the imagined global family of nations.

As the 1950s progressed, international friendship, voluntary action, and the family itself became weapons in the intensifying Cold War conflict. Yet they were cleverly concealed weapons. American workers suggested that good democratic citizens developed naturally as the result of child-rearing practices, such as providing orphans with a sense of family, already widely acknowledged by Americans to be in children's best interest. The insistence that good child welfare and good foreign policy were one and the same allowed voluntary workers to evade thorny questions about the scope and suitability of children's political action. After all, were the children of Monteflavio, who unseated the local Communist Party, really so different from Feng-ming, the Chinese girl who fought alongside the communist guerillas? American voluntary workers might have argued that the distinction lay in free choice as opposed to coercion, or that childish pranks in an Italian town square differed markedly from warfare in the rugged hills of China. But how much choice did children in any nation really have when it came to their own upbringing? And with the entire globe a Cold War battlefield, to what extent should—or could—children's participation in the conflict be limited? The entanglement of child rearing and international affairs permitted American voluntary agencies to simultaneously embrace and deny the political nature of their work. Child welfare programs abroad were thus at once benevolent expressions of American concern for the most vulnerable and partisan projects aimed at fortifying U.S. global hegemony. And children themselves were both innocents to be shielded from conflict and little cold warriors essential to the United States' defeat of communism.

CHAPTER FIVE

Forging the Free Child's Armor

ON OCTOBER 23, 1956, the *Korea Times* transported readers to a dark, drafty orphanage in Seoul. It introduced them to Pak, a four-year-old who had lost both of his parents during the recent war. The sorrowful child had little to look forward to, the paper reported, aside from a daily helping of porridge doled out by distracted attendants. Pak's life would change dramatically, however, with the arrival of Helen Tieszen and her colleagues. Tieszen did not patch the orphanage's paper doors or fix its splintering floor. Instead, she worked to reform the building's inhabitants. With support from two American voluntary organizations, Christian Children's Fund and the American-Korean Foundation, Tieszen and her fellow American educators trained Korean child-care workers in new ways of interacting with children. They urged native workers to treat children as individuals and taught them how to transform their institutions into loving homes. The Americans also played with Pak and his peers. They sought to arouse the children's imaginations, creating puppets and staging dramatic puppet shows. Once a forlorn child, the newspaper reported, Pak soon became a happy youngster who enjoyed "rollicking" games with his playmates.[1]

To American voluntary agencies, and to the United States Information Service photographer who captured his likeness for the newspaper, Pak's transformation was at once a personal and a political victory. The Cold War was a battle for hearts and minds, but it was also a struggle to create a certain type of heart and mind, a particular configuration of personal character. Through interventions in the lives of youngsters such as Pak, American workers during the 1950s and 1960s sought to mold children with the personal characteristics—emotional security, creativity, independent thought—that they thought would bolster democratic regimes across the globe. In the process, they transformed the family room, the playroom, and the classroom into key sites in the United States' battle against communism.

FREE CHILDREN AND AUTOMATONS

In December 1950, over five thousand social workers, educators, parents, and children convened in Washington, D.C., for the Mid-Century White House Conference on Children and Youth. A gathering of child-care professionals that met every decade throughout most of the twentieth century, the 1950 conference was organized by a committee composed of social scientists and child welfare experts, including Margaret Mead, Lawrence K. Frank, and Benjamin Spock. With the theme "a healthy personality for every child," the 1950 meeting represented the first White House conference to focus on children's emotional health and personality development.

Addressing conference participants on December 5, President Harry S. Truman spoke of "the tremendous struggle of our time—the struggle between freedom and Communist slavery." He described the principles of freedom, independent thought, and self-reliance on which American democracy rested. And he rooted the contrast between free and communist societies in the personal character of their citizens, forged during the formative years of childhood. "If children have a good home—a home in which they are loved and understood—and if they have good teachers in the first few grades of school, I believe they are well started on the way toward being useful and honorable citizens," Truman contended. He contrasted American methods of child rearing with those in communist lands: "The great weakness of dictatorships is that they enslave the minds and the characters of the people over whom they rule. And the effects of this enslavement are most serious in the case of children."[2]

Convened as the United States faced growing setbacks on the battlefields of Korea, the 1950 White House conference was an occasion for Americans to reflect on the global significance of children's personality formation. "We can only hope to achieve our ideal of a free society," noted Lawrence K. Frank, "through healthy personalities who are capable of bearing the burdens of freedom."[3] The *Washington Post* agreed; personal character, the newspaper opined in 1950, constituted the "free child's armor." The *Post* explained the significance of a healthy personality to the Cold War conflict, which had recently turned hot:

> For we are at last realizing that this is not only the best insurance against the warped mind that breeds the fanatic, the hatemonger, the tyrant, but is also the genesis of the responsible citizen upon whom the survival of free democratic government depends. . . . The free child finds himself greatly outnumbered by the hordes of the regimented. As he grows up he will find himself one of a relatively small brigade that must uphold mental enlightenment and human freedom against ruthless primitive masses seeking the slavery of the spirit. To do this he must be given the "strength of ten" through his emotional stability, maturity, self-discipline and creativeness.[4]

Creativity, independent thought, and emotional stability were personal characteristics long celebrated by American child-care experts. But their political salience had shifted over time. Previously a tool in the fight against fascism and authoritarianism in postwar Europe and Japan, these personality traits were now a shield that could effectively contain the spread of communism across the globe.

While Americans believed that the kinds of citizens Communist countries were seeking to shape—unthinking, obedient—were tremendously different from those that the United States sought to create, many recognized that Communist leaders shared their understanding of children's malleability. While citizens in Germany and elsewhere had to be taught that personal characteristics were shaped during childhood, not inborn, Communist leaders appeared to already recognize the transformative potential of child rearing—and they were eager to use it to their own advantage. Stories about Communist, particularly Soviet, efforts to indoctrinate children circulated widely in the United States. Headlines such as "Reds Brainwash Greek Tots" and "Red China's Children Brain-Washed Early" revealed nefarious communist plots to take advantage of youngsters during their formative years. "Children are the raw material from which good communists are molded," noted Foster Parents' Plan's Fred Mason in 1956.[5] This "raw material,"

American child-care experts fretted, could prove just as dangerous as the uranium in the superpowers' nuclear arsenals. Child rearing remained a means of reshaping the world "more powerful than the atomic bomb," but it was now a weapon wielded by Americans to effectuate the victory of the West, not a tool to usher in global harmony.

While Soviet, Chinese, and American leaders shared similar conceptions of children's malleability, the communist understanding of human development rested on a different theoretical basis than that of its Western counterparts. This incongruence had significant implications with regard to child-rearing practices. American social workers Herschel and Edith Alt, who visited the Soviet Union in 1956, noted that a longstanding reliance on the tenets of behaviorism meant that those caring for children placed a good deal of emphasis on learned behaviors but devoted little attention to youngsters' emotional lives. The elevation of Pavlov over Freud led parents and welfare workers to look to outside stimuli, rather than to internal disturbances, as explanations for deviant childhood behaviors. And it led them to attempt to correct these behaviors via collective social pressure rather than individualized counseling. "Nowhere did we find any recognition that stealing might be a symptom of a child's emotional conflict," the Alts recounted in a book relating their impressions of Soviet child welfare. "To them stealing is a product of insufficient or bad education that can be corrected by better education." The "emotionally disturbed" child, the Alts observed, was a figure Soviet child-care professionals refused to recognize. Pavlov also trumped Freud in China, observers noted, where state-run nurseries and schools adopted a system of "reflexive teaching," designed to mold youngsters into unthinking agents of the state.[6]

The contrast between American and communist child-rearing ideals was reminiscent of the opposition between behaviorists such as John Watson and proponents of the child guidance movement in the United States a generation earlier. Communist child-rearing wisdom resembled the advice dispensed by Watson and his peers during the 1920s and 1930s, advice that many mid-century experts in the United States had dismissed as outdated. Moreover, the communist understanding of personality development and the methods of dealing with children to which it gave rise supported the perceived goal of totalitarian regimes: to mold a populace guided not by internal motivations but by the external will of the state. "There has now developed in the Soviet Union a theory of child training internally consistent and showing a point-for-point congruence with Soviet political and social theory," noted Margaret Mead in a 1955 study of Soviet child-rearing ideals, coauthored with psychiatric social worker Elena Calas.[7]

American writers who visited China and the Soviet sphere often described the governments' systematic attempts to suppress children's independent thought and action. For example, an American journalist wrote of his visit to a Young Pioneer headquarters in Tashkent, Uzbek: "There were no bubbling, rambunctious kids such as one might expect to find in that age bracket in any large group. Somehow they seemed spiritless. . . . Gravely they did everything they were told to do without hesitation or questions." Writer Joseph Wechsberg described communist child rearing in similar terms in an article in the *Saturday Evening Post*. "Schoolteachers and kindergarten nurses," he wrote, "have been charged with the duty to turn the kids into communist robots with mechanical brains." Wechsberg recounted a Czech father's lament over the Communist government's influence on his son: "the communists are now making an automaton out of him. They don't want him to think. They want him merely to repeat what they are thinking." A visitor to China described observing a "procession of solemn children marching four abreast" one Sunday morning. He asked an interpreter where the children were headed. The children were going on a picnic, the surprised visitor was told.[8]

The Alts offered a less sensationalized assessment of childhood in the communist sphere, but they too emphasized the discipline and obedience expected of youngsters. "Where we would be concerned that our social institutions—the family and the school—provide the youngster with opportunities for expression of impulse, for experimentation, for creative expression and choice, the Soviet emphasis is on restraint, on the harnessing of impulse and directing it," they explained. "Most of us would assume," the Alts noted, "that the principles the Russians advocate and practice would most certainly produce a personality lacking in initiative and creativity and in spiritual aspirations."[9] As the Cold War intensified, the pernicious repercussions of the communist model of child development added new urgency to Americans' efforts to spread their own understanding of personality growth to their allies overseas.

CHILD CARE IN KOREA

The war in Korea provided a new focus for American humanitarian attention and an opportunity for child-care workers to put their methods of care into practice on the ground. At the conclusion of World War II, the Korean peninsula had been divided into the Soviet-occupied North and the U.S.-occupied South. In June 1950, Communist North Korea invaded its southern neighbor. With the outbreak of hostilities, thousands of families poured south of the 38th parallel, which divided North and South Korea, and many others fled homes in war-devastated areas. The number of orphaned and abandoned children expanded exponentially. American observers in South Korea described with pity and horror groups of emaciated waifs begging on street corners and huddled in train stations. In 1953, as hostilities concluded, the American-Korean Foundation dubbed Korea the "Land of Lost Children." Observers estimated that the war had produced over 100,000 orphans, about 40,000 of whom had found shelter in the orphanages that were rapidly springing up across the country. "Little boys and girls who but a short time ago enjoyed the love and warmth of home are today, because of this war, little urchins starving and suffering from exposure and cold," observed Verent Mills during a trip to Korea in 1952. "Their stomachs are swollen, while their necks, legs and arms look like bean poles." As in postwar Europe, homeless children in Korea served as a potent symbol of social chaos. But impressionable youngsters also offered hope for the country's reconstruction. In "securing the cause of democracy for the future, the children of Korea offer a gilt-edged investment," asserted Leonard Mayo, an American social worker who traveled to Korea in 1953.[10]

Foreign agencies seeking to reach the greatest number of needy people looked to institutions such as orphanages and retirement homes as an efficient means of channeling aid. As a result, such institutions, which had been few in number prior to the war, proliferated; by early 1953, Korea boasted an estimated 350 to 400 orphanages. Members of the American military supported many of these institutions. According to one account, American troops in Korea gave more than a million dollars in voluntary contributions to needy Koreans between July 1950 and October 1953; almost two-thirds of these contributions went to orphanages. American voluntary workers agreed that needy children were better housed in orphanages than living on the street. But they questioned the care these institutions provided. "It is doubtful if 50 of these 'orphanages' are giving a quality of care that would be comparable to the lowest standards tolerated in the United States," asserted an American committee that toured Korea in 1953 under the leadership of Howard Rusk, physician and president of the American-Korean Foundation. Korean child-care workers, American observers complained, had no knowledge of modern child-rearing precepts. CCF's William Asbury repeated to J. Calvitt Clarke a complaint he claimed to hear frequently: "Koreans don't know how to take care of children."[11]

In 1954, the Unitarian Service Committee sought to improve Korean social welfare by sponsoring three men to undertake advanced social work study at the University of Minnesota. When these men returned to Korea in 1957, they worked, with the assistance of USC funds, to organize a department of social work at Seoul National University. One of the men, Sang Nak Ha, who had previously managed PLAN's Seoul office, was instrumental in establishing the first child guidance clinic in Korea. Ha and the other Korean workers who launched the child guidance clinic saw it as playing a key role in their country's national development. "We soon came to realize that the future of our country, lies upon the shoulders of our youth," they noted. Indeed, the work of foreign voluntary agencies and the growing cadre of American-trained social workers in Korea helped reorient Korean social welfare away from a Confucian emphasis on the care of the elderly and onto a new concern for the welfare of children and youth.[12]

CCF, which already had a large presence in Asia, moved quickly to assist Korean youngsters. By 1952, the organization had extended aid to at least a quarter of Korea's orphans. As it had in Japan, the organization sought to introduce modern methods of child care in the orphanages it supported. To do this, the organization enlisted Helen Tieszen, an educator with degrees in childhood development and early childhood education from the University of Minnesota. Tieszen had volunteered to serve abroad with the Mennonite Central Committee, a voluntary organization affiliated with the Mennonite Church, and was in turn assigned to work with CCF. Upon arriving in Korea in early 1955, Tieszen learned that the American-Korean Foundation had been planning a similar project. The American-Korean Foundation's child welfare consultant was Rose Alvernaz, a former member of the United States Children's Bureau who had worked extensively in Brazil.[13]

Tieszen and Alvernaz decided to work together. Over the course of the next two years, they organized a series of courses for institution superintendents, child welfare workers, and infant caretakers. The need for these courses was great, Tieszen contended. In 1955, she reported on a visit to a typical Korean orphanage in which the children had put on a program for their guests. "During the entire program, housemothers were simply policemen for the children. In the long prayer which preceded the program, the children were expected to fold their hands and bow their heads. Those who did not maintain the correct posture were given a sharp rap on the head," Tieszen recounted. The staff, she told her American colleagues, was in need of "a good bit of re-education."[14]

In planning their courses, Tieszen and Alvernaz worked with the League of Social Workers, a semiofficial Korean organization of institution directors. In some instances, they collaborated with other voluntary agencies, such as PLAN and the American Friends Service Committee. Children's institutions throughout Korea served as hosts to the program so that trainees could observe the behavior of actual children while the courses were in session. Tieszen and Alvernaz worked to impart to their Korean colleagues an understanding of the psychological theories of child development developed by Anna Freud and her peers. They encouraged child-care workers to "think of what it means to a child to be deprived of his family" and urged them to transform their orphanages into homes. They spoke about the emotional roots of behavioral problems and imparted the fundamentals of child nutrition, sanitation, and health. A total of 369 Korean superintendents and child-care workers participated in the courses.[15]

Korean child-care workers were exposed not only to new information but also to new methods of teaching. Tieszen and Alvernaz required the active participation of their students, encouraging them, for example, to draw conclusions based on their observations of child behavior. Korean trainees "were accustomed to teachers who outlined each lecture for them to write in their notebooks. Being expected to think for themselves in class was a novel experience for them, and at first they thought they were learning nothing," Tieszen and Alvernaz recounted. A language barrier further complicated the women's teaching efforts. As neither spoke Korean, they conducted their courses using translators. Some child-care workers, Tieszen and Alvernaz noted, found new ways of thinking about children too difficult to assimilate. Others demonstrated little motivation to learn. "Many of our trainees," the women acknowledged, "were very poorly paid institutional personnel who had selected their occupation on the basis of having no other means of livelihood."[16]

But some participants responded enthusiastically. After participating in Tieszen and Alvernaz's course, a group of child-care workers at one institution formed the Bo A Yun Gu Whai, or Housemothers' Child Study Monthly Meeting. The workers met once a month to discuss methods and share problems relating to institutional child care. The idea soon spread to other children's homes. Some of the students who had been reticent during the training courses became active participants in these study groups, Tieszen reported. A bulletin on child care written by the Bo A Yun Gu Whai demonstrated a firm grasp of the psychological theories of child care Tieszen and Alvernaz had worked to impart. "No greater power could exist than love in the education of the child. This has been my faith in ordinary times, but through the lectures of Miss Alvernaz and Miss Tieszen in the training course, I became confident of it," one housemother wrote. "We should try to give love similar to that of their real parents and brothers, and our love should be trusted by all the children," she argued. A report by a Korean social workers' league offered a somewhat more measured assessment of the courses and their influence. The report noted that attendees had "learned much from the course" and "were greatly enlightened in social work knowledge." But although learning about the care of children in the United States was interesting and useful, the social workers noted, "we should never expect all of the American ways would apply to our present Korean situation as they are. Therefore, we must try to find out our way in caring [for] children."[17]

The child-care lessons imparted by Tieszen and Alvernaz informed all of CCF's operations in Korea. For example, Ernest Nash, the organization's director in Korea, chastised the director of an orphanage in Pusan whose wards had appeared unhappy during a recent inspection. "The 'school' discipline which is now enforced must be wholly replaced by the type of 'home' discipline which characterizes the great majority of our CCF homes," Nash insisted. He threatened to withdraw support from the orphanage if the superintendent did not work to ensure that his staff was "animated by a spirit of true home parenthood towards the children." By 1956, Nash insisted on calling all of the organization's Korean orphanages "homes" in order to better capture the "generally unregimented, happy, and carefree character of the 'home family.'"[18]

Tieszen's lessons in child care would touch several generations of Korean practitioners: she worked in Korea, with only a brief interruption, for more than four decades. During the 1960s, Tieszen conducted child-care training courses for workers in children's homes and day-care centers as a member of the Mennonite Central Committee's team in Taegu. In the 1970s, she taught in Yonsei University's newly created Department of Child and Family Studies, training instructors to teach courses in child development, home economics, and parent education. Tieszen continued to serve as an editor of a Korean journal of child studies until 2009.[19]

Tieszen was one of a growing cadre of women who would serve with voluntary agencies not only in Korea but elsewhere in Asia and the Middle East. These women faced both a distinct set of challenges and a unique set of opportunities. Unlike in the United States and Europe, social work in the East was not necessarily considered "women's work." In the mid-1950s, more men than women were enrolled in all the Asian schools of social work, with the exception of the Philippines. The student body at the Madras School of Social Work in India in 1960, for example, consisted of ninety men and only ten women. Women were also not a significant presence among native voluntary workers: in Middle Eastern countries with a tradition of purdah, in particular, women's participation in organized efforts outside the home was discouraged.[20]

American women working overseas found that their local counterparts were often men—and sometimes men who resented female authority. For example, Arlene Sitler arrived in Korea in 1954 to work for CCF. She found that her gender often put her at a disadvantage when interacting with Korean government officials and orphanage superintendents and, at times, when dealing with her American colleagues as well. "The snap judgment and quick change of mind on the part of a woman in this culture didn't advance the cause of female suffrage at all, and certainly not CCF's relations with the Ministry," complained an American male colleague when Sitler changed her mind about something during a meeting with a Korean minister. "Being a lady in Korea poses special problems as you well know, and many superintendents have said there ought to be a man in the job," the man related. By 1955, CCF had decided that a man should be appointed to take over Sitler's responsibilities, and Sitler had resigned in frustration.[21] Sitler's troubles might have stemmed from personality clashes as much as from outright gender discrimination, but being female was essentially a further strike against her. Disavowing gender prejudice as a pesky Eastern phenomenon allowed Sitler's American colleagues to embrace sexism while simultaneously denying their role in its perpetuation.

Among American agencies' country directors in the non-European world during the 1950s and 1960s, men generally outnumbered women. Women, however, predominated among child-care consultants. Moreover, men who served abroad with American agencies often brought along wives who performed important, if frequently unrecognized, work. Alma Mills assisted her husband, Verent—CCF's overseas director—with such tasks as letter writing. Robert Arculli, who served with CCF in India, reported that his wife had assumed responsibility for taking photographs that could be used in CCF advertisements. Harold Berrean was in charge of Save the Children Federation's program in Korea, but his wife, Sally, reviewed every translation and status report before it was sent out. The AFSC recognized the contributions made by wives, hiring couples to lead several of its overseas initiatives. A 1958 job description for an AFSC representative in the Arab Middle East called specifically for a "single man or married couple."[22]

Being a female worker abroad did have some advantages. Women workers often had better access to local mothers than did their male counterparts, particularly in countries where women traditionally had little contact with men outside the family. PLAN's executive director at the time, Gloria Matthews, noted that her gender helped her when "dealing overseas with bureaucracies in masculine cultures," as she was not perceived to be a threat. Matthews had joined PLAN in 1941 as a secretary. Although she lacked formal training in social work or child welfare, her enthusiasm for PLAN's work earned her the role of assistant director in 1951 and executive director in 1954. (Matthews would become the organization's first international executive director in 1973.) Matthews regularly visited PLAN's far-flung operations, traveling for four to five months out of the year. Women such as Matthews were often in a better position than their male colleagues to dispense advice regarding child rearing. Orphanage superintendents "apparently take it [child-care advice] from a lady, whereas they resent it coming from a man," noted one CCF worker in Korea in 1960.[23]

"A LIVING SYMBOL OF DEMOCRACY IN ACTION"

In addition to training foreign personnel, American agencies worked to inject a familial spirit into the architecture and organization of their children's homes overseas. In the United States, cottage-style homes had begun to replace large dormitory-style orphanages in the late nineteenth century.

Orphanages arranged on the "cottage plan" sought to replicate for children the experience of living in a family home. They grouped children of varying sexes and ages into "families," each of which lived in its own house under the care of a "cottage mother." Reformers praised cottage-style homes for offering children the love and individualized attention they needed to grow into healthy adults. Institutions organized according to the cottage plan were more costly to run than dormitory-style homes, but child-care experts insisted that the individual attention they provided to children was priceless. By 1937, the Child Welfare League of America endorsed the cottage system as the preferable means of caring for institutionalized children. But although cottage-style children's homes had gained widespread popularity in the United States by the mid-twentieth century, the idea had yet to take root in Asia or the Middle East.[24]

In 1952, CCF embarked on a project to build a model cottage-style home in Hong Kong. Children's needs in Hong Kong were acute. During the 1950s, hundreds of thousands of refugees fleeing China arrived on Hong Kong's shores. Many were women and children whose husbands and fathers had been killed by the communists. These refugees lived in flimsy hillside shacks or crowded into government-built concrete dwellings. Two thousand children resided in orphanages that offered—according to Western observers—a dubious level of care. "Psychology as yet, is an almost unknown science in Hong Kong," noted Penelope Brooke-Johnson, who worked for CCF in Hong Kong. The staffs of most orphanages, she observed, "were convinced that children were born either bad or good, and that nothing could be done to change them. The idea of trying to help a naughty child was very strange to them."[25]

CCF had run courses for orphanage superintendents and staff in Hong Kong that familiarized them with American methods of caring for children. The courses instructed workers to create a relaxed atmosphere in their homes and to offer children sympathy and understanding rather than punishment. But if strict discipline had no place among children, it was accepted with regard to employees: CCF instructors gave child-care workers two weeks to write an article explaining how the techniques they learned in the course could be applied in their own institutions. The articles were submitted to the CCF office, where they were assessed to determine workers' "interest and concern." Those who demonstrated reluctance to adopt the new techniques were fired.[26]

But the organization wanted to do more for Hong Kong's children. "Future citizens could be best developed under the influence of a mother-figure in a cottage-type home rather than the cold, austere, and loveless regimentation of an institution-type orphanage," the organization explained. Using funds collected from individual donors—77,000 of them—along with a construction grant from the Hong Kong government, CCF purchased a fifty-one-acre parcel of land near Kowloon, at the base of the Saddleback Mountain. On it, the organization constructed what it boasted was the "largest cottage-style children's home in the Far East." Named Children's Garden, the home opened in early 1958 with sixty-five cottages, each with four bedrooms, a living/dining room, a bathroom, and a kitchen. The cottages housed a total of 845 children, with 13 children per cottage. CCF praised Children's Garden not only as a model child welfare institution but also as "a living symbol of democracy in action on Communist China's doorstep." CCF's ideas about child care touched many of Hong Kong's institutionalized children: by the late 1950s, the organization was supporting more than two-thirds of the three thousand institutionalized children in Hong Kong in both cottage-plan homes such as Children's Garden and in more traditional dormitory-style homes.[27]

But some of CCF's Chinese staff members did not share the organization leaders' enthusiasm for the cottage system. CCF constructed a smaller cottage-style home, the Clarke Children's Home, in Hong Kong to replace a dormitory-style orphanage that it had been supporting. The orphanage's child-care workers were "violently opposed" to the new cottage-plan system, Penelope Brooke-Johnson related. If CCF officials saw the cottage system as an emblem of democracy, local workers viewed it as an unwelcome foreign imposition. The workers did not relish their new roles as cottage mothers and resented the child-care advice imparted by their Western colleagues. "It was clear at the outset that they would have great difficulty in accepting these ideas of the 'foreign devils,'" Brooke-Johnson reported. She expressed hope that the cottage system would eventually gain widespread acceptance among indigenous workers. Once it did, she asserted, it would bring about "a revolution in Child Care—not only for Hong Kong, but for the whole of the Far East."[28]

Several years after the institution opened, local attitudes toward Children's Garden remained mixed. Assistant Superintendent James Ming N. Ch'ien reported that many local citizens criticized Children's Garden for spoiling children with too much material comfort and thus making it difficult for them to adjust once they reentered the world outside the home. In addition, disciplinary problems, particularly with boys, were a recurrent problem, keeping many cottage families from enjoying the pleasant home life for which Children's Garden had been designed. While reaffirming the orphanage's commitment to providing children with "love and care" and to rearing them in a "democratic environment," Ch'ien noted plans for "tightening control and enforcing discipline." The institution added men to its staff in the hope that male guidance would help solve some of the home's disciplinary woes.[29] While CCF officials saw the care and affection provided by mothers as essential to the rearing of strong democratic citizens, local workers, frustrated with youngsters' perceived poor behavior, emphasized the importance of paternal discipline.

Despite its problems, Children's Garden would serve as a training ground for child welfare workers from across the continent. Welfare professionals visited the institution to study the operations of a cottage-plan orphanage and to observe "modern" methods of child care. CCF also constructed cottage-style children's homes in Korea, Japan, India, the Philippines, and Puerto Rico. At the Philippines home, also called Children's Garden, each cottage had a pet dog as a playmate for the children, and youngsters called their cottage mothers "Mommy." Hong Kong's Children's Garden would arouse the interest of people in places as far afield as Turkey. In 1959, the governor of Istanbul thanked CCF's Ernest Nash for sending him plans that would allow him to construct a Children's Garden in his city.[30]

The cottage system also took root in Korea. A cottage-style children's home stood as the centerpiece of the Central Social Workers' Training Institute in Seoul. Built with assistance from the U.S. and Korean governments, the United Nations Korean Reconstruction Agency (UNKRA), and private American agencies, the school trained Korean workers in social welfare methods. The U.S. government lauded the institution as the "first Center in Korea to provide courses of study, demonstration and good practice in child care." As many students at the center were expected to work in children's institutions after graduation, they conducted fieldwork in the attached cottage-style Un-dong children's home, which cared for youngsters "in the most modern methods." The training center emphasized children's need for individual attention and gave demonstrations of play techniques. It trained approximately 550 orphanage directors, social workers, and government officials in its first year of operation alone.[31]

Cottage-style homes were designed to provide children with the love and affection that would help them grow into confident, emotionally stable adults. Their proponents also hoped that they would combat the uniformity and collective mentality seen as plaguing traditional dormitory-style homes. Children reared in collective environments, many American experts argued, were more likely than their peers reared in families to follow the dictates of the crowd—even if the crowd chose to support a totalitarian leader. American commentators often cited respect for the dignity of each citizen as a defining feature of a democracy. They contrasted the American enshrinement of individual human rights with communist societies in which the needs of the collective took precedence. In order for democracy to fully take root in the East, Americans argued, citizens needed to learn to respect the needs and desires of each individual.

Child-care workers were on the front lines of this reorientation. Tieszen and Alvernaz noted that the first step in their child-care training program was to foster an interest "in each child as an individual having emotional, social, and spiritual needs. Only as this goal was achieved would the trainees be ready to modify constructively their ways of dealing with children." The women required trainees to observe the behavior of a single child and to write a paper based on these observations. The American Jewish Joint Distribution Committee, which ran day nurseries for young children in several countries in the Middle East and North Africa, also made an effort to encourage the individual personality development of each child under its care. "This is an age when a child can be molded easily," a JDC worker explained. "Their individuality can be easily taken away from them. We will then be turning out sausages, each one like the other, instead of children."[32]

Child-care workers' emphasis on children's individuality projected American ideals. But, set against the backdrop of the culture of conformity within the United States at the time, it also gave expression to American anxieties about personality development at home. To what extent could individual thought thrive in the climate of fear produced by the domestic anticommunist crusade? Was the United States itself producing "sausages" or children? America portrayed itself as the model of individual rights and freedom of expression on the global stage, but these ideals were in peril not only abroad but also within the borders of the United States itself.

Child sponsorship programs forced child-care workers to consider the personality of each youngster under their care, as American agencies required local staff to fill out detailed case histories for each sponsored child. These histories were then forwarded to American sponsors, giving them insight into the personalities and aspirations of their foster children. PLAN, for example, required orphanage staff to complete a questionnaire that asked not only about a child's familial and educational background but also about his or her "personal traits" and "what [he or she] want[s] to be."[33] Treating each child as an individual was at once good child-care practice, a method for molding democratic citizens, and a means of earning a child a place in an American sponsor's heart.

In 1959, Mildred Arnold, a U.S. Children's Bureau official, toured several Asian countries on her way to an international social work conference in Tokyo. Arnold was encouraged by the progress she observed. "The dignity and worth of the individual is beginning to be emphasized in these Asiatic countries. This is sharp contrast to the situation just a few years ago," she contended. Arnold recalled the international social work conference in India in 1952, when most Eastern countries were preoccupied with the mere struggle for survival. Now, she argued, a heightened standard of living had allowed a concern for the individual to come to the fore. Arnold recounted a query posed to her by a Japanese conference delegate: "The United States has achieved so well this concern for the individual. Won't you tell us how?"[34]

But not all observers lauded the perceived rise of individualism, as it signaled as well the decline of the traditional family system. In 1958, a Western priest in Korea criticized the proliferation of American-supported orphanages. These institutions, he charged, had helped to "disrupt the Confucian sense of family responsibility." The priest contended that the availability of institutions to look after orphaned children made family members less inclined to assume responsibility for their care. Ernest Nash dismissed the priest's criticisms. He argued that the war and the country's rapidly modernizing socioeconomic system—not American humanitarian groups—were to blame for the disintegration of the traditional Korean extended family. Orphanages were the response to, rather than the cause of, "the public disregard of Mr. Confucius," Nash maintained.[35]

Rose Hum Lee, an American professor of sociology who traveled around the world observing social welfare conditions, noted that new ideas about the relationship between the individual and the family had disseminated unevenly throughout many Eastern societies. As a result, few countries had developed a social welfare infrastructure concordant with new ideals. Lee described the plight of a divorced woman with children in Asia or the Middle East. "She and others of her generation have adopted the ideal of individualism and freedom from ancient fetters that bind her to male dominance and unsatisfactory interpersonal relations," Lee noted. But such a woman was likely to find herself ostracized by family and friends, unable to earn a living, and without any social welfare programs to assist her. Lee urged the establishment of more adequate public welfare systems in Eastern countries. But she acknowledged that the development of these systems was stymied by a dearth of trained workers, a lack of funds, and the instability of the political structures necessary to support them.[36] American commentators connected individual personality development to the social order writ large. But, as Lee understood, the line between personal and societal transformations was rarely direct or immediate.

FREEDOM IS CHILD'S PLAY

Child welfare experts located the roots of emotional security, creativity, and independent thought in the love and individualized attention children received within the familial setting. Another source of these personal attributes, experts argued, was creative play. To child welfare experts and voluntary workers alike, play epitomized childhood. As the nineteenth century waned, declines in child labor and infant mortality led to the development of a new conception of childhood. Parents and educators came to understand the early years as a distinct phase of life. They saw children as vulnerable beings, properly sheltered from the tribulations of the adult world, and placed a new premium on children's happiness. Childhood became a time of play rather than work. "War or peace, there are a few basic expressions which belong to the world of childhood," asserted author Clara Lambert. "The opportunity to play is one of these, as much as the opportunity to be fed, housed, clothed, kept in health, and sent to school." Play also served an important developmental purpose. By the postwar years, child welfare professionals understood play to be essential to children's healthy personality development. According to contemporary experts, play helped children work through difficult emotions, served as a rehearsal for life's tasks, and helped children develop their creative facilities. Play, argued Lambert, "is emotional education."[37]

The therapeutic value of children's play assumed heightened significance in the aftermath of the Second World War. "We are now living in a period when we all have been exposed in varying degrees to savagery and war," explained the Play Schools Association, a New York–based organization that offered advice regarding methods of stimulating children's creative play, in 1947. "As a result, children the world over are expressing themselves in aggressive play or are withdrawing into passivity or disassociation from the group." The association urged children's caretakers to encourage children's play in order to help them come to terms with their wartime experiences. Voluntary agencies working in Europe after World War II regularly used play therapy in the rehabilitation of the war's youngest victims. The AFSC translated American material on play therapy for use in its child guidance clinic in Wuppertal, Germany, and the JDC sent materials from the Play Schools Association to its overseas representatives. "Nursery equipment has been particularly helpful in overcoming the shy, unemotional and withdrawn defense mechanism resulting from Nazi brutality and terror," the JDC explained in a letter to a donor. "Toys are the tools used in releasing inner tension and directing energies into healthy constructive channels."[38]

In the aftermath of the war in Korea, voluntary workers continued to recognize play's therapeutic function. Helen Tieszen used play therapy to rehabilitate the conflict's young victims. Some children had been so traumatized by the upheaval of war and by familial separation that they did not know how to play, Tieszen recounted in a 1957 article in the child welfare journal *Children*. When a group of severely deprived orphans, aged five to seven, first encountered a permissive play situation, she wrote, "They had no skills at their command for adequately meeting the demands made upon them." The orphans refused to share play materials and had no concept of how to interact with other youngsters. They behaved "emotionally" in the manner of two-year-olds, Tieszen noted, though they had the memory and intelligence of children their own age. Tieszen worked to demonstrate to Korean child-care workers the therapeutic value of children's play. With the continued attention of patient adults, the orphans gradually learned to share their toys and to work together to build with blocks.[39]

Child-care experts' focus on play cloaked children in Korea and other Eastern countries, whose foreignness threatened to place them outside the realm of American concern, within the Western mantle of sentimentalized childhood. By presenting donors in the United States with images of youngsters at play around the world, American agencies promoted a universalized understanding of childhood that portrayed children everywhere as defined by the same needs and desires. "Children are alike," the Play Schools Association asserted, "in their need to play at all times and in all places." A booklet produced by the AFSC to raise funds for Korean children affected by the war introduced American youngsters to foreign counterparts very much like themselves. "In that land where a war has just been fought, do the children *still* play games, sing songs, go to school, help their mothers, or do any of the other things that *you* do?" the booklet queried. The answer, of course, was yes: "Right in the midst of bombed buildings boys and girls were doing what boys and girls everywhere have always done and what you and your friends do." More than a decade later, as the United States' involvement in Southeast Asia intensified, the AFSC produced a fact sheet on children in Vietnam that employed a similar tactic. By depicting youngsters flying kites, playing games with small stones, and receiving toys during the mid-autumn Festival of the Children, the AFSC underscored the similarities between Vietnamese children and those in the United States.[40]

Play also provided evidence of the universality of the stages of child development. Children's play—like children's physical, intellectual, and emotional development—followed a predictable developmental sequence, child welfare experts contended. As children grew, their play progressed naturally according to a set pattern. In fact, one expert noted, one feature of neurotic children was that their play did not follow a developmental sequence. So important was the progression of children's play according to a set pattern that Lambert instructed teachers and parents to allow children whose play had deviated from the pattern to "make up" the stages they had not experienced. "If they have missed, even though they are eight or nine, the play life of the four or five year old, they should be given time to catch up with themselves by playing like four or five year olds," Lambert recommended. American overseas workers reinforced the idea that children's play progressed according to a set sequence. In a book written for teachers in foreign day-care centers, for example, the JDC's child-care experts described the interests and abilities of three-, four-, and five-year-olds, recommending play activities appropriate for children in each age group.[41] The "play life" of a five-year-old, the JDC's experts implied, looked largely the same the world over.

While images of children at play emphasized the similarities between children in the United States and those around the world, depictions of play could also serve to highlight the different conditions under which children in the free world and those in communist countries were reared. Popular publications in the United States regularly carried stories recounting the pernicious encroachment of the communist state on the intimate sphere of children's play and games. In Poland, the *Saturday Evening Post* recounted, children played "Red Army soldiers and fascists" instead of cops and robbers. In Czechoslovakia, youngsters worked together to build with blocks—but they constructed only factories, never castles. Even children's fairy tales, American readers were told, received a communist overhaul: in the Czech retelling of Little Red Riding Hood, the heroine was a poor working girl and the wolf a capitalist. Sleeping Beauty's suitor recoiled upon discovering the privileged sleeping princess and instead of kissing her awake, went outside to join a parade of people "celebrating the victory of work." In China, kindergarten children pointed toy machine guns and rifles at imaginary capitalists and revisionists. And in Cuba, American readers learned, children's "first animal stories are set on collective farms," and "their first bogeymen are Yanqui imperialists."[42]

American descriptions of children at play both affirmed and denied the political salience of play and games. On the one hand, images of youngsters at play evoked a wholesome, "natural," and universal childhood on which the demands of the state dared not encroach. Descriptions of children at play in communist lands offended American sensibilities precisely because children's play in these countries had become politicized. On the other hand, however, experts saw children's play as a symbol of national development and as a constructive tool to be marshaled into service for the good of the country. American workers were rarely clear as to whether creative play was a learned behavior that required inculcation or an innate drive stifled by caretakers unschooled in its importance. But many agreed that children's play was essential not only to personal growth but also to national progress.[43]

In a 1963 book titled *Children's Games around the World as Enjoyed by the Children of the World-Wide "Family" of Christian Children's Fund*, CCF's Helen Clarke and her daughter Jeanne Clarke Wood took readers on a whirlwind tour of children's amusements across the globe. Just in time for Christmas, the book's lighthearted narratives introduced readers to a variety of indigenous children's songs, toys, and games. But the book also brought a critical eye to bear on foreign children's play behavior. Clarke and Wood subtly ranked countries along a scale of civilization, using children's play as a proxy for a country's level of development. At the top of the scale stood countries such as France, whose children enjoy a "repertoire of games as varied and lengthy as our own." At the bottom rested places such as Haiti, where youngsters "have known practically nothing of play and games as we know them. In fact, witchcraft and cockfighting are the only diversions some of them know." Clarke and Wood were surprised to find countries in which the state of children's play and national development were not in congruence: "In observing the spirited play of Paraguayan children," they noted, "one could wonder why the small country should be so far behind others in its development."[44]

Voluntary agencies were not alone in their concern for children's play overseas. The U.S. Children's Bureau sent pamphlets on creative play to interested parties abroad. The U.S. Information Agency also promoted children's play. The agency translated *Play Is Our Business,* a film about the importance of play made by the Play Schools Association, into twenty languages and distributed it around the world. The film portrayed children's play as essential to both individual development and to the well-being of the free world. Playing together taught children cooperation, an important democratic ideal. Play also helped children become emotionally stable, self-reliant, free-thinking, and creative people—the kinds of citizens on whom the survival of a democratic society depended. "Children are the raw materials of democracy," the film explained.[45] Their enrichment through creative play activities would be a boon to free countries everywhere.

American voluntary workers were confident that children given the opportunity for free play and creative expression would develop into strong democratic citizens. But play occupied a less exalted position in many countries around the world. American workers stationed in Asia and the Middle East were troubled to find that parents and child-care workers did not universally understand childhood as a time for carefree play. For example, Tieszen and Alvernaz found Korean orphanage workers resistant to the suggestion that they organize play activities for the children under their care. The Korean workers argued that "since these were poor children they needed to learn to work rather than play," the women recounted. Play materials were so alien to some Korean workers, Tieszen noted, that they placed gifts from children's sponsors directly into a cupboard, never distributing them to their intended recipients. JDC consultants reported a similar phenomenon in the organization's day nurseries in Morocco. "When some new toys were sent to [local teachers], such as donkeys and camels for imaginative play, they locked them up in the cupboard to await the next visit of the day care consultant, saying that [i]n their training course no one had instructed them how to use these toys," recounted Minette Jee, a JDC day-care consultant.[46]

Moroccan parents also took issue with the JDC day nurseries' program of play activities. "They think we 'spoil' the children, giving them too much freedom and not enough 'discipline'; they say that this form of education may be satisfactory in our western culture, but it does not equip the children to adjust to demands of schooling here," day-care consultant Mary Grist reported. But the JDC remained firm in its commitment to its creative program and to its emphasis on freedom. In 1959, Minette Jee worked to revise the curriculum of the JDC's day nurseries in Morocco to expand the five hours per week allotted to free play. But she found her efforts frustrated by a dearth of educational play materials and a cadre of local teachers who lacked the training necessary to engage children in meaningful play experiences. Jee conducted training courses with the nursery teachers that stressed the significance of children's play to their overall development. The absence of free play in the Moroccan nurseries, however, made it difficult to connect theory and practice. Many of the creative play activities encouraged by the JDC consultants, such as painting pictures and modeling with clay, were entirely alien to local teachers in North Africa and the Middle East. When the organization initiated its day nursery program in Tunisia in 1951, for example, the JDC consultant found she had to demonstrate to teachers how to rip paper to put on easels and how to roll clay into balls. The majority of the women teaching in the JDC's Moroccan nurseries, complained Mary Grist in 1962, "are literate rather than educated. Their schooling has demanded of them passivity and obedience and there is no wave of the magic wand that will bring an immediate response of creativeness and initiative."[47] Whether children under the care of these teachers could themselves develop into creative and independent adults was a question that remained to be answered.

In addition to creativity and cooperation, play intersected with another emblem of democracy: the free market economy. In the United States, many commentators looked to a booming consumer economy as a means of creating a more prosperous, happy, and egalitarian society. As industries reconverted to peacetime production in the years following World War II, middle-class Americans were treated to an unprecedented profusion of consumer goods. Many saw American capitalist abundance as a reproach to the communist planned economy and situated the country's well-stocked supermarkets and shiny time-saving appliances as the icons of democracy and free choice. Children were an integral part of this new mass consumption society, the beneficiaries of a proliferation of amusements that manufacturers promised would make youngsters smarter, happier, and more creative. Toys—preferably, those designed by experts in child development—were by mid-century firmly ensconced in the pantheon of childhood necessities.[48]

American organizations frequently rallied assistance by describing foreign children who had no toys with which to play. In a 1952 publication, for example, PLAN printed a large photograph of forlorn-looking refugee children in West Germany gathered around a large puddle. "With not one toy in the entire group, these child-refugees find enjoyment round a muddy puddle in Feldafing Camp (Bavaria). God sends the rain," the organization noted wistfully. "We could send them toys." In a description of a visit to a Korean children's home, voluntary worker LeRoy Bowman and his colleagues told of youngsters so desperate for toys that they "grabbed for burnt-out flash bulbs for playthings." CCF interpreted Pakistani children's lack of interest in playthings as an indictment of the country's child-rearing practices: "Children of Pakistan have not been nurtured in the cheerful warmth of childhood pleasures. For instance, newly arrived children in CCF affiliated homes and schools often do not know what to do with TOYS."[49]

Both PLAN and SCF ran doll contests as a means of drawing attention to the plight of children overseas. "How tragic the plight of little girls who never owned a doll and how wonderful the experience of the 'first doll,'" noted SCF. Partnering separately with *Seventeen* magazine, the organizations asked American girls to decorate and clothe dolls. Luminaries including Eleanor Roosevelt and Marian Anderson were called on to judge the girls' creations, awarding prizes to the best ones. The dolls were then donated to needy girls. PLAN saw the dolls as helping to "forge a chain of love and friendship between American girls and their counterparts overseas," and thousands of girls relished the gifts. But while PLAN was pleased with the publicity its doll contest generated, it noted that most of the letters it received in response "asked for PLAN help and not dolls." Many foreign families preferred to receive monetary assistance rather than toys.[50]

As PLAN noted, consumer goods—toys, but also clothing and other supplies—often served as a medium that connected foreign children with their American foster parents. The gifts sent by American sponsors to their children overseas were a tangible manifestation of the bonds of love and obligation that bound them together. In their letters to the United States, many children expressed love and gratitude. But for children who were more emotionally reticent, who were less adept at letter writing, or who had simply run out of things to say, describing in detail the gifts they received was a handy means of filling the required missive. Some children's letters read like inventories of goods received. "On Feb. 23, I received your Plan Grant in the amount of Hwan 10,360 ($8.00), and a sweater, three pairs of socks, five notebooks and a color painting-set and a school-bag," one Korean youngster told his foster parents. Several months later, he thanked them for "two bars of soaps, a bottle of insect repellant lotion, two toothbrush and a clothing." Descriptions of gifts written by children were, however, sometimes touching or humorous. "I am proud to possess such fine new underwear from America!" a refugee child in Germany wrote in an excited letter to his foster parents. Korean youngster Soon Ok reported in a letter to her foster mother: "I look so charming in my lovely swimming suit that you kindly sent me that everyone who sees me on the beach envies me with my swimsuit."[51] A Greek boy was equally thrilled by the gifts he received. He told his American sponsors:

> I want my good friends to know how I laugh and be glad that I do not get the old mended things nobody could wear any more. I got new shiny shoes and much new clothings. Oh, I laugh the whole time because I am so happy from my Foster Parents. I thank you from the whole of my heart.[52]

Foreign orphans brought to the United States to receive medical treatment or for publicity tours were often publicly showered with consumer goods. A pair of European orphans brought to New York by a women's organization for a fund-raising tour received brand-new wardrobes, courtesy of the B. Altman department store. Photographs of the children's shopping spree were splashed across the pages of *Life* magazine. An organization called the Federation for Orphans in Greece sent two seven-year-old girls maimed by communist grenades for plastic surgery in the United States. As they embarked on their well-publicized return trip to Greece, the girls wore pretty pink dresses and clutched bride dolls—a testament to American benevolence and to the robustness of the country's consumer economy.[53]

In 1954, SCF embarked on a project aimed at assisting the children of refugees fleeing Iron Curtain countries. The organization provided each child with a toy "as a welcome to the free world." In their emphasis on providing children with material goods, American organizations trained foreign children to be consumers. They reinforced gender-specific patterns of consumption—dolls for little girls—and imparted to children the connection between material abundance and political freedom. Child sponsorship programs invited Americans to help fight the Cold War as consumers. As Christina Klein has argued, American organizations essentially converted intangibles—a child's happiness, U.S. domination in the struggle against communism—into commodities available for purchase.[54]

American voluntary workers sometimes used the language of modern corporate transactions in describing their work. For example, J. Calvitt Clarke noted in a 1951 letter that CCF "tries to 'sell' the children to the public." William Asbury explained the organization's mission using similar language. "Our sponsors in effect buy a share of an orphanage with their $10 per month," he wrote in 1954. "They expect us to keep title in their holdings." A group of high school students in Seattle adopted a boy and raised money for him by selling "stock" in him under the name "Orphans Unlimited." For $1 per share, a stockholder received a photograph of the foster child and a copy of his case history.[55] American organizations and their supporters linked child welfare with capitalism and consumption. By applying the language and techniques of modern business to the private activity of rearing children, they domesticated corporate affairs. These groups implied that modern business techniques could enhance personal relationships rather than diminish them. Even as they encouraged the sharing of capitalist wealth with beneficiaries overseas, they suggested that a better world was, at least in part, available for purchase.

But the commodification of humanitarian action had its limits. In 1959, members of the Committee on Foreign Affairs in the U.S. House of Representatives were concerned by reports that packages donated by voluntary agencies to needy families overseas were being resold in retail stores in several countries in Asia. Similarly, officials from American child sponsorship agencies were deeply disturbed to learn that their model of sponsorship had given rise to a new type of business in Korea. Enterprising citizens with a knowledge of English had set up agencies patronized by poor families that collected the addresses of ordinary Americans and wrote letters to them pleading for assistance. The agencies charged the families a fee or took a portion of whatever assistance arrived from the United States.[56] These situations stripped

American assistance to foreign families of its affective cloak. They reduced humanitarian aid to a mere economic transaction, undermining the confluence of capitalism and sentiment advocated by child welfare agencies working overseas.

LESSONS IN FREEDOM

While American child-care experts believed that children learned many important democratic principles through family relations and creative play, schools also played a significant role in shaping the youngest citizens of the free world. As they had in Germany, American workers in Korea and other countries around the world saw cold, rigid relationships between children and their caretakers as conditioning citizens to accept authoritarian leadership in government. But as American efforts moved eastward, the locus of fears regarding authoritarian child rearing migrated from the family to the classroom. In some ways, this shift represented an expansive interpretation of Freudian ideas that applied to teachers and parents alike. American efforts to reform foreign classrooms also reflected the ways in which American fears about poor child rearing took on a class-specific dimension. In Asia and the Middle East (and later, in Latin America), American workers critiqued poor families for their apathy and ignorance, not for their authoritarian tendencies. Charges of authoritarianism came to rest instead with teachers, who were generally more educated than local parents.

In 1952, the Department of State approached the USC about the possibility of organizing a mission to help Korea improve its educational system. The request originated with the Korean Ministry of Education, which sought advice regarding how to reorient its schools along more "democratic" lines. The majority of Korean teachers had been trained during the Japanese occupation, which had ended in 1945. As a result, American observers contended, Korean teaching was plagued by "rigid, authoritarian methods." This manner of teaching did little to encourage children's learning and development; even worse, it was distinctly out of sync with the vision of a thriving democracy Americans hoped Korea would become. Teachers who nurtured children's confidence and creativity, however, could produce a population ready to take on the challenges of democratic citizenship. Through these teachers, USC team member Vester M. Mulholland contended, "a democratic nation can come into being."[57]

A number of groups, including the U.S. Army and the United Nations, participated in the effort to rebuild the Korean system of education. The war had devastated Korean schools. An estimated 80 percent of books, furniture, and school equipment had been destroyed. Nearly a million students were not attending school due to lack of facilities. Many Korean classrooms were housed in flimsy, unheated buildings with upwards of sixty students per class. Nonetheless, the USC rose to the challenge. "We feel that in this critical area of the world, a challenge such as this must be met," explained Helen Fogg. The organization had experience in taming "authoritarian" methods of dealing with children, and it drew on its experience running the Child Care and Education Institutes in Germany in planning its Korean project. Between 1952 and 1954, the USC sent three teams of educational experts to Korea. The project was supported in its first year by the Department of State; later, it received funding from UNKRA and the American-Korean Foundation. The USC's teams worked with Korean principals and teachers on revising school administration, teaching methods, and curricula. First, in a series of workshops, and later, working directly with teachers' training schools, they sought to impart the new theories of child development and education they saw as reinforcing Korea's nascent democracy. The Americans worked as a team in order to best demonstrate the process of cooperative decision making.[58]

The American educators urged their Korean counterparts to craft a holistic "experience curriculum" that invited children to learn through educational activities rather than by rote memorization. They encouraged teachers to abandon uniform curricula and to instead consider the individual learning style of each child. American advice often extended beyond teaching methods and into the realm of child development and psychology. "Children are born neither good nor bad," USC team member Elizabeth C. Wilson wrote in a handbook for Korean teachers compiled by the mission. Wilson blamed the educational system imposed by the Japanese for producing citizens who passively deferred to authority. A more flexible teaching style geared toward encouraging children's growth and creativity would help develop strong democratic citizens.[59]

The USC's efforts were far reaching: the organization estimated that it made contact with about a third of Korea's 54,000 teachers during its first year of work alone. The American embassy in Korea was pleased with the results of the program. "There are reports everywhere of changes in educational approach as a result of the institutes," noted an embassy official. In a hand-written letter to the USC, Korean teacher Eun Yong Ki thanked the organization for the program. "We have known already 'What is the real democratic education' but we could not realize it for we were too weak. From I attended this class of mission I get new self-confidence and courage," she wrote. But even enthusiastic teachers no doubt found their efforts to implement new methods of teaching hampered by lack of supplies and severely overcrowded facilities. A teacher could hardly consider individual learning styles in a classroom with sixty students.[60]

The JDC also sought to reform foreign schools. In Iran and Tunisia, where the organization ran large-scale programs to assist local Jewish communities, the JDC worked to transform the classrooms in which local schoolchildren were taught. In 1960, the organization embarked on a project to improve a first grade class in Tehran. The JDC had no control over the class's curriculum, which had been set by the government. Instead, the organization sought to change teachers' "attitude and understanding of children," promoting a friendly and relaxed student-teacher relationship that contrasted with the perceived rigidity plaguing most Iranian schools. The JDC developed a teacher-training program that focused on the classroom's emotional atmosphere, covering such topics as "how a child feels about the teacher"; "teachers have feelings"; and "understanding children's feelings." Many of the teachers were initially resistant to the lessons, JDC consultant Evelyn Peters reported. But some gradually accepted the precepts the JDC sought to impart. "I never knew how much I could affect a child's feelings," one teacher noted upon completing the course. "I never realized that a child could learn as much from a teacher when the teacher was kind as when the teacher was strict," commented another.[61]

A healthy emotional environment in the classroom, however, did not always correspond with traditional academic achievement. The JDC ran a similar program on an experimental basis in a preschool class in Tunis. At the end of the academic year, the school's principal observed that children in the JDC's class read and wrote with less fluency than did their peers in other sections. But, he noted, they were certainly happier. Peters praised the programs' effect on children's personality development. The graduates of the special class, she noted, were "lively, responsive, and alert," while those in the traditional classes were "apathetic, frightened and dulled." But some foreign educators complained that the JDC's "progressive" methods of imparting knowledge were less effective than traditional methods of learning by rote. In Tunis, admitted the JDC's chief day-care consultant, Dorothy Beers, "there is little enthusiasm for this experimental class anywhere but in JDC."[62]

Both the USC's and the JDC's educational programs attempted to spread overseas a model of progressive education that had long been popular in the United States but that by the mid-1950s had become subject to growing criticism. Promoted by turn-of-the-century philosopher and educational re-former John Dewey, progressive educational methods were designed not only to impart knowledge but, more importantly, to shape youngsters' personalities. Dewey and his followers eschewed curricula that emphasized rote memorization and blind submission to the authority of teachers in favor of experiential learning programs that encouraged children's creativity, curi-osity, and independent thought. "Teachers must help parents to see that per-sonality adjustment and good-quality living take priority over learning to read at any particular age or other traditional subject-matter goals," argued William Heard Kilpatrick, a student of Dewey and a prominent progressive educator, in 1949. During the first half of the twentieth century, the tenets of progressive education assumed a prominent place in classrooms across the country.[63]

By the mid-1950s, however, progressive education had become caught up in the politics of the Cold War. Some conservative critics blamed the per-ceived privileging of social and emotional development at the expense of in-tellectual rigor for the United States' lagging place in the technology race, particularly following the Soviet launch of Sputnik. To many educators and child welfare experts, however, progressive education promised to mold citi-zens with the personality characteristics essential to the perpetuation of a free society. They asserted that traditional methods of imparting knowledge, such as rote memorization, were doing little to cultivate the creativity chil-dren would need to compete effectively on a global scale.[64]

The perceived political significance of creative learning to progressive ed-ucators was particularly evident in a teacher-training program organized by the USC in Cambodia. Shortly after the organization completed its work in Korea, the U.S. Foreign Operations Administration asked it to assist Cam-bodia in improving its primary education system. On a fact-finding tour in 1955, Helen Fogg was dismayed to find the majority of Cambodian teachers relying on stern discipline and a series of interminable verbal recitations. "The whole business is a matter of rote learning and memory, of question and answer, of endless correction which, if it results in the child saying the right words, is deemed successful," Fogg recounted. Over the next few years, Fogg and her colleagues would work to train Cambodian educators in new ways of interacting with young children. Working in collaboration with the United States Operations Mission and the Royal Government of Cambodia, the USC constructed a teachers' training college in the village of Kompong Kantuot. The school, which opened its doors in December 1957, imparted to young would-be teachers the importance of involving students in learning activities instead of forcing them to engage in rote memorization. The USC saw the training center as a means of shaping young citizens who would go on to strengthen the newly independent nation. "If the Center can function successfully in the kind of an educational program it attempts, it can be a powerful tool in the drive to instill in citizens a desire to be free and independent," the USC argued.[65]

The USC was particularly concerned with training educators to encourage children's creative expression. In 1960, the organization hired a Kentucky artist, William G. Boaz, to serve as an art consultant to the training school. Boaz was assistant professor of Art at Murray State College, where he taught art education and sculpture. He had previously developed art curricula for public schools. Boaz saw the training school's art program as serving a larger national purpose. "There was a feeling on the part of some Cambodians that although Cambodia had obtained its independence from France seven years earlier, its people were still not 'emotionally' free," Boaz explained. The USC sought to help Cambodian teachers create art programs that would cultivate national pride and help children "become more free and creative individuals." Boaz was displeased with the teaching methods he observed among his Cambodian counterparts. Cambodian art teachers insisted on "imposing the patterns of French culture" rather than encouraging students to take pride in their own national artistic tradition. Boaz tried to demonstrate to these teachers the importance of getting students to draw from their own experiences. In a nod to burgeoning understandings of cultural integrity, he urged them to abandon their requests for expensive art supplies and to work instead with local materials, such as clay. He argued that encouraging children to express their emotions freely was much more important than creating impressive-looking works of art.[66]

Boaz saw children's artistic expression as essential to the creation and maintenance of a free country. "Boys and girls can through art experiences be-

---

YBP Library Services

FIELDSTON, SARA, 1983-

RAISING THE WORLD: CHILD WELFARE IN THE AMERICAN
CENTURY.
                                Cloth   316 P.
CAMBRIDGE: HARVARD UNIV PRESS, 2015

EXAMINES POLITICAL ELEMENT OF POST-WAR CHILD
WELFARE AGENCIES.
  LCCN 2014028417
  ISBN 0674368096   **Library PO#** GENERAL APPROVAL
                                List   39.95   USD
  5461 UNIV OF TEXAS/SAN ANTONIO   **Disc**   17.0%
  App. Date   5/27/15   SWK.APR   6108-11 **Net**   33.16   USD

SUBJ: CHILD WELFARE--U.S.--HIST.--20TH CENT.

CLASS HV881   DEWEY# 362.7   LEVEL ADV-AC

come free (from the inside) and consequently produce free free [*sic*] expressions. . . . Free thinking and acting boys and girls make way for free adults; thus a free society," Boaz explained. But Boaz found Cambodian teachers resistant to his methods and philosophy. Art instructors at the teachers' training center were unenthusiastic and reluctant to try new approaches, Boaz complained to his colleagues in the United States. When forced to use the lesson plans Boaz created, they simply followed them mechanically. The associations between creativity and political freedom so apparent to Boaz seemed not to resonate with the Cambodian teachers. He returned to the United States frustrated that he had been unable to accomplish more.[67]

By training child-care workers, redesigning children's homes and schools, and providing children with opportunities for play and creative expression, American voluntary workers sought to equip youngsters overseas with the "free child's armor"—a personality healthy enough to withstand the challenges of democratic citizenship. The personality traits celebrated by American workers were not new ideals at midcentury: the emphasis on creativity, independent thought, and emotional health would have found an eager audience among John Dewey and his peers during the opening decades of the twentieth century. But these traits gained newfound political significance in the context of the Cold War. Voluntary workers' efforts to promote creativity and independent thought were a rebuke to the perceived communist goal of molding children into unthinking agents of the state. Their emphasis on building emotionally stable children through individualized attention and familial love contrasted sharply with communist child-rearing tenets that allegedly gave little attention to children's individual personalities or to their emotional lives.

The ideal democratic citizen projected by American child welfare workers showcased American values; however, it also betrayed hints of deeper fears and insecurities. During the 1950s and 1960s, many American commentators decried the creeping conformity infecting American life. They voiced fears that the rise of big corporations and the growth of mass consumerism signaled the death knell of individuality and creative life. Child-care experts, in particular, expressed fears that a popular emphasis on group adjustment was producing citizens without the backbone to defend their own beliefs. And even as Americans looked to the family to produce strong citizens, social workers lamented the perceived disintegration of the family unit. Attendees at the 1960 White House Conference on Children and Youth described the family as "threatened, weakened, imperiled, crumbling, deteriorating, disintegrating, exposed to the acids of carelessness and selfishness."[68] Perils internal to the free world, just as much as the foreign communist menace, threatened to erode the "free child's armor."

In their efforts to assist children overseas, American voluntary agencies portrayed democracy not as a form of government but rather as a state of thinking and feeling. Democracy, argued William Heard Kilpatrick, "now reaches beyond the legal aspects of government into the animating spirit of ethics and friendship. Such a democracy is founded primarily on respect for human personality."[69] Spreading democracy meant rearing children who were, in the words of William Boaz, "free (from the inside)." It meant enlisting caregivers, teachers, and parents in the mission to protect the free world. It meant crafting environments—families, children's homes, schools—that would produce emotionally healthy, freethinking, and creative people. American agencies never openly contemplated the possibility that such people might choose communism over democracy.

CHAPTER SIX

Training the Natives
of the Future

ON DECEMBER 14, 1957, Harvard social psychologist David C. McClelland presented a paper to the Conference on Community Development and National Change, organized by the Massachusetts Institute of Technology's (MIT) Center for International Studies. McClelland proposed a new framework for approaching development projects overseas. In recent years, the psychologist noted, American experts had devoted unprecedented attention to efforts aimed at raising the standard of living in so-called underdeveloped countries. They had overseen the construction of roads and irrigation systems, introduced new agricultural methods, and worked tirelessly to improve public health. But these projects, McClelland argued, were missing a crucial element: "a careful consideration of psychological factors." Economic growth, he suggested, was contingent not on external variables—available capital, political structures, technical know-how—but on a deeply rooted personality structure he called "*n* Achievement," or an individual's innate impulse to achieve.

A society could progress only as far as its own citizens' desire for development, McClelland maintained. Therefore, underdeveloped societies were unlikely to achieve self-sustaining economic growth without a change in their populations' fundamental attitudes and worldviews. The best way to achieve this change, McClelland contended, was by intervening during early childhood, the critical period in which *n* Achievement was formed. "The family is the key institution which carries cultural values and sees to it that the next generation is brought up to share the values of its elders," Mc-Clelland noted. "To produce real cultural change, one must get at the family, one must, for example, change the attitudes of parents toward achievement and self-reliance in their children."[1]

McClelland's paper—which would soon circulate among overseas workers and receive a write-up in the *Washington Post*—cast the issue of economic underdevelopment primarily as a problem of personality. McClelland erased the history of colonialism and economic exploitation that had marked much of the newly characterized developing world. He downplayed the importance of political institutions, economic infrastructures, and a population's ability to fulfill basic needs such as nutrition and health care. Instead, he located the source of developing countries' economic backwardness in the psyche, molded during the first few years of life. "A whole new perspective is opened up—the possibility of social planning in terms of its psychological effects as well as in terms of its more rational economic or political effects," McClelland later noted. "The shortest way to achieve economic objectives might turn out to be through changing people first."[2] And the most effective means of changing people, McClelland asserted, was by intervening in the rearing of children.

By the late 1950s, combating poverty and guiding the modernization of so-called underdeveloped societies had assumed a central place on the U.S. foreign aid agenda. Emergency relief efforts directed at war-torn Europe and Asia were gradually replaced by programs aimed at ameliorating the deeply entrenched problems, such as poverty, disease, and lack of access to education, that plagued developing regions. This shifting focus was due in part to a global landscape transformed by the wave of decolonization precipitated by the Second World War. Within the first five years following the war, ten countries gained independence. By 1960, approximately 800 million people resided in about forty newly independent nations. According to contemporary experts, large swaths of Asia, Africa, and Latin America—about 120 countries comprising some 2 billion people—could be characterized as "developing" or "underdeveloped," lacking the infrastructure necessary to provide their residents with an adequate standard of living.[3] Rural parts of Europe, too, sometimes fell into the category of underdeveloped. Countries' underdevelopment intersected with Cold War geopolitics: American officials were aware that new and impoverished nations could easily subscribe to the communist, rather than the capitalist, model of development.

American definitions of "development" were often vague as to the term's particulars. Some writers stressed the importance of economic growth, while others emphasized social or political progress. But if the term itself was nebulous, foreign populations' desire for a better standard of living—and the lure of communism if Western models were unable to deliver it—was clear. Many observers saw it as the duty of the United States to help underdeveloped regions achieve orderly economic growth and technological development. American social scientists, including McClelland and others associated with MIT's Center for International Studies, sought to respond to this challenge. The body of ideas they produced—modernization theory—constitutes what historian Nils Gilman has called the "most explicit and systematic blueprint ever created by Americans for reshaping foreign societies."[4]

Modernization theory saw all societies progressing along a linear path from tradition to modernity. The pattern of development appeared well demarcated: the history of the United States served as a model for how modernization should play out. But developing regions, theorists argued, risked being waylaid, succumbing to communism rather than progressing along the path to democracy and industrial capitalism. Indeed, nations in the process of modernization were seen as inherently unstable, making them vulnerable to communist lures. Therefore, theorists contended, it was the responsibility of the United States to guide developing regions as they shed the passive, superstitious trappings of traditionalism and transformed into the cosmopolitan, secular, and economically complex embodiments of modernity.[5]

The collapse of biological theories of human difference gave rise not only to new ideas about child development but also to novel ways of looking at the development of whole populations. No longer were certain groups seen as innately incapable of progress; instead, all peoples of the world, given the proper tutelage, might advance along the path to modernity. Modernization theory's liberal version of anticommunism was fueled by optimism in the global potential for progress and confidence in the United States' own brand of modernity. By the early 1960s, modernization had become a veritable "ideology," a way of viewing the world that informed not only social science research but also foreign policy and humanitarian work overseas.[6]

Modernization propelled a massive expenditure of American effort and capital on infrastructure and technical assistance projects across the developing world in the two decades following World War II. With the active support of the U.S. government, American experts dammed rivers, constructed factories, and brought electricity to remote villages. They sponsored programs to help local populations grow more crops, breed better livestock, and eradicate diseases. But, as McClelland's ideas demonstrate, some saw modernization as involving changes of a more psychological nature.[7] They understood these changes as most effectively implemented not through large-scale infrastructure projects but through interventions in the private domain of the family—in the lives of parents and children.

American voluntary workers established day nurseries and programs of family assistance across the developing world. They worked to train mothers and child-care workers in new ways of interacting with children that would arouse youngsters' creativity and independent initiative—character traits they understood to be essential not only to the promotion of a free society but also to the stimulation of economic growth. American agencies also looked to child sponsorships to stimulate children's aspirations for a better life, fund education and vocational training, and provide youngsters with a sense of the world beyond their seemingly limited horizons. Just as they viewed personal, emotional transformations as a means of promoting democracy and fighting communism, American workers rooted economic development and modernization in the intimate realm of children's psychological development. From the 1950s through the early 1970s, American overseas workers attempted to mold a generation psychologically equipped to launch the underdeveloped world into the future.[8]

As they sought to mold modern minds, however, American programs for children revealed the limits of grounding larger political and economic transformations in personal psychological development. Even if children themselves were as malleable as experts insisted, external structures—particularly political institutions and economic realities—would continue to shape youngsters' lives in ways that child-care experts were often loath to acknowledge. At issue, ultimately, was the transformative power of the human psyche itself.

"THE ARDUOUS PROCESS OF 'GROWING UP'"

The notion of modernization—of bringing technological, economic, and social advances to "backward" regions—was not a product of the Cold War, though it assumed increased importance in the context of the conflict and the geopolitical shifts of the post–World War II years. Efforts to promote overseas development received federal mandate in 1949, when President Harry S. Truman announced in his inaugural address what would become known as the Point IV program. Point IV is best known for making available U.S. technical assistance to developing regions around the world, mainly in the fields of agriculture and industry. But the initiative also sought to improve the care of children overseas. Point IV sent child welfare experts to India and Pakistan, where they met with indigenous experts, advised children's aid organizations, and taught courses in social work and child care. The U.S. Children's Bureau also organized programs of study and observation in the fields of child health and welfare for foreign trainees who came to the United States through Point IV and other foreign exchange programs. Point IV was at once an effort to relieve suffering by improving social conditions abroad and a means of guiding developing countries along the road to American-style development. By throwing a spotlight on the misery—and the potential threat—of underdevelopment, Point IV helped make modernization a watchword of foreign aid efforts both public and private.[9]

During the early 1960s, development programs overseas received a renewed place on the federal agenda. "To those peoples in the huts and villages of half the globe struggling to break the bonds of mass misery," President John F. Kennedy announced in his inaugural address in 1961, "we pledge our best efforts to help them help themselves." The Kennedy administration's efforts to promote development overseas, among them the Peace Corps, positioned the United States as a guide to nations striving to partake of the benefits of modernity. These programs also strengthened the associations between international social welfare and anticommunism forged during the previous decade. American efforts dovetailed with a larger global emphasis on uplifting the developing world, epitomized in the United Nations' declaration of the 1960s as the "Decade of Development."[10]

Although not everyone shared McClellend's conviction about the centrality of child rearing to national development, many theorists agreed that underdevelopment was at base a problem of personality. Political scientist Lucian Pye, sociologists Alex Inkeles and Daniel Lerner, and other scholars joined McClelland in describing modernization as hinging on individual psychological transformations. "The great dramas of societal transition," Lerner argued, "occur through individuals involved in solving their personal problems and living their private lives." While some proponents of modernization looked to properly reared children as the future developers of large-scale public works, others lauded infrastructure projects themselves as altering the mentality of entire regions. David Lilienthal, former head of the Tennessee Valley Authority and champion of large-scale international development projects, argued that modern infrastructure could produce a "change in spirit" that affected whole communities. New roads or dams, Lilienthal argued, would unleash the "self-reliance, independence and creativity" that would help propel the developing world into the modern age.[11]

American understandings of the mentality of developing countries drew on a long-standing Orientalist discourse that cast the East as a site of sensuality and languor. But modernization theorists, social workers, and educators viewed the Eastern personality (and, by extension, the mentality of the developing world more generally) through a clinical, rather than a romantic, lens. In an article in the *New York Times Magazine* titled "Is It the Mysterious—or Neurotic—East?," Iranian American writer Fereidoun Esfandiary ascribed the origins of the Eastern personality—"xenophobic, apathetic, withdrawn and fatalistic"—to the tense and hostile environment in which children were reared. "How can a child grow up undisturbed—how can he grow up at all—when his parents, his many brothers and sisters and, indeed, all those with whom he first forms relationships are ignorant and confused, foisting upon him their suspicions, prejudices, fears and superstitions?" Esfandiary queried. If German families had been plagued by a tradition of authoritarianism, parents in developing countries suffered from the opposite: a centuries-long habit of apathy and inertia.[12]

Burgeoning ideas about the "culture of poverty" gaining currency in the United States during the 1960s shaped the way American theorists and overseas workers understood development. Scholars such as anthropologist Oscar Lewis blamed the perpetuation of poverty on social structures that inculcated youngsters into a subculture with an aberrant value system. "By the time slum children are age six or seven," Lewis argued, "they have usually absorbed the basic values and attitudes of their subculture and are not psychologically geared to take full advantage of changing conditions or increased opportunities which may occur in their life-time."[13] Lewis's "culture of poverty" thesis, like the culture-and-personality school's theories, described poverty as rooted in culture and perpetuated through child-rearing practices. Scholars such as McClelland took these cultural explanations for poverty and placed them within modernization theory's evolutionary framework. Breaking the cycle of poverty, then, required a decisive movement away from the traditional fatalistic worldview that shackled the developing world to the past and toward a new system of modern values that stressed change and purposeful action.

If development was dependent in large part on psychological changes, then children were among the most promising agents of modernization. Children's perceived malleability continued to render them attractive objects of American aid. By the 1960s, the notion that early childhood served as a critical period of personality formation had gained widespread acceptance and begun to shed its associations with psychoanalytic thought. "Without resorting to Freudian theories, is it not universally admitted that the physical and mental health of the individual, his physiological and psychic development, even his cultural pre-conditioning, are greatly influenced by the first period of his life?" queried Georges Sicault, a UNICEF official, in 1964. Sicault urged countries to focus on the needs of the child as a means of facilitating national development. "His health, his physical and moral strength, his education and his personality will determine the future of the whole nation," Sicault asserted.[14] In the years immediately following World War II, writers seeking to make a case for children's mental malleability had often referred to the findings of "modern psychology." By the 1960s, however, the notion that childhood was a formative period during which personality congealed no longer required the overt scaffolding of science. Many writers simply took children's plasticity as a given.

Ideas about the malleability of childhood often found expression in advice manuals for overseas workers. Among the experts offering advice was Margaret Mead, who edited a 1953 manual titled *Cultural Patterns and Technical Change*. Just as she had insisted that youngsters were the key to reforming Germany after the war, Mead argued that children would determine the future of the developing world. Her manual urged overseas workers to focus on families, noting an "urgent need for agencies which will help parents develop new ways of being parents, and children develop new ways of growing up." Anthropologist Conrad M. Arensberg and research scientist Arthur H. Niehoff echoed these sentiments in a 1964 manual titled *Introducing Social Change*. "In general, changes will be accepted more readily by the young than by the older people," Arensberg and Niehoff contended. "This is true of all cultures, but the phenomenon of the 'generation effect' is doubly pronounced in the underdeveloped countries because they are receiving concentrated doses of Westernization and modernization in such a short time."[15]

Experts looked to methods of child rearing as a means of shaping people with the type of personality conducive to national development. "Innovation and entrepreneurial capacity, which have been widely stressed as being essential ingredients of economic development, depend heavily on the kind of upbringing and education which children and youth have," noted participants in a 1964 symposium convened by UNICEF on planning for the needs of children in developing countries. Assistance to children in developing countries also made sense demographically, noted International Cooperation Administration (ICA) director James Riddleberger: due to high birth rates and low life expectancies, nearly half the population in many developing countries was under fifteen years of age.[16]

The application of child psychology overseas was a central component of the United States' modernization mission. Indeed, modernization encompassed two related and often intersecting goals: the development of humans and the development of nations. Both goals were premised on the existence of a series of universal developmental stages. And both sought to apply scientific principles to the process of guiding a vulnerable being through the often unruly process of maturation. The language of human development pervaded the work of modernization theorists. "Countries, like people, are not handed identities at birth, but acquire them through the arduous process of 'growing up,' a process which is a notoriously painful affair," argued sociologist Seymour Martin Lipset in 1963. Economist Walt Rostow, best known for his influential treatise on the stages of economic development, also analogized the development of nations to the development of children. Just as it was "possible to specify in broad terms the kinds of problems which, inevitably, must be confronted by an infant of nine months; a child of five; an adolescent of fourteen; a young man of twenty-one," Rostow noted, "the study of economic development, to the extent that it can be called a science, consists primarily in identifying the sequence of problems to be overcome and the kinds of efforts to solve them which have succeeded or failed at different times in different nations." Rostow described economic development, like child development, as proceeding through a series of orderly preordained stages: the "traditional society"; the "preconditions for take-off"; the "take-off" phase; the "drive to maturity"; and, finally, the "age of high mass consumption."[17]

Analogies between human development and national growth expressed optimism about the developing world's potential for progress. But they also drew on a deeply rooted tradition of Western paternalism. While the language of child development abandoned overt racial hierarchies, it naturalized the imbalance of power between the so-called First and Third Worlds and legitimized—in fact, mandated—Western guardianship and guidance.[18] The parallelism between national and human development held particular significance for American agencies whose work focused on children: interventions on behalf of youngsters overseas seemed to serve as a meaningful way, both literally and figuratively, to guide a developing nation toward maturity.

MAKING MODERN CHILDHOODS

The majority of voluntary workers may have been unfamiliar with the central texts of modernization theory, but the theory's main tenets—that modernization unfolded according to a fairly predetermined course, that modernity involved a psychological component, and that developing countries required the assistance of the United States in order to progress—animated the work of many American agencies working with children overseas. Moreover, there was some direct interaction between voluntary workers and modernization scholars themselves. David McClelland's interest in the relationship between child rearing and economic development was not merely academic. An active Quaker, McClelland was deeply involved in the American Friends Service Committee for many years. In the 1940s, shortly after earning his PhD at Yale, McClelland served on the AFSC staff. In the 1950s, while teaching at Harvard, he served on the organization's Social and Technical Assistance Committee, which directed many of its social welfare activities overseas. McClelland's association with the AFSC provided added impetus and scientific grounding to its work with children overseas. "David McClelland . . . [says] that the most important contribution which AFSC can make to the economic development of the poorer countries is to give primary attention to children," noted AFSC official Lorraine Cleveland in a 1959 letter to Joy Ash, who ran a day nursery supported by the organization in Dacca, East Pakistan.[19]

McClelland described certain methods of child rearing as conducive to national development. He argued that children instilled with a sense of independent initiative from an early age would become the entrepreneurs who would drive economic growth across the developing world. Denying children the opportunity to become self-reliant could have devastating consequences. McClelland suggested that the decline of ancient Greece could be traced to the point in time at which economic prosperity had allowed parents to purchase slaves to help them rear their children. Children with slaves had little incentive to do things for themselves, McClelland argued, and the Greek population's desire for independent achievement consequently plummeted. The downfall of the civilization was not far behind.[20]

McClelland located a laboratory for teaching children independence and self-reliance in a series of day nurseries run by the AFSC to provide day care to children in Acre, Israel, and Dacca, East Pakistan. Children in the nurseries spent their days building with blocks, constructing sand castles, and drawing pictures with crayons. These creative activities, McClelland argued, instilled in children a sense of confidence and autonomy. The nurseries' emphasis on "self-actualization, self-reliance, and development of one's own potential," he contended, contrasted sharply with traditional methods of early childhood education, whereby students simply learned by rote. Youngsters who had the benefit of the nursery experience, McClelland speculated, would become the entrepreneurs who would launch their countries into the future.[21]

Even as McClelland stressed the importance of self-reliance, however, he also emphasized the need to train children in cooperative group action. In a 1959 letter to Cleveland, McClelland noted the importance of group play in cultivating the personality characteristics that drove development. "I have found that the ratio of group to individual play . . . is definitely associated with more rapid economic development," McClelland wrote. "The more group activities reported by the children the faster the rate of development." Playing together, McClelland contended, helped children learn to cooperate in order to exert control over nature. Group activities also taught youngsters to be responsive to one another. These functions made group play essential to national development. "Getting the child to pay attention to what others think early in life through . . . group activities appears to be one of the foundation-stones of political democracy and economic development," McClelland argued in his 1961 book *The Achieving Society*.[22] McClelland's assertion that play was a vehicle for cultivating both independence and cooperation shows how childhood and the activities associated with it could be marshaled in the service of diverse and sometimes contradictory aims.

The AFSC was not the only voluntary agency that looked to day nurseries as a means of shaping youngsters with the personality characteristics that facilitated development overseas. The American Jewish Joint Distribution Committee ran a series of nurseries for poor Jewish children in Iran, Morocco, and Tunisia. The JDC's chief day-care consultant was Dorothy Beers, an American day-care expert who had formerly directed a day nursery in New York City and served as a consultant for the Child Welfare League of America. Beers saw day nurseries as a means of ridding children of the pernicious listlessness that she and others saw as the bane of the developing world. She recounted the behavior of children in a nursery in Morocco during a period of outdoor play: "These children who were supposed to be turned loose and to run and play with great animation and glee simply walked right over to the sunshine and sat in it, in the same postures in which their fathers and grandfathers have been sitting for years." The children's "closed-in" world, Beers argued, coupled with malnutrition and disease, "has produced a personality that is absolutely flat and lethargic and that has no initiative at all." Moroccan children, Beers contended, "come from a world that is 2,000 years behind the times."[23]

At the JDC's day nurseries, Beers and her colleagues tried to mold a new generation characterized by vigor rather than apathy. By the early 1960s, the JDC oversaw more than thirty nurseries serving over 6,500 children.[24] It hired local women to serve as teachers and directors, and worked in cooperation with committees of local citizens—often middle-class women—in each city where a nursery had been established. Even so, the organization retained responsibility for many of the practical aspects of running the nurseries, including the development of curricula and the training of indigenous teachers and directors.

The JDC saw its day nurseries as beacons of modernity in the poor foreign communities in which they were established. Katya Roberts, a day-care consultant with the JDC's day nursery program in Tunisia, described a nursery established on the isolated island of Djerba as "a breath of the twentieth century."[25] In Marrakech, Morocco, noted day-care consultant Mary Grist, the nursery contrasted sharply with the ghetto that surrounded it:

> Here is a different range of experience, an environment of squalor and poverty that no stretch of imagination can conjure up. Built to exclude the sun, the alleyways are like slits between high walls; many are only about two yards

across and some are even narrower. . . . To reach the [nursery] you walk these little streets turning abruptly round first one corner and another. After the first few visits you become adept at skirting around piles of decaying rubbish, dead rats, donkey droppings, etc. and practice enables you to breathe deeply at the strategic moment before squeezing past the donkey-drawn refuse cart.

The JDC nursery served as a welcome refuge from the disorder of the streets. Pushing open its heavy door, Grist noted, "is like stepping into a different world where, in contrast to the neglect and deprivation outside, every human effort is made to give the children the health and happiness that is their due."[26] The nursery was a lone haven of modernity amid a primitive landscape.

The JDC's day nurseries served children nutritious meals with the help of surplus commodities received free of charge from the U.S. government under the Food for Peace program. They provided them with baths, haircuts, and medical care. But many in the organization saw the social and emotional aspects of the nurseries as outweighing the health benefits they provided. Children in the nurseries were exposed to a variety of creative experiences: they played in a model house, constructed with blocks, painted at easels, modeled with clay, danced to music, listened to stories, and amused themselves with educational toys. These stimulating activities stood in sharp contrast to the perceived monotony and listlessness that characterized children's home lives. Upon first entering the nursery, Beers contended, children were completely devoid of mental curiosity or personal initiative. "If I were to seat one on a chair at that stage," Beers told a reporter, "he would stay there all day without moving unless we started him in his new way of life." The JDC's day-care consultants saw their nurseries as providing the catalyst to propel children along a new path of active development—to enter a personal "take-off" phase, to borrow a phrase from Rostow. As Beers explained, "When we take these youngsters into the nursery, . . . we have to think about how we can wake them up as well as about how we can feed them and how we can cure them. We have to think about how we can introduce them gradually to new ideas, to a new way of thinking, to a new way of acting, to having some initiative, to being able to think for themselves a little bit."[27] To Dorothy Beers and David McClelland alike, children's creative play was key to opening new horizons and to molding individuals who would take the initiative to reshape the world around them.

If modernity was situated in children's minds, it was also inscribed on their bodies. Many American workers were preoccupied with physical cleanliness, and health and hygiene occupied a prominent place on the agenda of the AFSC, the JDC, and other American agencies working in the developing world. American workers distributed soap to families and consistently imparted to mothers lessons in health and sanitation. Day nurseries often provided children with a bath or shower. American-led health and sanitation programs drew on long-established ideas that associated cleanliness with enlightenment and civilization, and local children's transformations from filth to cleanliness often assumed a symbolic importance. When youngsters first arrived at the AFSC's day nursery in Dacca, reported its director, Joy Ash, "it took many days to get them clean and even then we were not sure that they were as clean as they ought to be." Even playtime became a lesson in sanitation. "We make a habit of washing the dolls, clothes [and] the pots and pans very frequently so as to give early training in self help and cleanliness," Ash explained.[28]

The JDC maintained that its day nurseries made a significant imprint, both physically and psychologically, on the youngsters who benefited from their care. In Morocco, reported Dorothy Beers in 1961, a very real change was obvious in children who had been in the nurseries for three years: "They are cleaner, they are more alert, they have more personality, and they are much more active." Nurseries provided evidence of children's remarkable malleability, Beers contended. "In the oldest classes of the Parvareshgah [day nursery in Iran] are children who have had the benefit of the program for three consecutive years, and they provide the most convincing proof of the influence of environment on the total development of a child," she noted. Beers was enthusiastic about the nurseries' ability to influence society at large. "The kind of thing that can happen to a . . . child as a result of this experience," she asserted, "seems to me to be one of the greatest hopes that we have for the future of the world."[29]

David McClelland's final assessment of the AFSC's day nurseries was more ambiguous. In 1958, McClelland embarked on a research project designed to test his theories about the role of nurseries in inculcating n Achievement in children. McClelland hypothesized that the nursery programs' emphasis on creative activities, coupled with the warm relationships cultivated between teachers and their charges, had instilled in nursery students a need to achieve that surpassed that of their counterparts who had not attended the nursery.

Using the AFSC's day nursery in Acre, Israel, as his laboratory, McClelland conducted tests designed to measure the level of n Achievement in children who had spent three years in the nursery. Tests designed to measure n Achievement in children assumed a variety of forms. In some situations, researchers asked youngsters to draw free-form doodles; their works were then coded and analyzed for graphic expressions that supposedly correlated with n Achievement. In other scenarios, researchers asked children to participate in a ring-toss game, then analyzed the children's behavior and strategies for indications of their innate motivations. McClelland tested a number of children who had previously attended the AFSC's day nursery in Acre, some of whom had graduated from the nursery as many as five years earlier. He also measured n Achievement in local children who had not attended the nursery.[30]

Those children who had been students at the nursery, McClelland reported in his 1961 book, *The Achieving Society,* "appeared more at ease in the situation, adapted more readily to the testing conditions, and were in a sense more 'open' to such a strange procedure introduced by an outsider." But McClelland found that levels of n Achievement in former nursery students did not differ significantly from those of their local peers. McClelland attributed the failure of the nursery to inculcate higher levels of n Achievement to its "partial" character. "After all," he noted, "the nursery school experience is very minor as contrasted with the major shaping influences of the family to which the child returns every day and of the general Arab culture in which he was completely immersed after he left the nursery school."[31]

The results of his tests in Acre forced McClelland to come to terms with the importance of parents, in addition to American-trained teachers, in shaping children's personalities. He urged the AFSC to try to extend the day nurseries' child-rearing methods into local homes. "David stated that he now feels it is absolutely [imperative] to get involvement on the part of the parents in the approach of the nursery school so that the home life of the child will also be such as to be conducive to the development of high achievement motivation," Lorraine Cleveland wrote to William Channel, who led the AFSC's programs in Acre and later in Hong Kong, in 1961.[32] Although McClelland emphasized the involvement of parents, his focus on child-rearing implicitly placed mothers, not fathers, on the front lines of modernization efforts overseas.

MODERN MOTHERHOOD

McClelland was not alone in widening his focus from the child to the family. By the late 1950s and early 1960s, voluntary agencies working with children overseas increasingly expanded their programs of assistance to include the parents and siblings of the individual youngsters they had initially targeted. The community development programs that had begun on a small scale during the 1950s expanded significantly during the next decade. In addition to the desire to extend to parents the lessons imparted to youngsters in day nurseries and other children's institutions, the broadening focus of American work with foreign children had several underlying causes. First, the notion of indigenous self-help gained increasing currency during the 1950s. Kennedy's 1961 promise to help developing nations "help themselves" drew on ideas already in wide circulation among foreign aid workers. The theory that local populations could, when given the proper tools, propel their countries along the path to modernity added impetus to efforts aimed at empowering children and adults alike.[33]

In addition, by the late 1950s, child welfare workers began articulating a new understanding of the causes of child abandonment overseas. As the war-torn regions of Asia recovered, many American workers expected to witness a declining number of children in orphanages. American child welfare professionals had long viewed the institutionalization of children, even in cottage-style homes, as less preferable than legal adoption or foster care, due to the emotional benefits of family life. Many saw orphanages as a temporary measure that would dwindle as foreign nations recovered from the ravages of World War II, the Korean War, and the Chinese refugee crisis. But instead of declining, orphanage populations remained on the rise. In Korea, the number of children abandoned per year increased from an estimated 715 in 1955 to almost 8,000 by 1965; a total of 69,000 children resided in Korean orphanages by 1967.[34] Studies revealed that many of the children living in orphanages were not, in fact, orphans. At a Christian Children's Fund–supported orphanage in Japan in 1960, only slightly more than 21 percent of the residents were orphans; the remaining residents had been institutionalized as a result of poverty or broken homes. A 1965 study conducted on a sampling of orphanage residents supported by CCF in Korea indicated that 40 percent of youngsters had a living parent or relative.[35] Many of the waifs arriving on orphanage doorsteps, American workers were forced to admit, were the victims of poverty, not war. This understanding of child abandonment encouraged American child welfare workers to align their efforts with those of technical assistance experts attempting to combat economic underdevelopment overseas.

Finally, orphanages—particularly "modern" ones designed on the cottage plan—required huge capital outlays to build and were costly to run. Children living with parents or relatives could be supported for less money per child, with the funds benefiting the entire family. American support to foreign orphanages did not end in the late 1950s and 1960s; CCF, in fact, continued to support orphanages into the 1970s. But many organizations at that time began placing new emphasis on programs intended to assist entire families: parent education programs directed at the mothers of children attending day nurseries, and family assistance programs that delivered monthly cash grants to needy families. The grants, sometimes supplemented with gifts of commodities, were earmarked for the care of a particular child, with a portion often going to cover school expenses. But the money and other gifts were seen as contributing to the overall well-being of both children and their families. Sponsors in the United States, who served as foster parents to an individual child in the family, often provided the funds.[36] Local caseworkers generally met with children and their mothers monthly to assess their progress and to oversee the use of the grant money.

Family assistance programs abroad closely resembled the Aid to Dependent Children (ADC) program, which provided public assistance to needy families in the United States (in 1962, the program was renamed Aid to Families with Dependent Children, or AFDC). In fact, one of CCF's first Family Helper Projects, established in Korea in the late 1950s, was modeled on the ADC program. Among the program's architects were several American-trained Korean social workers, including Sang Nak Ha, who had been introduced to ADC while studying at the University of Minnesota. Upon their return to Korea, these social workers shared their knowledge of the workings of the ADC program with their American colleagues at CCF, who had been contemplating initiating a program of assistance that would help children remain with their families.[37]

In addition to supporting children, some family assistance programs offered services to participating families, such as medical and dental care and vocational training. Foster Parents' Plan's program in the Philippines, established in 1961, had by 1965 set up a vocational training center that parents and siblings of sponsored foster children were eligible to attend. The Foster Parents' Plan Opportunity Vocational Training Project taught such skills as automotive and diesel mechanics, electrical engineering, carpentry and cabinet making, dressmaking, cosmetology, and hairdressing. SCF's Family Self-Help Program—which, beginning in 1957, operated in Greece, Finland, France, Korea, and Lebanon—offered families loans to help them improve crops and livestock or to start small businesses.[38]

Some agencies providing financial assistance to families described their programs not only as providing material aid but also as helping families acquire the mental outlook that would help launch them and their countries along the path to development. "Our job, in addition to material and financial help," noted PLAN's Frank Ryan, "is helping our clients bridge the gap between traditional and modern ways of life." Ryan's colleague in Peru, B. L. Weisbart, described modernization as rooted not in the development of institutions but in the transformation of people. "Development," Weisbart asserted in a 1967 speech commemorating the two-year anniversary of PLAN's work in Peru, "is an individual obligation."[39]

As American agencies expanded their child welfare programs during the late 1950s and 1960s, they also widened their geographic reach. In addition to ongoing programs in Asia and rural Europe, the two largest child sponsorship agencies, CCF and PLAN, initiated programs in Central and South America. American agencies remained active as well in the Middle East and North Africa. Programs for children in sub-Saharan Africa remained somewhat slower to develop. A number of factors might have contributed to this: fear of political instability in newly independent countries, unfamiliarity with the area, lingering racism. By the early 1960s, however, voluntary agencies sponsored small numbers of children in the region.[40]

Programs of assistance to families sought to spread new methods of child rearing—and, in particular, a new model of motherhood. The passivity and seclusion that traditionally defined the lives of women in many countries, American workers lamented, hindered their ability to grasp new methods of child care. Some theorists argued that women's roles as the transmitters of values to a new generation sometimes even justified their work outside the home. As McClelland asserted, "No matter how Westernized Moslem men may become, . . . there is unlikely to be much over-all value and motivational change in the community so long as their wives stay locked up in Purdah insulated from such matters and therefore unable to transmit new values and motives to their children." Women's employment outside the home, McClelland argued, would expose them to new values that they would then pass on to their offspring.[41] Modernization was thus contingent upon the status of women.

Mothers were often on the front lines of efforts designed to alter indigenous ideas about fate and human ability. As ICA director James Riddleberger noted in 1959, "Since the mother often proves to be the most important member of the family in bringing about acceptance of social change . . . family and child welfare services assume particular importance."[42] An American-sponsored home economics manual prepared by a local worker for rural women in Korea insisted that mothers had the power to determine the fate of their children. Some rural mothers still insisted that children died due to destiny, the manual noted: but "often babies die because their mothers were not looking after them well—carelessness and nonchalanc[e]." The manual instructed mothers in new methods of infant feeding and care that would prevent illnesses and help babies grow into healthy children. It drew parallels between child rearing and agriculture, which had also benefited from recent innovations:

> Farming (agriculture) has developed—you get better result (harvest) by newly developed scientific method of farming which was totally depended upon weather (nature) in good old day. You mothers are facing new era, which you should make effort to accept scientific methods on bringing children up—with less labor, and have better result.[43]

Margaret Mead expressed similar sentiments, portraying the human psyche as a vast untapped resource. "Just as the results of scientific inquiry can enable us to grow twenty bushels of wheat where two grew before or to travel as far in a day as we once did in two months," Mead noted in 1952, "so also by increasing our knowledge of human behavior and applying that knowledge responsibly, we can draw on the great untapped sources of human potentiality." The notion that humans could achieve mastery over nature—be it crops and rivers or human health and personality—was, according to American theorists, a key component of a modern outlook. "When people realize that it is in their power to improve the conditions under which they live and under which their children will live," asserted UNICEF in 1963, "a great deal of progress becomes possible."[44]

Roberta Channel, who ran the AFSC's community center in Acre, Israel, along with her husband, William, believed strongly that the status of women was connected to the state of national development. Channel was particularly committed to raising the status of Arab women and girls in Acre and in the nearby village of Tamra. "Is the status of Arab women one of the reasons for the seeming deterioration of what was once a glorious civilization?" she suggested in 1959. "It is rather a coincidence that in recent years in Tamra, as the men are slowly beginning to recognize the need to raise the literacy of women in their village, the village appears to be a better village than those surrounding it." Channel was heartened to find that a meeting to explain to local mothers "the value of education for girls in this modern age of ours" brought thirty-six new female pupils to the village school. Not all voluntary workers championed gender equality as forcefully as Channel. But the fact that American voluntary organizations extended services and support to boys and girls on an equal basis was not insignificant, particularly in countries where girls had traditionally been excluded from education. PLAN's program in Hong Kong, for example, was committed to assisting exceptional students, both male and female, in pursuing higher education, even though Chinese families traditionally devoted more effort to educating sons than they did to daughters.[45]

When the Channels transferred from Acre to Hong Kong in 1960, they brought with them their interest in the status of women. As the AFSC's field director in Hong Kong, William Channel oversaw the development of a new day nursery for the children of working mothers. Many were the children of the many refugees who had fled China in the aftermath of the Communist revolution. In designing the day nursery, Channel and his colleagues heeded McClelland's advice regarding the importance of extending the child-care methods of the nursery into local homes. The AFSC ran the nursery on a semicooperative system; mothers who wished to enroll their children were required to assist in the nursery for half a day per week or for two full days per month. This gave AFSC workers the opportunity to work with mothers and teach them new child-care methods. The organization sought to train mothers to interact more actively with their children through such activities as storytelling, singing, and playing games. They imparted basic information on children's growth as well as on hygiene and nutrition.[46] The AFSC also ran a mothers' club, at which local women had the opportunity to meet their neighbors, engage in creative activities, receive homemaking advice, and learn skills that would help them augment the family income.

AFSC workers in Hong Kong strove to make the day nursery and the mothers' club a lesson in the principle of self-help. Work with indigenous mothers served as a stepping-stone to larger efforts to help local people help themselves. The mothers' club, explained William Channel, taught women "to plan cooperatively to meet common needs, a program which we would hope to gradually expand to involve increasing numbers of people and attacking increasing numbers and varieties of problems."[47]

But mothers often appeared to be less malleable than their children. Some mothers, AFSC workers complained, were "lazy"; many, burdened by economic hardships, came to the nursery "unwillingly" and were resistant to the new methods of interacting with children that AFSC workers sought to impart. Only a small group of "better educated" mothers attended monthly meetings. Moreover, local child-care workers often resented working alongside untrained women. By 1967, disappointed with mothers' lack of involvement in the day nursery, AFSC voluntary workers initiated a series of mandatory courses to teach mothers child care and other subjects. A meeting of mothers themselves decided that those who did not attend the courses or arrived late would be subject to fines and penalties. Voluntary workers' efforts to use child care as a means of stimulating cooperation and self-help among local women ultimately evolved into a program that made American aid contingent on mothers' willingness to adopt new child-rearing methods.[48]

The JDC also sought to train mothers whose children attended its day nurseries in new ways of caring for their youngsters. The organization's day-care consultants held parent education courses in many of the nurseries. The JDC even attempted to extend its lessons in creative free expression to parents. In 1962, the agency's day nursery in Tehran held a parents' meeting in which mothers and fathers were encouraged to experiment with finger paints and modeling clay. But even as they looked to mothers to shape the generation of the future, JDC workers were often disappointed with women's inability to adopt new methods of child rearing. "A mother of 22, with 5 children, and pregnant living in primitive conditions does not have time to know her children's daily life in all its wonderfully revealing details," noted a JDC worker in Iran.[49] Despite voluntary workers' best hopes, mothers—poor, culturally isolated, and burdened with the strain of caring for large families—often appeared ill equipped to rear a new generation of modern children.

Indeed, mothers sometimes appeared to serve as obstacles to national development. While American voluntary workers saw creative play as a tool for stimulating personal development and national growth, many local mothers greeted children's play with indifference or even suspicion. In Acre, Israel, Roberta Channel noted, Arab mothers often stifled children's games by yelling at boisterous youngsters to stop and be quiet. "It's a pity to stop them when they are laughing," Channel commented. Children unable to play, she mused, "seem so trapped." Voluntary workers in Dacca, East Pakistan, where the AFSC ran a day nursery and a neighborhood center, also encountered mothers seemingly ignorant of the importance of childhood play. When workers at the center tried to organize a recreational group for girls in 1960, they found that the youngsters' heavy household duties made it impossible for them to participate. The center decided to send an emissary to visit the girls' mothers, who succeeded in obtaining the children's "release from water, wood and baby carrying for one afternoon a week" so the girls could play ball and skip rope at the neighborhood center. The Dacca center's recreational programs were well attended by neighborhood children. But AFSC workers noted that parents were not uniformly pleased with the organization's activities for youth. In a meeting at the neighborhood center, some fathers expressed "some criticism of our emphasis on recreation, play, and dancing," noted Bernhard Klausener, the center's director. To many local families, the AFSC's emphasis on recreation was not in harmony with their own ideas about the relative importance of work and play. When social workers from the Dacca center asked local families what kinds of recreational activities they preferred, Klausener reported, "many were insulted."[50]

To many of the American workers, parents throughout the developing world seemed to lack the necessary mind-set to raise a generation prepared for modern life. George Ross, who led PLAN's Hong Kong program in the early 1960s, was frequently frustrated by the seemingly low level of care parents afforded to children enrolled in the organization's family assistance project. "The parents of a good number of our children have no concept of a decent standard of living," Ross complained in 1961. "With these I am equally sure that we shall have to <u>force</u> them to provide the surroundings for their children that we think essential."[51]

American voluntary workers looked to native parents as agents of development, imbuing children with the personality characteristics conducive to national growth. But they also feared that parents would be unwilling or unable to alter their ways, hindering the development of children—and of the developing world more generally. A 1962 handbook written by JDC consultants to assist communities in developing countries establish day nurseries insisted that the nurseries were not intended to replace children's families. But the handbook's description of the wide range of services that should be offered by nurseries—educational, medical, emotional—placed a heavy burden on trained teachers and left little to be provided by mothers. "If parents are unable to give the kind of care which will make a child grow into a healthy, happy, responsible adult," the handbook argued, "then the community has an obligation to provide that care." The plasticity of early childhood, JDC consultants contended, made it imperative that children receive the best care possible: "If a child's life experiences during these early years are crippling ones, we cannot make it up to him later on, for he has lost beyond recall the years of his life when he is most impressionable."[52]

The JDC's handbook reached a wide audience. In less than two years following its publication, overseas workers from various agencies, including the Peace Corps, requested it for use in twenty-six countries around the world.[53] Although shaped by JDC consultants' experiences in North Africa and the Middle East, the handbook was used by overseas workers in countries ranging from Taiwan to Peru. Texts such as the JDC handbook promoted an understanding of children's needs as universal and helped to construct the underdeveloped world as a coherent, uniform entity.

Like the authors of the JDC handbook, a group of experts convened by UNICEF in 1966 to discuss the place of children and youth in national development in Latin America looked askance at native parents' child-rearing practices. They dismissed as futile efforts to reform them:

> As he grows up, the child needs affection; suitable conditions in which to develop physically, mentally and emotionally; employment opportunities; and social acceptance. His parents' inability to satisfy these requirements in full measure stems from the shortcomings of their own childhood (which are irremediable) and the inadequacies of the social system that provides for them, which can be improved upon.

The experts cast Latin American parents as incapable of rearing a generation adequately prepared for modern life. They recommended that young children in their impressionable years receive supplementary care in nurseries or preschools that could provide them with the values and thought patterns essential to modernization and national progress. "Because of the characteristics of families in the lower-income brackets, especially in rural areas where the parents are often illiterate and are largely unfamiliar with the basic elements of modern culture, the family environment cannot be regarded as any sort of substitute for pre-school education," the experts noted.[54]

If psychological theories of child development supported a buoyant optimism about the malleability of human nature and the potential of all people for progress, experts' comments regarding native parents reveal the dark underside of these theories. Children in all nations were seen as capable of acquiring the psychological outlook necessary for modern life. But adults—especially those whose personalities had been irrevocably shaped by their own culturally and economically impoverished childhoods—had little hope for change. Their personal deficiencies had become "irremediable."

Even as agencies began to move away from the institutionalization of children, CCF in some cases determined that children would be better served living in orphanages than with their parents. "Some parents," asserted Clarke in 1957, "are worse than none at all." Ernest Nash agreed: "Many homes will not care for [children] as adequately as some orphanage will." In 1962, CCF extended support to an orphanage-school for blind children in India. Among the home's residents was ten-year-old Joseph John. Although his parents, severely impoverished workers, were living, CCF agreed with superintendent Reverend Father Abraham that the boy was best served in the home. Voluntary officials, in fact, blamed the boy's parents for his predicament. "It is just possible that the child had lost its eyesight as a baby due to the neglect of some serious affectation of the eye due to the ignorance and poverty of the parents," the boy's case history noted. Twelve-year-old Murthy, another resident of the home, had resorted to begging in order to supplement his family's meager income. Concerned about the level of care the boy was receiving after spotting him on the street, Abraham attempted to persuade Murthy's parents to relinquish the boy to the orphanage. After ten continuous days of petitioning, Murthy's parents at last gave their consent. Voluntary officials were heartened by the child's adjustment to the orphanage but stressed to CCF the importance of the boy's continued residence in the home. "He can maintain his progress only so long as he is in this School," the boy's case history noted. "If he were permitted to return to his parents it is not difficult to visualize his relapse into old habits due to financial necessity." Clarke was inspired by Murthy's story and considered using the boy in an advertisement. But he decided that a tale that centered on rescuing a child from parents who were reluctant to give him up might not sit well with the American public.[55]

In cases in which children remained in the care of their parents, American agencies tried to influence the children's home environments. PLAN social workers in Colombia scolded a mother whose home appeared "untidy" and pressured her to stop selling liquor in the small store she ran out of her home, noting that it set "a bad example for the children." The agency also exerted substantial oversight with regard to the use of cash gifts given by sponsors. Agency caseworkers generally went shopping with mothers and children to ensure that they spent the funds in a responsible manner. In 1963, Colombia director Keith Turner solved the problem of supervising the use of cash gifts during the busy Christmas season by giving families vouchers that could be spent only at the Sears, Roebuck store. The store opened two hours early on several days in December, during which time Sears supervisory personnel and PLAN social workers assisted foster children and their families with their purchases. The system was so successful that the organization decided to continue the use of Sears vouchers throughout the year. "We are pleased with this system, for it gives us a total control of the use of the gift money," Turner explained.[56]

American workers' interactions with mothers and local child-care workers reflected their complicated relationship with the notion of indigenous self-help. Even as they lauded the goal of helping foreign people help themselves, American workers were often ambivalent about relinquishing control to parents and local child-care workers. CCF held annual meetings with Korean orphanage superintendents to discuss issues related to child care and administration. When a group of superintendents formed themselves into a representative body outside CCF in 1956, agency officials were concerned. The idea of an organized representative body of superintendents "sounds wonderful—American in spirit, democratic and all that—but you had better order a carload of aspirin and be prepared for some severe headaches if such a body is formed," cautioned J. Calvitt Clarke. Clarke worried that superintendents might "gang up" on CCF and make demands that the organization was not prepared to meet. "There could be built up a group that might advocate and even insist upon some change or concession that would actually be against their own interests," he argued. Clarke articulated his opposition to increased indigenous power with an analogy to contemporary nationalist struggles. "There could be a situation where Korean superintendents would try and sieze [*sic*] a 'Suez Canal,'" Clarke fretted in a letter written less than three weeks after Egyptian president Gamal Abdel Nasser's July 1956 decision to nationalize the Suez Canal. At the Superintendents' Conference in 1958, CCF's Korean director, Ernest Nash, warned participants that organization "for its own sake" was "a mistaken concept of the purpose of democratic procedures." "The Korean group, in a tactful way, must be taught that they are not running CCF," Clarke insisted in 1959. "I think the Superintendent's [*sic*] Conference sometimes gets a little bit out of hand if it is not watched."[57]

Because of children's perceived adaptability, voluntary workers sometimes looked to children to serve as their parents' instructors. This was particularly true regarding health and sanitation efforts. One mother reported that since coming to the AFSC-supported nursery, her child would not eat until she had washed her hands. When Dimitrios, a young Greek boy, returned to his village after being fitted by PLAN for an artificial limb, the agency reported, "his first remark to his mother was, 'you must wash your hands every day.'" Two Italian girls who had enjoyed a vacation at a children's colony in 1958, courtesy of PLAN, liked their morning shower so much that they constructed a shower for themselves out of a large old tin can upon returning to their village. Children at the JDC's day nurseries in Iran said that their favorite activity was taking a bath. But children's reported love of hygiene did not always influence the standards of their parents. For example, the JDC considered curtailing its bathing and haircutting programs in Iran but found that local parents could not be relied on to maintain the agency's standards of cleanliness. When the organization stopped providing these services, Beers observed, "children arrived at school dirty and with nits in their hair."[58] Health and sanitation efforts showcased children's ability to serve as modernizers, bringing new standards of living into their homes and communities. But they also revealed the limits of children's role as the agents of modernization. Youngsters ultimately had little say regarding the care provided to them by their parents.

Many families across the developing world accepted American assistance for their children even as they failed to adopt the child-rearing practices advocated by American agencies. Some families, however, harbored deep-seated misgivings about accepting U.S. aid. The United States' global power colored

American humanitarian ventures, and Americans' perceived authority troubled some local mothers. In Colombia, for example, some mothers greeted PLAN social workers with stones and angry dogs, fearful that American foster parents would take their children away from them. Foster parents in the United States were often displeased when children's parents or guardians did not use gifts of cash exactly as specified. During the 1960s, CCF replaced the word "adoption" with the term "sponsorship" in all of its advertisements, hoping to "correct the assumption of complete possession."[59] American agencies struggled to balance efforts to improve child care and please American donors with the imperative to accord local families a measure of independence and free choice.

Programs for children in the developing world reveal the ways that understandings of modernity were mapped onto—and sometimes helped deepen—distinctions of class. For example, the JDC entrusted the care of children in nurseries to child-care workers who had completed training courses given by American consultants in "modern" child-care techniques. They delegated oversight of the nurseries to committees composed of middle-class citizens, often women. The nurseries provided new professional opportunities for local child-care workers, and they served as a venue for middle-class women's civic participation. In the process, however, they often marginalized mothers, who were overwhelmingly poor and uneducated. Middle-class Ladies' Committees exerted control over local child-care workers, who often hailed from more modest socioeconomic backgrounds. Meanwhile, training in American-style child care gave local child-care workers a means of asserting their superiority over mothers. In Morocco, Dorothy Beers complained, the nursery staff's "insecurity" with and "hostility" toward local mothers hindered the JDC's goal of educating parents through the nursery. Child-care workers in Marrakech were hesitant to even admit parents into the nursery building, finally doing so only at the urging of the American day-care consultant.[60]

In a 1967 article in *Redbook* magazine, Margaret Mead reflected on recent decades' efforts to uplift developing nations. She discussed the rapid progress made by countries across the globe in improving the standard of living enjoyed by their citizens, challenging theories that saw certain peoples as biologically or culturally incapable of progress. Instead of focusing on the dichotomy of advanced and primitive civilizations, she argued, observers should look at the differences between parents and their children.

Adults in all countries struggled to find their way in a world newly shaped by advanced technology. But children across the globe effortlessly acquired fluency in new ways of living and thinking that remained alien to their elders. "All children, in whatever part of the world they are growing up, are native to a kind of world in which they take for granted the thinking toward which their parents can only grope," Mead argued. American voluntary agencies' programs for children in the developing world challenged the opposition implicit in modernization theory that associated women with traditionalism and men with modernity. But they ultimately promoted a new dichotomy that broke down along the lines of age and class rather than gender. Children, whose minds were still malleable, were the bearers of the future. Their parents, who struggled to escape poverty and adopt a modern mentality, remained shackled to the past.

"THE BEAUTIFUL AMERICANS"

If children's own parents were unable to help them grow into modern men and women, perhaps American foster parents were up to the task. "This is the age of jet propulsion, the breaking of sound barriers . . . the annihilation of space and time," asserted PLAN publicity director Lenore Sorin in 1958. "The far ends of the earth are joined together in seemingly no time at all. But, Foster Parents' Plan knows of many areas which are seldom if ever reached by the progress and plenty of this new world. There are thousands and thousands of children who are not even touched by this great forward march." Sorin called on American families to "join the march of progress" by acting as foster parents to children overseas.[61]

Child sponsorship organizations often looked to American foster parents as long-distance agents of modernization. Sponsors' perceived modernizing influence was evident in a family assistance project established by PLAN in 1965 on the outskirts of Chimbote, Peru. The children enrolled in the project, wrote field director Robert H. K. Walter, had "almost unimaginably limited experience. The great majority have come from tiny villages in the Andes, where life was primitive to a degree that people in the U.S. and Canada can hardly visualize." Many of the children had never even ventured inside the city of Chimbote. They had never seen books, magazines, television, or movies. "They have no idea," Walter contended, "of what the great world holds." Even a trip to the PLAN office in Chimbote to receive their grants was a new and exciting experience for the children. "When I went to receive the help, I saw a typewriter, a filing cabinet and many more things," one youngster noted enthusiastically in a letter to his foster parents. "I saw a circular light for the first time in my life," another child reported. Americans matched with Peruvian children planned to send them scrapbooks of pictures clipped from magazine stories and advertisements, Walter reported, "which will help these children stretch their ideas of what the world is like, and what they may aspire to achieve in it." Walter saw correspondence with Americans as a means of introducing children to the modern world.[62]

When American foster parents visited their sponsored children in person, they often exposed youngsters from small, isolated villages to exciting new worlds. When journalist Ned Calmer met his twelve-year-old Italian foster child, Vincenzo, in Rome in 1952, the village boy was "practically stunned" by the city, Calmer reported. Vincenzo was fascinated by his first encounter with a record player and enjoyed eating ravioli—four helpings' worth—for the first time. New experiences were also in store for Edita, a seven-year-old Filipino girl, when the group of naval officers who served as her foster parents paid her a visit in 1965. The officers treated the girl and her mother to an expensive Chinese lunch and took them on a visit to the zoo. Edita, who had never ridden in an automobile or been to the zoo, got sick several times. "The whole thing was a bit bewildering for the poor child," admitted country director Robert Sage.[63]

But even as child sponsorship agencies positioned American foster parents as the bearers of modern life, they acknowledged that Americans themselves were sometimes just as interested in learning about seemingly exotic countries as they were in leading their youngest citizens along the path to national development. During the 1960s, *CCF World News* ran a feature called "Armchair Traveler," which transported readers to different locations across the globe where the agency was assisting children. Through the column, readers could vicariously experience flying over the jungles of Vietnam or spotting a monkey from the window of a Jeep climbing a twisting road through the Himalayas.[64]

While American foster parents introduced their children to new experiences and ideas, foreign youngsters also expanded the worlds of their American supporters. Sponsoring a child overseas served as a form of cultural education. "Do you know what you are responsible for?" a Minnesota man asked in a letter to his Greek foster daughter. "You have made me get educated about Greece. I've been reading about your country in the encyclopedias. I have never dreamed there could be so many islands anywhere. There must be more than a thousand. Why, it would take a man two lifetimes just to visit them all." In another letter, he confided, "You can't imagine how much I envy you, little daughter. I am an ancient twenty-three years old and I have never in my life seen the sea. You must write and tell me all about it, in one of your next letters."[65] If American foster parents transmitted "modern" values, children in developing countries sometimes reminded their friends in the United States that modernity was always relative and that shared human emotions transcended time and place. For example, a man in Vermont told CCF about his experience corresponding with his foster daughter in India:

> I have tried to tell her about the life of a country doctor in Vermont, and she has taught me much more in her letters about the mind and life of a young lady in India. For example, I wrote and did my best to describe the miracles of the 3rd generation computor [sic] in the local medical center; how one needed only to touch a plate of glass and instantly a patient's name and all the facts of the patient's illness would be printed instantly on the plate of glass. Her response was: "I know the thrill you had doing such a thing. I had such a thrill the first time I turned on an electric light bulb." I shall never forget that line.[66]

American agencies' work with foreign children reaffirmed long-cherished notions of American exceptionalism. American theorists and workers' reverence for autonomy and self-reliance resurrected an ethos of rugged individualism at a time when American commentators increasingly lamented the decline of individuality at the hands of big corporations. If children were the key to the developing world's future, it was a future that bore a striking resemblance to the imagined American past. However, a commitment to exporting American values was never absolute or uncontested. The development of personal relationships often undercut the one-way transmission of "modern" values. And, because they centered directly on molding personalities, child-care projects forced voluntary workers to grapple with the cultural and psychological effects of American development initiatives overseas.

Overseas workers were often uncomfortable with the negative stereotypes about American hubris that preceded them. The publication of *The Ugly American* in 1958, in particular, catalyzed debates regarding Americans' cultural sensitivity. Eugene Burdick and William J. Lederer's best-selling political novel presented a biting indictment of American foreign aid officers, whose arrogance and lack of respect for local culture poisoned the United States' image abroad. Keenly aware of Americans' reputation overseas, some voluntary workers sought to portray their work as an antidote to, rather than a manifestation of, the "Ugly American" phenomenon. In a 1960 newsletter, for example, SCF invited readers to meet "the Beautiful American," represented by a selection of foster parents. "Save The Children Federation believes that the Federation Family constitutes a force of more than 50,000 Americans whose influence is the antithesis of those described in the best-seller," the organization asserted. In his 1961 book *Yankee Si!*, CCF's Edmund Janss portrayed the organization's benevolent efforts as garnering gratitude for the United States around the world. "The world says 'thanks,'" Janss wrote, "and each American is no longer so ugly."[67]

When David McClelland approached William Channel about the possibility of conducting *n* Achievement tests on youngsters in Acre in 1958, Channel bristled at the notion that the center's day nursery promoted Western values. He took issue with the nature of McClelland's proposed tests, which he saw as measuring progress solely in terms of economic development. He worried, too, about the social and cultural changes that inevitably accompanied economic progress. "Does high *n* Achievement bring a high TV and tail-fin culture?" Channel queried in a letter to AFSC headquarters. Responding to Channel's charges, McClelland argued that new methods of child care could not be isolated from the Western values that gave rise to them. Children in the Acre day nursery, he contended, experienced a manner of child rearing unknown to their peers. They spent the day playing and engaging in creative activities under the supervision of warm and caring teachers, while their counterparts sat "around the 'teacher' learning to memorize and recite aloud the Koran (and only the Koran)." "I can readily understand why you would not want to think that you were promoting Western values through the nursery school," McClelland noted in a letter to Channel, "but I also think you are probably doing so by the mere fact of having a nursery school at all."[68] McClelland cast the principle of cultural integrity as largely incompatible with efforts to raise the standard of living in developing countries. Since culture was perpetuated via patterns of child rearing, any effort to improve the manner in which children were reared would invariably tamper with indigenous culture, McClelland argued.

Nonetheless, many American overseas workers were determined to demonstrate respect for local customs, even as they sought to modify certain elements of traditional cultures. JDC workers in the Middle East viewed cultural retention as important to children's psychological well-being. "There is a richness in the environment of these children, despite the physical poverty, which our program ignores or, at the best, uses insufficiently," Mary Grist argued in 1963. JDC workers sought to provide children with toys that reflected their lived experiences. In Tehran, they combed local markets and shops for appropriate materials and asked local teachers for suggestions regarding methods for "Easternizing" play equipment.[69] The organization explained in its handbook for teachers:

> We want children to use familiar objects closely resembling those used in their homes. Doll corners *should* differ from country to country. It means nothing to a child to find a toy washing machine in the doll corner when his mother washes clothes by rubbing them on stones in the river; it means nothing to a child to find telephones in a doll corner when there are no telephones in his neighborhood.[70]

Margaret Mead's manual suggested that careful research and acute sensitivity on the part of overseas workers could facilitate the introduction of technical innovations without destroying local cultures. When introducing new methods into a society, *Cultural Patterns and Technical Change* recommended, "it is desirable to strip these technical practices of as many extraneous cultural accretions (from the lands of origin) as possible."[71]

But Western "cultural accretions" were sometimes what local people found most appealing about new child-care methods. In Korea, reported Helen Tieszen in 1957, "one orphanage considers itself a model of American democracy because children have bread for breakfast and are called by Western names. Its big attraction is the lovely oven for baking bread." The outward trappings of Western culture were not necessary components of modern child care, Tieszen insisted. She constructed dolls and doll dishes in a typically Korean style and insisted that bread need not replace kimchi in children's diets. Although the JDC tried to "Easternize" play equipment, the middle-class women who made up the membership of the local Ladies' Committee in Tehran preferred that the nursery reflect Western traditions. The committee banned from the playhouse a child-size chador, the traditional covering worn outside by children's mothers, insisting that the nursery students "grow up in a modern fashion." "Ladies Committees want Western equipment and they want their parvareshgahs [day nurseries] to look 'modern' and up to date regardless of what psychology might dictate is better for the child," day-care consultant Evelyn Peters complained.[72]

Conflicting understandings of children's best interests in the context of modernization also came to a head in a disagreement regarding the publication of a children's storybook. Troubled by the dearth of indigenous storybooks for children in Iran, Peters endeavored to write her own, using traditional Persian elements in her tales. But when the Ladies' Committee contemplated publishing the stories in 1962, its members criticized a set of "charming typically Persian illustrations" and endorsed only "the one rather 'American' story with 'American' illustrations."[73]

For the Ladies' Committee, Western culture served as a marker of education and middle-class identity. Local women hindered American workers' attempts to promote their vision of cultural integrity. And while many American workers sought to create materials for children that spoke to their own national traditions, toys and storybooks were themselves artifacts of a philosophy of child rearing alien to most developing countries. Efforts to improve the care of children overseas raised thorny questions about the limits of cultural integrity in the context of child rearing, the appropriate scope of American interventions overseas, and the nature of modernity itself.

JOINING THE "REVOLUTION OF RISING EXPECTATIONS"

While early childhood programs emphasized the development of creativity and self-reliance, those for school-age children often stressed academic achievement as the road to personal—and national—betterment. "Any country striving to reach a self-sustaining level of development needs a large reservoir of skilled and semi-skilled man power," opined Frederick Chaffee, assistant director of PLAN's program in Vietnam, in 1967. "Here in Viet Nam a real contribution could be made if upon cancellation [of PLAN support] there were skilled workers and not just day laborers, who could read and write." "There is an intimate link between poverty and illiteracy and between education and economic progress," agreed Fram Jehangir, who worked for CCF in India, in 1968.[74] Youngsters who received the proper education and training could drive and direct the industries that would lift developing countries out of poverty.

In Hong Kong, CCF was dismayed to learn that Chinese refugee children were ineligible for public education. The organization came up with a creative solution, constructing classrooms on the flat rooftops of the concrete apartment buildings that housed many refugee families. Funds from American foster parents provided the students with uniforms, school supplies, and food. Between seven thousand and eight thousand children received an education in the rooftop schools. PLAN's Hong Kong office also stressed academic achievement, awarding prizes to sponsored children who came out among the top three students in their class at the end of the school year. Since many students in Hong Kong lived in crowded quarters and lacked adults who could assist them with their schoolwork, the agency set up after-school study centers to provide sponsored children and their siblings with homework assistance and individual tutoring. Frank Ryan, who ran PLAN's Hong Kong program in the late 1960s, described PLAN's study centers as providing "the kind of assistance that middle class Chinese parents extend to their children, which is unfortunately mostly missing in families which we support." Poor families, Ryan noted, "do not take an interest in their children's school work in providing necessary time for homework and study at home, and do not encourage school progress beyond primary grades."[75] Conceptions of modernity were also conceptions of class.

Foreign foster children appear to have recognized the premium placed by American foster parents on educational achievement: many letters from children focused on their performance in school. "There are 45 students in our class and I came out the 12th of the whole class. What do you think of my result?" queried Tai Ho, a youngster in Hong Kong, in a 1964 letter to her foster parents. Jaime of Santiago, Chile, noted proudly in a 1965 letter, "I have been back at school for a week now. We are doing lots of homework and I want to study really hard."[76]

The efforts of child sponsorship agencies and their supporters to promote children's achievement bore fruit: by the early 1960s, the ranks of former foster children in Europe and Asia included doctors, nurses, civil servants, teachers, and ministers. A 1959 study of CCF graduates in Hong Kong revealed that the majority of the 1,270 former orphans surveyed were employed as textile workers (15%), shop attendants (10%), schoolteachers (10%), students (10%), and domestic servants (7%). The remaining graduates were employed in smaller numbers as sundry workers, factory workers, rattan workers, tailors, restaurant waiters, shoemakers, policemen, drivers, nurses, or church workers. Even if not wildly successful by Western occupational standards, most graduates did manage to become self-supporting—not a small feat for former destitute youngsters. Reflecting on PLAN's twenty-fifth anniversary in 1962, former foster children thanked their American sponsors not only for their material contributions but also for their moral support. Jacqueline, a former foster child who became an actress, noted that the agency gave her "courage." Former Italian foster child Arturo, a television-radio technician, credited PLAN with instilling in him "a great impulse to succeed." California governor Edmund G. Brown commended the agency for saving children not only from the horrors of war, hunger, and homelessness but also from an equally dire "lack of purpose."[77]

But if American agencies succeeded in instilling in children a desire for personal achievement—what David McClelland might call n Achievement—programs for youngsters sometimes made rising aspirations themselves a condition of aid. Agencies noticed that sponsors' continued support was often contingent on a child's academic success and purposeful planning for the future. American donors' interest in their foster children's academic achievement made PLAN reluctant to continue support to youngsters who appeared to lack the motivation to succeed. In Hong Kong, Frank Ryan hired an educational specialist to help children improve their academic performance and to educate parents about the importance of children remaining in school. "Probably a big reason for foster parents who cancel out is disappointment in educational progress of their foster children," Ryan explained. PLAN's program in Hong Kong tried to select children "with average or better intellectual ability and whose parents are interested in and sincerely desire education for their children."[78]

PLAN's Gloria Matthews noted that many foster parents chose to curtail support to their children at age sixteen, even though support was encouraged until the children's eighteenth birthdays, because "they believed their help wasn't accomplishing anything for the child who was making no effort to get somewhere." In considering whether to continue support to older children, Matthews noted, the organization had to consider youngsters' personal drives and aspirations. "Will we be merely feeding a boy or girl," Matthews queried, "or are they striving toward some goal?" PLAN officials ultimately recommended that all country directors cancel children at age sixteen "unless the children were showing some effort to improve their lots." In countries ranging from Colombia to Italy to Vietnam, agency workers canceled several children each month due to "apathy."[79] A "modern" outlook was more than the end goal of American programs for children. For PLAN, it had become a prerequisite for assistance.

Moreover, as programs for children began to address the needs of families as well as youngsters themselves, children's eligibility for aid sometimes became contingent not only on their own perceived worthiness but also on their families' motivation for progress. SCF, for example, tried "to select needy children in families which are determined to do everything possible to help themselves." PLAN also aimed to enroll families who were motivated to achieve self-support. Frank Ryan likened the organization's program to a hospital with a limited number of beds for tuberculosis patients. "We have 7,500 'beds' to offer to a larger number of needy cases, and we want 'patients' who possess a reasonable chance for recovery," Ryan explained in 1965. Gloria Matthews recommended that PLAN focus on children from families that were "poor but honest." If children "come from families who along with being poor don't give a damn what happens to them or their children, I'm afraid we couldn't do very much for these children," Matthews argued.[80]

But children's aspirations—along with those of their parents and foster parents—often ran up against hard economic realities. In many developing countries, even educated youngsters had difficulty finding jobs after graduation. In Korea, for example, only an estimated 5 percent of college graduates secured employment. In addition, few developing countries boasted free public education, even at the elementary level, and a dearth of openings in high schools often resulted in intense competition among students for secondary schooling. Some foster parents continued to support their children through college or vocational training, even after the conclusion of agencies' official programs of support. Increasing numbers of sponsors expressed a desire to support their children through college, CCF's J. Calvitt Clarke reported in 1962. In fact, several sponsors specifically asked for children to educate.[81] In the absence of highly motivated sponsors, however, American aid generally extended only to a child's eighteenth birthday. This put higher education beyond the reach of many youngsters.

While American theorists such as McClelland sought to foster entrepreneurship, by the mid-1960s some voluntary workers tried to prepare children for industrial labor, which appeared to them to provide the best chance of upward mobility. This was particularly true with regard to agencies working in urban areas, namely CCF and PLAN, which committed to supporting children through adulthood. In Hong Kong, PLAN tried to guide children toward vocational training that would prepare them for industrial jobs, even though their parents often preferred for the youngsters to receive a more classical education. In Korea, PLAN director Frank Ryan initiated an innovative program that trained older children and their older brothers and sisters for work in the rapidly expanding industrial sector. Ryan worked with a large manufacturer in Pusan to determine its employment needs. In exchange for the promise of jobs, PLAN provided the young men and women supported by the agency with suitable industrial training. Boys took courses in fields such as lathe operation, while girls studied subjects such as radio assembly and embroidery. "Korea has a bright future as a reservoir of skilled but low-priced labor," Ryan asserted in 1965.[82] PLAN contributed to the development of an industrial (and sex-segregated) workforce in Korea. Industrial jobs endowed children and their families with a measure of self-sufficiency. But on some level, they called into question the personal characteristics child-care workers sought to cultivate. Factory work demanded discipline and the ability to follow orders far more frequently than it required the creativity and independent thought long championed by American voluntary agencies.

Not all children, however, had access to industrial jobs. PLAN's director in Greece, Ismene Kalaris, admitted that the organization was unable to assist many youngsters in securing employment after graduation. "Here," Kalaris argued, "we fail as a child welfare agency." "It is a shame to take a child from the streets and bring it up and then, on Graduation Day, just sort of cast it off," agreed J. Calvitt Clarke in 1962. The policy of automatically canceling eighteen-year-olds rankled some sponsors, who saw discrepancies between agencies' rhetorical emphasis on achievement and their actual ability to help all youngsters reach their full potential. In 1957, for example, a foster parent penned an angry missive to PLAN upon the organization's cancellation of his sponsorship of Ezio, an eighteen-year-old Italian boy. Education had helped the youngster rise above his primitive background, the man argued. An agency representative had told him that the boy could "no longer return to being a humble peasant, and his love for studies burns deeply within." But while American aid had succeeded in raising the boy's aspirations, the foster parent charged, it had ultimately failed in helping him to fulfill his dreams. The man expressed hope that Ezio "will not become antagonistic towards the United States because one of its organizations failed to keep faith with him."[83] If the "revolution of rising expectations" powered national development, it also exposed a dangerous discordance between youngsters' soaring goals and their ability to achieve them.

These frustrations revealed the limits of theories that grounded economic progress in individual psychological development. Voluntary workers might, by their own lights, help imbue children with the ambition to live a life different from that of their parents and grandparents. They could do little, however, to bring about the larger economic conditions that would help them to do so. If development was, as PLAN director B. L. Weisbart had suggested, "an individual obligation," voluntary workers' experiences with older children increasingly highlighted the extent to which people's success depended not only on individual character but also on the opportunities made available by the larger economic and political environment. The tensions between personal and societal change would only become more evident in the years to come.

Like programs aimed at promoting peace and fighting communism, American child welfare agencies' efforts to stimulate national development and modernization looked to interventions in the process of personality development as a means of achieving larger political goals. But voluntary workers' understandings of the personality traits that drove national development were at times inconsistent. American workers celebrated the self-reliant entrepreneur, but they also looked to the cooperative group member and to the pliant industrial worker as the agents of democracy and progress. American-led programs exposed local families to increased scrutiny and judgment even as an emphasis on self-help gave foreign parents a key role to play in improving the lives of their children and their countries at large. Voluntary agencies extolled efforts directed at helping entire families, but children's perceived malleability continued to render them more attractive recipients of aid than their parents. And even as American programs for children sought to bring about the modern mentality they saw as essential to promoting economic growth, they also betrayed hints that the developing world might need more than a psychological overhaul. Voluntary agencies could marshal convincing anecdotal proof of their programs' success in winning friends for the United States, but the evidence supporting their influence on economic development was somewhat flimsier. While international friendships flourished in the absence of extensive government involvement—indeed, some argued, *because of* the absence of government involvement—the challenge of assisting older children to achieve self-support increasingly highlighted the importance of external political and economic structures in launching the developing world into the future.

American efforts to help children overseas exposed fundamental tensions within modernization theory itself. American agencies' reluctance to allow self-help projects to progress to the logical end point of indigenous self-rule reflected a deeper ambivalence among modernization theorists about local populations' capacity for self-determination. On some level, helping children solved modernizers' dilemma of how to intervene in foreign nations without violating the principles of democracy and self-determination they championed. Children, by virtue of their vulnerability and immaturity, could never be accorded the level of independence and free choice to which indigenous adults could lay claim.

U.S.-led programs for children in developing countries ultimately reflected not only an effort to usher in a modern era abroad but also a struggle to define the values that characterized modern life at home. "We all live in a world which is being transformed before our eyes by new inventions, new forms of communication," noted Margaret Mead in 1955. "Attention to the more dramatic instances in which the culture of a people is transformed sharpens our realization of what is happening to us."[84] Programs for children overseas reflected tensions within American society at large, revealing competing and sometimes inconsistent visions of what constituted children's best interests in a rapidly changing world. Child rearing ultimately served as a site on which the meaning of modernization was both shaped and contested. Youngsters might light the way to the future, but it was a future whose contours were, and would increasingly become, uncertain.

CHAPTER SEVEN

Challenging the Global Parent

AT 10:45 IN THE MORNING on May 21, 1969, a group of twenty protesters marched into the Unitarian Universalist Service Committee's (UUSC) three-story brownstone in Boston and interrupted the opening of the organization's executive committee meeting. Like so many protesters that year, the group that burst through the doors of 78 Beacon Street was angry about American actions in Vietnam. But unlike their counterparts in cities across the country who condemned the actions of the U.S. military, the demonstrators were focused on the activities of an American aid organization. Specifically, their wrath was directed at the UUSC's neighborhood center in Saigon, a venue for child welfare, social work training, and recreational activities. Established in late 1968 with a grant from the U.S. Agency for International Development, the UUSC's neighborhood center represented the culmination of the organization's nearly three decades of experience in overseas social welfare. Agency officials envisioned a center that would promote "neighborhood cohesion" and provide uprooted families living in a government housing project with a "sense of belonging." In addition to supplying families with needed social services, the center served as an important locus for social work training. But children and youth stood at the heart of the center's work: UUSC workers established a well-baby clinic, ran play groups, and trained teenagers to lead younger children in recreational activities. They organized a youth club, where youngsters took sewing and English lessons and staged performances of Vietnamese folk songs and puppet shows.[1]

UUSC officials described the neighborhood center in Saigon—like its predecessors in postwar Germany and elsewhere around the world—as a means of relieving human suffering and training local citizens in methods of democratic self-help. The protesters argued that the UUSC's social welfare programs buttressed U.S. military aims in a misguided and morally objectionable war. They denounced the center for helping to prop up the "dictatorial" South Vietnamese regime and demanded the organization's immediate withdrawal from its Vietnam program. After presenting their demands to the UUSC executive committee, the protesters occupied a "liberated zone" on the first floor of the organization's headquarters, where they were joined by dozens of supporters.[2]

The UUSC did not immediately withdraw from its neighborhood center in Saigon. But the demonstration did help bring to the fore criticisms of the project already long brewing within the organization itself. Some UUSC officials, too, worried that the agency's cooperation with USAID would compromise its commitment to political neutrality and appear to constitute support of a war to which many of its employees and supporters were strongly opposed. Some charged that the project was not really politically neutral, as the UUSC worked only in South Vietnam and had never made any overtures toward assisting those in the North. Others assailed the program for failing to help the neediest citizens. The families residing in the housing project where the center was located were largely middle class, they argued; the neighborhood center thus neglected the poorest Vietnamese citizens. Finally, some affiliated with the UUSC questioned whether American social work theory and practices could—or should—be transferred intact from the United States to a foreign country.[3]

The UUSC was not the only voluntary organization whose overseas child welfare and social work programs had become the subject of growing scrutiny. The criticisms leveled at the UUSC neighborhood center, both by outside observers and by agency officials themselves, were emblematic of those that would be directed at American child welfare projects overseas over the course of the late 1960s and 1970s. In the two decades following World War II, American voluntary organizations' focus on children—at once victims and agents in the global arena—had allowed them to slip easily between the political and the humanitarian realms. Their work had been buoyed by the goals they shared with the U.S. government and by the perceived symbiosis between personal and national development.

By the late 1960s and early 1970s, however, this consensus was rapidly unraveling. For many Americans, the atrocities of the Vietnam War, coupled with the mixed success of many modernization programs abroad, prompted a reassessment of the appropriate nature and scope of U.S. interventions overseas. As American foreign aid became increasingly controversial both at home and abroad, voluntary agencies reexamined their relationship to the U.S. government and worked to disentangle overseas child welfare from U.S. foreign affairs.

CHILD WELFARE IN VIETNAM

American voluntary agencies began work in Vietnam shortly following the end of French colonial rule and the division of the country into Northern and Southern zones in 1954. As in Korea and other political hot spots across the Asian continent, American programs for children in Vietnam served as a showcase for U.S. benevolence in the face of Communist aggression. In 1957, Foster Parents' Plan proudly publicized an English and Vietnamese rendition of "God Bless America" sung by youngsters at the Thu Duc orphanage upon the visit of an American foster parent. The same year, Christian Children's Fund's Verent Mills described his organization's Family Helper Projects in Vietnam as guiding local families along the road to democracy. "To gain the confidence of the local populace for the cause of democracy means we have to meet the Vietnamese welfare needs," Mills explained. "The one who wins the socio-economic war is really going to win the ultimate victory." By the early 1960s, CCF was running advertisements soliciting funds for Vietnam featuring families such as the Hiets, whose father had been murdered by the Communists.[4]

In the mid-1960s, as the U.S. military presence in Southeast Asia escalated, the welfare of Vietnamese children increasingly moved to the forefront of American concern. During the summer of 1965, as President Lyndon B. Johnson sent growing numbers of American combat troops to Vietnam, the percentage of new foster parents asking PLAN for Vietnamese children rose from 7 to 20 percent. By 1967, CCF was receiving more requests for sponsorships of Vietnamese youngsters than the organization could fill.[5]

American government officials widely regarded the war in Vietnam not only as a military conflict but also as a battle for "hearts and minds." Since communism was seen as appealing to hungry, suffering people, social welfare programs were integral to the U.S. strategy for victory. "A nation cannot be built by armed power or by political agreement. It will rest on the expectation by individual men and women that their future will be better than their past," argued President Johnson in 1965. Vice President Hubert Humphrey lauded foreign aid workers in Vietnam as "the ones who are going to win this war." "As you know here in Vietnam there is a struggle going on to win the mind of the people, by the communist[s]," Army Sergeant Bruce O. Gilmore wrote in a 1965 letter to CCF seeking support for a boys' orphanage. "If these you[ng] men are allow[ed] to grow up without guidance, how many will be entice[d] to join the communist movement? No one know[s]."[6]

Gilmore was not alone in placing children at the center of the American effort to win "hearts and minds." U.S. military officials looked to children as a means of winning friends for the United States among the local population. "If the South Vietnamese ever contain the Viet Cong, they will have to do so by long-term development of [their] youth," one U.S. official opined. A military news release described a new playground constructed by U.S. troops for children in the hamlet of Nam Thien, "formerly an area of concentrated VC activities," as key in turning the tide of local opinion in favor of the United States. Whereas residents once regarded the U.S. military advisory team "with hostility and suspicion," the news release noted, after the playground was built, the children were friendly and the adults nodded their heads or waved as one of the team members drove through the hamlet. In villages across Vietnam, U.S. military and aid officials constructed schools and playgrounds; distributed books, soccer balls, and badminton rackets; organized children's athletic competitions; and supported troops of Boy and Girl Scouts. U.S. officials also called on American military personnel to volunteer with Vietnamese youth groups during their time off as a means of establishing better understanding between the Vietnamese people and the U.S. armed forces. "The children are a natural, low key way to reach the adult population, and the work with children gains credit for the government, stimulates morale and draws the people together toward constructive goals," explained a U.S. Army official in a 1969 memorandum to Vietnamese provincial officials. "The children," he noted, "can also be exploited as an excellent source of intelligence."[7]

Some voluntary agencies and their supporters also looked to child welfare activities as a means of fighting communism and building support for the United States among the local population. "The conflict in Vietnam is more than a clash of arms," explained Verent Mills in 1966. "We are combating an ideology aimed at undermining and overthrowing all democratic forms of government. In order to win the heart of the peasant and counteract the enemy's propaganda, it is essential that we protect his bowl of rice." An Illinois woman seeking to sponsor a war-injured Vietnamese girl she had seen in a newspaper photograph wrote in a 1965 letter to PLAN: "We have to do something constructive in order to overcome communism. Here is a victim of communism, twice a victim. I would be delighted if I could have that child."[8]

But American interest in the welfare of South Vietnam's children did little to stem the overwhelming tide of youngsters in need of care and protection. Estimates in 1966 and 1967 placed the number of refugee children between 200,000 and 800,000. The war drew fathers into the military, forced impoverished mothers to seek paid employment, and produced staggering numbers of civilian casualties. "The situation is so chaotic, ungoverned and so unsettled by the war that hundreds if not thousands of children are scrambling through childhood without the attention, the care, the guidance nor the love that life should offer them," fretted PLAN's director in Vietnam, Elizabeth Brown. As families disintegrated, the ranks of orphanages began to swell. By 1966, about 10,000 children resided in institutions; by 1973, the number had more than doubled. American experts denounced the living conditions of institutionalized children as "deplorable." Vietnamese orphanages were "unbelievable, as bad or worse than the plight of the orphans during the Korean War," CCF officials noted.[9]

In many ways, child welfare efforts in Vietnam during the initial years of the war were reminiscent of those in Korea more than a decade earlier. A number of the same child welfare experts, including Howard Rusk and Leonard Mayo, brought their knowledge to bear on the situation in Vietnam. American child welfare efforts again centered not only on feeding, clothing, and housing needy children but also on upgrading the professional standards in the fields of social work and child care more generally. " 'Welfare' as a concept is still poorly defined," observed Kenneth W. Kindelsperger, dean of the University of Louisville's Kent School of Social Work, upon visiting Vietnam in early 1966. "It tends to fluctuate between the 'lady bountiful' act of charity to a rudimentary custodial responsibility for the residual problems that cannot be handled by the individual or his family."[10]

American agencies worked to professionalize the field of social work and to train child-care workers in "modern" methods of caring for children. PLAN served as a center for fieldwork training so that students at the Caritas School of Social Work in Saigon could observe the workings of a professional child welfare organization. CCF also trained local citizens to serve as the agency's caseworkers. At the UUSC's neighborhood center in Saigon, American social workers cooperated with their Vietnamese colleagues to compile the first social work training materials written in Vietnamese. American workers in Vietnam were also joined by an increasingly international group of colleagues. The United Nations Bureau of Social Affairs supported the work of Belgian child welfare expert Yvonne Lemaire, who was stationed in South Vietnam from 1964 through 1967. Lemaire assisted the Vietnamese government in developing an in-service training course for orphanage workers and helped establish a community center and day-care program where social work trainees could gain practical work experience.[11]

The American Friends Service Committee, which established a day-care center (the term "day nursery" had largely fallen out of use by the late 1960s) for children in the city of Quang Ngai, held a series of training courses for Vietnamese child-care workers in 1967 and 1968. The courses were led by Jill Richards, an American social worker who was the wife of the director of the AFSC's program in Quang Ngai. Like her predecessors in Korea, Germany, and other countries around the world, Richards designed the courses to provide local workers with a better understanding of child psychology and human development. Richards's lessons were rooted in the particular circumstances of Vietnamese families, but they drew heavily on the theories developed by psychologists more than two decades earlier. Indeed, Richards registered her delight that Co An, the Vietnamese day-care center director, "has already read some Freud!!"[12]

Richards emphasized the importance of love and familial security, rather than heredity, in shaping children's personalities. "Temperament—that which one inherits from one's parents—is only a part of our character," Richards explained in a note to the trainees. "There are other reasons why the child is so passive . . . reasons of physical, emotional, social development . . . if a child does not have a lot of love, he might become timid, passive, sad." The AFSC deliberately restricted enrollment in the day-care center despite the great numbers of youngsters in need of care so that the staff could develop a warm "personal relationship" with each of the children. The organization aimed to train not only child-care professionals but also mothers in new methods of caring for children. The day-care facility in Quang Ngai served as a demonstration center that instructed mothers in better cooking and hygiene practices and hosted home economics courses that taught girls needlework and cooking skills.[13]

American efforts to train Vietnamese social workers, child-care practitioners, and mothers produced mixed results. AFSC workers noted that their efforts to raise the standards of child care in refugee families' homes were often unsuccessful. Students in the home economics course were mainly interested in acquiring salable skills such as needlework, AFSC director Jack Richards reported, not in bringing home new domestic standards. When the organization's day-care center reopened after a hiatus of several weeks, Richards noted, the children were "hungry, their clothes torn and dirty, their hair unkempt and lousy, and their nails uncut."[14]

Elizabeth Brown observed that many Vietnamese child-care workers welcomed the opportunity to receive training, and she hailed the success experienced by teams of American and other foreign professionals in raising the child-care standards in orphanages. However, she questioned the large-scale impact of such efforts. "One wonders how new young workers with the limited training available can make much progress against entrenched old fashioned methods," Brown noted. Moreover, the small numbers of local workers receiving training represented only a tiny fraction of the total number needed to deal effectively with the country's vast social welfare problems. "Not even if we flooded the country with trained and experienced workers could we meet all the needs of the people," one observer commented.[15]

While child welfare efforts in Vietnam were reminiscent of those in Korea in their emphasis on training welfare workers in "modern" methods of child care, they also bore evidence of the shifts in child welfare practice that had taken place during the course of the 1950s and 1960s. In the aftermath of the Korean War, many had seen American support for orphanages as a testament to U.S. friendship and generosity. But by the late 1960s, the rescue of Korean children had come to represent a cautionary tale. Korean institutions established in the aftermath of the war were still in existence over a decade later, dependent on foreign support and caring for vast numbers of children—69,000 by 1967—many of whom, experts recognized, were not truly orphans.[16] By the late 1960s, American child welfare professionals increasingly shunned institutional care in favor of programs aimed at supporting children within their own families.

Indeed, study after study revealed that the vast majority of children residing in Vietnamese orphanages were not orphans. Instead, they were "extra" children, placed in institutions by parents too poor, or too unsettled, to care for them at home. Parents often placed children in institutions temporarily, returning to reclaim them when their living situations improved. A study of a sampling of orphanages conducted by the South Vietnamese Ministry of Health, Social Welfare and Relief in 1966 found that 75 percent of institutionalized children had either one or both parents or a close relative living.[17]

Seeking to learn from the lessons of Korea, American agencies established day-care centers and initiated or expanded programs of family support that would allow families to care for children at home instead of relinquishing them to institutions. "The Vietnamese family must not be permitted to become another casualty of war," declared the AFSC's David Stickney upon dedicating the organization's day-care center in Quang Ngai in 1966. Many experts placed the family at the center of efforts to improve child welfare in South Vietnam. In a 1966 statement of suggested principles governing the care and protection of children in war-torn countries, for example, the United States Department of Health, Education, and Welfare (HEW) recommended the care of children within their own family or kinship group "if at all possible." The American Council of Voluntary Agencies for Foreign Service, an umbrella group of voluntary agencies working overseas, agreed. "The preservation and strengthening of family life should be the primary guiding principle for all agencies seeking to help and serve children in Vietnam," it noted in 1967. In 1969, acting on the advice of American welfare experts, the South Vietnamese Ministry of Health, Social Welfare and Relief issued a directive restricting the establishment of new orphanages. Although the directive failed to curtail the growth of new children's institutions, it signaled a growing international consensus that situated the institutionalization of youngsters even in wartime as the child-care method of last resort.[18]

The family had long played a key role in American efforts to rear and rehabilitate foreign children. But these efforts had often privileged substitute or virtual families—institutional "cottage families," American foster parents—over children's biological kin. American child welfare workers were frequently ambivalent about the ability of parents to care adequately for their children, and this ambivalence remained a consistent undercurrent as the 1960s progressed. By the late 1960s, however, child welfare workers increasingly sought to facilitate the care of children within their families of origin. This was in part a practical move: supporting the care of children in their own homes was more cost effective than creating institutions and substitute families in which to rear them, especially within war-torn Vietnam.

The growing focus on supporting the care of children within families was also due to a growing effort to preserve native culture that had occupied American overseas workers since the publication of *The Ugly American* a decade earlier. Cultural preservation was particularly important in the context of programs for children, on whom the perpetuation of indigenous cultures depended. "The culture and traditions of the country have a direct bearing on family life and thus are of paramount importance. Plans and programs for children should be developed within this context and in cooperation with officials of the country," noted HEW in its 1966 statement of principles governing the care and protection of children in war-torn countries.[19]

Experts had situated the family as the wellspring of children's emotional well-being for many years. By the late 1960s, native culture was becoming the second pillar of children's psychological health. So paramount were the principles of familial care and cultural preservation that many agreed they should not be violated, even in the case of temporarily removing children from their country of origin to receive medical treatment. Numerous child welfare experts argued that children should not be uprooted, even if doing so meant receiving a higher level of physical care. "Our prime concern is for the individual and his best possible rehabilitation and we would not wish to pursue a program activity which on the one hand might result in good physical recovery but which might have severe emotional and psychological upheaval," explained the AFSC's Frank Hunt.[20]

Even organizations that did work to bring groups of war-injured children to the United States for treatment took into consideration the principles of cultural and familial preservation. Groups such as the Friends Meeting for the Sufferings of Vietnamese Children promised to take measures to protect Vietnamese children from "cultural shock." In order to preserve children's sense of familial security, the group planned to send them abroad in groups of six under the care of "a Vietnamese woman of sufficient maturity, capability and 'motherliness' to act as a parent-substitute throughout their sojourn abroad." Intercountry adoption also became increasingly controversial among child welfare experts. Although many people in the United States expressed interest in adopting Vietnamese youngsters, American child welfare experts largely agreed that children should be sent abroad for adoption only when it was impossible to make adequate provisions for their care within their country of origin. Vietnamese experts were also wary of foreign schemes that removed children en masse from the country for adoption, medical care, or education. In 1968, the South Vietnamese government issued a decree banning any group or mass emigration of children, although it continued to issue exit visas for youngsters on an individual basis.[21]

On one level, discussions about the best means of caring for youngsters in Vietnam revealed a broad consensus among Americans and their foreign colleagues regarding what constituted children's best interests. All observers expressed concern for youngsters' psychological well-being, cited the importance of bolstering the Vietnamese family, and agreed that children must retain their cultural heritage. But on another level, efforts on behalf of Vietnamese children revealed larger tensions within the American child-saving project long masked by the seeming congruence of private and national aims. For years, many American voluntary agencies had portrayed their work as both humanitarian and political: support for needy foreign children fit fairly seamlessly with official U.S. foreign policy and international development objectives. As the 1960s progressed, however, U.S. military aims seemed to supplant, rather than buttress, American efforts to assist children overseas. Just as the escalating war in Vietnam undermined President Johnson's ambitious Great Society programs on the home front, military objectives increasingly appeared to take precedence over international social welfare goals. "If the man power and the money, at three million dollars a day being spent on war, could be transformed into a constructive effort," complained Elizabeth Brown in 1965, "a lot of people would benefit, and a more genuine victory for freedom be won." CCF challenged its supporters to demonstrate a humanitarian commitment to Vietnam that rivaled their country's military one. "If we can afford to send planes and bombs," the organization asserted in 1966, "surely we can also send food, clothing, medicine—and our love."[22]

American voluntary workers in Europe, Japan, and Korea had worked in the aftermath of devastating wars. But workers in Vietnam labored in the midst of an ongoing conflict. The war made routine matters, such as visiting client families, perilous. The roar of jets overhead forced the cancellation of intake interviews, and errant shells destroyed records and children's thank-you notes. "This is not . . . an old-fashioned war with a front behind which to work," Elizabeth Brown noted. In particular, local workers employed by American agencies risked becoming the targets of Vietcong aggression. Vietnamese social workers often hid their case records when traveling by bus out of Saigon on account of persistent Vietcong harassment. Some of the families assisted by PLAN were visited by the Vietcong and lectured about the merits of communism and the reasons why they should refuse aid from an American organization. On June 29, 1971, one of Save the Children Federation's local field workers, Dang Van Tran, was traveling to a tiny village near Qui Nhon in the Binh Dinh province to discuss the federation's programs with the villagers. When he arrived, he was stopped by a Vietcong patrol, which took him prisoner and accused him of working on behalf of "American imperialists." After a kangaroo court trial, Tran was taken to the center of the village, tied up, and executed. SCF described its continued commitment to work in Vietnam as a fitting tribute to a man who had dedicated his life to assisting his fellow citizens.[23]

The surprise Tet Offensive in late January 1968 shattered even the relative safety of Saigon, where many American agencies had their headquarters. CCF's director in Vietnam, John Fitzstevens, watched some of the fighting from the window of his home. In the months that followed, the CCF office in Saigon was frequently in the range of sniper fire and missile attacks. Members of the AFSC's team in Quang Ngai discovered that their day-care center had been used as a fortress forming part of a strategic line of defense during the Tet Offensive battles. South Vietnamese soldiers had built a bunker and operated a machine gun on its roof. During the summer of 1971, vehicles belonging to UNICEF and the U.S. government were firebombed within a half block of PLAN's office. Continuous warfare made many improvements in child welfare transitory at best. Surveying Vietnamese families' losses of lives and homes in the aftermath of the Tet Offensive, PLAN's assistant director in Vietnam, Frederick Chaffee, lamented the "work of many years wiped out." Almost two-thirds of SCF's Vietnamese program was destroyed in a 1972 offensive that forced the agency to consolidate its programs near Saigon. A Vietnamese child wrote in a letter to her American foster parents: "In the place where we live every night we hear mortar shells blow up, so we have to hide in the shelter. Fighting is going on in our country. We are very worried and do not know what will come next."[24]

Even more harmful than attacks by the Vietcong was harassment on the part of the very citizens whom American workers were attempting to help. "The hardest thing about working in Viet-Nam is the hatred that the Vietnamese people have for Americans," the AFSC's Louis Kubicka noted in a letter to friends. One AFSC worker was spat on by locals; another was forced off the road by South Vietnamese Army trucks while riding a bicycle. A group of Vietnamese teenagers hit CCF's John Fitzstevens in the back with a large rock. "The common people are not behind this government and as a result I am encountering more and more anti-American feeling," Fitzstevens noted. American workers' efforts on behalf of children did little to exempt them from rising anti-U.S. sentiments. Fitzstevens's attackers, he reported, "knew who I was and the work I represent and that I speak their language." "The great American effort 'to win the hearts and minds!' of the Vietnamese," argued the AFSC's David Stickney in a letter to Senator Edward Kennedy, "is failing."[25]

By the late 1960s and early 1970s, American agencies working with children in Vietnam faced a growing sense of disenchantment, both among supporters and among voluntary workers themselves. "If we are winning this thing as the press indicates we are and the men in Washington think we are—then why are things worse in all areas when you talk first hand to people who live there? Good question huh?" queried John Fitzstevens in a 1968 letter to a colleague. Beginning that year, requests for Vietnamese youngsters among CCF sponsors began to decline. "There is here on the home front a growing malaise and disillusionment with our effort in [Vietnam]," the organization's Edmund Janss explained. Some observers questioned whether American-led child welfare programs in Vietnam were capable of exerting any long-term influence. "Fundamentally, these programs function more to ease our own guilt feelings than they do to change the living structure in that country," one visitor to Vietnam observed in 1967. The AFSC admitted that in the face of overwhelming need, its efforts were "mainly a gesture." "We have tried to act as a catalyst in Vietnam and have failed. Perhaps it is because we have taken a system and attempted to mold a foreign tradition and culture to it rather than vice versa," wrote PLAN's Frederick Chaffee in 1968. "Changes will come in Vietnam," Chaffee predicted, "but they will come from within and will be radical and sweeping."[26]

Some saw the failures in Vietnam as evidence of the fundamental discordance of military and social welfare goals. "Here in Viet Nam we have had the anachronism of military aid, which maintains the status quo, being carried on at the same time as civilian aid, which should work for change," noted Elizabeth Brown in 1969. Others saw welfare programs as furthering the aims of a military undertaking they understood to be wrong-headed and immoral. These programs, some observers argued, postponed the end of the war by relieving suffering and reducing anti-American sentiment to a level that allowed U.S. official efforts to continue. Welfare programs, particularly those directed at children, also supported an image of the United States as a beneficent presence in Vietnam that could serve to quell opposition to the war at home.[27]

Domestic opposition to the war in Vietnam, however, continued to mount. As it did, many voluntary agencies tried to distance their work from that of the U.S. government. It was an argument they had made successfully in the past: throughout the 1950s and early 1960s, American organizations had emphasized their private status as evidence both of U.S. citizens' disinterested generosity and of the superiority of American free enterprise. But voluntary agencies' work was not, and rarely had been, entirely private. Organizations registered with the Advisory Committee on Voluntary Foreign Aid received government-subsidized ocean freight for relief supplies and were entitled to commodities through the Food for Peace program. Even agencies that did not take advantage of these benefits were dependent on the U.S. government in Vietnam—as they had been in Korea, Japan, and Germany— for logistical support, transportation, and security guidance. The U.S. government also supported the work of certain agencies in Vietnam more directly. The AFSC's day-care center was constructed with cement, steel, and roofing provided by USAID, and lumber and paint provided by the U.S. Navy.[28] The UUSC and SCF ran their Vietnamese programs with the assistance of USAID grants.

In 1967, the United States Operations Mission placed private voluntary agencies operating in Vietnam under the jurisdiction of a new organizational structure called Civil Operations and Revolutionary Development Support (CORDS), under the command of General William Westmoreland. The U.S. Operations Mission promised voluntary agencies independence—its agreement with private organizations working in Vietnam stated that it would respect "voluntary agency requirements for identity and freedom of action"— but some voluntary workers felt that the government failed to live up to its statement in practice. One voluntary agency official complained to a newspaper reporter of "a steady and subtle effort to make us become part of the Government's war effort." "It's one thing to operate and get along with the military. It's another thing to start worrying about your agency's sovereignty. This whole situation is very, very difficult," stated Elizabeth Brown in 1967.[29]

Private organizations' cooperation with the U.S. government had rarely raised eyebrows in the past. But as growing numbers of the American public viewed Washington with suspicion, voluntary agencies' relationship with the government became subject to increasing scrutiny. PLAN's executive director Gloria Matthews explained the risks posed to voluntary agencies accepting U.S. government funds in a 1970 letter to a colleague:

> [The U.S. government] will use this in publicity and willy nilly, PLAN is an arm of the U.S. Government! We KNOW that is not so—but put yourself in the place of a reader of this news. Those who think that the USAID program is swell are delighted. But those who do not take out their hangups on us . . . and it is this tightrope we must walk. This is not to say we do NOT take help from the government. If it will help the children I'll take it from the devil himself. But in the publicity, that's where we have to be careful.[30]

Once forced by public opinion to take a stance against communism, PLAN now felt pressure to publicly repudiate its connections with U.S. foreign policy.

For Matthews, the issue of accepting government funding was largely a problem of publicity. But for other groups, it was a matter of conscience. No one grappled more with the dilemma of whether or not to accept U.S. government assistance than members of the AFSC, whose Quaker values led them to oppose war in all its forms. The AFSC had been an outspoken opponent of the war in Vietnam since its outset. But the organization's opposition to the conflict did not stop it from attempting to relieve some of the human suffering it left in its wake. The AFSC opened its day-care center in 1966; a year later, it established a rehabilitation facility that provided physical therapy and prosthetic limbs to war-wounded civilians, about half of whom were children.[31] The AFSC did not receive any direct funding from the U.S. government, but like other voluntary groups in Vietnam, its workers depended on the government for some supplies and for logistical support.

AFSC officials divided over whether the acceptance of any assistance from the American government meant condoning the conflict and furthering U.S. official aims. Some felt that any coordination with the military furthered the U.S. war effort. Others disagreed. "We hope that it is our principles which say what needs saying, and not the fact of our using certain U.S. facilities," noted a group of AFSC representatives. "The good must always be gleaned from a world wherein good and evil are bound up together, and often about as easy to separate as it is to chemically distinguish cancer cells from normal cells," mused Louis Kubicka in a 1968 statement on the AFSC's relationship with the U.S. military in Vietnam. "While it is true that we are dependent for other services, it seems clear that as long as we do not, by accepting these services, slip into being controlled by the military, that our position is one of simply putting to good purpose what might otherwise be wasted or worse," Kubicka argued. As the war progressed, however, the AFSC increasingly attempted to safeguard its independence from the U.S. military. When an army representative requested information on the AFSC's team members and its facilities for use in case of an emergency requiring the evacuation of American citizens, AFSC team leader Eric Wright refused to supply it. "We are especially concerned that should fighting occur in the town, no 'rescue' efforts be undertaken on our behalf which might endanger either the soldiers sent out to rescue us or the 'enemy' they would be rescuing us from," he wrote to military officials in late 1969.[32]

American organizations' efforts to separate their work in Vietnam from that of the U.S. government did little to affect their reception on the ground. Most rural people did not make a distinction between the U.S. military, aid workers, and private voluntary groups, reported a team of American social welfare experts who visited Vietnam in 1969—they were simply opposed to all Americans. Neither did the North Vietnamese accept the contention that child welfare work in the South was nonpolitical. When AFSC representative William D. Lotspeich met with a National Liberation Front official to offer civilian aid to North Vietnam, the official rebuffed the AFSC's offer of assistance because of the organization's association with the American military. Lotspeich's argument that the AFSC's work in South Vietnam was "with children" and outside the realm of politics fell on deaf ears.[33]

AMERICAN HUMANITARIANISM UNDER FIRE

The experience of American voluntary workers in Vietnam was mirrored around the world. From the Philippines to Morocco to Peru, rising nationalism and anti-American sentiments rendered even private aid increasingly controversial and unwelcome. Some foreign governments seeking to limit U.S. influence within their borders went as far as to arrest or expel American child welfare workers. The American Jewish Joint Distribution Committee's Katya Roberts was ousted from Tunisia in 1967, for example, after being accused by the government of traveling around the country much more than her responsibilities as a day-care consultant merited.[34]

American child welfare programs were sometimes targets for violent displays of anti-Americanism. In 1967, the outbreak of the Six Day War triggered a wave of anti-foreign and anti-Jewish sentiment in Tunisia that led to the destruction of one of the JDC's classrooms, along with the American and British embassies, by a mob. On December 6, 1971, groups of angry students in Colombia—"anti-gringo and anti-imperialism and anti anything else [they] happen to think of at the time"—stoned one of PLAN's vehicles and set the other one on fire. In Peru, PLAN was shocked to find even its own local employees emboldened by nationalist fervor. In 1973, PLAN staff in Peru took hostage American organization officials for three hours in an effort to intimidate the Americans into dropping their opposition to a proposed union made up of agency employees. American aid to children overseas, some observers noted, increasingly resulted in hatred and resentment rather than fealty and gratitude. "We in America . . . have spent millions of dollars to help these countries," puzzled Henry F. Harvey, director of the U.S.-based child welfare agency Compassion. "Yet, it seems that at every turn of the road we are hated and despised and stoned and spit upon."[35]

Foreign commentators criticized the publicity surrounding American aid to children as undercutting their countries' abilities to assume a dignified and independent place on the global stage. "This face, recorded in 'The New Yorker,' is all that many gringos know about us," complained a Colombian journalist in response to an advertisement depicting a poor Colombian girl that SCF ran in American magazines. Greek authorities were so embarrassed by photographs of ill-clad Greek children depicted in American advertisements that they asked PLAN in the early 1970s to remove Greece from the list of countries in which the agency operated. PLAN phased out its Greek program in 1974. Korea, too, had grown tired of the "orphan image" it developed over two decades of receiving child welfare funds from American agencies. By the early 1970s, the South Korean government attempted to subject the foreign voluntary agencies working within its borders to greater scrutiny.[36]

Some took issue not only with the publicity that surrounded American aid to children overseas but also with the manner in which such aid was administered. One Peruvian writer accused PLAN's program, which exercised considerable oversight with regard to the ways in which recipient families reared their children, of "substituting for the father" and "endangering the family structure." If social work's connection with democracy had encouraged its export in earlier years, it would by the 1970s render it a symbol of American cultural blindness and overreach among critics. Some charged that the orientation of American social work, particularly its emphasis on individual psychology, had little relevance to the social structures and local problems in developing countries. In 1969, Dutch social worker Jan F. de Jongh, who in 1950 had looked eagerly to the adoption of American-style social work in Europe, questioned its relevancy to the developing world. "I wonder whether in many cases our methods may be more uprooting than helpful, more alienating and isolating than integrating," de Jongh mused. "It does not seem unwarranted to assume that the confrontation of Western social work with many of the Afro-Asian cultures creates cultural shock-effects which explain the lack of visible results, the feelings of uneasiness and uncertainty after twenty years of technical assistance." By the early 1970s, many within the American social work establishment agreed with Rosa Peric Resnick's characterization of Western social work as "too culture-bound and too inextricably conditioned by its economic and political origins to serve as a universally acceptable model." Casework and social work methods more generally were increasingly coming under fire within the United States as well. Some activists within the social work profession rejected casework's emphasis on individual emotional adjustment and urged their colleagues to work to ameliorate the difficult social conditions they understood to be at the root of many of their clients' distress.[37]

Critics in both the United States and abroad argued that American social work methods not only disregarded the needs of less developed countries but actually hindered their progress toward self-sufficiency. Lynn Harold Vogel and Betty Vos Vogel, American social workers who were stationed in Vietnam in 1969 and 1970, accused the American welfare workers who flocked to the country during the 1960s—and not the war itself—with issuing the first blow against the integrity of Vietnamese society. American workers' disregard for indigenous social welfare structures and their inability to fully relinquish power to local workers probably did "more to curb the rise of initiative and trust among the Vietnamese than to encourage it," the Vogels argued. In Korea, where foreign aid workers had by the 1970s been a presence for two decades, a similarly critical view emerged. Sei-Jin Nam, a professor of social work at Seoul National University, accused foreign agencies of assuming social welfare responsibilities that should have been met by the government and indigenous agencies. The presence of foreign voluntary organizations, he argued, slowed the implementation of public welfare provisions, inhibited the growth of a sense of civic responsibility among the general population, and discouraged local social workers from developing theories appropriate to Korean culture and society.[38]

In the face of mounting criticisms, many Americans concerned with the promotion of child welfare abroad, particularly in Vietnam, attempted to depict their work as divorced from international politics. Susan Gardner, a college student who spearheaded a drive to raise funds for Vietnamese orphans, described her work as politically neutral. "These children don't know who hurt them—just that they were hit when a mine went off, or they were shot by a soldier, or burned," Gardner explained. "People may be against the war, but they're not against children." Even CCF backed away from its once enthusiastic support of U.S. foreign policy aims. In a 1966 article in *CCF World News* titled "Why Are We in Vietnam?," executive director Verbon Kemp insisted that CCF had no interest in influencing international politics. "For Christian Children's Fund the answer has nothing to do with political pressures or maintaining a military balance of power. CCF is in Vietnam for one simple reason: the children need our help," Kemp wrote. Three years later, he reemphasized CCF's political neutrality: "The Christian Children's Fund as a corporate body takes no position whatsoever regarding the war in Vietnam. Our ministry is to assist children without regard to the circumstances motivating their needs." More common than Kemp's statements was silence. Once eager to connect their work with foreign affairs, many groups simply stopped talking about the larger political implications of their work.[39]

Portraying aid to foreign children as an apolitical expression of America's responsibility to the helpless shielded child welfare work from criticisms regarding the United States' conduct in the Vietnam War. It allowed voluntary groups to rally support for their work even as foreign aid increasingly fell into disrepute. But this discursive strategy ultimately rested on shaky ground. In Vietnam, in particular, many Americans found it difficult to overlook the fact that foreign children's suffering was directly related to the military and foreign policy decisions of the United States. After World War II, American commentators had argued that the United States' new position as a preeminent global power compelled each and every citizen to contribute to the welfare of suffering populations overseas. If American responsibility to children abroad was now disconnected from the U.S. government's actions in the global arena, then what compelled Americans to help the less fortunate around the world?

Even as voluntary groups sought to distance their work from American foreign affairs, the U.S. government continued to look to international child welfare as a political tool. In 1974, it insisted that UNICEF, which was committed to aiding children on a nonpartisan basis, refrain from using American money to finance a series of new programs to assist children in North Vietnam and in communist-held areas in the South. Many Americans found the government's actions distasteful. The *New York Times* denounced government officials for putting "politics before children."[40] Helping children overseas as a means of fighting communism was a vastly different project than withholding aid from them in an effort to accomplish the same goal.

As American voluntary agencies attempted to isolate child welfare from unpopular U.S. foreign policy, international child welfare was itself losing some of its political utility. In the late 1960s, thousands of protesters—many of which were young people—took to the streets in cities across the globe to protest the Cold War status quo. Directly assailing the powers that be, these activists demanded social and political revolutions that were immediate and far-reaching. In contrast, programs that promised to change the world by carefully molding the next generation appeared quaint and ineffectual. In fact, American programs for foreign youngsters sometimes aimed to curtail young people's participation in protest movements. In 1969, for example, PLAN's program in the Philippines sought to draw "restive youth" into group activities during the summer months "in order to direct excess energies toward constructive goals." "Our teen-agers soon found the goings-on in and outside of PLAN's Youth Center more diverting than betaking themselves to the scene of, or perhaps even participating in, a demonstration or riot that may have been staged somewhere in the big city," the program's director, Robert Sage, reported.

Among some observers, the actions of young protesters served as an indictment of the child-rearing methods long championed by many American child-rearing experts. Conservative leaders, including U.S. Vice President Spiro Agnew, denounced the youthful protests as an end result of the "permissive" parenting advocated by child-rearing experts such as Benjamin

Spock, who himself had become a prominent antiwar activist. Child-rearing methods had indeed transformed society, Agnew and others argued: they had created a generation disrespectful of authority and utterly devoid of discipline.[41]

Also transforming the ties between child rearing and international politics were new ideas about women's work and motherhood. The growing global feminist movement made acceptable a form of women's activism disconnected from motherhood and child rearing. For example, the Ladies' Committee in Tehran had collaborated with JDC day-care consultants for many years. For these women, work with the JDC nursery had, during the 1950s and 1960s, been a socially acceptable venue through which to participate in public life. By the 1970s, however, the women's interest veered from child rearing to women's rights. By 1973, day-care consultant Evelyn Peters noted, the Ladies' Committee's involvement in the JDC's nursery had waned, replaced by "a prodigious correspondence concerning women's rights."[42] For women and other citizens alike, direct activism had eclipsed work with children as a means of political participation.

Moreover, the rate of global population growth had by the late 1960s become a source of worldwide concern. Many experts fretted that the world population was expanding at a rate that would soon prove to be unsustainable. Fears of a "population explosion" increasingly cast foreign children not as agents of political and economic development but as consumers of scarce resources. American efforts to save children in developing countries competed for attention and funding with programs seeking to prevent many such children from being born in the first place.[43] Curtailing population growth and offering aid to children overseas were not mutually exclusive; by the 1970s, most of the American child sponsorship agencies were also helping families gain access to birth control. Some experts cast family planning as a means of improving child welfare, as smaller families allowed parents to provide each child with the love and individual attention he or she required. But the surge of interest and public attention that surrounded organizations such as International Planned Parenthood made supporting family planning, rather than the efforts of international child welfare agencies, appear to be the responsible choice for the globally minded. A sponsor wrote to PLAN in 1972 after being assigned a three-year-old foster child with two younger siblings, "we feel sure that this family needs help, but we also feel that the kind of help they (and the world community!) need most is the prevention of additions to their family."[44]

International child welfare work was also affected by a new national mood. As feminists and members of the counterculture assaulted the family as a bastion of conservatism and experimented with new social configurations, the family no longer offered a comforting metaphor for the United States' relationship to the world. To many Americans, the image of the United States as a "global parent" began to appear more paternalistic than compassionate. The sentimentalism that had once made American work with foreign young-sters so popular appeared by the 1970s to be cloying and inauthentic. A sense of optimism that had driven American social welfare projects overseas during the 1950s and early 1960s had by the 1970s given way to cynicism. The per-ceived misconduct of the United States in Vietnam, coupled with rising anti-American sentiments around the world, shattered public confidence in the United States' position as a force for good within the world community. "The burst of enthusiasm, of consideration, money and attention to help the un-derdeveloped world that came after World War II has somehow been dissi-pated," noted Elizabeth Brown in 1969. "There have been disillusionment and discouragement in many places over foreign programs, a withdrawal, and a belief that domestic problems have increased and should have atten-tion." David McClelland worried that "a kind of emotional revulsion from overseas involvement" might stifle American groups' ability to work effec-tively overseas. "We are living in a time when there is an almost overpow-ering feeling among young people that we should get out of all involvements abroad because everything we do seems to produce evil effects," McClelland noted ruefully in 1969.[45]

To some, uneasiness regarding interventions abroad reflected a deeper am-bivalence about the nature of American life at home. On the domestic front, the social reformist impulse of previous years had fallen into disarray. By the late 1960s and early 1970s, Johnson's Great Society had unraveled, riots rocked cities across the United States, and student protesters assailed the policy decisions of their elders. Many observers questioned whether the United States' brand of modernity was a goal to which other nations should aspire. Nor were many U.S.-led projects abroad living up to the hopes of their founders. Instead of serving as a showcase for American-style technological and social progress, critics charged, modernization programs in the devel-oping world had wrought widespread cultural and ecological destruction and done little to alleviate foreign poverty. To theorists and foreign aid workers alike, the very notion that all societies must follow a single path to moder-nity appeared increasingly misguided.[46]

Indeed, voluntary workers began to turn a critical eye on long-standing American prescriptions for national development. Industrialization, many argued, had done little to improve the lot of poor families. "Growing industrialization and commercial economies tend to improve conditions of the upper and middle class before having any effect on the very poor" and actually "narrow[ed] even further the probabilities of a better life for foster children," observed PLAN's field director for Brazil, David Youmans, in 1974. Ordinary Americans also began to look askance at efforts to bring "progress" to the less developed world. In a 1974 publicity letter, Verent Mills, who had assumed the position of CCF's executive director in 1970, proudly described the organization's work among the Mangyan, an indigenous tribe that lived in the remote mountains of the Philippines. Mills told readers about devoted CCF workers who sought to teach Mangyan children to read and write; to instruct their parents in the basic elements of health, hygiene, and nutrition; and to convince tribespeople to exchange their garments made of leaves and vines for modern clothing. "They require a great deal of specialized assistance, because they must be helped [to] make the difficult transition from a hidden primitive culture to the complex life of the twentieth century— where men walk upon the moon!" Mills explained.[47]

A decade earlier, Mills's letter might have inspired a flood of donations. In 1974, it provoked a stream of angry letters. CCF supporters took issue with the organization's seeming disregard for the sanctity of native culture and with its perceived attempt to force a group of isolated people to enter the modern age. In his response to the critical letters, Mills emphasized CCF's cultural sensitivity. "If it were possible to simply leave these tribe folks alone, protect them and let them develop their own culture without interference from 'civilization,' then CCF would be in favor of such action," Mills insisted.[48] CCF quickly realized that donors now preferred to promote cultural diversity rather than American-style modernization. Around this time, CCF also shed its religious identity. By the mid-1970s, the organization no longer engaged in proselytizing or restricted its assistance to Christian homes and projects. As it distanced itself from its religious roots, CCF moderated its conservative politics.

If working with vulnerable children had largely shielded American agencies from the anticommunist crusade during the 1950s, it now rendered their work the subject of increased federal scrutiny. In 1973, Senator Walter Mondale, the chairman of the Senate Labor and Public Welfare Committee's Sub-

committee on Children and Youth, launched an investigation into the operations of American voluntary organizations that worked with children
overseas. The investigation eventually narrowed its targets to five organizations. Mondale investigated CCF, PLAN, and SCF, which were the three
largest American child sponsorship agencies, as well as the American-Korean
Foundation, which by the 1970s had expanded its work into Vietnam, and
the Holt Adoption Program, which facilitated intercountry legal adoptions.
These five groups were by no means the largest American charities; in fact,
they together received less than six one-hundredths of one percent of the funds
administered by agencies registered with the Advisory Committee on Voluntary Foreign Aid. But their work with youngsters, and their prominent
use of children's images in publicity materials, rendered them of particular
interest to legislators. At the request of Senator Mondale, investigators from
the U.S. government's General Accounting Office (GAO) scrutinized the
agencies' financial records, fund-raising methods, and programs, and visited
a number of their overseas field offices.[49] Agency representatives testified at a
Senate hearing held in October 1974.

The GAO's final report, released in late 1974, did not uncover any illegal
activity. But it did note several instances in which funds collected from American donors did not reach their intended recipients. This problem was particularly pronounced in connection to the work of CCF. The largest child
sponsorship organization in the United States, CCF had witnessed phenom-
enal growth during the 1960s. By 1974, about 192,000 children in sixty-
two countries were cared for under the aegis of what Verbon Kemp once
referred to proudly as a "vast benevolent empire." But with CCF's huge geo-
graphic reach came inevitable difficulties in oversight. At one school in Hong
Kong supported by the organization, GAO investigators found, American
donors were unwittingly sending money to 118 children who were no longer
enrolled. At a CCF project in Kenya, local administrators had decided to
divide a cash gift from a sponsor among several children, even though the
sponsor had earmarked the gift for the benefit of one particular child. In
addition, CCF supported a number of projects for which investigators felt
the organization lacked sufficient information.[50]

CCF's inability to effectively monitor its overseas projects was shared to
a lesser degree by the other groups under investigation. None of the agencies,
the GAO noted, had established clearly measurable goals that could be used
to evaluate progress in accomplishing overall objectives. As a result, statements

made about the effect of their work on the lives of foreign youngsters and their families were based largely on feelings rather than facts. The GAO also uncovered some discrepancies between child welfare agencies' advertisements and their actual practices. In some instances, the GAO noted, child welfare programs selected those children they deemed most likely to be able to improve their own lots, rather than extending aid to the very neediest recipients, as their advertisements suggested. In the past, the GAO report noted, CCF advertisements had used children's case histories that were several years old.[51]

Although voluntary agencies' seemingly close ties to the U.S. government had rendered their work controversial in recent years, Mondale's investigation uncovered how tenuous government oversight of private organization activity really was. Since the conclusion of World War II, the U.S. government had coordinated the activities of private voluntary organizations working overseas through its Advisory Committee on Voluntary Foreign Aid. Registration with the ACVFA was voluntary; agencies that chose to register submitted regular reports and financial disclosures in exchange for the ability to take advantage of benefits such as government-subsidized ocean freight for relief supplies. Although the U.S. government had stated previously that an agency's registration with the ACVFA indicated "United States Government approval of the aims and purposes of that agency," in truth the ACVFA lacked enough information about most of its registrants to make an accurate assessment about the nature of their operations. When a CCF supporter wrote to the ACVFA in 1974 wondering if the agency "is all it says it is," an ACVFA official admitted, "we are unable to make a definitive statement at this point."[52]

Coming directly on the heels of the Watergate scandal, the GAO audit met an American public already frustrated by the seeming lack of transparency in public life. Press coverage of the investigation delighted in exposing the gaps between international child welfare agencies' carefully cultivated public images and their actual practices, expanding the discrepancies noted by GAO investigators into accusations of gross financial mismanagement and false advertising. "The renowned Christian Children's Fund, like the old lady who lived in the shoe, has so many children it doesn't know what to do. Worse, the fund doesn't know what it did with $25 million, which was raised to feed, clothe and educate needy children around the world," wrote journalist Jack Anderson in an article in the *Washington Post*. In a different political climate, the GAO report could have been framed as an endorsement of international child welfare agencies' work: despite the groups' far-flung operations and vast numbers of beneficiaries, investigators found very few instances of serious operational deficiencies. But the cynical tenor of the press coverage surrounding the investigation instead rendered the report yet another exposé on public subterfuge—a case made all the more shameful due to the involvement of vulnerable children. For CCF, in particular, unfavorable press coverage further diminished an already shrinking donor pool.[53]

At the heart of Mondale's investigation stood a growing mistrust of the "people-to-people" programs that had long been promoted as the optimum means of administering foreign assistance. In the two decades following World War II, U.S. officials and voluntary agencies alike lauded programs that promoted international friendship in addition to facilitating the exchange of material aid as a testament to American generosity and goodwill. But in the skeptical climate of the 1970s, "people-to-people" programs—particularly child sponsorships that involved monthly gifts—appeared to some critics to be less about friendship and more about securing a continuous stream of donations. Some experts criticized sponsorship programs as an exceedingly inefficient means of promoting child welfare overseas. Overseeing thousands of individual relationships required a vast army of social workers, translators, and other support staff. The National Information Bureau, a watchdog organization for charities, denounced child sponsorship as "a cumbersome and expensive form of relief-aid." "Person-to-person relief is so complex that the CCF has had to install a computer," the bureau marveled in 1973.[54]

Critics also charged that sponsorship programs were inherently unfair, as they arbitrarily elevated some children in a community above others. Many of the foreign institutions receiving sponsorship funds "in fact believe that they can do a better job for all the children within their institution if they take an individual contribution and spread it," Mondale noted during the hearings. These criticisms were not new—the JDC had articulated a similar critique of child sponsorship programs in the late 1940s—but they became more pervasive than ever before. By the mid-1970s, growing numbers of voluntary officials themselves questioned the efficacy of international friendship programs as a means of administering aid. Connie Widyatma, who worked with CCF's program in Indonesia, noted that some of her colleagues found the task of facilitating written correspondence between children and their sponsors to be so time-consuming that it hindered their ability to develop meaningful programs for children locally.[55] In 1975, Verent Mills downplayed the significance of correspondence with the United States in the context of child sponsorship:

> While the correspondence is beneficial, the financial assistance is even more essential to the services the project provides. We hope that the personal attention and community services (such as schooling) which the child and family receive as a result of CCF's sponsorship will in the long run prove to be the more significant aspect of these sponsorships; the relationship with the <u>local</u> caring persons is, developmentally, the more significant to the child. (Again, this is not to discount the significance of having also a distant friend.)[56]

Once portrayed as the most important element of CCF's work, children's relationships with distant foster parents had become little more than a pleasant added benefit.

In an article published in the journal *Child Welfare* in 1975, CCF's director of child and family services, David Herrell, conceded that "agencies that use the sponsorship system to raise funds for child welfare programs do not win the universal admiration of the social work profession." Sponsors' interest in being emotionally important to their children, he noted, threatened to overshadow youngsters' own needs. In addition, foster parents' desire to cultivate a long-term relationship with children risked foreclosing an agency's ability to modify or shift its programs as needs changed. Locating sponsors for special-needs children, such as mentally handicapped youngsters, often proved difficult. Moreover, sponsors' attachment to their own assigned child sometimes led to a reluctance to see their support distributed among a whole family or a community at large. Finally, sponsorship ran the risk of facilitating paternalism. "Some sponsors may not understand the broad international economic and social forces that have placed certain countries and cultures at a disadvantage in economic development. . . . The goal of building international understanding and good will on an individual person-to-person basis can backfire, having an adverse effect on both the sponsor and child," Herrell wrote.[57]

Herrell maintained, however, that child sponsorship programs could be administered in a manner that allowed their advantages to outweigh their drawbacks. Sponsorship offered emotional benefits to children, Herrell argued; in many instances, a child's behavior and school performance improved when he or she began corresponding with a sponsor. The child-sponsor relationship served as an excellent venue for cross-cultural education and communication. And, of course, sponsorship assured organizations of continuous funding. Herrell recommended that child sponsorship programs emphasize the parity of the relationship between children and their sponsors and that they take care to educate sponsors about the differences between child sponsorship and permanent legal adoption. He suggested that child sponsorship agencies focus their attention on communities in the "lesser-developed of the underdeveloped areas," where the limited amount of assistance provided by sponsorship funds could make an outsized impact.[58]

Once a testament to American generosity and global responsibility, the letters exchanged between foster parents and their foreign children had become one exhibit in an increasingly crowded museum of American hubris. Within the course of a few years, child welfare programs overseas had slipped from a source of American pride to an example of U.S. overreach in the global arena. From the streets of Saigon to the chambers of Congress, American organizations' work with foreign children had become a target for scrutiny and criticism. A vocal chorus of critics challenged traditional centers of authority both within the United States and abroad, rewrote understandings of the family, and called into question the methods of humanitarian assistance that American voluntary agencies had employed for over two decades. The United States had become a very much embattled parent to the world.

CHAPTER EIGHT

Globalizing a Happy Childhood

CHILDREN'S GARDEN—CHRISTIAN CHILDREN'S Fund's monumental orphanage in Hong Kong—was intended to be the organization's crowning achievement overseas. Completed in 1958 at a cost of over $1 million, the institution cared for more than eight hundred children in dozens of buildings scattered across fifty-one picturesque acres at the base of the Saddleback Mountain. It boasted its own school system, complete with chemistry and physics laboratories, a 1,600-seat auditorium, a well-equipped playground and athletic facilities, and sixty-five cozy cottages surrounded by flower beds and vegetable gardens. As the first orphanage in Asia arranged on the "cottage plan," Children's Garden served as a training center for child-care workers from across the continent seeking to give their institutions a more affectionate, familial feeling. CCF proudly ferried sightseers across Tolo Harbor on its own boat, the *Lady Clarke,* to tour the facility and witness modern child care in action.[1]

But only a decade after constructing Children's Garden, CCF officials began actively searching for ways to divest themselves of the institution. By the late 1960s, Children's Garden had morphed from a model child welfare institution into an embarrassing albatross. The institution, child welfare experts charged, was isolated and overcrowded. Although impressive—and expensive to run—it was becoming increasingly clear that Children's Garden was doing little to meet the particular needs of its residents, most of whom were not actually orphans. A survey conducted by the United Nations in the late 1960s found that 77 percent of the children residing at Children's Garden had one or both parents living, suggesting that the institution was doing more to facilitate family breakdown than it was to provide cutting-edge care to children.[2]

Indeed, by the late 1960s, CCF's many orphanages overseas were increasingly becoming a source of embarrassment and expense rather than pride. In 1968, the agency sought to transfer ownership of Children's Garden, along with an additional twenty-six children's homes in its possession, to qualified local agencies in the countries in which the facilities were located. In 1970, CCF donated Children's Garden free of charge to the Chinese YMCA for use as a camping facility, conference center, and boarding school.[3] Once a "living symbol of democracy in action on Communist China's doorstep," Children's Garden had become an emblem of the folly of American overreach abroad.

The demise of Children's Garden marked the beginning of a decade that witnessed seismic shifts in American child welfare work overseas. The sinking profile of "people-to-people" and modernization efforts, coupled with rising anti-American sentiments around the world, had constituted a crisis for American agencies working with children. During the 1970s, these organizations reconsidered the nature of their work and ultimately revised and reframed their missions. Once eager to publicize their identity as American organizations, voluntary groups now increasingly sought to work through local agencies, to promote indigenous leadership, and to widen their base of supporters beyond the borders of the United States. Previously drawn to political hot spots across the globe, American international child welfare agencies shifted their focus to the areas with the greatest poverty and apparent need. Redoubling their efforts to preserve native culture, American organizations eschewed large-scale projects and worked to tailor their programs to meet the particular needs of the communities in which they worked.

But even as Children's Garden's impressive buildings ceased to house American child welfare programs, the ideas that the institution had fostered did not fade away. The notion that familial love and creative play were the birthright of every child—and the conviction that they were essential not only to personal but also to national development—would continue to animate American child welfare workers and their colleagues around the world during the 1970s and throughout the decades that followed. While standardized prescriptions for international development fell by the wayside, the perceived universality of child development continued to lend weight to child welfare efforts rooted in Western notions of what constituted a proper upbringing. American agencies working with children overseas ultimately reframed, rather than discarded, their ambitions to reshape the world.

MEETING CHILDREN'S "BASIC NEEDS"

CCF's decision to dismantle its huge network of orphanages was a sign of the shifting times. By the early 1970s, as U.S. foreign aid programs became increasingly controversial both at home and abroad, the American government and private agencies alike began to reexamine their projects overseas and to overhaul the means by which they delivered aid. In 1973, Congress revised the Foreign Assistance Act, substituting an emphasis on top-down, large-scale infrastructure projects with a focus on programs that involved local people and addressed fundamental human needs such as nutrition and food production, health, rural development, and population planning. Dubbed "New Directions," the amendments to the Foreign Assistance Act called for USAID to work increasingly through private voluntary agencies in providing assistance to populations overseas. The new mandate offered government grants to help voluntary agencies shift their focus from relief to long-term development. New Directions reflected President Richard Nixon's ambitions for a scaled-back foreign aid program in the aftermath of the unpopular Vietnam War and in the wake of the perceived failure of the large-scale modernization projects of earlier years.[4]

Many child welfare organizations continued to operate largely independently of government funding (though during the 1970s, Save the Children Federation did accept USAID grants). Nonetheless, the evolution of their work paralleled shifting official foreign aid priorities. Voluntary agencies, too, placed a new emphasis on tailoring their programs to meet the specific needs and particular social patterns of local communities. Just as the U.S. government's New Directions mandate eschewed large-scale infrastructure projects in favor of smaller, community-based approaches, child welfare organizations moved away from an emphasis on grand model institutions and focused instead on smaller projects that were an integral part of the communities in which they were situated.

The new focus on meeting local needs was particularly evident in American child welfare organizations' policies regarding education. During the 1950s and 1960s, American voluntary workers lauded children's educational achievements as the key to launching the developing world into the future. But by the late 1960s and 1970s, many questioned the relevancy of Western-style education to the needs of lesser-developed countries. "We have often wondered if we were educating for goals not consistent with those of the culture. It would be helpful and pertinent for us to know how we could more realistically train staff and provide a program better suited to the society in which the children live," the American Jewish Joint Distribution Committee's Evelyn Peters noted in 1968. Foster Parents' Plan's Robert Walter also questioned his organization's policy to "encourage—almost to force—those FC's [foster children] who finished primary school to try to continue on to junior high school." Most children in developing countries had little use for the academic skills imparted, Walter argued in 1973, and emerged from the experience frustrated and no better positioned to earn a living than their peers who had not attended school. "We're beginning to think . . . and practice . . . that teaching a fisherman to be a better fisherman is more realistic than helping him to an academic education," noted PLAN's Gloria Matthews in 1974.[5]

Instead of providing youngsters in developing countries with access to formal education, as they had been doing for decades, American agencies began promoting vocational or agricultural training that would teach children the skills necessary for them to become economically independent while remaining within their own communities. New educational models reflected the declining profile of modernization theory, which had cast urbanization and industrialization as necessary and inevitable corollaries to economic progress. New methods of schooling sought to provide children with training that would allow them to thrive in rural environments and thus forestall the movement of populations into cities. CCF noted that it had been "in a small way . . . also contributing to the move to the cities and the over-professionalization in developing countries." The agency reduced its emphasis on formal education, often delivered in the form of boarding schools, and focused instead on local programs designed to teach children skills that would help them improve their own communities. PLAN, too, began to focus on teaching children skills relevant to rural life. In 1973, the agency opened a practical secondary school in Bali to train youngsters in farming, fishing, and cottage industries after determining that its current vocational programs, which taught trades such as auto mechanics and typing, were resulting in an exodus of young people from rural areas. In Colombia, PLAN even spearheaded a "back to the farm program," which provided misguided urban migrants with the agricultural skills necessary to allow them to return to their rural communities.[6]

Vocational and agricultural education also represented renewed efforts to preserve and promote native culture, which increasingly came to the fore during the 1970s. Academic schooling, noted CCF's David Herrell, tended "to siphon off children from their own communities and backgrounds." Education tailored to the needs of developing areas, however, reinforced indigenous cultural patterns. Indeed, argued CCF executive director Verent Mills in 1975, programs for youngsters "should be on a level so that the children will not be maladjusted within their culture." In Gaza, the American Friends Service Committee trained teachers to teach children traditional folk songs and dances. Summer campers in a PLAN-sponsored camp in Manila were encouraged to take an interest in local traditions through activities with themes such as "Taking Pride in Our Heritage" and "A Tourist in Your Own Country."[7] CCF formalized its commitment to cultural integrity in a series of guidelines for projects serving indigenous communities in 1980:

> We feel that members of an indigenous community have the right to retain their culture, value system, language as they choose. We also feel that CCF affiliated projects should encourage those programs which help enhance the indigenous people's feelings of self-worth, personal dignity, cultural pride and identity.

CCF urged local workers to use native therapeutic systems and lines of authority where possible. The agency also encouraged projects to teach children in their native language and to assist in the preservation of the oral history, folk celebrations, and music of the indigenous community.[8] This focus represented the culmination of efforts to preserve native culture that had been underway since the late 1950s, even as it foreshadowed a new politics of multiculturalism that would come to the fore in the United States during the next decade. By emphasizing cultural integrity and diversity, American agencies cast themselves as the bearers of a new brand of culturally sensitive internationalism.

American agencies had long employed local citizens as child-care workers, caseworkers, and translators. By the 1970s, efforts to encourage indigenous leadership intensified, and greater numbers of local citizens were recruited to help run American agencies' programs. Promoting local leadership was a goal inherent in the New Directions mandate, and it was at once good social welfare practice and good politics. Placing native people at the helm of agency programs made them more likely to address the most pressing local needs in a culturally sensitive manner. Encouraging indigenous leadership also mitigated growing fears that Western aid to the developing world was stunting local initiative and creating long-term dependency on foreign assistance. Moreover, Western leadership had increasingly become a source of resentment among local workers. When CCF decided to appoint a native Korean to lead its Korean field office in 1970, for example, the agency's Edmund Janss noted that the appointment "will help our image here tremendously." Two years later, he reaffirmed the decision to select a native to lead the Korean office. "The outlook of the office and staff morale is changed 100% since Dr. Song took over!" Janss reported in 1972.[9]

American agencies not only hired locals as employees but also attempted to incorporate into their program designs the needs and desires of families receiving aid. SCF and CCF established local community committees, broadly representing the local population, that met regularly to define their needs and priorities and assist with the implementation of projects. "We want to help countries, their own agencies, and their citizens eventually have the capacity to serve the needs of the children in their own areas. If CCF goes in, organizes, finances, and provides the service in its own name, the accomplishment of that goal is retarded," David Herrell explained. Although many local projects were slow in fully incorporating beneficiaries into their planning and representational board structure, Herrell noted after a visit to CCF's field offices in the Philippines in 1974 that "the communication gap between the formerly-dispossessed and the benevolent providers is narrowing." PLAN also increasingly adopted a "bottom up" approach that required the direct participation of clients in the development of relevant programs. Through meetings with social workers and community workers, PLAN's recipient families in the Philippines even collaborated on the field office's budget for the 1978 fiscal year.[10]

As in the past, however, native workers' ambivalence regarding the ability of poor local families to care adequately for their children hindered American

agencies' efforts to promote indigenous rule. Indeed, efforts to include ben-
eficiary families in program planning were sometimes resisted most emphat-
ically by native workers. After visiting a number of CCF-supported projects
in Mexico in 1977, for example, Herrell was disappointed to find "somewhat
condescending and paternalistic attitudes on the part of staff toward the
poor." Staff members, Herrell noted, were reluctant to share leadership with
parents and resistant to suggestions to involve families in decisions regarding how project resources should be allocated. CCF's Sarah Manning
criticized staff in the agency's field office in Manila for their failure to allow
local projects to develop their own programs and priorities. "What came out
in their relationships to projects was like a big mother hovering over her children," Manning complained. Herrell admired two CCF-supported projects
in Brazil that decided to finance the construction of a community center by
deducting a portion of each family's monthly cash subsidy. But he worried
that the community council that had made the decision to do so was composed of local elites who did not necessarily appreciate the importance of
cash subsidies to the poorest families.[11] American agencies were successful
in promoting local leadership, but these efforts would continue to be plagued
by indigenous socioeconomic divides.

The need to adapt programs to local conditions was particularly evident
in Africa, a region on which many American child welfare organizations increasingly focused during the 1970s. The prevalence of polygamous families and nonmonetary economies confounded American voluntary workers
accustomed to channeling funds through nuclear family units. In lieu of
monthly cash grants to certain children and their families, many child-aid
programs in Africa funded community development projects that—like their
predecessors in the 1950s and 1960s—benefited all the inhabitants of an area.
In Mali, for example, PLAN established credit schemes and community
health and education projects. In Upper Volta, the organization dug wells;
planted trees; and provided local families with donkeys, plows, and construction materials. The model of aid to whole communities increasingly set the
standard for aid to children not only in Africa but also across the globe. In
communities across Latin America and Asia, too, voluntary agencies dug
wells; constructed irrigation systems; planted trees and vegetable gardens;
and built medical clinics, libraries, and schools. "As the community pros-
pers," SCF explained, "so will all the children."[12]

As international child welfare efforts increasingly focused on uplifting entire communities, programs for foreign youngsters began to occupy a smaller place on the agendas of the voluntary agencies that had never focused solely on child-care work. Enrollment in the JDC's nurseries declined sharply during the 1970s due to Jewish emigration from Iran and North Africa. Although the JDC, along with the AFSC, continued to support child welfare programs in the Middle East—the AFSC in the Gaza Strip and the JDC in Israel—both groups placed a growing emphasis on helping local populations obtain adequate housing, nutrition, and health care. The Unitarian Universalist Service Committee's formerly expansive international child welfare program had by the 1970s been replaced with efforts to promote health and human rights. Even child sponsorship organizations, which focused first and foremost on youngsters, sought to embrace new, broader identities as international development organizations charged with assisting both children and their communities at large.

American agencies' rationales for choosing which countries to assist also evolved. U.S. foreign aid, both government sponsored and private, had long targeted nations with seemingly precarious political futures. By the 1970s, however, methods of determining where to work changed. Frustrated by political insecurity that hindered their ability to work effectively, voluntary agencies now looked to nations that enjoyed relative political stability. In 1973, for example, a CCF official endorsed the agency's expansion to Brazil due to the country's "good and stable government" but questioned the advisability of working in the "less stable" countries of Bolivia, Chile, and Peru. Furthermore, the existence of poverty would come to dominate many agencies' global plans for expansion. PLAN, for example, began using statistics from the United Nations and its agencies as guidelines for determining new countries for expansion. Scrutinizing figures such as the number of doctors, the literacy rate, and the per capita daily caloric intake, PLAN officials sought to select the neediest countries on which to focus their energies. CCF also aimed to work not in political hot spots but—as David Herrell put it—in "the lesser-developed of the underdeveloped areas." "It is very important in our work to keep our assistance relevant to need," Verent Mills noted in 1974, pointing to Africa, India, Indonesia, and South America as "the areas of greatest need." CCF issued guidelines in 1976 that recommended comparing a country's per capita income to that of the United States in order to determine its level of poverty. The agency's emphasis was now on helping the "poorest of the poor." SCF, too, sought to assist the neediest populations around the world. Among the criteria considered by the agency in determining where to establish programs was inclusion on the United Nations' list of poorest nations. The bulk of the new programs initiated by the agency during the 1970s were located in the two dozen countries identified by the UN as "fourth tier," where annual per capita income was $200 or less.[13]

Poverty and political instability were not mutually exclusive, and American voluntary agencies did not entirely avoid political hot spots during the 1970s. In Ethiopia, for example, PLAN established a program that did not find favor among some of the socialist revolutionaries who overthrew Emperor Haile Selassie in 1974. In 1977, several PLAN staff members, including the agency's field director, Leslie Fox, were arrested. Fox, who was accused of being a CIA agent, was jailed for six weeks. The agency terminated its Ethiopian program shortly thereafter.[14] On the whole, however, voluntary agencies now tended to address welfare needs related to war or other political crises through short-term emergency efforts rather than long-term projects such as child sponsorships.

Integral to American voluntary agencies' efforts to assist the "poorest of the poor" were programs that helped augment families' long-term ability to earn a living. In New Delhi, CCF helped families purchase farm animals; trained parents in skills such as knitting, embroidery, tailoring, and umbrella making; and proffered loans to help families buy raw materials for making crafts. In Manila, the agency trained parents in income-generating activities such as duck raising, mushroom growing, and selling salted and pickled shellfish, a popular local delicacy. In Bali, PLAN supported projects ranging from poultry production to furniture manufacturing to pottery works. Children were also incorporated into income-generating projects. In the Dominican Republic, SCF ran youth club projects that taught youngsters poultry and hog production, sewing, embroidery, beekeeping, and rabbit raising. From Korea to Thailand to Mexico, American agencies helped mothers and fathers launch small income-generating enterprises. They also worked to establish institutions, such as credit unions, that would provide local families with the capital to start new businesses.[15] Efforts to establish income-generating schemes signaled American workers' enduring faith in entrepreneurship as a means of fighting global poverty, even as more overt efforts to cultivate *n* Achievement fell by the wayside.

Women in developing countries played a prominent role in income-generating projects. Once seen as essential to national development due to their role in shaping the next generation, women had by the mid- to late-1970s assumed a new significance due to their potential as economic producers. In a keynote speech delivered at a conference of CCF field representatives in 1977, Verent Mills quoted scholar and activist Irene Tinker: "Women . . . are not only the bearers of children, but also participants in economic activities that are essential to the family unit." CCF promoted education and vocational training for women in developing countries. SCF also worked to help unlock women's economic potential. The organization provided women's groups around the world with small business training and with loans to initiate income-generating projects, such as pig raising, sewing, basket weaving, and fruit canning. In addition, SCF made an effort to recruit more female employees. In 1976, the organization urged its field offices to hire local women to coordinate social development activities and provided funds for recruitment and training. "Women have been the single most overlooked and undervalued factor in the development process," SCF asserted.[16] The agency affirmed women's centrality to national development even as it erased two decades of efforts to marshal motherhood into the service of modernization.

In 1978, AFSC representative William Pierre questioned the effectiveness of the organization's day-care centers in Gaza in influencing children's long-term development. But he argued for the centers' continuation on the basis of their impact on the lives of teachers. "If we wish to justify the investment of money in the kindergarten program it is not because it serves 1300 children but because it gives meaningful, and valuable careers to a group of women who would otherwise have no future to look forward to other than marriage and an endless string of babies," Pierre asserted. "We are unlocking new doors, developing new careers, shaking up traditional ways of thinking about what women should and can do," CCF's David Herrell asserted in 1979. SCF noted that it followed the lead of local women in determining the appropriate scope and nature of women's labor outside the home.[17] But an emphasis on women's empowerment inevitably undermined efforts to preserve native culture and suggested that American agencies' understanding of cultural integrity remained circumscribed. Only certain elements of native culture, women's programs implied, were worthy of preservation.

Viewing women's relevance to national development in terms of income production rather than child rearing signaled a new understanding of the causes of poverty and the appropriate means of stimulating economic growth. American overseas workers increasingly located the main source of poor foreign families' woes not in deficient psychology or culture—the product of methods of child rearing—but in their material hardships. This shift reflected the declining stature of psychoanalysis within American culture by the 1970s. In a 1974 letter to a colleague, for example, PLAN's George Ross noted that many of the foreign families the agency assisted had little use for casework. "The major problem with most of our families," Ross explained, "is a lack of money and a lack of skill to earn money." When PLAN's Asbjorn Osland established a new field office in Upper Volta in 1976, he elevated the delivery of basic services over the more expansive psychologically oriented assistance long favored by the organization. "It's unlikely that social group or casework will play a role in that it's assumed one must have a modicum of physical satisfaction of human needs such as water and food prior to working with inter and intra personal difficulties," Osland noted. Augmenting parents' earnings, some voluntary workers suggested, might be the best way to improve the lives of children. "If [parents] can learn to obtain higher incomes," argued welfare consultant David P. Beverly in 1978, "they will obtain educations, health services, and better living conditions." Efforts to alter families' mentality did not go away completely—voluntary workers continued to complain of local people's "fatalism" as hindering their progress—but an emphasis on psychology was increasingly eclipsed by a focus on satisfying material needs.[18]

Focusing on communities' physical, rather than psychological, deficiencies helped American agencies distance themselves from the overt efforts to mold model citizens that had animated foreign aid projects in the past. In an era wary of master narratives of national development and skeptical of America's ability to serve as a force for good on a global scale, American agencies embraced the seemingly narrower project of meeting foreign populations' "basic needs."

A UNIVERSAL HAPPY CHILDHOOD

The notion that all countries must progress along a single path to modernity had by the 1970s been discredited. But another master narrative, that of child development, still retained its currency. Indeed, even with the decline of psychoanalysis during the late 1960s, most experts continued to conceptualize human development as a series of predetermined physical and emotional milestones along the path to adulthood. The universality of child development—the notion that a four-year-old in New York had the same physical and emotional needs as his counterpart in Nairobi—tempered the efforts of voluntary agencies to create community-specific programs for children. Even as they backed away from top-down, universal models of national development, voluntary agencies continued to promote a specific vision of happy childhood that transcended national lines. And even as they eschewed overt efforts to intervene in other nations' affairs, voluntary workers remained steadfast in their belief that child welfare was a means of reshaping the world.

The child-rearing wisdom that had informed the previous three decades of child-saving work continued to shape American-led programs for youngsters in developing countries during the 1970s, finding expression among both U.S. personnel and indigenous workers. As they had in the past, American agencies promoted free play and creative activities. In 1972, for example, AFSC workers in Gaza conducted an in-service training course for day-care workers that included instruction in singing and rhythm instruments, as well as a session in an "experiment room" where teachers could explore creative materials such as magnets, water, papier-mâché, sorting games, blocks, and construction materials. "In our kindergartens we encourage children to be creative, inventive," asserted the AFSC's Clara Hurn in 1978. PLAN's program in the Philippines enrolled young children in a toy orchestra to develop their musical talents and encouraged children as young as four to engage in painting and other creative art activities. As the American military withdrew from Vietnam, PLAN's Frank Campbell labored to create an "educational play area" for local children.[19]

"When faced with seriously malnourished children can one really justify authorizing funds, even though very limited, for a teeter-totter?" queried PLAN's Albrecht Hering in 1975. Hering answered his own question in the affirmative, lauding children's participation in recreational programs as a means of developing self-discipline and basic social skills. In Sudan in 1977, PLAN funds purchased construction materials for classrooms, the services of a veterinarian to vaccinate cattle, pipelines for water delivery systems—and a Ping-Pong table. Even as CCF increasingly focused on using culturally sensitive methods to assist "the poorest of the poor," a new set of standards for agency-supported day-care centers circulated to all CCF field offices in 1980 recommended a dizzying array of toys and educational materials.

The standards called for equipment such as "games, blocks, puzzles, art material, play equipment, etc. . . . in abundance," as well as equipment for science, art, music, water and sand play, and outdoor recreation. "Play is a way of learning for a child and has the same meaning for him that work or play does for an adult," the standards noted. "If we are to move from superficial care to meaningful day care, then centers must be willing to invest in equipment and materials."[20] Creativity, play, and toys remained essential ingredients of a happy and constructive childhood.

Voluntary workers also continued to emphasize the importance of providing children with love and understanding rather than discipline. In 1974, for example, PLAN's field office in Ecuador ran training sessions for parents on how to handle their children that emphasized the cultivation of "mutual respect" over the use of "a big stick." American-led programs also continued to stress the importance of love and emotional security during youngsters' formative years, a sentiment now often echoed by local workers. "We could use the term 'unfinished' in referring to a child, that his development will depend upon his environment, in his acceptance by others, and upon his relationship with people, objects, and situations. . . . He must be loved to learn to love those who surround him," noted Maria Angela Gama, a Brazilian social worker, in a 1977 article published in CCF's newsletter. Case histories of families written by indigenous social workers in Latin America in 1980 gave as much attention to families' emotional relationships as to their material hardships. Social workers in Bolivia praised a family in which "the mother acts as a friend and companion of her daughters" and criticized another in which the father "is a little severe and treats his family with no[t] much kindness." From India to Iran, American voluntary workers and their indigenous colleagues continued their efforts to provide children with a sense of love and familial security.[21]

In a 1973 training guidebook for indigenous CCF caseworkers, Edmund Janss provided a veiled suggestion that child-rearing practices were crucially dependent on class- and national-specific living conditions and values. "Middle Class families in the Western World often place great stress on permissiveness and gentleness. These parents can afford this, since there is enough room in the homes, there are usually few children, carefully spaced, and they live in good neighborhoods, etc.," he wrote. But although Janss noted that families in different cultures might feed, hold, or swaddle babies in various manners, nowhere in his guidebook did he suggest that native parents and child-care workers depart from the "permissiveness and gentleness" that characterized middle-class child rearing in the West.[22]

Voluntary workers also continued to laud the transformative power of letters from foster parents. The winter 1977 issue of CCF's *World News* carried anecdotes from around the world about young emotional lives transformed by simple missives from across the ocean. Nine-year-old Ah Yu, a disabled boy in Hong Kong, was belligerent and failing in school until he began corresponding with American foster parents: "It changed his whole life to know that someone cared about him besides his mother." Three-year-old Maria in Argentina, neglected by her new stepfather, was also a changed child after she was matched with a sponsor in the United States. "Although her home conditions are no different, these are more than compensated for by the knowledge that she is wanted by someone she has never even seen," an Argentinean field representative asserted. Upon receiving letters from her sponsor, Noreen, a shy, withdrawn child in India, became an "active, cooperative child," who took a new interest in her studies and extracurricular activities. "The love and concern of her sponsor," asserted field representative C. I. Mathunni, "had brought about this remarkable change in Noreen's life." Notes from foster parents acquired an almost mystical quality, thoroughly transforming the lives of their young recipients. Voluntary workers also described the act of letter writing itself as serving a therapeutic function for children. At a 1977 conference of CCF field representatives, some workers described children's correspondence with sponsors as a means of helping children to express their feelings, especially in cultures that generally put a premium on emotional reticence.[23]

Child sponsorship continued to serve as an important means of cross-cultural communication, exposing both children and their foster parents to ways of life entirely different from their own. But cross-cultural communication was not always easy to facilitate. In some nations, particularly in Africa, the act of writing letters had no place in native culture. Nor were American foster parents universally well equipped to write meaningful letters to their sponsored children. "The focus of much donor correspondence, while reflecting general good-will, is uninformed, sometimes culturally insensitive, and often self-interested," SCF noted. But rather than abolish letters in cultures in which they were alien, child sponsorship agencies decided instead to train local workers and children in the art of correspondence. In 1978, PLAN organized a letter-writing course for indigenous workers in Sierra

Leone who had never before penned a missive. A conference of CCF workers from South Asia and Africa also devoted a day to improving the quality of children's letters. Voluntary workers identified the problems and the positive features of children's correspondence, studied a model letter, and engaged in role-playing. Since thank-you notes were incongruous to Asian culture, local CCF workers decided to call them "child expression letters."[24] Efforts to preserve native culture ultimately faltered when it came to abolishing letters, which were the financial and emotional lifeblood of child sponsorship agencies.

Indeed, while American organizations encouraged cultural integrity, their commitment to the preservation of native culture in the context of child rearing went only so far. This was evidenced in a controversy surrounding the Children's Garden in the Philippines in 1974. Like its larger counterpart in Hong Kong, Children's Garden in Manila had been constructed by CCF during the 1950s on the "cottage plan" in an effort to provide orphaned and abandoned children with a sense of familial security. By the mid-1970s, CCF no longer owned or operated the institution, but the agency still provided it with financial support. In 1974, at CCF's request, Ahti Hailuoto, one of the vice presidents of the International Union for Child Welfare, inspected the institution.

Hailuoto's assessment of Children's Garden in Manila, as reported by field director Alton Gould, was bleak. Hailuoto expressed concerns about the general atmosphere of the home, which he characterized as far too rigid. Youngsters were expected to look after themselves and to perform all of the household chores. The children, Hailuoto complained, were never allowed to relax; they were expected to rise at 5:00 or 5:30 in the morning and go to bed at 9:30 in the evening, even on vacation. Housemothers were untrained and displayed a marked ignorance of child-care principles, sometimes resorting to corporal punishment. The home did not have any psychologists or psychiatrists on staff. Moreover, Hailuoto charged, the children were accorded absolutely no privacy, which stifled their imaginations. "Children love to 'day dream.' This is conducive to growth but in the Garden a child is not allowed to 'dream or have any personal privacy,'" Gould reported.[25]

Ester Pangindian, Children's Garden's superintendent, denied the charges of inappropriate punishment and the hiring of untrained workers. But she defended the other child-care practices criticized by Hailuoto as an expression of native cultural values. "You know our set-up here regarding the cottages," Pangindian wrote in a 1974 letter to Verent Mills. "It was not really made for individual private rooms like an American home but patterned after our own culture the Filipino way."[26] A club consisting of both native Filipinos and American expatriate women who volunteered at Children's Garden rallied to Pangindian's defense. They, too, used the language of cultural integrity, noting in a letter to CCF:

> To expect sudden "modernizations" or changes of method according to the latest American practices is unreasonable when imposed upon this very ancient and totally different culture. Mrs. Pangindian prepares her children to live in their own culture, at their own level. A foreigner coming in for even a few days or weeks could not possibly understand the ramifications of her problems.[27]

But arguments for cultural integrity did not hold much clout in the context of perceived breaches of acceptable child welfare practices. CCF officials paid little heed to cultural justifications.[28]

While many of the programs for children advocated by American workers during the 1970s differed little from their predecessors in previous decades, others reframed traditional child-rearing wisdom. For example, efforts to combat world hunger increasingly assumed a place on voluntary agencies' overseas agendas. In 1976, CCF initiated Hope for the Hungry, a dedicated effort to fight hunger around the globe. This initiative, funded separately from the agency's sponsorship programs, distributed high protein foods and educated families regarding the kinds of local fare most nutritious for children. In 1978, the JDC collaborated with two other voluntary agencies to found the Interfaith Hunger Appeal, which focused on relieving world hunger.[29] Nutrition programs such as Hope for the Hungry and the Interfaith Hunger Appeal emphasized long-term development rather than relief, aiming to combat malnutrition in lieu of feeding children made hungry due to war or other catastrophic events.

Nutritional programs provided hard data regarding their results, allowing agencies to address one of the chief points of criticism that had emerged from the Mondale investigation: the lack of quantifiable evidence of accomplishments. In 1976, for example, PLAN's field office in Tumaco, Colombia, established a Height and Weight Control Program for undernourished children. The agency provided children with nutritional supplements and their mothers with lessons in child feeding. Voluntary workers weighed and measured children monthly to gauge the effectiveness of the program. If a child's growth pattern appeared to be stunted, PLAN workers met with mothers to devise an appropriate nutritional intervention.[30] Nutritional programs provided quantifiable evidence of their effectiveness in the form of added pounds and inches. In addition, they helped American agencies situate their work with children overseas in the seemingly dispassionate realm of nutritional science.

But nutritional programs did not represent a complete break from the past. Psychoanalysts had long cast early childhood as a crucial period of personality formation, describing the loving bonds between mothers and their children as the key to youngsters' healthy personality development. New research in the field of nutritional science reaffirmed the importance of early childhood interventions, portraying nutritional intake during children's youngest years as a pivotal determinant of future health. "Recent biological research indicates that protein deficiencies in the early years of life have a depressing effect on future physical and mental development," a task force on international development reported to President Richard Nixon in 1970. Voluntary workers echoed these sentiments. "Recent research has shown that children under two years of age are particularly vulnerable to brain damage as a result of poor nutrition and that such damage is not reversible," PLAN's Frank Ryan asserted in 1977. A set of guidelines circulated among PLAN workers on combating malnutrition in the preschool child stated that "a child's entire life is determined in large measure by the food his mother gives him during his first five years." Substituting "love" for "food," the sentence could have been penned by John Bowlby in 1951. Although nutritional programs acknowledged that malnutrition was often the result of poverty, they sometimes blamed mothers just as much as food shortages. PLAN's guidelines, for example, advised workers to "attack the scourge of infant malnutrition at its source—maternal ignorance." Understandings of malnutrition updated and recast long-standing discourses regarding maternal responsibility and blame. Indeed, nutrition provided a scientific justification for early childhood interventions just as strictly psychoanalytic rationales were falling out of favor.[31]

Like income-generation and other poverty-alleviation projects, nutritional programs were emblematic of American agencies' efforts to focus narrowly on "basic needs" and to distance themselves from the overtly political goals, such as combating communism, that had animated welfare programs in the past. But the consistencies between child welfare programs at midcentury and those of the 1970s demonstrate just how successful American agencies had been in expanding the very definition of children's basic needs to include elements—familial affection, toys, opportunities for creativity—that arguably went beyond the basic requirements for child survival. While rhetorically embracing a pared-down, culturally sensitive program of child assistance, voluntary organizations continued to promote methods of child rearing rooted in Western conceptions of childhood. Even as they sought to strip child welfare of its connections to democracy and capitalism, child rearing remained a means of reshaping the world and its inhabitants.

A NEW GLOBAL POLITICS OF COMPASSION

During the 1970s, American agencies attempted to broaden their pool of donors, setting their sights beyond the borders of the United States. This move was prompted in part by a shrinking base of supporters within the country, resulting from the economic downturn and the declining profile of foreign aid. Efforts to recruit foreign donors also reflected a conscious move on the part of American-based agencies to cultivate a more international identity. Once eager to represent the United States abroad—Charles R. Joy had requested that his agency's overseas donations be stamped with the American flag in 1947—American voluntary organizations were by the 1970s attempting to move beyond their national affiliation in favor of an increasingly global one. Child sponsorship agencies, in particular, began to actively seek out foreign nationals to serve as foster parents. As the 1970s progressed, Canadian, Australian, Dutch, Danish, German, Taiwanese, Japanese, and Korean citizens joined the ranks of sponsors. Foreign foster parents sometimes supported needy children within their own countries, as in the case of Taiwan. But in most instances they, too, supported child welfare efforts overseas.[32]

American child sponsorship agencies' internal organization evolved to meet the needs of their increasingly global donor base. In 1973, PLAN created a new entity, Foster Parents Plan International, which coordinated the activities of fund-raising branches in the United States, Canada, and Australia, as well as a number of field offices overseas. As some of the nations assisted by CCF acquired the ability to care for their own needy children, the agency encouraged them to develop local independent affiliates. During the 1970s and 1980s, citizens in Australia, Canada, Denmark, Great Britain, Germany,

Japan, Korea, Hong Kong, and Taiwan established locally funded agencies that set their own aid-giving priorities and functioned as CCF's "international partners." SCF did not itself solicit international sponsors, but the organization worked to cultivate a more global identity. In the late 1970s, SCF joined together with Save the Children agencies in Canada, Great Britain, Norway, and Denmark to establish the International Save the Children Alliance, an umbrella organization that facilitated collaboration across national lines. The national agencies in the alliance had long shared the Save the Children moniker but had worked entirely independently from one another. Alliance members met yearly and cooperated on fund-raising and field projects.[33]

An increasingly international profile of donors and affiliates helped American organizations shed their associations with U.S. foreign policy and forge a new global humanitarian identity. But memories of American prominence in the field of overseas aid took longer to fade. When a group of German CCF representatives visited a community social welfare project in Brazil supported by German sponsors in 1979, for example, they found that the youngsters in the project had no idea that their benefactors were not Americans. "It was evident that the children didn't know that Germany was not in the USA. The German sponsors are always understood to be Americans. For these children apparently only one foreign country exists, and this is the United States," the representatives noted.[34]

Even as child welfare agencies sought to transcend narrow nationalistic concerns, national histories of imperialism and occupation continued to shape their programs in subtle ways. Foster parents in the Netherlands overwhelmingly preferred to sponsor children in Indonesia, a former Dutch colony. CCF's Japanese affiliate, the Christian Child Welfare Association of Japan (CCWA), chose to sponsor children in Korea and the Philippines, nations once occupied by the Japanese. "CCWA is in Korea and the Philippines because we Japanese are very conscious of what we did in the war," explained Takeshi Kobayashi, the agency's national director. Many of CCWA's most enthusiastic sponsors were former soldiers.[35]

Child sponsorship provided citizens with a means of atoning for their nations' perceived imperial sins, even as it naturalized the notion that certain countries reserved the right to intervene in other nations. Sponsorship agencies cultivated a more global identity, but they also reified the division between recipient and benefactor, between the global North and South. Indeed, the countries extending support to children overseas were precisely those that had by the 1970s become part of the developed world, with relatively robust economies and a sizable middle class. The internationalization of child sponsorship situated the act of aid-giving itself as an emblem of development and a signification of stature within the world community. International child welfare remained deeply embedded in larger global relations of power.

*   *   *

In March 1979, as Israeli Prime Minister Menachem Begin and Egyptian President Anwar Sadat marked the signing of a Middle East peace treaty in Washington, D.C., their wives ventured elsewhere in the U.S. capital. Aliza Begin and Jehan Sadat paid a joint visit to the Capital Children's Museum to commemorate the United Nations' proclamation of 1979 as the International Year of the Child (IYC). The women's decision to celebrate the IYC in the midst of affirming their countries' desire to make peace was not coincidental. Established by UN proclamation in December 1976, the IYC reflected a growing global awareness of the perceived connections between child development and global peace, prosperity, and progress. The yearlong event, commemorated by 160 nations around the world, was an opportunity for nations and private agencies alike to focus their attention on the needs of children and to mobilize resources on their behalf. "The full and effective realization of the rights of the child," noted the secretary-general of the UN, Kurt Waldheim, "have a direct bearing on the economic and social development of every community and every nation and would thus help to make ours a richer and more tranquil world." Tara Ali Baig, the president of the International Union for Child Welfare, expressed similar sentiments: "Care for each stage of every child's growth is imperative if nations are to prosper."[36]

The IYC showcased an increasingly universalized vision of childhood. "There is a growing global consciousness that children everywhere are alike and that the world of children is indivisible," noted Estefania Aldaba-Lim, a clinical psychologist and former secretary of social services and development in the Philippines, who served as a special representative for the IYC.[37] The advocacy work and publicity surrounding the IYC highlighted the extent to which the vision of childhood advocated by American agencies and their foreign allies had become the global standard to which all childhoods were held. Familial affection, individualized attention, and creative play had become the universal recipe for a happy and healthy childhood—and a widely accepted prerequisite to national development.

The IYC demonstrated the increasingly global character of international child welfare efforts, but it also highlighted continuities between American child-saving efforts at midcentury and those of the late 1970s. American voluntary agencies had expanded their programs, changed their emphases, and overhauled the means by which aid to children was delivered. But agencies' understandings of the core tenets of a good childhood remained largely constant. While uniform prescriptions for international development fell out of favor, an understanding of child development that saw the needs of children as the same everywhere retained its currency. And even as voluntary workers disentangled child welfare from efforts to fight communism and promote democracy, the conviction that helping children was a route to uplifting nations would bind a new generation to the American mission of raising the world.

Epilogue

Raising Children, Uplifting the World

DURING THE SUMMER OF 1962, the missile cruiser USS *Boston,* docked in Boston harbor, prepared to depart for a mission to the Mediterranean. The ship had served as part of the Pacific fleet during World War II, supporting the invasion of Guam, the raid on Okinawa, and the assault on Japan. During the 1950s, after being outfitted with antiaircraft missile launchers, the cruiser participated in NATO exercises in the North Atlantic and in the U.S. military intervention in Lebanon. But on this warm day in August 1962, as Captain Richard G. Colbert welcomed aboard a group of seven civilians, the USS *Boston* was preparing for a very different type of mission. Upon arriving at the ports of Athens and Naples, the ship's crew would be hosting parties for Greek and Italian children sponsored by American families. On this August day, the men of the USS *Boston* shared their plans for the celebrations with seven Boston-area foster parents and appointed seven sailors to serve as "special emissaries" to the foster children overseas. Crew members looked at children's photographs and letters and promised to convey the love and good wishes of the seven foster parents to their sponsored youngsters on the other side of the world.[1]

The symbolic retrofitting of the USS *Boston* as a site for children's celebrations is a powerful emblem of the way in which American child welfare supported the United States' growing global hegemony during the decades following World War II. American voluntary agencies working with children overseas filtered American power through the soft prism of familial love, seeking to connect the United States and its allies around the world through the bonds of international friendship. By matching foreign youngsters with foster parents in the United States, American agencies endeavored to create ties of fictive kinship that would prove more durable than political alliances forged by governments. They also looked to child sponsorships, and to child rearing more generally, as a form of social engineering. Marshaling the insights of the sciences of child psychology and human development in the service of U.S. foreign relations, American workers attempted to mold youngsters with the personal characteristics—emotional security, creativity, self-reliance—they understood to be conducive to international development and progress.

American-led programs for foreign children cloaked the United States' global ascendance in the mantle of humanitarianism. But while American child welfare workers appropriated the rhetoric and aims of U.S. anticommunism and modernization efforts, they also reworked these ideas to suit their own ends. So, too, did the hundreds of thousands of ordinary families, both in the United States and around the world, who participated in American agencies' child welfare programs. Poor foreign families enrolled their children in U.S.-supported day nurseries, attended mothers' meetings, encouraged their children to write to foster parents, and accepted American material aid when it was proffered. But they often failed to rear their children according to the precepts prescribed by the American workers with whom they interacted. Even parents and child-care workers who appeared to adopt new methods in whole or in part sometimes did so in different ways, or for different reasons, than American experts anticipated.

Programs for children overseas broadcast American agencies' confidence about American child-rearing methods and about American society as a whole. Voluntary workers' reverence for creativity, self-reliance, and freedom of thought served as a rebuke to the repressive Communist state. Their reliance on mothers and fathers (or substitute parents) to rear good citizens contrasted sharply with the perceived low regard in which the family was held in Communist lands. But American efforts on behalf of foreign children also betrayed larger insecurities and inconsistencies. American agencies lauded the self-reliant entrepreneur and the creative freethinker at a time when the rise of big corporations and the culture of conformity led many commentators to question the viability of these character types within the United States itself. And even as American agencies advanced a vision of the family as the optimal site for rearing children, voluntary workers designed programs that removed children from the influence of their parents. Day-care centers and schools trained children in new habits of thought and action. Foster parents in the United States tried to impart new ideals from across the sea. And American-supported orphanages offered material and educational benefits that many mothers and fathers were unable to provide themselves, leading scores of poor parents to relinquish their children in hopes of securing for them a better life.

Children themselves were the objects of American assistance, but they were also agents who shaped the outcomes of U.S.-led programs across the globe. Sponsored children cultivated individual relationships with foster parents, relationships that frequently spanned multiple years and sometimes evolved in ways unanticipated by either voluntary agencies or participants themselves. Through thousands of letters sent around the world, American foster parents might have been successful in cultivating in the minds of some foreign youngsters a new image of the United States. But so, too, did children around the globe reshape Americans' understandings of the world and of their place within it.

In the years following World War II, American agencies portrayed their efforts on behalf of children as fulfilling both humanitarian and political aims. Since familial love, individualized attention, and creative play were considered to be conducive both to healthy personality development and to the promotion of democracy, American organizations were able to serve at once as apolitical child savers and as Cold Warriors and modernizers. During the late 1960s and early 1970s, the unpopular war in Southeast Asia, rising anti-American sentiments worldwide, and the sinking profile of U.S. foreign aid led American agencies working with children overseas to attempt to distance themselves from official U.S. foreign policy goals. But American international child welfare work had become too closely tied to global politics to successfully retreat behind a shield of disinterested benevolence. Indeed, less than five years after the footsteps of American-sponsored children echoed on its decks, the USS *Boston* was back in the Pacific, firing thousands of rounds of shells at targets in North and South Vietnam.

By the mid-1970s, American international child welfare agencies had come to espouse a novel set of foreign-aid dictates. Many American organizations eschewed work in political hot spots and focused instead on assisting the citizens of the world's poorest nations in gaining access to basic needs such as adequate nutrition, clean water, and medical care. While projects during the post–World War II period focused on saving individual war orphans, the programs of the 1970s aimed more frequently to aid youngsters by assisting whole communities. Whereas earlier projects often met emergency needs, those initiated during the 1970s took as their goal long-term development. Programs in the past had highlighted American leadership, while more recent endeavors sought to draw on local resources and personnel. What remained consistent throughout the history of American efforts to assist children overseas was the conviction that helping youngsters was not only an end unto itself. The notion that programs on behalf of children were a means of molding nations and, ultimately, reshaping the world animated several generations of American overseas workers and foster parents alike.

A potent symbol of the inextricable entanglement of American humanitarianism and U.S. global expansionism, the USS *Boston* also serves as a reminder of the tenuous nature of American power, and the ongoing adaptation and reinvention necessary to remain relevant globally. In 1970, shortly following her tour of duty off the coast of Vietnam, the USS *Boston* was decommissioned; her technology had become obsolete. Five years later, she was sold for scrap metal.

* * *

On September 23, 1990, as twilight descended slowly across the globe, thousands of men and women gathered together in parks and other public places, lit candles in hand. In 1,200 cities and towns across the United States and around the world, candlelight vigils aimed to bring attention to the needs of a group both quite specific and remarkably broad—the children of the world. In particular, the vigils were a show of support for the World Summit for Children, a meeting to be held at the United Nations in New York the following weekend.[2]

The largest gathering of heads of state ever to convene at the UN, the World Summit for Children drew more than seventy world leaders, including U.S. President George Bush and Soviet President Mikhail Gorbachev. Participants discussed the needs of children worldwide, approving a declaration containing a set of ambitious goals that included reducing infant and maternal mortality, combating malnutrition, and providing all children with access to safe drinking water and a basic education. At the heart of the World Summit for Children was the conviction that improving the lives of children was essential to the development and progress of all nations.[3]

When the World Summit for Children convened, the Soviet grip on Eastern Europe had loosened, the Berlin Wall had fallen, and just the next year, the Soviet Union itself would cease to exist. Some attendees voiced hope that the end of the Cold War might free up money that would have been spent on armaments to be devoted instead to the well-being of children. Most nations' military spending had long dwarfed their social welfare budgets, and the calls for a "peace dividend" for children were timely. But these calls also effectively erased child welfare's long entanglement with the Cold War itself. The global conflict had added impetus to American child welfare efforts, even as the project of amassing the arsenals of war drew resources that might have otherwise been devoted to social welfare programs. American programs on behalf of foreign children had been at once humanitarian gestures and a means of achieving U.S. dominance within a divided world order.

The World Summit for Children and the activism surrounding it showcased the paramount position of the "world's children" in the late twentieth-century popular consciousness, not only in the United States but also across the globe. It demonstrated the persistent—if now often unstated—connections between child welfare and international development and peace. The summit also highlighted the extent to which "the world's children" had become a discrete, unified entity. The World Summit meeting and the candlelight vigils that preceded it rested on the notion that youngsters the world over had the same needs, rights, and desires, and that the welfare of children was a responsibility that fell on governments and private organizations alike. These were ideas that American child welfare agencies working abroad had helped put into circulation during the decades following the Second World War.

During the closing decades of the twentieth century and the opening decades of the twenty-first, American child welfare organizations' programs overseas continued to reflect both the evolution of humanitarian aid giving and the shifting currents of world politics. As the twentieth century wound down, American organizations maintained a focus on assisting the poorest nations, but they also reached out to assist children affected by political upheavals and other disasters. They worked to help Southeast Asian refugees; South African children traumatized by violence; youngsters in Bosnia-Herzegovina and Rwanda; and, in the aftermath of the collapse of the Soviet

Union, families in the former Soviet republics. Indeed, the disintegration of the Soviet Union gave American agencies a new opportunity to promote democracy through programs of child welfare. American agencies also devoted growing attention to groups of foreign children in need of particular forms of assistance, such as children with special needs. As the international aid community became increasingly concerned with promoting gender equity during the 1990s, some U.S.-based groups designed programs to help eliminate the particular obstacles faced by female children.

In 2013, an estimated 9.14 million children received support through formal programs of child sponsorship; millions of additional children received assistance through other child welfare programs spearheaded by international organizations. While the lion's share of sponsored children today receives support through U.S.-based agencies, agencies in the United Kingdom, France, Canada, Italy, Australia, Denmark, Spain, Germany, and other countries also support children in significant numbers. A recent study conducted by three economists—one of the first to empirically analyze the long-term effects of child sponsorship—found that children in six developing countries who had participated in a sponsorship program remained in school for longer than their peers had and were, as adults, more likely to have white collar jobs. The economists described the most significant impact of the sponsorship program they studied as psychological. "It may be that the internal constraints of the poor also contribute to poverty traps in important ways," they wrote.[4] Children's minds remain a fertile site for interventions aiming to uplift the world.

As American experts continue to draw on the sciences of child psychology and human development in efforts to improve society, they increasingly set their sights on the United States in addition to the world at large. A growing number of American physicians and psychologists argue that a stressful familial environment during early childhood, or even before birth, can undermine children's mental development and predispose them to developing personality characteristics that make it more difficult to escape poverty. Today, as in the past, many commentators position familial love and affection during early childhood as both a prerequisite to adult mental health and a means of reshaping the social order. In a recent column, *New York Times* writer Nicholas D. Kristof dubbed attentive and affectionate parenting "a poverty solution that starts with a hug." "The most cost-effective way to address poverty isn't necessarily housing vouchers or welfare initiatives or prison-building,"

Kristof wrote in another column. "Rather, it may be early childhood education and parenting programs." Indeed, Save the Children (as Save the Children Federation is now known) runs programs in Appalachia that train mothers to more actively interact with their children through hugs, storytelling, and reading books. Love and attention during early childhood, this program and others imply, have the power to shape a generation equipped to pull itself out of poverty.[5]

By rooting social and economic development in the nursery, American commentators continue to endow the role of parents, particularly mothers, with far-reaching significance. But in locating the roots of deep-seated societal ills in the soil of the family circle, they persist in encouraging outside intervention into the intimate sphere of the family in the name of social progress. By focusing on personal transformations, they also serve to downplay (often unintentionally) the importance of government-supported social welfare programs. The perceived connections between poverty and early childhood development demonstrate the sustained entanglement of child-rearing methods with notions of class: the methods of child care advocated by experts as a means of fighting poverty are most easily adopted by parents with the resources, education, and time needed to put them into practice.

To many today, the idea of building world peace and global development through programs of assistance to children may appear trite or clichéd. Images of suffering foreign children routinely peer down at us from billboards; they lurk in the advertisements at the corners of our computer screens as we browse the Internet. E-mail and social media have accelerated communication across continents, facilitating the growth of international friendships and encouraging public participation in activism and aid projects. But foreign children are at once closer than ever and even more remote. Just as child sponsorship promised Americans the satisfaction of helping a needy child while reducing the burden of parenting to a monthly letter, contemporary aid efforts now often ask little more of their supporters than the click of a cursor.

Now, as in the past, child welfare agencies portray helping children as more than a mere act of benevolence: assisting a youngster remains a way to reshape, if only slightly, the contours of the world order. But the current ubiquity of the idea that children are key players in achieving international harmony and progress obscures the radical potential that the notion held at midcentury. In the aftermath of World War II, the idea that methods of child rearing had the potential to forestall another global cataclysm unleashed un-bridled optimism about the future of the international community and about the nature of humanity itself. The notion that monumental societal changes had their roots in the malleable clay of human personality catalyzed a gen-eration of Americans—child welfare professionals and ordinary citizens alike—to work toward improving the world by intervening in the lives of children. Americans' commitment to reshaping the global order by molding its youngest members would remain constant even as the vision of the new world they sought to create was reconfigured by the tensions of the Cold War and by the political shifts of the Vietnam era. The frequency with which children assume a central role in contemporary appeals for international de-velopment and peace is, at least in part, a testament to the success of Amer-ican agencies in forging a persistent link between global politics, childhood, and the science of human development.

Abbreviations

Andover-Harvard Theological Library • Cambridge, Massachusetts
   Charles Rhind Joy Papers, bMS 347 (CRJ)
   Records of the Unitarian and Unitarian Universalist Service Committees (USC)
      Unitarian Service Committee Administrative Records, bMS 16011
      Unitarian Service Committee Administrative Records, bMS 16035
      Unitarian Service Committee Administrative Records, bMS 16171
      Unitarian Service Committee Medical Missions Records, bMS 16103
      Unitarian Service Committee Records of the Director, Child and Youth
         Projects, bMS 16036
      Unitarian Service Committee Social Work and Education Overseas Project
         Records: Cambodian Teacher Education Project, bMS 16008
      Unitarian Universalist Service Committee Administrative Records, bMS 16102
      Unitarian Universalist Service Committee, International Programs
         Administrative Records: International Service Projects, bMS 16026
      Unitarian Service Committee Medical Programs—Director, Administrative
         Records, bMS 16025

Arthur and Elizabeth Schlesinger Library on the History of Women in America, Radcliffe Institute
for Advanced Study, Harvard University • Cambridge, Massachusetts
   Martha May Eliot Papers (ME)

Center for Creative Photography, University of Arizona • Tucson, Arizona
   Helen Gee Papers (HG)

ChildFund International • Richmond, Virginia
   Records of Christian Children's Fund (CCF)

Columbia University Rare Book & Manuscript Library • New York, New York
   Katharine F. Lenroot Papers (KL)
   Paul Baerwald Papers (PB)

Girl Scout National Historic Preservation Center (GS) • New York, New York
   Defense Collection
   American Legion Controversy Collection

Harry S. Truman Library • Independence, Missouri
   Alice H. Pollard Papers (AHP)

Harvard University Archives • Cambridge, Massachusetts
   David C. McClelland Papers (DM)

Library of Congress • Washington, DC
   Margaret Mead Papers (MM)

Minnesota Historical Society (MHS) • St. Paul, Minnesota
   St. Cloud State Reformatory Subject Files
   Walter F. Mondale Papers

National Archives and Records Administration (NA) • College Park, Maryland

RG 43 Records of International Conferences, Commissions, and Expositions

RG 59 General Records of the Department of State

RG 84 Records of the Foreign Service Posts of the Department of State

RG 102 Records of the Children's Bureau

RG 306 Records of the U.S. Information Agency

RG 331 Records of Allied Operational and Occupation Headquarters, World War II

RG 466 Records of the U.S. High Commissioner for Germany

RG 469 Records of U.S. Foreign Assistance Agencies, 1948–1961

RG 472 Records of the United States Forces in Southeast Asia, 1950–1975

New York Public Library, Astor, Lenox, and Tilden Foundations • New York, New York

CARE Records (CARE)

Ernst Papanek Papers (EP)

United China Relief Records

New York Public Library for the Performing Arts, Dance Collection, Astor, Lenox, and Tilden Foundations • New York, New York

José Limón Papers (JL)

Save the Children • Westport, Connecticut

Records of Save the Children Federation (SCF)

State Historical Society of Missouri Research Center, University of Missouri • St. Louis, Missouri

Margaret A. Hickey Papers (MH)

Tamiment Library & Robert F. Wagner Labor Archives, New York University Library • New York, New York

Jewish Labor Committee Records (JLC)

United Nations Archives • New York, New York

International Year of the Child, Container S-0990-009: United Nations Emergency and Relief Operations

University at Albany, State University of New York, M. E. Grenander Department of Special Collections and Archives • Albany, New York

Records of the Psi Gamma Sorority and Alumnae Association, Inc. (PG)

University of Rhode Island, Special Collections Department • Kingston, Rhode Island

Casey Miller (Foster Parents' Plan) Letters (CM)

Records of Foster Parents Plan International, Inc., Volume 1 (FPPv1)

Records of Foster Parents Plan International, Inc., Volume 2 (FPP)

Wisconsin Historical Society • Madison, Wisconsin

Rod Serling Papers (RS)

Yale University Divinity School Library, Special Collections • New Haven, Connecticut
   Records of the China's Children Fund (CCFY)

Yeshiva University, Mendel Gottesman Library, Special Collections • New York, New York
   Rescue Children, Inc. Collection (RC)

YIVO Institute for Jewish Research, Center for Jewish History • New York, New York
   Records of the German-Jewish Children's Aid, RG 249 (GJCA)

Notes

PROLOGUE

1. Soon Ok to Casey Miller, January 1968, Folder 4, Box 1, CM.

2. Soon Ok Case History, March 1959, ibid.

3. Michael Barnett, *Empire of Humanity: A History of Humanitarianism* (Ithaca, NY: Cornell University Press, 2011), 112; Michael H. Hunt, *The American Ascendancy: How the United States Gained & Wielded Global Dominance* (Chapel Hill: University of North Carolina Press, 2007); Nicolaus Mills, *Winning the Peace: The Marshall Plan & America's Coming of Age as a Superpower* (Hoboken, NJ: John Wiley & Sons, 2008); Samuel Hale Butterfield, *U.S. Development Aid—an Historic First: Achievements and Failures in the Twentieth Century* (Westport, CT: Praeger Publishers, 2004); John Fousek, *To Lead the Free World: American Nationalism and the Cultural Roots of the Cold War* (Chapel Hill: University of North Carolina Press, 2000); Donald W. White, *The American Century: The Rise & Decline of the United States as a World Power* (New Haven, CT: Yale University Press, 1996). On the history of American overseas philanthropy, see also Merle Curti, *American Philanthropy Abroad: A History* (New Brunswick, NJ: Rutgers University Press, 1963).

4. "Evelyn Peters," 2001, Folder JDC Admin., Personnel, Indiv., Peters, Evelyn 1/2001, JDC.

5. Helen Tieszen, telephone interview by author, December 12, 2011.

6. Ann Laura Stoler, ed., *Haunted by Empire: Geographies of Intimacy in North American History* (Durham, NC: Duke University Press, 2006); Naoko Shibusawa,

America's Geisha Ally: Reimagining the Japanese Enemy (Cambridge, MA: Harvard University Press, 2006); Laura Briggs, "Mother, Child, Race, Nation: The Visual Iconography of Rescue and the Politics of Transnational and Transracial Adoption," *Gender & History* 15, no. 2 (August 2003): 179–200, and "Making 'American' Families: Transnational Adoption and U.S. Latin America Policy," in *Haunted by Empire,* 344–365; Ann Laura Stoler, *Carnal Knowledge and Imperial Power: Race and the Intimate in Colonial Rule* (Berkeley: University of California Press, 2002); Emily S. Rosenberg, *Financial Missionaries to the World: The Politics and Culture of Dollar Diplomacy, 1900–1930* (Durham, NC: Duke University Press, 2003), and *Spreading the American Dream: American Economic and Cultural Expansion, 1890–1945* (New York: Hill and Wang, 1982). See also Donna Alvah, *Unofficial Ambassadors: American Military Families Overseas and the Cold War, 1946–1965* (New York: New York University Press, 2007); Christian G. Appy, ed., *Cold War Constructions: The Political Culture of United States Imperialism, 1945–1966* (Amherst: University of Massachusetts Press, 2000); and Cynthia Enloe, *Bananas, Beaches, and Bases: Making Feminist Sense of International Politics,* updated ed. (Berkeley: University of California Press, 2000), 93–123.

7. "Adventures in World Friendship," 1947–1948, Louisville Public Schools, Louisville, Kentucky, Folder AYFWY 1948, Box 13, EP.

8. On transnational adoption, see, for example, Laura Briggs, *Somebody's Children: The Politics of Transracial and Transnational Adoption* (Durham, NC: Duke University Press, 2012); Karen Balcom, *The Traffic in Babies: Cross-Border Adoption and Baby-Selling between the United States and Canada, 1930–1972* (Toronto: University of Toronto Press, 2011); Karen Dubinsky, *Babies without Borders: Adoption and Migration across the Americas* (New York: New York University Press, 2010); Diana Marre and Laura Briggs, eds., *International Adoption: Global Inequalities and the Circulation of Children* (New York: New York University Press, 2009); Arissa Oh, *To Save the Children of Korea: The Cold War Origins of International Adoption* (Redwood City, CA: Stanford University Press, 2015), and "A New Kind of Missionary Work: Christians, Christian Americanists, and the Adoption of Korean GI Babies, 1955–1961," *Women's Studies Quarterly* 33, no. 3/4 (Fall 2005): 161–188; Catherine Ceniza Choy and Gregory Paul Choy, "Transformative Terrains: Korean American Adoptees and the Social Constructions of an American Childhood," in Caroline Levander and Carol Singley, eds., *The American Child: A Cultural Studies Reader* (New Brunswick, NJ: Rutgers University Press, 2003), 262–279. Two recent works that consider international child welfare outside the context of transnational adoption are Tarah Brookfield, *Cold War Comforts: Canadian Women, Child Safety, and Global Insecurity* (Waterloo, Ontario: Wilfrid Laurier Press, 2012), and Tara Zahra, *The Lost Children: Reconstructing Europe's Families after World War II* (Cambridge, MA: Harvard University Press, 2011).

9. Emily S. Rosenberg, "Rescuing Women and Children," *Journal of American History* 89, no. 2 (September 2002): 456–465; Briggs, "Mother, Child, Race,

Nation: The Visual Iconography of Rescue and the Politics of Transnational and Transracial Adoption." See also Karen Dubinsky, "Children, Ideology, and Iconography: How Babies Rule the World," *Journal of the History of Childhood and Youth* 5, no. 1 (Winter 2012): 5–13, and Margaret Peacock, *Innocent Weapons: The Soviet and American Politics of Childhood in the Cold War* (Chapel Hill: University of North Carolina Press, 2014).

10. On the idea of "Republican Motherhood," which endowed women with political significance through their roles as mothers charged with raising virtuous citizens, see Linda Kerber, *Women of the Republic: Intellect and Ideology in Revolutionary America* (Chapel Hill: University of North Carolina Press, 1980). On "orphan trains," see Stephen O'Connor, *Orphan Trains: The Story of Charles Loring Brace and the Children He Saved and Failed* (New York: Houghton Mifflin Company, 2001), and Linda Gordon, *The Great Arizona Orphan Abduction* (Cambridge, MA: Harvard University Press, 1999). On schools for Native American children, see Clifford E. Trafzer, Jean A. Keller, and Lorene Sisquoc, eds., *Boarding School Blues: Revisiting American Indian Educational Experiences* (Lincoln: University of Nebraska Press, 2006). On the connections between child rearing and citizenship, see Sonya Michel, "Children and the National Interest," in Dirk Schumann, ed., *Raising Citizens in the "Century of the Child": The United States and German Central Europe in Comparative Perspective* (New York: Berghahn Books, 2010), 27–49.

11. Miss D. E. Emerson, "Bureau of Woman's Work," 42nd Annual Report of the American Missionary Association and the Proceedings at the Annual Meeting held in Providence, Rhode Island, October 23–25, 1888 (New York: American Missionary Association, 1888), 46. There is an extensive literature on American missionaries, and female missionaries in particular. Key works include Lisa Joy Pruitt, *A Looking-Glass for Ladies: American Protestant Women and the Orient in the Nineteenth Century* (Macon, GA: Mercer University Press, 2005); Dana L. Robert, ed., *Gospel Bearers, Gender Barriers: Missionary Women in the Twentieth Century* (Maryknoll, NY: Orbis Books, 2002); Dana L. Robert, *American Women in Mission: A Social History of Their Thought and Practice* (Macon, GA: Mercer University Press, 1996); Ruth A. Tucker, *Guardians of the Great Commission: The Story of Women in Modern Missions* (Grand Rapids, MI: Academie Books, 1988); Patricia R. Hill, *The World Their Household: The American Woman's Foreign Mission Movement and Cultural Transformation, 1870–1920* (Ann Arbor: University of Michigan Press, 1985); and Jane Hunter, *The Gospel of Gentility: American Women Missionaries in Turn-of-the-Century China* (New Haven, CT: Yale University Press, 1984). On aid to children during World War I, see Dominique Marshall, "Children's Rights and Children's Action in International Relief and Domestic Welfare: The Work of Herbert Hoover between 1914 and 1950," *Journal of the History of Childhood and Youth* 1, no. 3 (Fall 2008): 351–388.

12. Dominique Marshall, "Humanitarian Sympathy for Children in Times of War and the History of Children's Rights, 1919–1959," in James Marten, ed.,

Children and War: A Historical Anthology (New York: New York University Press, 2002), 184–200, and "The Construction of Children as an Object of International Relations: The Declaration of Children's Rights and the Child Welfare Committee of the League of Nations, 1900–1924," *International Journal of Children's Rights* 7, no. 2 (1999): 103–147; Kathleen Alaimo and Brian Klug, eds., *Children as Equals: Exploring the Rights of the Child* (New York: University Press of America, 2002). Save the Children Fund's newsletter, covering the activities of the British and Commonwealth organizations, was *The World's Children*. Save the Children Federation's newsletter was the *SCF World Reporter*.

13. Jonathan Todres, Mark E. Wojcik, and Cris R. Revaz, eds., *The U.N. Convention on the Rights of the Child: An Analysis of Treaty Provisions and Implications for U.S. Ratification* (Ardsley, NY: Transnational Publishers, 2006); Mark Ensalaco and Linda C. Majka, eds., *Children's Human Rights: Progress and Challenges for Children Worldwide* (New York: Rowman & Littlefield Publishers, 2005); Philip E. Veerman, *The Rights of the Child and the Changing Image of Childhood* (Boston: Martinus Nijhoff Publishers, 1992).

14. Viviana A. Zelizer, *Pricing the Priceless Child: The Changing Social Value of Children* (New York: Basic Books, 1985); Bernard Wishy, *The Child and the Republic: The Dawn of Modern American Child Nurture* (Philadelphia: University of Pennsylvania Press, 1968), vii; Kathleen Jones, *Taming the Troublesome Child: American Families, Child Guidance, and the Limits of Psychiatric Authority* (Cambridge, MA: Harvard University Press, 1999); Ann Hulbert, *Raising America: Experts, Parents and a Century of Advice about Children* (New York: Alfred A. Knopf, 2003).

15. On the dissemination of a particular conception of childhood from the global North to the South, and its repercussions, see Jo Boyden, "Childhood and the Policy Makers: A Comparative Perspective on the Globalization of Childhood," in Allison James and Alan Prout, eds., *Constructing and Reconstructing Childhood: Contemporary Issues in the Sociological Study of Childhood* (New York: Falmer Press, 1990), 184–215.

16. For more on this argument, see Christina Klein, *Cold War Orientalism: Asia in the Middlebrow Imagination, 1945–1961* (Berkeley: University of California Press, 2003).

17. David Ekbladh, *The Great American Mission: Modernization and the Construction of an American World Order* (Princeton, NJ: Princeton University Press, 2010), 5. On historians' explorations of modernization as a psychological project, see, for example, Ellen Herman, *The Romance of American Psychology: Political Culture in the Age of Experts* (Berkeley: University of California Press, 1996), 136–148.

18. David C. Engerman and Corinna R. Unger make this point in "Introduction: Towards a Global History of Modernization," *Diplomatic History* 33, no. 3 (June 2009): 383–384. One work that does provide a sustained focus on women is Matthew Connelly's *Fatal Misconception: The Struggle to Control World Population*

(Cambridge, MA: Harvard University Press, 2008); Connelly's focus, however, is on reproduction, not child rearing. J. K. Galbraith, "India Between Two Worlds," *Reporter,* May 16, 1957, 40, quoted in Nick Cullather, "The Third Race," *Diplomatic History* 33, no. 3 (June 2009): 509–510; Catherine V. Scott, *Gender and Development: Rethinking Modernization and Dependency Theory* (Boulder, CO: Lynne Rienner Publishers, 1996), 23–32.

1. MANUFACTURING THE CITIZENS OF THE WORLD

1. "Report of a Conference on Germany after the War," Folder Country Germany Reports and Letters on Conditions in 1945, Box Foreign Service 1945-Germany, AFSC. For more on the conference, see Peter Mandler, *Return from the Natives: How Margaret Mead Won the Second World War and Lost the Cold War* (New Haven, CT: Yale University Press, 2013), 189–195, and Uta Gerhardt, "A Hidden Agenda of Recovery: The Psychiatric Conceptualization of Re-education for Germany in the United States during World War II," *German History* 14, no. 3 (1996): 312–319.

2. "Report of a Conference on Germany after the War," Folder Country Germany Reports and Letters on the Conditions in 1945, Box Foreign Service 1945-Germany, AFSC; "Germany after the War. Roundtable—1945," *American Journal of Orthopsychiatry* 15, no. 3 (1945): 381–441.

3. Joanne Meyerowitz, " 'How Common Culture Shapes the Separate Lives': Sexuality, Race, and Mid-Twentieth-Century Social Constructionist Thought," *Journal of American History* 96, no. 4 (March 2010): 1059.

4. David Starr Jordan, "Prenatal Influences," *Journal of Heredity* 5, no. 1 (January 1914): 39, quoted in Hamilton Cravens, *The Triumph of Evolution: The Heredity-Environment Controversy, 1900–1941* (Baltimore: Johns Hopkins University Press, 1988), 46; Daniel J. Kevles, *In the Name of Eugenics: Genetics and the Uses of Human Heredity* (Cambridge, MA: Harvard University Press, 1985); Margaret O'Brien Steinfels, *Who's Minding the Children? The History and Politics of Day Care in America* (New York: Simon and Schuster, 1973).

5. John Watson, *Behaviorism* (New York: W. W. Norton & Company, 1925), 82; and *Psychological Care of Infant and Child* (New York: W. W. Norton & Company, 1928), 69–87.

6. Kathleen Jones, *Taming the Troublesome Child: American Families, Child Guidance, and the Limits of Psychiatric Authority* (Cambridge, MA: Harvard University Press, 1999), 140–141; "Modern Attitude Toward Behavior of Children Discussed for Teachers," *Hartford Courant,* September 25, 1934, 21; Lawrence A. Cremin, *The Transformation of the School: Progressivism in American Education, 1876–1957* (New York: Random House, 1961).

7. Meyerowitz, " 'How Common Culture Shapes the Separate Lives' "; Mandler, *Return from the Natives.*

8. Greg Eghigian, Andreas Killen, and Christine Leuenberger, "Introduction: The Self as Project: Politics and the Human Sciences in the Twentieth Century," *Osiris* 22 (2007): 1–25, quotes at 10 and 2. On personality in the twentieth-century United States, see also Warren I. Susman, "'Personality' and the Making of Twentieth-Century Culture," in *New Directions in American Intellectual History,* ed. John Higham and Paul Keith Conkin (Baltimore: Johns Hopkins University Press, 1979), 212–226. Susman draws a distinction between personality, with its focus on self-expression and self-presentation, and character, which he sees as connected to morality and self-control. Postwar child welfare experts' understanding of personality development incorporated elements of both "personality" and "character" as Susman defines them. Therefore, I use the terms interchangeably.

9. Meyerowitz, "'How Common Culture Shapes the Separate Lives,'" 1077; Katherine Bain to Gregory Bateson, May 14, 1943; Gregory Bateson to Martha Eliot, April 21, 1943; Martha Eliot to Gregory Bateson, March 29, 1943; and Memorandum from Martha Branscombe to Martha Eliot, Subject: "Conference with Dr. Margaret Mead," March 26, 1943, Folder 22-3-1-0, Box 201, Record Group 102, Records of the Children's Bureau, NA; Harold Orlansky, "Infant Care and Personality," *Psychological Bulletin* 46, no. 1 (January 1949): 1–48; Ann Hulbert, *Raising America: Experts, Parents, and a Century of Advice about Children* (New York: Alfred A. Knopf, 2003), 202.

10. On new postwar child-rearing ideas, see Nicholas Sammond, *Babes in Tomorrowland: Walt Disney and the Making of the American Child, 1930–1960* (Durham, NC: Duke University Press, 2005); Hulbert, *Raising America.*

11. Anna Freud, "Questionnaire for Personnel of All Colonies," March 16, 1941; Dorothy Burlingham, "Questionnaire for Personnel of All Colonies," March 16, 1941; and George Godwin, "New Homes for Old: Britain's Residential Nurseries are Real Homes," undated, Folder 22, Box 303, FPPv1. For additional information on the Hampstead Nurseries, see Ellen Herman, *Kinship by Design: A History of Adoption in the Modern United States* (Chicago: University of Chicago Press, 2008), 260–261.

12. Anna Freud and Dorothy T. Burlingham, *Young Children in Wartime* (London: George Allen & Unwin Ltd., 1942); Anna Freud and Dorothy T. Burlingham, *War and Children* (New York: Medical War Books, 1943); Anna Freud and Dorothy T. Burlingham, *Infants without Families: The Case for and Against Residential Nurseries* (New York: International Universities Press, 1944).

13. Freud and Burlingham, *Infants without Families,* 103.

14. John Bowlby, *Maternal Care and Mental Health* (Geneva: World Health Organization, 1951), 157. Bowlby published an abridged version of this work in 1953 as *Child Care and the Growth of Love,* abridged and edited by Margery Fry (Baltimore: Penguin Books, 1953). For an account of the reception of Bowlby's

ideas in the United States, see Marga Vicedo, "The Social Nature of the Mother's Tie to Her Child: John Bowlby's Theory of Attachment in Post-War America," *British Journal for the History of Science* 44, no. 3 (September 2011): 401–426; Hulbert, *Raising America*, 205.

15. Benjamin Spock, *The Common Sense Book of Baby and Child Care* (New York: Duell, Sloan and Pearce, 1946), quote at 19.

16. On the Americanization of psychoanalysis, see Nathan G. Hale Jr., "From Berggasse XIX to Central Park West: The Americanization of Psychoanalysis, 1919–1940," *Journal of the History of the Behavioral Sciences* 14, no. 4 (October 1978): 299–315. William Graebner, "The Unstable World of Benjamin Spock: Social Engineering in a Democratic Culture, 1917–1950," *Journal of American History* 67, no. 3 (December 1980): 612–629; Evelyn Eisenstadt to Mina Ross, February 10, 1949, and Evelyn Eisenstadt to Mina Ross, March 8, 1949, Folder The Pocket Book of Baby and Child Care, Box 11, Record Group 306, Records of the U.S. Information Agency, NA.

17. "General Report Adopted by the Conference," in U.S. Department of Labor, Children's Bureau, *Proceedings of the White House Conference on Children in a Democracy*, Children's Bureau Publication No. 266 (Washington, DC: Government Printing Office, 1940), 70; Sonya Michel, "American Women and the Discourse of the Democratic Family in World War II," in Margaret Randolph Higonnet et al., eds., *Behind the Lines: Gender and the Two World Wars* (New Haven, CT: Yale University Press, 1987), 154–167.

18. "Report by Conference of Consultants on Services to Children in Germany to the Department of State and the Department of the Army" and "Addendum to Report of Conference on Services to Children in Germany," undated (probably 1949), Folder 602, Box 43, ME.

19. *Health and Human Relations in Germany: Report of a Conference on Problems of Health and Human Relations in Germany, Nassau Tavern, Princeton, NJ, June 26–30, 1950* (New York: Josiah Macy Jr. Foundation, 1950), 43.

20. Ibid., 61.

21. Bertram Schaffner, *Father Land: A Study of Authoritarianism in the German Family* (New York: Columbia University Press, 1948), 4; Institut für Sozialforschung, *Studien über Autorität und Familie* (Paris: Félix Alcan, 1936); Wilhelm Reich, *The Mass Psychology of Fascism* (New York: Farrar, Straus and Giraux, 1970 [1946]). For a discussion of *Studien über Autorität und Familie* and its reception in the United States, see Thomas Wheatland, *The Frankfurt School in Exile* (Minneapolis: University of Minnesota Press, 2009), 208–211.

22. Ruth Benedict, *The Chrysanthemum and the Sword: Patterns of Japanese Culture* (Boston: Houghton Mifflin Company, 1946), 48, 57.

23. Theodor W. Adorno et al., *The Authoritarian Personality* (New York: Harper and Brothers, 1950), 385.

24. Weston LaBarre, "The Age Period of Cultural Fixation," *Mental Hygiene* 33 (April 1949): 211. Emphasis in original.

25. "Report of a Conference on Germany after the War," Appendix 7, "Long-Term Procedures in the Management of Germany," 10–11, Folder Country Germany Reports and Letters on Conditions in 1945, Box Foreign Service 1945-Germany, AFSC. Peter Mandler speculates that Mead was most likely the author of the appendix. Mandler, *Return from the Natives,* 193.

26. On the reception of the conference report, see "Conference on Germany after the War (Replies to Report)," Folder 1, Box M32, MM.

27. "Boys and Girls Share . . . in the Program of the Unitarian Service Committee," undated, Folder AYFWY-Publicity Material, N.D., Box 13, EP.

28. D. N. (Mrs. Oscar) Schnabel to Ernst Papanek, March 24, 1945, Folder Refugee Children Correspondence 1945; Ernst Papanek, "Some Highlights of the Situation of the Children in Europe," undated, Folder Refugee Children-Misc. General Info On, Box 5, ibid.; Frank Spooner Churchill, "The Children of Germany and Lasting Peace: A Home-School Plan," June 1944, 13, Folder 22-3-1-12, Box 201, Records of the Children's Bureau, NA.

29. Katharine Lenroot, "Interview with Mlle. S. Gouin, Bureau Information Ouvries Social," October 21, 1945, Folder 7, Box 21, KL; "Juvenile Delinquency in Germany," *Social Service Review* 20, no. 4 (December 1946): 570; Herschel Alt, "Observations on Juvenile Delinquency in Germany," *Social Service Review* 23, no. 2 (June 1949): 184; Yoshihiro Shimizu, "The Problems of Juvenile Delinquency in Post-War Japan," *Journal of Educational Sociology* 26, no. 1 (September 1952): 32; John Patrick Carroll-Abbing, *A Chance to Live: The Story of the Lost Children of the War* (New York: Longmans, Green, 1952); Dorothy Macardle, *Children of Europe: A Study of the Children of Liberated Countries: Their War-Time Experiences, Their Reactions, and Their Needs, with a Note on Germany* (Boston: Beacon Press, 1951), 260–268, quote at 267; Melvin A. Glasser, "Fact-Finding for the White House Conference on Children and Youth," *Social Security Bulletin* 13, no. 11 (November 1950): 15.

30. Regina Kunzel, *Fallen Women, Problem Girls: Unmarried Mothers and the Professionalization of Social Work, 1890–1945* (New Haven, CT: Yale University Press, 1993), 147–148; Leslie Leighninger, *Social Work: Search for Identity* (New York: Greenwood Press, 1987), 86, 152; Elizabeth Ann Danto, "'A New Sort of Salvation Army': Historical Perspectives on the Confluence of Psychoanalysis and Social Work," *Clinical Social Work Journal* 37, no. 1 (2009): 67–76; Cora Kasius, "Casework Developments in Europe," *Social Casework* 32, no. 7 (July 1951): 281–288. On social work training in Germany in particular, see David R. Hunter and Howard R. Studd, "Postwar Social Services in Berlin," *Social Service Review* 22, no. 2 (June 1948): 157. On the influence of American psychology on social psychology in Europe, particularly in the Netherlands, see Pieter J. van Strien, "The

American 'Colonization' of Northwest European Social Psychology after World War II," *Journal of the History of the Behavioral Sciences* 33, no. 4 (Fall 1997): 349–363. On social work in Japan, see Toshio Tatara, "1400 Years of Japanese Social Work from Its Origins through the Allied Occupation, 552–1952" (PhD diss., Bryn Mawr College, Graduate School of Social Work and Social Research, 1975).

31. "Child Care Program Prospectus," 1951, Folder 15, Box 3; Frances Burns, "Germans Say War Didn't Upset Their Nerves, but Blood Pressure and Ulcers Contradict Them: Nightmares and Tantrums Show Effects of Bombings on Children," *Boston Daily Globe,* October 1, 1949, Folder 5, Box 4, bMS 16036, USC; Edrita G. Fried and Marjorie Fiske Lissance, "The Dilemmas of German Youth," *Journal of Abnormal and Social Psychology* 44, no. 1 (January 1949): 55.

32. Gunnar Dybwad, "Mission on Maternal and Child Health and Welfare, United States Zone of Germany, February and March, 1949, Report of the Child Welfare Section," quotes at 8 and 26, Folder 602, Box 43, ME.

33. Gisela Konopka, "Report, Public Welfare Consultant Gisela Konopka, June 15 to September 8, 1950," September 5, 1950, 5, Folder Experts, American Continental German, Box 3, Record Group 466, Records of the U.S. High Commissioner for Germany, NA.

34. Bowlby, *Maternal Care and Mental Health,* 13. Gunnar Dybwad, "Child Care in Germany," undated, Folder 5, Box 4, bMS 16036, USC. On American overseas workers' attitudes toward the biological orientation of German child welfare, see, in particular, Helen Fogg, "1950 Education and Child Care Institute, Newsletter No. 3, Berlin Session," Folder 9, Box 4, bMS 16036, USC and Perry J. Gangloff, "The Public Welfare Program in Berlin Military Government: A Way of Interpreting Democracy," *Social Service Review* 24, no. 2 (June 1950): 204.

35. *Health and Human Relations in Germany,* 27. Even young adults who had not yet started families expected to rear their children according to "semi-authoritarian principles," psychologists reported. In a study of German youth between the ages of eighteen and twenty-eight, "less than ten of the subjects said, in discussing how they would handle disobedience, that they would first look for its causes." Instead, these prospective parents reported that they would rely on punishment as a means of correcting their children's bad behavior. Fried and Lissance, "The Dilemmas of German Youth," 53–54; Dybwad, "Mission on Maternal and Child Health and Welfare," 9.

36. Alt, "Observations on Juvenile Delinquency in Germany," 187; Dybwad, "Mission on Maternal and Child Health and Welfare," 32.

37. Hertha Kraus, "The Role of Social Casework in American Social Work," *Social Casework* 31, no. 1 (January 1950): quotes at 10 and 9.

38. Jan F. de Jongh, "A European View of American Social Work," *Social Casework* 31, no. 4 (April 1950): 152; Kraus, "The Role of Social Casework in American Social Work," 8.

39. John W. Dower, *Embracing Defeat: Japan in the Wake of World War II* (New York: W. W. Norton & Company, 1999), 62–64.

40. "Father Flanigan [*sic*] Dead in Berlin: Founder of Boys Town in 1917 Stricken with Heart Attack While Touring Germany," *New York Times,* May 15, 1948, 15; "'Flanagan Day' Decreed: Japan's Major League to Honor Founder of Boys Town," *New York Times,* May 26, 1947, 27.

41. Edward Joseph Flanagan, "Child Welfare Report (Japan and Korea)," 1947, Folder Refugee Children Reports by Others, Box 9, EP; Norman Lloyd, "Flanagan Tells Macarthur Aim: Christian Japan," *Chicago Daily Tribune,* July 10, 1947, 9.

42. Emilie Baca Putnam, "Japan . . . Its Children's Welfare," *Survey* 88, no. 3 (March 1952): 123.

43. Ibid., 119.

44. Martha M. Eliot, Jessie M. Bierman, and Gunnar Dybwad, "Report of the Mission on Maternal and Child Health and Welfare, United States Zone of Germany," February and March 1949, Folder 604, Box 43, ME.

2. READING DR. SPOCK IN POSTWAR EUROPE AND JAPAN

1. Alice Pollard to William Clayton, March 16, 1948, Folder 0-4-1-1, Box 57, Record Group 102, Records of the Children's Bureau, NA.

2. William Clayton to Alice Pollard, March 21, 1948; Ellen S. Woodward to Charles E. Saltzman, July 9, 1948; and Katharine Lenroot to Ellen S. Woodward, December 28, 1948, ibid.; Alice Pollard, "Postscript—1977," January 22, 1977, and Alice Pollard, "Memorandum on Progress of Plan to Date," January 25, 1949, Folder Progress Reports 1949, 1951, 1977, Box 2, AHP.

3. "Child Guidance Curatorium, Wiesbaden," May 25, 1951, Folder Child Guidance Clinics Activities Reports, Box 1; Gisela Konopka, "Report, Public Welfare Consultant Gisela Konopka, June 15 to September 8, 1950," September 5, 1950, 5, Folder Experts, American Continental German; and "Application for Participation in Personnel Exchange Program," Folder Exchange Program Pending, Box 3, Record Group 466, Records of the U.S. High Commissioner for Germany, NA. For more information on American welfare experts sponsored by the Office of the U.S. High Commissioner for Germany, see Folder Exchange Programs Information on U.S. Experts, Box 2, ibid.; and Petra Goedde, *GIs and Germans: Culture, Gender, and Foreign Relations, 1945–1949* (New Haven, CT: Yale University Press, 2003), 127–165.

4. For more information on the Arbeiterwohlfahrt, see Christiane Eifert, "The Forgotten Members of the Arbeiterwohlfahrt: Jews in the Social Democratic Welfare Association," *Leo Baeck Institute Yearbook* 39, no. 1 (1994): 179–209.

5. Unitarian Service Committee, Board of Directors meeting minutes, October 27, 1950, Folder 1, Box 1, and "Section II-Report of the Second Week,

Second Session, Report #V," Folder 6, Box 4, bMS 16036; Unitarian Service Committee Staff, Bremen, "Memorandum: For Use of USC Staff, Boston, on Significance of Institute," September 1951, Folder 8, Box 14, bMS 16011, USC.

6. Helen Fogg, "Report #III, Final Report–First Session–Child Care Institute," July 27, 1949, Folder 6, Box 4; "Report #1 First Course, July 1–July 10, Berlin," July 12, 1951, Folder 2, Box 1; "These Three Years," 1951, Folder 8, Box 4, bMS 16036; "Unitarian Service Committee," Folder 7, Box 14, bMS 16011; Katharine Taylor and Marianne Welter, "Field Work Record, KT and MW, Stuttgart, January 25 and 26, 1952"; "Field Work Record, KT and MW, Erlangen, January 31 to February 2, 1952"; "Field Work Record, KT and MW, Haiger, February 6 to 8, 1952"; and "Field Work Record, KT and MW, Bielefeld, February 11 and 12, 1952," Folder 7, Box 11; Helen Fogg to Exchanges Division, U.S. High Commissioner for Germany, "Report—Child Welfare Program of the USC in Germany," 1952, Folder 17, Box 14, bMS 16011, USC.

7. "Child Care Program Prospectus," 1951, Folder 15, Box 3, bMS 16036; Katharine Taylor to Helen Fogg, November 29, 1949, Folder 4, Box 3, bMS 16171, USC; John McCloy to Secretary of State, telegram, October 26, 1950, Folder 0-1-0-7-2, Box 314, Records of the Children's Bureau, NA.

8. "Project Suggestions for Relief Work in Germany," July 13, 1945, Folder Country Germany Policy and Work in Germany 1945, Box Germany, AFSC/ UNRRA Team, AFSC.

9. For more information on the American Friends Service Committee during its early years, see Clarence E. Pickett, *For More Than Bread: An Autobiographical Account of Twenty-Two Years' Work with the American Friends Service Committee* (Boston: Little, Brown, 1953). "October 1-Wuppertal Nachbarshaftsheim," 1950; Rose Porter, "Wuppertal-Nachbarshaftsheim-November 1950"; and Georges M. Weber to Sharon L. Hatch, "Darmstadt Neighborhood Center, Report for Period April 1–April 30," Folder American Friends Service Committee, Unitarian Service Committee, Brethren Service Committee—Welfare Branch, Box 15, Records of the U.S. High Commissioner for Germany, NA; Rose Albert Porter, "Neighborliness Rediscovered," *Survey* 88, no. 2 (February 1952): 79; Irma Skorczewski, "Report on Plans and Preparative Work for the Neighborhood Center to Be Set Up in Berlin," December 9, 1946, and "What Is Mittelhof?," September 10, 1947, Folder Country Germany, Project, Center Berlin 1947, Box Foreign Service 1947, Country— Germany (Projects), AFSC.

10. Henrietta Buchman to Clara Simon, February 1, 1949, and Henrietta Buchman to MacEnnis Moore, September 13, 1948 (microfilm: file 1028, frames 1035–1036 and 1047), JDC 45/54.

11. "Notes on the Proposed Mental Hygiene Service," April 29, 1946 (microfilm: file 259, frame 848); "Notes on a Mental Hygiene Service," June 14, 1946 (microfilm: file 259, frame 844); AJDC Paris to Robert Pilpel and Paul Friedman,

AJDC New York, "Mental Hygiene Activities," June 14, 1946 (microfilm: file 259, frame 843), ibid.

12. "Jewish Unit Plans School in France," *New York Times,* June 11, 1949, 5; Zachariah Shuster, "Turning Point in Europe," *Committee Reporters,* December 1949, Folder PB47, Box 2, PB; "Paul Baerwald School of Social Work, Bulletin of Information, 1949–1950, Preliminary Draft," August 1949 (microfilm: reel MKM 8.12, folder 224), GJCA.

13. Philip Klein, "The Paul Baerwald School of Social Work," reprinted from *Jewish Social Service Quarterly* 26, no. 4 (June 1950), Folder C15-PB46 and "Baerwald School to Offer Courses in Six Countries," *JDC Digest,* September 1951, Folder C15-PB45, Box 2, PB.

14. "Report on Child Care Department, Office for France, October 1946– October 1948" (microfilm: file 248, frames 557 and 560), JDC 45/54. On the American Jewish Joint Distribution Committee in France and its influence on the practices of local organizations, see Maud S. Mandel, "Philanthropy or Cultural Imperialism? The Impact of American Jewish Aid in Post-Holocaust France," *Jewish Social Studies* 9, no. 1 (2002): 53–94.

15. Hilde Loos, "Quaker Jugendheim, Koln, Report for October, 1950"; "Quaker Jugendheim, Koln, Report for the Month of December, 1950"; "Quaker Jugendheim, Koln, Report for March 1951"; "Quaker Jugendheim, Koln, Report for the Month of April, 1951"; "Quaker Jugendheim, Koln, Report for August, 1951"; Virginia Chapman, "Darmstadt Neighborhood Center, Report for June 1–30"; and Georges and Marjorie Weber, "Darmstadt Neighborhood Center, Report for Period May 1–31, 1950," Folder American Friends Service Committee, Unitarian Service Committee, Brethren Service Committee—Welfare Branch, Box 15, Records of the U.S. High Commissioner for Germany, NA; Helen Fogg, "1950 Education and Child Care Institute, Newsletter No. 3, Berlin Session," Folder 9, Box 4, bMS 16036, USC.

16. Marianne Welter, "Auermühle Children's Home, Unitarian-Universalist Service Committee, Monthly Report, July–August 1948," Folder 14, Box 28, bMS 16035, USC.

17. "Opening of Hana Benes Children's Home," February 16, 1947, Folder 6, Box 14; Karel Haspl to Raymond Bragg, "Monthly Report, March 1947," March 25, 1947, Folder 5, Box 8; and Jeannette Novak, "Final Report on Olesovice," September 24, 1947, and Ernst Papanek to Raymond Bragg, "Memorandum RE: Children's Home at Olesovice, Czechoslovakia," November 21, 1947, Folder 1, Box 8, ibid.

18. Eunice Minton, "Observation Programs in the United States: A Meeting of Social Work Colleagues," *Social Casework* 32, no. 7 (July 1951): 288–294; Hertha Kraus, "The Role of Social Casework in American Social Work," *Social Casework* 31, no. 1 (January 1950): 3.

19. Peter Melvyn to Paul Baerwald School faculty, March 29, 1951, and Joel Katz to Henry Selver, February 20, 1951, Folder C15-PB45, Box 2, PB.

20. Katharine Lenroot to Martha Eliot, January 12, 1949, Folder 599, Box 42, ME; *Health and Human Relations in Germany: Report of a Conference on Problems of Health and Human Relations in Germany, Nassau Tavern, Princeton, NJ, June 26–30, 1950* (New York: Josiah Macy Jr. Foundation, 1950), 157.

21. Jeannette A. Margolies, "A Study in the Development of Multiple Services for Young Immigrants," undated, 11 (microfilm: reel MKM 8.31, folder 585), GJCA. For another example of children reluctant to discuss their feelings with caseworkers, see Lotte Marcuse, Jeannette Margolies, and Hilda Meyerowitz, "Report of the EJCA," March 2, 1949 (microfilm: reel MKM 8.2, folder 37), ibid.

22. Cora Kasius, "Casework Developments in Europe," *Social Casework* 32, no. 7 (July 1951): 284; Georges and Marjorie Weber, "Darmstadt Neighborhood Center, Report for Period May 1–31, 1950"; Edward E. Merone to Public Affairs Division, Education & Cultural Relations Branch, "Community Activities Report for June 1951," June 29, 1951, and "Community Activities Report for July 1951," July 31, 1951, Folder Women's Affairs Reports, Box 127; Georges M. Weber to Sharon L. Hatch, "Darmstadt Neighborhood Center, Report for Period April 1– April 30," Folder American Friends Service Committee, Unitarian Service Committee, Brethren Service Committee—Welfare Branch, Box 15; Liesel Miltenberger, Application for Participation in Personnel Exchange Program, January 15, 1950, Folder Personnel Exchange Program Training in Social Work, Box 6, Records of the U.S. High Commissioner for Germany, NA.

23. Edward Ross Dickinson, *The Politics of German Child Welfare from the Empire to the Federal Republic* (Cambridge, MA: Harvard University Press, 1996), 245–261.

24. On the history of CCF, see Larry E. Tise, *A Book about Children: The World of Christian Children's Fund, 1938–1991* (Falls Church, VA: Hartland Publishing for the Christian Children's Fund, 1993). "That War Is Over, but the Battle for Needy Youngsters Lingers On," undated, CCF.

25. Verent Mills, "Jiai No Mura," undated, CCF; Maud O. Powlas, *Gathering Up the Fragments* (Greenville, NC: Era Press, 1978); China's Children Fund, "Japan," *China News* 5, no. 2 (Winter 1948): 3, and China's Children Fund, "Japan," *China News* 7, no. 3 (Spring 1950): 4, CCFY.

26. Arissa Oh, "A New Kind of Missionary Work: Christians, Christian Americanists, and the Adoption of Korean GI Babies, 1955–1961," *Women's Studies Quarterly* 33, no. 3/4 (Fall–Winter 2005): 161–188. See also Oh, *To Save the Children of Korea: The Cold War Origins of International Adoption* (Redwood City, CA: Stanford University Press, 2015).

27. Lawrence S. Wittner, "MacArthur and the Missionaries: God and Man in Occupied Japan," *Pacific Historical Review* 40, no. 1 (February 1971): 77–98, quote at 82; Thomas S. Rogers, "The *Licensed Agencies for Relief in Asia*: Esther B. Rhoads

and Humanitarian Efforts in Postwar Japan, 1946–1952," *Quaker History* 83, no. 1 (Spring 1994): 18–33; "Plan for Civil Information Activities on Child Welfare," Folder Child Welfare General References Informational Materials, Box 2853, Record Group 331, Records of Allied Operational and Occupation Headquarters, World War II, NA.

28. Milton J. Evans, "Child Welfare," November 12, 1949, Folder Child Welfare General References Informational Materials, Box 2853, Records of Allied Operational and Occupation Headquarters, World War II, NA.

29. Headquarters Eighth Army, Subject: "Transmittal of Plan for Civil Information Activities on Child Welfare," January 21, 1949, and "Plan for Civil Information Activities on Child Welfare," ibid.; Headquarters Eighth Army, United States Army, Military Government Section, for Civil Information Officer: "In Order to Bring Up Good Children," distributed May 20, 1949, and Headquarters Eighth Army, United States Army, Military Government Section, for Civil Information Officer, Recognition Copy: Poster on Child Welfare Week, Prepared by Welfare Ministry, Translation, Folder Child Welfare 50-B, Box 5222, ibid.

30. Donald V. Wilson, General HQ SCAP Public Health and Welfare Section, Memorandum for the Record: Subject: "Training Program for Day Nursery Personnel, March 8, 1948," Folder Training Program for Day Nursery Personnel, Box 9348, ibid.; Crawford F. Sams, *Medic: The Mission of an American Military Doctor in Occupied Japan and Wartorn Korea* (Armonk, NY: M.E. Sharpe, 1998), 162; Toshio Tatara, "1400 Years of Japanese Social Work from Its Origins through the Allied Occupation, 552–1952" (PhD diss., Bryn Mawr College, Graduate School of Social Work and Social Research, 1975), 439–440.

31. Powlas, *Gathering Up Fragments,* 186.

32. Tsuyako Shimada, "Aspects of Japanese Parent-Child Relationships," in Dorothy Dessau, ed., *Glimpses of Social Work in Japan* (Kyoto: Social Workers' International Club of Japan, 1968), 176–184. Shimada's article was reprinted from an earlier edition published in 1958. Tatara, "1400 Years of Japanese Social Work," 501, 546–557; "Plan for Civil Information Activities on Child Welfare." On casework with families in Japan during the 1950s and 1960s, see Tatsuro Hatakeyama, "Problem Treatment at the Family Welfare Research Institute of Meiji Gakuin," and Dorothy Dessau, "The Clinic at 9 Miyagawa-cho," in *Glimpses of Social Work in Japan,* 116–133.

33. Tatara, "1400 Years of Japanese Social Work," 541.

34. Regina Kunzel, *Fallen Women, Problem Girls: Unmarried Mothers and the Professionalization of Social Work, 1890–1945* (New Haven, CT: Yale University Press, 1993), 165–170. See also Janice L. Andrews, "Female Social Workers in the Second Generation," *Affilia* 5, no. 2 (Summer 1990): 46–59, on the declining power of women within the social work profession.

35. Robyn Muncy, *Creating a Female Dominion in American Reform, 1890–1935* (New York: Oxford University Press, 1991); Kriste Lindenmeyer, *"A Right to Childhood": The U.S. Children's Bureau and Child Welfare, 1912–46* (Urbana: University of Illinois Press, 1997); "The International Activities of the Children's Bureau," 1960, 17, Folder 10, Box 21, KL; Martha Eliot to Philip Jessup, July 26, 1943, and enclosed memorandum, "The Type of Personnel Needed to Deal with the Problem of Child Care, and the Qualifications Which the Relief Worker Should Have Whose Task Will Be to Deal Primarily with Children and Mothers," Folder 22-0-10-1, Box 200, Records of the Children's Bureau, NA. On recommendations of female welfare workers, see, for example, Katharine Lenroot to Fred K. Hoehler, January 5, 1943, ibid., and Mary Eva Duthie to Martha Branscombe, June 11, 1943, Folder 22-3-1-5, Box 201, Records of the Children's Bureau, NA.

36. On the influence of European, particularly German, models of social insurance on the development of the American welfare state, see Daniel T. Rodgers, *Atlantic Crossings: Social Politics in a Progressive Age* (Cambridge, MA: Harvard University Press, 1998). On the relationship between the emergence of large-scale state welfare programs and the rise of women's social action movements, see Seth Koven and Sonya Michel, "Womanly Duties: Maternalist Politics and the Origins of Welfare States in France, Germany, Great Britain, and the United States, 1880–1920," *American Historical Review* 95, no. 4 (October 1990): 1076–1108. Hertha Kraus, "A Neighborhood Center: Plan for a Standard Service Unit Which May Fit into Many Different Foreign Communities," submitted to the American Friends Service Committee on January 24, 1943, excerpt, and Alice Pollard to Katharine Lenroot, August 2, 1948, Folder 0-4-1-1, Box 57, Records of the Children's Bureau, NA.

37. Helen Fogg, "Section II, Second Session, Third Week," August 1949, Folder 6, Box 4, bMS 16036, USC; Louise Proehl Shoemaker worked at the Elliot Park Neighborhood House in Minneapolis; Maria Barbara Ladd worked at the Huntington Neighborhood Association Neighborhood House in Syracuse, NY; and Lillie Peck served as executive secretary of the National Federation of Settlements from 1934 to 1947 and president of the International Federation of Settlements from 1949 to 1951. See Curriculum Vitae, Miss Lea Demarest Taylor; Curriculum Vitae, Mrs. Bryce (Louise Proehl) Shoemaker; and Curriculum Vitae, Mrs. Edward T. Ladd, Folder 15, Box 14, bMS 16011, USC.

38. Helen Fogg, draft of application to Ford Foundation, March 5, 1951, Folder 10, Box 11, bMS 16011, ibid.

39. For a short biography of Hertha Kraus, see Beate Bussiek, "Hertha Kraus: Quaker Spirit and Competence," in Sabine Hering and Berteke Waaldijk, eds., *History of Social Work in Europe (1900–1960): Female Pioneers and Their Influence on the Development of International Social Organizations* (Opladen, Germany:

Leske + Budrich, 2003), 53–64; Kraus, "A Neighborhood Center: Plan for a Standard Service Unit Which May Fit into Many Different Foreign Communities."

40. The AFSC established neighborhood centers in Berlin, Bremen, Brunswick, Cologne, Darmstadt, Frankfurt, Ludwigshafen, and Wuppertal. James F. Tent, "Simple Gifts: The American Friends Service Committee and the Establishment of Neighborhood Centers in Post-1945 Germany," *Kirchliche Zeitgeschichte* 2, no. 1 (May 1989): 64–82; "Friends in Germany," *Military Government Weekly Information Bulletin* 115 (October 20, 1947): 5–6; F. J. Dallett Jr., "American Friends in Germany," *Information Bulletin: Monthly Magazine of the Office of the U.S. High Commissioner for Germany* (January 1952): 23–25; "What Is Mittelhof?"; "Quaker Jugendheim, Koln, Report for the Month of April, 1951"; Georges and Marjorie Weber, "Darmstadt Neighborhood Center, Report for Period June 1–30, 1950"; "October 1-Wuppertal Nachbarshaftsheim"; Rose Porter, "Wuppertal-Nachbarshaftsheim-November 1950"; and "Progress Report, October 1950, Wuppertal Nachbarshaftsheim," Folder American Friends Service Committee, Unitarian Service Committee, Brethren Service Committee—Welfare Branch, Box 15, Records of the U.S. High Commissioner for Germany, NA.

41. Porter, "Neighborliness Rediscovered," 79; Nancy Good to Hertha Kraus, January 13, 1947, Folder Country-Germany, Centers Project Frankfurt, 1947, Box Foreign Service 1947, Country—Germany (Projects), AFSC.

42. "Japan, Supplement to Manual for Finance Secretaries," 1959, Folder Japan Administration Finance International Centers Program, Box Foreign Service Japan 1959, and "The Farewell Address to Mr. and Mrs. Foulke," January 20, 1950, Folder Japan Personnel Foulke Thomas and Eliza, Box Foreign Service Japan 1950, AFSC; Anna Brinton, "The American Friends Service Committee," in B. L. Hinchman and Robert W. Wood, eds., *The Japan Christian Yearbook 1953: A Survey of the Christian Movement in Japan through 1952* (New York: Friendship Press, 1953), 299–302.

43. Florence Brugger, "The Citizens' Welfare in Japan," *Mount Holyoke Alumnae Quarterly* (August 1951): 42–43; Tatara, "1400 Years of Japanese Social Work," 417; Eiji Takemae, *The Allied Occupation of Japan* (New York: Continuum International Publishing Group Ltd., 2003), 420.

44. Harriet Eager Davis, "How Not to Raise Our Children," *Parents'* 20 (August 1945): 122.

45. Rebecca Jo Plant, *Mom: The Transformation of Motherhood in Modern America* (Chicago: University of Chicago Press, 2010); Philip Wylie, *Generation of Vipers* (New York: Farrar & Rinehart, 1942).

46. Alma Luckau, "Suggestions for Introducing Cooperative Work at Verden Adolescent Home," undated [probably 1948], Folder 4, Box 28, bMS 16035, USC.

47. Elaine Tyler May, *Homeward Bound: American Families in the Cold War Era* (New York: Basic Books, 1988), 14.

3. BUILDING INTERNATIONAL FRIENDSHIP IN AN ORPHAN AGE

1. "'ERP' of Cub Scouts Pleases Marshall," *New York Times,* February 11, 1948, 3; quotes from "7 Boys Presenting Own Aid Program Hear Special Talk," *Washington Post,* February 11, 1948, 1; "Cubs Praised by Marshall," *Baltimore Sun,* March 20, 1948, 10.

2. Wendell Willkie, *One World* (New York: Simon and Schuster, 1943).

3. United Service to Holland, *Dutch Messenger* 2, no. 4 (September 1948): 3, Folder Refugee Children—American Friends Service Committee, Box 6, EP; Saul Pett, "Openhearted America Forges Bonds of Foreign Friendship," *Milwaukee Journal,* August 8, 1948, 4; David Morris, *A Gift from America: The First 50 Years of CARE* (Marietta, GA: Longstreet Press, 1996), 18. For more information on CARE, see Wallace J. Campbell, *The History of CARE: A Personal Account* (New York: Praeger, 1990).

4. Pett, "Openhearted America Forges Bonds of Foreign Friendship."

5. "To Help U.S.-Jap Friendship Cause Through Children: American Church Committee to Urge That Dolls Be Sent to Japan," *Hartford Courant,* October 18, 1926, 5; "New World Friendship Project for Children and Young People," *Christian Science Monitor,* October 6, 1932, 6; Elizabeth Cobbs Hoffman, *American Umpire* (Cambridge, MA: Harvard University Press, 2013), 210; "Five Girl Scouts, Back from Trip Abroad, Satisfy Yearning for Ice Cream Sodas," *New York Times,* September 12, 1938, 24.

6. "Tomorrow's Leaders of Men—Are They Expendable?," Unitarian Service Committee, 1946, Folder AYFWY-Publicity Material, N.D., Box 13, EP; "The Brotherhood of Children," Foster Parents' Plan for War Children, Inc., Folder 4, Box 85, FPP.

7. "Saving the Children Is Most Urgent Need," *World Service,* USC, January 1947, no. 16, Folder AYWY Clippings and Rebecca S. Wolter to "Friend of Children," undated, Folder Refugee Children-American Friends Service Committee, Box 13, EP. Emphasis in original.

8. "Dear World," *American* 149 (January–June 1950): 104; "Pen Pal Society Deluged by Iranians Seeking American Friends," *Bangor Daily News,* November 28, 1986, 38; Joan McPartlin, "60,000 Abroad Write Here Seeking Pen Pals," *Daily Boston Globe,* August 1, 1948, C9.

9. On the history of PLAN, see Henry D. Molumphy, *For Common Decency: The History of Foster Parents Plan, 1937–1983* (Warwick, RI: Foster Parents Plan International, 1984).

10. J. Calvitt Clarke to Chang Ah The, March 30, 1951, Folder 3, Box IB1, CCF; Interview with George Kennan, February 19, 1953, Harry B. Price Papers, Harry S. Truman Library, quoted in Nicolaus Mills, *Winning the Peace: The Marshall Plan and America's Coming of Age as a Superpower* (Hoboken, NJ: John Wiley & Sons, 2008), xii.

11. Rescue Children, Inc., appeal for funds, reprinted from *Women's Wear Daily,* November 7, 1946, Folder 9, Box 16, RC; Ruza L. Stuerm, ed., American Friends of Czechoslovakia, *News of Czechoslovakia* 9, no. 150 (June 1947): 3, Folder Refugee Children Czechoslovakia, Box 6, and unknown writer to Madam, January 28, 1946, Folder 1946, Jan.–Feb., Box 12, EP.

12. Edna Blue to Lucille M. Borschke, November 21, 1947, Folder Foster Parents Plan, May 16, 1946, to –, A–B, Box 22, Record Group 469, Records of U.S. Foreign Assistance Agencies, NA.

13. Catherine Varchaver, "The Letters of European Jewish Children," *Jewish Social Service Quarterly* 23, no. 2 (December 1946): 119.

14. Catherine Varchaver, "Rehabilitation of European Jewish Children Through Personal Contact," *Jewish Social Service Quarterly* 24, no. 4 (June 1948): 411.

15. Catherine Varchaver to Henrietta Buchman, November 9, 1948 (microfilm: file 1034, frames 252–254), JDC 45/54; Varchaver, "Rehabilitation of European Jewish Children Through Personal Contact," 408; Foster Parents' Plan for War Children, Inc., appeal for funds, April 1950, Folder 4, Box 85, FPP.

16. Catherine MacKenzie, "Democracy's Basis Seen in Childhood," *New York Times,* September 29, 1946, 29; "Minutes, Child Welfare Conference, June 6, 1946, Morning Session" (microfilm: file 1030, frame 1193), JDC 45/54.

17. Ernest O. Hauser, "The Dead-End Kids of Cologne," *Saturday Evening Post,* June 16, 1945, 18; Anna Caples to Ernst Papanek, June 15, 1945, Folder Refugee Children Correspondence 1945, Box 5, EP; American Friends Service Committee Program in School Affiliation Service to American Schools, Subject: "German Affiliations," November 5, 1947, Folder School Affiliation Service, Germany School Material 1947, Box Foreign Service 1947, School Affiliation Service (F) to U.S. Government, AFSC; "General Clay Will Help Needy German Children," *New York Times,* October 4, 1949, 12.

18. Benjamin B. Goldman to Albert A. Rutler, September 27, 1948 (microfilm: file 1034, frame 260); Edward Phillips to Robert P. Jacobs, March 10, 1947 (microfilm: file 1034, frames 338–339); Louis H. Sobel to Catherine Varchaver, August 6, 1946 (microfilm: file 1030, frames 1150–1152); and Louis H. Sobel to Sidney S. Cohen, May 13, 1946 (microfilm: file 1030, frames 1214–1215), JDC 45/54.

19. Henrietta Buchman to Catherine Varchaver, October 27, 1948 (microfilm: file 1034, frames 258–259), and Catherine Varchaver to Henrietta Buchman, November 9, 1948 (microfilm: file 1034, frames 252–254), ibid.

20. On the JDC's "school adoption" program, see AJDC New York to AJDC Brussels, May 14, 1947 (microfilm: file 150, frame 820), and Beatrice Vulcan, AJDC Belgium to Edward Phillips, AJDC New York, April 1, 1947 (microfilm: file 151, frames 826–833), ibid. On Joseph Schwartz's approval of letter-based children's adoption programs, see Edward Philips, "Conference with Dr. Joseph Schwartz on Child Care Matters," August 19, 1946 (microfilm: file 1030, frame

1144), ibid. The organization also described the adoption of an eleven-year-old Belgian girl in one of its children's homes by a regiment of American soldiers in a November 1945 press release. "From the JDC Orphanage, Yvonne Became the 'Daughter' of the Regiment," November 16, 1945 (microfilm: file 150, frames 762–763), ibid.

21. Anna Freud and Dorothy T. Burlingham, *War and Children* (New York: Medical War Books, 1943).

22. "Foster Parents' Plan for War Children, Inc.," August–September 1952, Folder 13, Box 85, FPP; Transcript from Rescue Children, Inc., dinner honoring Herbert Tenzer, July 15, 1947, Folder 3, Box 15, RC.

23. Weston LaBarre, "The Age Period of Cultural Fixation," *Mental Hygiene* 33 (April 1949): 211.

24. Ernst Papanek, "Some Highlights on the Situation of the Orphans, Displaced and Destitute Children after World War II," September 1947, Folder Refugee Children—Typescript, Box 12, EP; United States Committee for the Care of European Children, Monthly Statistical Report ending September 1951 (microfilm: reel MKM 8.11, folder 205); Deborah S. Portnoy, "The Adolescent Immigrant," paper given at the National Conference of Jewish Social Welfare in Atlantic City, NJ, May 1948 (microfilm: reel MKM 8.31, folder 585); "Meeting," January 9, 1951 (microfilm: reel MKM 8.12, folder 271); and Lotte Marcuse to Mrs. B. Deitman, December 1, 1950 (microfilm: reel MKM 8.12, folder 232), GJCA. On the practice of religious matching in adoptions in the United States, see Ellen Herman, "The Difference Difference Makes: Justine Wise Polier and Religious Matching in Twentieth-Century Child Adoption," *Religion and American Culture: A Journal of Interpretation* 10, no. 1 (Winter 2000): 57–98.

25. Edna Blue to supporters, April 1945, Folder Refugee Children—Foster Parents Plan for War Children, Box 6, EP.

26. Robert S. to World Jewish Congress, October 16, 1945, in "Correspondence Service for Jewish Children, Child Care Division, World Jewish Congress," no. 1, January 1946, Folder Refugee Children-World Jewish Congress, Youth Aliyah, Box 7, EP.

27. Charles R. to Mrs. Victor J. W., March 3, 1946, Folder 1946 Mar–June, Box 12; Yichak S. to Mrs. Anna L., January 1, 1948, in World Jewish Congress, "Child Care Division Report," January 1948, Folder Refugee Children-World Jewish Congress, Youth Aliyah, Box 7; and Tamara B. and Natan S. to "Friends," January 8, 1946, Folder 1946, Jan.–Feb., Box 12, ibid.

28. Elsie Thomas Culver, "Germany," April 1, 1946, 6, Folder Refugee Children-UNRRA, Box 7 and Jacob G. to Ted P., March 20, 1946, Folder Refugee Children—Correspondence with Organizations, 1946, Box 5, ibid.

29. D. K. to "Godmother," December 29, 1946, Folder 1946, Aug.–Dec., Box 12, ibid.

30. Etsuys H., March 27, 1948, in "Adventures in World Friendship," 1947–1948, Louisville Public Schools, Louisville, Kentucky, Folder AYFWY 1948, Box 13, ibid.; American Junior Red Cross, "American Junior Red Cross Gift Boxes," Folder 5, Box 3, bMS 16035, USC.

31. Zsusi F. to "Friend," February 12, 1946, Folder Refugee Children—World Jewish Congress, Box 7 and Tony M. to "My Dear Little Friends of the United States," August 18, 1945, Folder 1945, Box 12, EP.

32. Dorothy Barrus to Henry H. Marter, April 25, 1947, Folder School Affiliation Service, Italy, Letters to and from 1947 and Memorandum from Alfred E. Stearns to Henry H. Marter, Subject: "Your Memo of February re: Problems of Correspondence," February 18, 1947, Folder School Affiliation Service, Letters from A. E. Stearns, January to December 1947, Box Foreign Service 1947, School Affiliation Service (F) to U.S. Government, AFSC.

33. "George W. Morris Children Send Candy to Poland," in "Adventures in World Friendship," 1947–1948, Louisville Public Schools, Louisville, Kentucky, Folder AYFWY 1948 and Jeanette D. to Carol L., December 22, 1945, Folder AYFWY-History of (Publicity) 1946, Box 13, EP.

34. Memorandum from Stearns to Marter, Subject: "Your Memo of February re: Problems of Correspondence."

35. Outline of the Child "Adoption" Program of the JLC (from the field office, Detroit, 1954); "Our Children," ed. Ida Alter, Jewish Labor Committee Child "Adoption" Program, undated; and quote from Z. Lichtenstein, "Report of the Child Care Department," undated, Folder 24, Box 117, JLC.

36. Stephen Baran to Gentlemen, January 30, 1946, Folder 1946, Jan.–Feb., Box 12, EP; Benedict Anderson, "Long Distance Nationalism," in *The Spectre of Comparisons: Nationalism, Southeast Asia, and the World* (New York: Verso, 1998), 58–74.

37. School Affiliation Service of the American Friends Service Committee, June 15, 1948, Folder 1948, June, Box 12, EP.

38. "The Twenty-Fourth Annual Report of the Save the Children Fund Incorporated," 1942–1943, 13, Folder Refugee Children England, Box 6, EP; Judy Mason to Edna Blue, June 18, 1945, Folder 202, Box 33, FPP.

39. Reinhold Schairer, "World Friendship Activities," *Journal of Educational Sociology* 20, no. 1 (September 1946): 52–59, quote at 54; "4000 Children Showered with Gifts from Americans," *Le National,* December 18, 1945, and "Santa Claus in Uniform," *L'Ordre,* December 18, 1945, excerpts prepared by Frank Dominique, Folder 1945, Box 12, EP.

40. "AJC to Sponsor Gifts for European Children Program," *Hartford Courant,* October 11, 1945, 13; "World Festivals for 1947 Planned," *New York Times,* September 11, 1947, 33; "World Friendship among Children," 1948, Folder World

Festivals for Friendship, Box 110, Record Group 59, General Records of the Department of State, NA.

41. Gerda Schairer, "Progress Report No. 2 of the World Christmas Festival," Folder 15, Box 27, bMS 16007, USC; "4000 Children Showered with Gifts from Americans"; quote from Reinhold Schairer, "World Friendship Activities," 55.

42. Alice Pollard to William Clayton, March 16, 1948, Folder 0-4-1-1, Box 57, Record Group 102, Records of the Children's Bureau, NA.

43. Pett, "Openhearted America Forges Bonds of Foreign Friendship"; F. I. Kaye, "The Children of Europe and the Foster Parents of America: Mrs. Roosevelt Visits Her European Foster Children, the Polish Girl Janina, the Spaniard Herman, and the Little English Boy Tommy," Folder 29, Box 86, FPP; Statement of Mr. J. D. Zellerbach, Chief of ECA Mission to Italy, July 20, 1949, Folder 1, Box 48, bMS 347, CRJ.

44. Lawrence K. Frank, "Good-Will to the Children," *New York Times*, December 12, 1948, SM44; China's Children Fund, "Japan," *China News* 5, no. 2 (Winter 1948): 3, CCFY; Irmgard P. (for the girls) and Dr. Hertha D. (for the teachers) to Kaufmann's Department Store, January 31, 1952, Folder Children's Book Fund Austria Thank-You Letters, 1951–1952, Box 480, CARE.

45. LaBarre, "The Age Period of Cultural Fixation," 216; Harriet Eager Davis, "Boys and Girls Are Working for Peace," *Parents'*, July 1947, Folder AYFWY Publicity Material 1947, Box 13, EP.

46. Interview, Miss Henderson and Miss Miller with Capt. Myron L. Brown, Re-Orientation Branch, Civil Affairs Division, War Department, Washington, DC, August 7, 1946, Folder 6, Defense Box 5, GS; Memorandum from Lois E. Wells, CRALOG Office, Public Welfare Branch, to Whom It May Concern, Subject: "'Affiliation' of American Schools with German Schools," January 17, 1947, and "Sunday, January 9" meeting notes, Folder School Affiliation Service, Germany, Program 1947, Box Foreign Service 1947, School Affiliation Service (F) to U.S. Government, AFSC; Harald Thomas Oskar Leder, "Americans and German Youth in Nuremberg, 1945–1956: A Study in Politics and Culture" (PhD diss., Louisiana State University, 1997), 534; "100,000 Friendship Letters Awaiting Delivery in Sweden: Many Inquiries Agreed to Handle," *Christian Science Monitor*, May 7, 1949, 18; McPartlin, "60,000 Abroad Write Here Seeking Pen Pals"; Dorothy Whipple to Mrs. Ray Archer, May 1, 1957, Folder Letter Writing Committee Children's Plea for Peace, Box 23, and Ethel Schroeder to Miss Faucett, June 10, 1953, Folder Pen Pals A–Z, Box 7, Record Group 306, Records of the U.S. Information Agency; Richard Walsh to William Phillips, May 19, 1951, and William Phillips to Edna MacDonough, June 13, 1951, Folder 125 International Friendship League, Box 15, General Records of the Department of State, NA.

47. "Theodore Ahrens Trade High School Sends Treasure Chests to Holland," in "Adventures in World Friendship," 1947–1948, Louisville Public Schools, Louisville, Kentucky, Folder AYFWY 1948, Box 13; Andre T. to Madam, undated, Folder N.D., Box 12; and Oscar M. to Ernst Papanek, February 14, 1946, Folder 1946, Jan.–Feb., Box 12, EP.

4. RAISING LITTLE COLD WARRIORS

1. Fraser Wilkins, Political Counselor of Embassy, Foreign Service Despatch No. 1734, from American Embassy New Delhi, India to Department of State, Washington, Subject: "The HIGH International Study Conference on Child Welfare (convened by the International Union for Child Welfare in Cooperation with the Indian Council for Child Welfare) held in the Sir Cowasji Jehangir Hall, Bombay, India, December 5–12, 1952," February 5, 1953, Folder Child Welfare, International Study Conference & 6th Social Work Conference, Bombay— Madras, December 1952, Box 31, Record Group 43, Records of International Conferences, Commissions, and Expositions, NA.

2. "Report on International Study Conference on Child Welfare," Folder Child Welfare, International Conference On, Bombay, December 5, 1952, ibid.; Wilkins, "The HIGH International Study Conference on Child Welfare."

3. Telegram from Chester Bowles, New Delhi, to Secretary of State, July 1, 1952, Folder Child Welfare, International Conference On, Bombay, December 5, 1952; Oscar Ewing to Lindsay Warren, January 19, 1953, Folder Child Welfare, Inter. Study Conf. & 6th Social Work Conference, Bombay—Madras, Dec. 1952; Department of State Memorandum of Conversation, Subject: "International Study Conference of Social Work," March 20, 1952; Memorandum, "United States Representation at the International Study Conference on Child Welfare, Bombay, December 5–12, 1952, and at the Sixth Session of the International Conference of Social Work, Madras, December 14–19, 1952," November 3, 1952; Telegram from John Hickerson to Chester Bowles, American Embassy New Delhi, November 17, 1952; and Memorandum for Files, Subject: "Excerpt from a letter from Ambassador Bowles Relative to United States Participation in the Social Welfare Conferences in India," February 5, 1953, Folder Child Welfare, International Conference On, Bombay, December 5, 1952; Evelyn Hersey to Mr. Kerry and Miss Kernohan, "Supplementary Information re: Mr. Lester Granger," September 5, 1952, Folder Child Welfare, Inter. Study Conf. & 6th Social Work Conference, Bombay—Madras, Dec. 1952, Box 31, ibid.

4. Charles R. Joy, "Report on Poland," November 3, 1947, Folder 19, Box 47, bMS 347, CRJ.

5. Charles R. Joy to Mel Arnold, June 23, 1953, Folder 8, Box 48, ibid.; J. Calvitt Clarke to William G. Taylor, Jr., November 20, 1950, Folder 16, Box IB21, CCF.

6. Verent Mills to J. Calvitt Clarke, January 2, 1951, and Verent Mills to J. Calvitt Clarke, January 12, 1951, Folder 1; Verent Mills to J. Calvitt Clarke, June 6, 1951, and Verent Mills to Helen Clarke, January 17, 1951, Folder 5, Box IB1, CCF; "China," 1949, Folder 81, Box 114, FPP; Larry E. Tise, *A Book about Children: The World of Christian Children's Fund, 1938–1991* (Falls Church, VA: Hartland Publishing for the Christian Children's Fund, 1993), 24, 28–30.

7. Daniel Polig, Introduction, in Edmund W. Janss, *Yankee Si! The Story of Dr. J. Calvitt Clarke and His 36,000 Children* (New York: William Morrow & Company, 1961), quotes at viii and 3.

8. Lack of funds also contributed to the USC's decision to end its program in Czechoslovakia. Helen Fogg, untitled report, Folder 6, Box 68, bMS 16103; Raymond Bragg to Kathryn Fenn, December 20, 1948, and Raymond Bragg to Karel Haspl, December 27, 1948, Folder 11, Box 23, bMS 16035, USC; Letter from Edna Blue to Foster Parents of Polish Children, 1949 [possibly October], Folder 4, Box 85, FPP; "Jewish Charity Groups Slated to Leave Poland: Voluntary Agencies Are Being Ousted," *Chicago Daily Tribune,* November 4, 1949, 12; " 'Curtain' Falls on U.S. Help to Red Satellites: Its Flow Is Cut Down to a Trickle," *Chicago Daily Tribune,* April 16, 1950, 18; Edna Blue to Friends, Draft letter, September 1950, Folder 4; quote from "Foster Parents' Plan for War Children, Inc.," pamphlet, August–September 1952, 22–23, Folder 13, Box 85, FPP.

9. J. Calvitt Clarke to Verent Mills, August 10, 1951, Folder 7, Box IB1, and "Two Yank's Encounter Outside a Barbershop—and the Result," probably April 1953, Folder 8, Box IB2, CCF; Janss, *Yankee Si!* 27.

10. William F. Asbury, "General Report, Lapland and Finland," December 2, 1954, Folder 4, Box IB15, and "A Verbal Report Presented to the CCF HK Policy Committee by Mr. J. J. De Ryke at a Regular Meeting Held on July 25, 1963, at the First National City Bank Office," Folder 6, Box IB5, CCF.

11. Letter from Foster Parents' Plan for War Children to all members of Foster Parents' Plan, Inc., April 17, 1956, Folder 14, and Lenore Sorin to Thomas L. O'Hagan, June 20, 1956, Folder 20, Box 3, FPP.

12. Ruth Fisher to Verent Mills, January 5, 1951, Folder 1, Box IB1, CCF.

13. " 'Friendship Fallout'—a Sponsorship Review," *SCF World Reporter,* Fall 1959, Folder 1960s, SCF.

14. Clarence E. Pickett, "AFSC Looks Forward," *American Friends Service Commission Bulletin,* November 1948, Folder American Friends Service Committee, Box 7, EP.

15. Fred Mason to Edna Blue, March 29, 1949, Folder 279, Box 138, and Fred Mason, "Field Report-New Areas in Italy," April 9, 1951, Folder 453, Box 158, FPP.

16. In 1951, Pentz was transferred from the Children's Bureau to the Point IV program. Martha Eliot to Ruth Shipley, September 29, 1952; "Country: India, Field: Social Security and Social Service," undated; and Deborah Pentz to Sarah

Dietrick, January 25, 1953, Folder 0-1-5-4-6, Jan. 1955 India, Box 545, Record
Group 102, Records of the U.S. Children's Bureau, NA.

17. Harriet Hyman Alonso, "Women Peace Activists during the McCarthy
Era," in Joanne Meyerowitz, ed., *Not June Cleaver: Women and Gender in Postwar
America, 1945–1960* (Philadelphia: Temple University Press, 1994): 128–150; Ellen
Schrecker, *Many Are the Crimes: McCarthyism in America* (Princeton, NJ: Princeton
University Press, 1999).

18. Telegram from Rabbi Zalman Schneerson to Edward Warburg, January 20,
1953 (microfilm: file 297, frames 400–401); Beatrice Vulcan, AJDC Belgium, to
AJJDC New York, Re: "Your letter No. 214 of March 14, 1947 and No. 216 of March
25, 1947," April 1, 1947 (microfilm: file 151, frames 826–833); and Adolph Held to
Alexander Kahn, December 22, 1952 (microfilm: file 297, frame 403), JDC 45/54;
"Red Paper Continues Attack Against Agency," *Hartford Courant,* January 19, 1953, 6.

19. Robert LeFevre, "Even the Girl Scouts," in "The Girl Scouts, the United
Nations and Our Own Constitution," in Extension of Remarks of Hon. Timothy P.
Sheehan of Illinois in the House of Representatives, Friday, July 2, 1954, *Congres-
sional Record—Appendix,* A4941–A4942, Folder American Legion Congressional
Record, and Confidential Memorandum from Leonard Lathrop to Regional
Directors, Subject: "Criticisms of Girl Scout Organization," April 9, 1954, Folder
American Legion Controversy, Criticism of the Girl Scouts, Box American Legion
Controversy, Communism and "Un-American" Activities Correspondence to
Criticism of the Girl Scout Handbook; "Resolution 33, Girl Scouts of America,"
American Legion Department of Illinois, 36th Annual Convention, Chicago,
Illinois, August 6, 1954, Folder American Legion Controversy, General, 1953–1954,
Box American Legion Controversy, General, 1953–1956, Atlantic Monthly
(American Legion) Attack, GS.

20. Bert Alcott to Mrs. J. H. Parsons, undated [probably 1954], Folder Amer-
ican Legion Controversy, Criticism of the Girl Scouts, Box American Legion
Controversy, Communism and "Un-American" Activities Correspondence to
Criticism of the Girl Scout Handbook, ibid.; Eleanor Roosevelt, "My Day," August
11, 1954, available online at http://www.gwu.edu/~erpapers/myday/displaydoc.cfm?
_y=1954&_f=md002930; Herb Block, *Washington Post,* August 11, 1954; Alice C.
Carney to Nina Squier, August 19, 1954, Folder American Legion Controversy,
American Legion Attack, Box American Legion Controversy, General 1953–1956,
Atlantic Monthly (American Legion) Attack; Lillian Moller Gilbreth, "Girl
Scouting: One Answer to Communism," in Extension of Remarks of Hon. Robert
W. Kean of New Jersey, House of Representatives, Wednesday, July 21, 1954,
Congressional Record—Appendix, A5288, and Anne L. New to Robert W. Kean,
July 19, 1954, Folder American Legion Congressional Record and "Girl Scouts
in Wonderland," April 15, 1955, Folder American Legion Controversy, Criticism
of the Girl Scouts, Box American Legion Controversy, Communism and

"Un-American" Activities Correspondence to Criticism of the Girl Scout Handbook; Memorandum from Mary J. Shelly to National Staff at Convention, Subject: "Facts about the Handbook Controversy," October 1955, and "Changes in the Girl Scout Handbook Intermediate Program (1953 edition)," Folder American Legion Controversy Handbook Criticism/Revision 8/54–12/54, Box American Legion Controversy, Handbook Criticism to Illinois American Legion Resolution, GS.

21. Louis M. Lyons, "From WGBH Broadcast," November 26, 1954, Folder American Legion Controversy Radio Reports, Box American Legion Controversy, Newspaper/Magazine Articles to Radio Reports, GS.

22. "The Retreat of the Girl Scouts," *New York Post,* December 28, 1954, Folder American Legion Controversy Newspaper and Magazine Clippings, Box American Legion Controversy Newspaper/Magazine Articles to Radio Reports; Shelly, "Facts about the Handbook Controversy"; "Criticisms of the Girl Scouts," Folder American Legion Controversy, Criticism of the Girl Scouts, Box American Legion Controversy, Communism and "Un-American" Activities Correspondence to Criticism of the Girl Scout Handbook; Ruth W. Clark to the President and Board of Directors, January 27, 1955, and Charles S. Milligan to Girl Scouts of the United States of America, March 5, 1955, Folder American Legion Controversy Region I, Box American Legion Controversy Region I to Region IX, ibid.

23. Ismene Kalaris to Fred Mason, December 14, 1954; Ismene Kalaris to Fred Mason, December 15, 1954; Gloria Matthews to Fred Mason, March 15, 1955; Fred Mason to Gloria Matthews, February 10, 1955; Fred Mason to Gloria Matthews, April 22, 1955; and Gloria Matthews to Fred Mason, April 26, 1955, Folder 300, Box 140, FPP.

24. Henry La Cossitt, "The Amazing Brats of Monte Flavio," *Parents' Magazine and Family Home Guide* 32 (February 1957): 39, 118–120.

25. Lenore Sorin to Elma Baccanelli Laurenzi, September 5, 1956, Folder 454, Box 158, and Lenore Sorin to Friends, undated, Folder 35, Box 86, FPP.

26. Clarence Pickett, "Proposals for Peace, VII," *Nation* 176, no. 8 (February 21, 1953): 166; "Japan," 1953, Folder Japan Administration Finance International Centers Program, Box Foreign Service Japan 1959, AFSC.

27. Signed into law by President Eisenhower in 1954, Public Law 480 (the Agricultural Trade Development and Assistance Act) provided an avenue by which U.S. agricultural products could be used for foreign aid. President Kennedy renamed the program Food for Peace in 1961.

28. *22nd Annual Report, Save the Children Annual Report for the Fiscal Year Ending June 30, 1953,* 16; Lewis M. Hoskins, "Voluntary Agencies and Foundations in International Aid," *Annals of the American Academy of Political and Social Science* 329 (May 1960): 66.

29. Ibid.; Richard P. Saunders, "Children in Europe in an Age of Anxiety," *Journal of Educational Sociology* 28, no. 7 (March 1955): 298; Helen Fogg to Joan

Kain, July 3, 1956, Folder 6, Box 1, bMS 16036; Jay E. Daily, "The Unitarian Service Committee, Report from Korea," undated, Folder Home Office—Korea—Education Mission, Box 21, bMS 16011; Helen Fogg to Samuel C. Adams, September 23, 1955, Folder Cambodia Teacher Education Project, Box 1, bMS 16008, USC.

30. Ernest Nash to J. Calvitt Clarke, "Children's Garden—Hospital," December 31, 1958, and "Visit to the Children's Home," undated, Folder 6, Box IB6, CCF.

31. "Advisory Committee on Voluntary Foreign Aid," September 15, 1953, Folder Home Office—U.S. Department of State—Advisory Committee on Voluntary Foreign Aid, Box 33, bMS 16011, USC; *FOA and U.S. Voluntary Agencies* (Washington, DC: Foreign Operations Administration, undated), (microfilm: file 1184, frame 630), JDC 55/64.

32. Dwight D. Eisenhower to Anna Lord Strauss, May 29, 1956, quoted in Helen Laville, "The Importance of Being (In)Earnest: Voluntary Associations and the Irony of the State-Private Network during the Early Cold War," in Helen Laville and Hugh Wilford, eds., *The U.S. Government, Citizen Groups and the Cold War: The State-Private Network* (New York: Routledge, 2006), 53; American Council of Voluntary Agencies for Foreign Service, Inc., Committee on Korea, Minutes of Meeting, February 14, 1958, Folder Korea Committees and Organizations, A.C.V.A. (American Council of Volunteer Organizations), Box Foreign Service Japan 1958, AFSC.

33. Campbell Craig and Fredrik Logevall, *America's Cold War: The Politics of Insecurity* (Cambridge, MA: Harvard University Press, 2009), 160; Andrew Tully, "Our Personal Foreign Aid," *ICA Digest* 61, no. 11 (December 1960): 4.

34. *22nd Annual Report, Save the Children Annual Report for the Fiscal Year Ending June 30, 1953,* 12.

35. Helen Tieszen, "Play Behavior in Deprived Korean Children," *Children* 4, no. 1 (January–February 1957): 20; Helen Tieszen and Rose Alvernaz, "Technical Assistance for Child Welfare in Korea," *Children* 5, no. 4 (July–August 1958): 134–139, quote at 135; "Tehran Demonstration Children's Home, Joint Project of the Ministry of the Interior, Municipality of Tehran and the U.S. Operations Mission Iran," August 17, 1956, Folder 0-1-5-4-8, Iran, 1953–1956, Box 546, Records of the Children's Bureau, NA; LeRoy Bowman, Benjamin A. Gjenvick, and Eleanor T. M. Harvey, *Children of Tragedy: Church World Service Survey Team Report on Intercountry Orphan Adoption* (New York: National Council of Churches, 1961), 18; Ernest T. Nash, "Report on Conference between Superintendents of CCF Korea Homes and the Staff of CCF Korea Office Held from August 28 to August 31, 1956," Folder 5, Box IB9; Penelope Brooke-Johnson, "Child Care in Hong Kong," July 1958, Folder 3, Box IB7; Ernest T. Nash, "Lessons from a Hong Kong Visit," 1958, Folder 2, Box IB10, CCF.

36. Jal F. Bulsara, "Toward Human Welfare . . . the Eastern Way," *Survey* 88, no. 2 (February 1952): 59; Ernest F. Witte, "Developing Professional Leadership for

Social Programs," *Annals of the American Academy of Political and Social Science*
329 (May 1960): 123–136. Verent Mills led a committee appointed by the British
governor in Hong Kong that studied child welfare problems and drafted a child
welfare act. See John C. Caldwell, *Children of Calamity* (New York: John Day
Company, 1957), 57. A child welfare committee in Korea composed of representatives from foreign voluntary agencies and U.S. and Korean government officials
advised the Korean government on child welfare matters and urged it to adopt a
child welfare law. See "Child and Family Welfare in Korea," undated, Folder
Central Social Workers Training Institute, Box 2, Record Group 469, Records of
U.S. Foreign Assistance Agencies, 1948–1961, NA. See also Korea Child Welfare
Committee c/o Ministry of Health and Social Affairs, "Petition," November 9,
1959, Folder 714 Child Welfare Committee Minutes etc. '57 thru, Box 3, ibid.

37. Louis Schneider, "Verbatim Report to Refugee Committee," January 5,
1959, Folder Hong Kong Foreign Service Reports 1959, Box Hong Kong Foreign
Service 1959; William Channel to Dave Elder, January 9, 1962, and David Elder
to William Channel, November 2, 1962, Folder ISD Refugee Program Overseas
Hong Kong Letters to and from Hong Kong 1962, Box International Service
Division Refugee Program Overseas 1962, AFSC.

38. Earl McCoy to Jane Bennett, June 6, 1958, Folder Israel, Social & Tech-
nical Assistance, Letters From, 1958, Box Foreign Service Israel 1958; J. Philip
Buskirk, "Israel Unit October 1959/September 1960," Folder ISD-STA Middle East
Program, Israel: Reports, Monthly 1960, Box Foreign Service Israel 1960; Lorraine
Cleveland to Bernhard Klausener, October 6, 1961, Folder ISD STA Pakistan
Programs Pakistan—E (Dacca)—Reports Quarterly, Box Pakistan 1961, ibid.

39. J. Calvitt Clarke to Norman Turner, May 16, 1962, Folder 8, Box IB5;
Ernest Nash to J. Calvitt Clarke, May 8, 1956, Folder 2, Box IB9; and Seiji Giga,
"Japan," *CCF and Our World Today,* October 1968, CCF.

40. On the importance of cultivating self-help in underdeveloped areas, see
Bulsara, "Toward Human Welfare," 59; Michael E. Latham, *Modernization as
Ideology: American Social Science and "Nation Building" in the Kennedy Era* (Chapel
Hill: University of North Carolina Press, 2000), 123; Michael E. Latham, "Intro-
duction: Modernization, International History and the Cold War World," in David
Engerman et al., eds., *Staging Growth: Modernization, Development and the Global
Cold War* (Amherst, MA: Amherst University Press, 2003), 7; Robert Sage to
Thomas O'Hagan, October 17, 1957, Folder 3, Box 24, FPP; Lucy W. Adams, "The
Community Development Program in Korea: Review and Forecast," undated
[possibly 1960], Folder A Ten Year Plan for Community Development in Korea,
Box 1, Records of U.S. Foreign Assistance Agencies, NA.

41. *Twenty-Third Year of Service to Children, Annual Report of the Save the
Children Federation for the Fiscal Year Ending June 30, 1954,* 7; "'Always We Have
Dreamed': From Dream to Reality—the Story of Self-Help," *SCF World Reporter,*

Fall 1959, Folder 1960s, and Glen Leet, "A Special Message from Our Program Director," *SCF World Reporter,* Spring 1959, Folder 1950s, SCF.

42. *Training for Social Work,* Third International Survey (United Nations: Department of Economic and Social Affairs, 1958), 93.

43. International Cooperation Administration Manual Order 2710.1, quoted in Louis Miniclier, "Community Development as a Vehicle of U.S. Foreign Aid," *Community Development Journal* 4, no. 1 (1969): 8; "Village Self-Help Program Is Changing the Lives of Children," *SCF World Reporter,* Spring 1960, and Richard P. Saunders, letter, *SCF World Reporter,* Fall 1959, Folder 1960s, SCF.

44. "And Now the Children?," *Time* 78, no. 14 (October 6, 1961): 269; Margaret Mead, *A Creative Life for Your Children* (Washington, DC: United States Department of Health, Education and Welfare, Social Security Administration, Children's Bureau, 1962), 28.

45. Joseph Wechsberg, "They're Afraid of Their Own Children," *Saturday Evening Post,* April 18, 1953, 134; Joseph Wechsberg, "Communism's Child Hostages," *Saturday Evening Post,* April 1, 1950, 126; Ann Su Cardwell, "Poles Mark Children's Day by Accent on Communism," *Christian Science Monitor,* June 19, 1952, 14.

46. "Visitor to USSR Reports on Soviet Women's Status," August 1953, Women's Packet number 6, Feature Packets, Recurring Themes, Box 19, RG 306, Records of the U.S. Information Agency, NA, quoted in Laura A. Belmonte, *Selling the American Way: U.S. Propaganda and the Cold War* (Philadelphia: University of Pennsylvania Press, 2008), 144–145; Herschel and Edith Alt, *Russia's Children: A First Report on Child Welfare in the Soviet Union* (New York: Bookman Associates, 1959), 101; William H. Wilbur, "Russia Weans Babies from Family's Love: Molds Young to Communism," *Chicago Daily Tribune,* January 31, 1957, 6.

47. Margaret Wylie, *Children of China* (Hong Kong: Dragonfly Books, 1962), 16, 35, 88; Pearl S. Buck, in Wylie, *Children of China,* introduction. On debates about public responsibility for child care in the United States in the post–World War II era, see Emilie Stoltzfus, *Citizen, Mother, Worker: Debating Public Responsibility for Child Care after the Second World War* (Chapel Hill: University of North Carolina Press, 2003).

48. Board of Community Relations, Buffalo, New York, *Building the Community Through Family Life,* 1955, Folder Building the Community Through Family Life, Container 4, Records of the U.S. Information Agency, NA. For a detailed analysis of the USIA's use of images of gender and the family in official propaganda, see Belmonte, 136–158.

49. Ernest Nash to J. Calvitt Clarke, December 1, 1955, Folder 9, Box IB8, CCF.

50. Christina Klein, *Cold War Orientalism: Asia in the Middlebrow Imagination, 1945–1961* (Berkeley: University of California Press, 2003), 151; Janss, *Yankee Si!* 126. On the connections between domestic ideals and U.S. foreign policy during

the Cold War, see Elaine Tyler May, *Homeward Bound: American Families in the Cold War Era* (New York: Basic Books, 1988); Laura Briggs, "Mother, Child, Race, Nation: The Visual Iconography of Rescue and the Politics of Transnational and Transracial Adoption," *Gender & History* 15, no. 2 (August 2003): 179–200; Donna Alvah, *Unofficial Ambassadors: American Military Families Overseas and the Cold War, 1946–1965* (New York: New York University Press, 2007). A growing body of scholarship explores the role of gender ideals in bolstering U.S. expansionism or imperialism more generally. See, for example, Mary Renda, *Taking Haiti: Military Occupation and the Culture of U.S. Imperialism, 1915–1940* (Chapel Hill: University of North Carolina Press, 2001); Kristin Hoganson, *Fighting for American Manhood: How Gender Politics Provoked the Spanish-American and Philippine-American Wars* (New Haven, CT: Yale University Press, 2000); Laura Wexler, *Tender Violence: Domestic Visions in an Age of U.S. Imperialism* (Chapel Hill: University of North Carolina Press, 2000); Emily Rosenberg, " 'Foreign Affairs' after World War II: Connecting Sexual and International Politics," *Diplomatic History* 18 (Winter 1994): 59–70.

51. "Orphanage 'Athanase Coquerel' Crosne (near Villeneuve-St-Georges)," April 23, 1952, Folder Children's Book Fund—Package Contents, Cost, Distribution Abroad, Box 480, CARE; Constance Capron Fucito as told to John Carlova, "I Am Grateful to My International 'Family,' " *Reader's Digest,* January 1959, 59–63, Folder 1960s, SCF; "Report on Korea," *China News* 8, no. 1 (Winter 1950–51): 1, CCFY.

52. Gennaro B. to Our Little Friends, the American Students, August 18, 1945, Folder 1945, Box 12, EP; Soon Ok to Casey Miller, June 1962, Folder 3, Box 1, CM.

53. "I.N. Bloom School Makes Friends with Children in Lille, France," in "Adventures in World Friendship," 1947–1948, Louisville Public Schools, Louisville, Kentucky, 17, Folder AYWFY 1948, Box 13, EP; Faith Graves to J. Calvitt Clarke, March 20, 1956, and Mrs. Ellis (Faith) Graves to J. Calvitt Clarke, August 5, 1956, Folder 11, Box IB14, CCF; "Foster Parents' Report," May 1954, Folder 17, Box 86, FPP.

54. "Plan-Aid=Self-Help" and "A Smile from Flor Cecilia," Foster Parents' Plan Report, December 1965, 3, 9, Foster Child Scrapbook, Subseries 2.4, Box 1, PG.

55. "Chief Petty Officer Meets His Foster Children," Foster Parents' Plan Report, September 1965, 4–5, ibid.

56. Betty Jo Ramsey, "The Greatest Gift of All," *Good Housekeeping* 153 (December 1961): 44, 46; "Sponsors See SCF at Work in Korea," *SCF World Reporter,* Summer 1959, Folder 1960s, SCF; "Chief Petty Officer Meets His Foster Children."

57. "Survey of American Correspondents of Letters Abroad," October 1955, Folder Letter Writing Committee, Letters Abroad, Box 23, Records of the U.S. Information Agency, NA.

58. "800 Penitentiary Inmates 'Adopt' 2 Asian Children," *Baltimore Sun,* March 7, 1959, 28; Robert H. Terte, "P.S. 80 Adopts Korean 'Sister'; 1,100 Write Composite Letters," *New York Times,* October 6, 1960, 36; "It's Children First on Navy Ship Here," *New York Times,* May 17, 1953, 32.

59. "Miss Gloria Matthews, Director in United States and Canada, Visits the Children in Europe," 1957, and Van to Foster Mother, quoted in Harry F. V. Edward, "Viet Nam-1957," September 1957, 5, Folder 27, Box 86; Memorandum from Elizabeth Whitmore to Director, Foster Parents' Plan, Subject: "Quarterly Report. Period: July 1–September 30, 1956, Supplementary to Report submitted for 2nd Quarter," October 1, 1956, Folder 12, Box 2, FPP.

60. Chung-lan to Eunice H. and Mattie F., July 2, 1949, Folder 84, Box 115; Lin-hui to Dr. Harold S. and Dr. Ednita B., October 29, 1949; Yu-sze to Muriel H., Secretary, October 19, 1949; and Van-un to Mrs. R. H. J., Secretary, October 24, 1949, Folder 38, Box 46; Fu-kun to Foster Parents, July 11, 1949, Folder 87, Box 115; King-tsai to Foster Parents, July 11, 1949, Folder 84; Feng-ming to Joy C., November 9, 1949, Folder 86; and Fu-kun to Foster Parents, July 11, 1949, Folder 87, Box 115, FPP.

61. Klein, *Cold War Orientalism,* 153; Verent Mills to J. Calvitt Clarke, February 9, 1952, Folder 11, Box IB1; J. Calvitt Clarke to Verent Mills, October 12, 1952, Folder 4, and J. Calvitt Clarke to Verent Mills, April 1, 1953, Folder 7, Box IB2; J. Calvitt Clarke to Verent Mills, April 19, 1951, Folder 4, Box IB1, CCF; Henry D. Molumphy, *For Common Decency: The History of Foster Parents Plan, 1937–1983* (Warwick, RI: Foster Parents Plan International, 1984), 248; George Ross to Robert Walter, Re: "Brazil and Negro FC's," January 26, 1967, Folder 61, Box 112, FPP. By 1961, Christian Children's Fund sponsored children in Africa, Haiti, and Jamaica. See Janss, *Yankee Si!* CCF opened an African office in Nairobi, Kenya, in 1973 (Tise, 297). Save the Children Federation opened its first major African program in 1962 in Tanganyika, following initial forays into Cameroon and Ghana (Unpublished history of Save the Children Federation, 1986, 11, SCF). Foster Parents' Plan started enrolling black children in 1965 when it initiated a small program in Buenaventura, Colombia. PLAN did not expand into Africa until 1974 (Molumphy, *For Common Decency,* 248, 281). On the relationship between American race relations and the Cold War, see also Penny Von Eschen, *Satchmo Blows Up the World: Jazz Ambassadors Play the Cold War* (Cambridge, MA: Harvard University Press, 2004); Thomas Borstelmann, *The Cold War and the Color Line: American Race Relations in the Global Arena* (Cambridge, MA: Harvard University Press, 2001); Mary Dudziak, *Cold War Civil Rights: Race and the Image of American Democracy* (Princeton, NJ: Princeton University Press, 2000).

62. On transnational adoptions from Korea, see, for example, Arissa Oh, *To Save the Children of Korea: The Cold War Origins of International Adoption* (Redwood City, CA: Stanford University Press, 2015); Rachel Winslow, "Colorblind Empire:

International Adoption, Social Policy, and the American Family, 1945–1976" (PhD diss., University of California, Santa Barbara, 2012); Eleana Kim, "The Origins of Korean Adoption: Cold War Geopolitics and Intimate Diplomacy," *U.S.-Korea Institute at SAIS Working Paper Series,* WP 09-09, October 2009; Catherine Ceniza Choy and Gregory Paul Choy, "Transformative Terrains: Korean American Adoptees and the Social Constructions of an American Childhood," in Caroline Levander and Carol Singley, eds., *The American Child: A Cultural Studies Reader* (New Brunswick, NJ: Rutgers University Press, 2003), 262–279. For the statistic on the total number of foreign-born children adopted by Americans, see Howard Altstein and Rita J. Simon, eds., *Intercountry Adoption: A Multinational Perspective* (New York: Greenwood Publishing Group, 1991), 3.

63. Henry La Cossitt, "We Adopted a War Orphan," *Saturday Evening Post,* December 15, 1951, 103; Janss, *Yankee Si!* 57; Janet C. to J. Calvitt Clarke, June 29, 1962, Folder 9, Box IB5, CCF; Tallulah Bankhead as told to Henry La Cossitt, "My Daughter, Barbara," *Cosmopolitan* 136 (April 1954): 79.

64. Arissa Oh suggests that child sponsorships helped build connections between Americans and Korean children and thus helped initiate international adoptions from Korea. See Oh, *To Save the Children of Korea;* J. Calvitt Clarke to Verent Mills, March 31, 1954, Folder 2, Box IB3, CCF; "Korean Waif Becomes Real American Boy," *Los Angeles Times,* January 10, 1955, 19.

5. FORGING THE FREE CHILD'S ARMOR

1. "Miss Tieszen and Orphan Pak: No Longer Alone," *Korea Times,* October 23, 1956, Folder 5, Box IB9, CCF.

2. Melvin A. Glasser, "Fact-Finding for the White House Conference on Children and Youth," *Social Security Bulletin* 13, no. 11 (November 1950): 15–16; Mary Ann Callan, "White House Parley: Better Children's World Promised," *Los Angeles Times,* December 29, 1950, B1; Harry S. Truman, "Address Before the Midcentury White House Conference on Children and Youth," December 5, 1950, available online by Gerhard Peters and John T. Woolley, *The American Presidency Project,* http://www.presidency.ucsb.edu/ws/?pid=13677.

3. Dorothy Barclay, "Parent and Child: The Youth at Midcentury," *New York Times,* December 31, 1950, SM9.

4. "Free Child's Armor," *Washington Post,* December 4, 1950, 8.

5. William L. Ryan, "Reds Brainwash Greek Tots," *Christian Science Monitor,* April 14, 1955, 4; P. K. Padmanabhan, "Red China's Children Brain-Washed Early," *Los Angeles Times,* August 10, 1960, A12; Fred Mason to Thomas L. O'Hagan, November 16, 1956, Folder 13, Box 2, FPP.

6. Herschel Alt and Edith Alt, *Russia's Children: A First Report on Child Welfare in the Soviet Union* (New York: Bookman Associates, 1959), 202–204, 216;

Padmanabhan, "Red China's Children Brain-Washed Early." See also Joseph Wortis, *Soviet Psychiatry* (Baltimore: Williams and Wilkins, 1950), especially "Child Psychiatry," 103–128, and Nancy Rollins, *Child Psychiatry in the Soviet Union: Preliminary Observations* (Cambridge, MA: Harvard University Press, 1972), 1–25.

7. Margaret Mead and Elena Calas, "Child-Training Ideals in a Postrevolutionary Context: Soviet Russia," in Margaret Mead, ed., *Childhood in Contemporary Cultures* (Chicago: University of Chicago Press, 1955), 179–203, quote at 195. Recent scholarship has explored Soviet programs aimed at molding children into members of the collective. See, for example, Ann Livschiz, "Growing Up Soviet: Childhood in the Soviet Union, 1918–1958" (PhD diss., Stanford University, 2007), and Gleb Tsipursky, "Pleasure, Power, and the Pursuit of Communism: State-Sponsored Youth Popular Culture in the Soviet Union, 1945–1968" (PhD diss., University of North Carolina at Chapel Hill, 2011).

8. William L. Ryan, "Reds Train Bright Youngsters to Form Hard Core of Party," *Miami Daily News,* December 30, 1953, 16-A; Joseph Wechsberg, "They're Afraid of Their Own Children," *Saturday Evening Post,* April 18, 1953, 38; Joseph Wechsberg, "Communism's Child Hostages," *Saturday Evening Post,* April 1, 1950, 125; Frank Moraes, "China Visit Bares Robot Education Imposed by Reds, Indian Declares," *New York Times,* June 13, 1952, 4.

9. Alt and Alt, *Russia's Children,* 203, 236.

10. Advertisement for the American-Korean Foundation in *Report of the Rusk Mission to Korea,* March 11–18, 1953 (New York: American-Korean Foundation, 1953); Leonard W. Mayo, "2,000,000 Reasons to Help South Korea," *New York Times,* August 2, 1953, SM10; Memorandum from Verent Mills to J. Calvitt Clarke, Subject: "Inspection of Orphan Homes in Korea Sponsored by Christian Children's Fund," November/December 1952, Folder 4, Box IB2, CCF.

11. Helen R. Tieszen, "Child Welfare Education, Christian Children's Fund, Inc., Korea 1955–1957," April 5, 1957, Folder Welfare Training and Education, Box 15, Record Group 469, Records of U.S. Foreign Assistance Agencies, 1948–1961, NA; *Report of the Rusk Mission to Korea;* William F. Asbury, *Military Help to Korean Orphanages: A Survey Made for the Commander-in-Chief, United Nations Forces, Far East, and for the Chief Chaplains of the United States Army* (Richmond, VA: Christian Children's Fund, 1954); William Asbury to J. Calvitt Clarke, September 17, 1953, Folder 4, Box IB2, CCF.

12. Ha Sang Nak to Peggy Hitchcock, January 26, 1959, and Frank Z. Glick to Ha Sang Nak, February 4, 1959, Folder 1959 Korean Social Work, Box 52, bMS 16103, USC; "Seoul Child Guidance Clinic," undated, and "Child Guidance Clinic in Seoul," undated, Folder 713 Child Guidance Clinic & Mental Health; "Child and Family Welfare in Korea," undated, Folder Central Social Workers Training Institute, Box 2, Records of U.S. Foreign Assistance Agencies, NA; Taekyoon Kim,

"State Provision via Voluntarism: The State-Voluntary Welfare Mix in South Korea" (December 2009), 12, WIAS Discussion Paper Number 2009–003, dspace.wul.waseda.ac.jp/dspace/bitstream/2065/36650/1/KotoKenkyujo_2009_Kim.pdf.

13. William Asbury, "'Adopt' War Orphans," *Christian Century,* January 16, 1952, 80; Helen Tiezsen, telephone interview by author, December 12, 2011.

14. Helen Tieszen and Rose Alvernaz, "Technical Assistance for Child Welfare in Korea," *Children* 5, no. 4 (July–August 1958): 134–139; Helen Tieszen, "Report on Institutions Visited in Kyong Sang Nam Do," August 1955, Folder 8, Box IB8, CCF.

15. Helen Tieszen, "Play Behavior in Deprived Korean Children," *Children* 4, no. 1 (January–February 1957): 20; Rose Alvernaz and Helen Tieszen, "Report on the Child Welfare Leaders' Course Held in Kunsan," March 5–10, 1956, Folder 2, Box IB9, CCF; Tieszen, "Child Welfare Education, Christian Children's Fund, Inc., Korea 1955–1957."

16. Tieszen and Alvernaz, "Technical Assistance for Child Welfare in Korea," 135–136.

17. Memorandum from Helen Tieszen to Ernest Nash, Re: "Meeting with Housemothers Who Took Anyung Training Course," February 29, 1956; Helen Tieszen to J. Calvitt Clarke, February 29, 1956; and Helen Tieszen to J. Calvitt Clarke, "Recent Developments in the Training Program," April 19, 1956, Folder 2; Kim Song Kyong, "Management of the New Child," in "Summary of the Bo A Yun Gu Whai Ji (Housemother's Child Study Bulletin)," First Issue, July 25, 1956, Folder 4; Cholla Pukto Social Workers League, "The Report on the First Child Welfare Leaders Course Submitted by Mr. Kim Chyun Pae, Chairman of the Cholla Pukto Social Workers League," undated [1956], Folder 1, Box IB9, CCF.

18. Ernest Nash to Kim Eung Sang, Superintendent, Kyung Nam Boys' School, Pusan, November 16, 1956; Ernest Nash to Kim Eung Sang, October 26, 1956; and Ernest T. Nash, "Annual Report on Korea Operations, Year Ending July 1956," July 15, 1956, Folder 4, ibid.

19. Mennonite Central Committee, "Christian Child Care Training, Plans for Training 1967," Folder 18, Box IIB5, ibid.; Helen Tieszen, telephone interview by author, December 12, 2011.

20. *Training for Social Work, Second International Survey* (New York: United Nations Bureau of Social Affairs, 1955), 21; Jack Lightman to John O. Moore and Staff, January 28, 1960, Folder India Social Welfare July 1, 1957, Box 3, Records of U.S. Foreign Assistance Agencies, NA; Rose Hum Lee, "Social Welfare: East and West," *Journal of Human Relations* 8, no. 1 (Autumn 1959): 70.

21. Dick Erman to Bill Asbury, September 14, 1954, Folder 4; Noel Braga to Verent Mills, February 25, 1955, Folder 6; Arlene Sitler, "Report on the CCF, Inc. Program in Korea during the Period Arlene Sitler Assignment February 1, 1954–August 8, 1955," Folder 8, Box IB8, CCF.

22. Among the country directors employed by Foster Parents' Plan in 1962, for example, there were five men and three women; the women were exclusively in charge of European programs (Germany, Greece, and Italy), while the men led programs in Asia and Latin America (Colombia, Hong Kong, Korea, the Philippines, and Vietnam). Women would, however, lead PLAN's programs in Hong Kong from 1964 to 1966 and in Vietnam from 1963 to 1974. See Henry D. Molumphy, *For Common Decency: The History of Foster Parents Plan, 1937–1983* (Warwick, RI: Foster Parents Plan International, 1984), 327–329. Among the country directors employed by Christian Children's Fund in 1968 was one woman—stationed in England and responsible for a territory consisting of Europe, Africa, and the Middle East—and six men. See *CCF and Our World Today,* October 1968, CFF. Verent Mills to J. Calvitt Clarke, January 20, 1952, and Verent Mills to J. Calvitt Clarke, February 9, 1952, Folder 11, Box IB1; Robert Arculli to J. Calvitt Clarke, March 7, 1955, Folder 9, Box IB3, CCF; "Meet: Harold Berrean, a Profile of Our SCF Field Director for Korea," *SCF World Reporter,* Winter 1959, Folder 1960s, SCF; Memorandum from Jeanne Scanlon to Allen White, Subject: "Job description for AFSC Representative in Arab Middle East," September 19, 1958, Folder Country—Middle East, Foreign Service 1958, Box Foreign Service 1958, AFSC.

23. Sarah S. Dietrick, Memo for the Record, Subject: "Afghanistan, July 15, 1957," Folder 0-1-5-4-0 Asia (Near, Far East) General 1953–56, Box 544, Record Group 102, Records of the Children's Bureau, NA; Unknown writer to J. Calvitt Clarke and Helen Clarke, October 14, 1960, Folder 1, Box IB11, CCF.

24. Howard W. Hopkirk, *Institutions Serving Children* (New York: Russell Sage Foundation, 1944), 18–21; Child Welfare League of America, *Standards of Foster Care for Children in Institutions* (New York: Child Welfare League of America, Inc., 1937), 20; Ernest T. Nash, "Overseas Annual Report," August 1, 1959, Folder 8, Box 1B4, CCF. For more information on cottage-style children's homes, see Timothy A. Hacsi, *Second Home: Orphan Asylums and Poor Families in America* (Cambridge, MA: Harvard University Press, 1997), especially 166–170, and Matthew A. Crenson, *Building the Invisible Orphanage: A Prehistory of the American Welfare System* (Cambridge, MA: Harvard University Press, 1998). Crenson suggests that in addition to a desire to promote a sense of family life, early American reformers promoted the cottage plan as a means of improving institutional discipline, because housing children in smaller groups made it easier to segregate troublemakers. See Crenson, 138–139.

25. Larry E. Tise, *A Book about Children: The World of Christian Children's Fund, 1938–1991* (Falls Church, VA: Hartland Publishing for the Christian Children's Fund, 1993), 41; Louis Schneider, "Verbatim Report to Refugee Committee," January 5, 1959, Folder Hong Kong Foreign Service Reports 1959, Box Hong Kong Foreign Service 1959, AFSC; Penelope Brooke-Johnson, "Child Care in Hong Kong," July 1958, Folder 3, Box IB7, CCF. Emphasis in original.

26. Verent Mills to J. Calvitt Clarke, July 20, 1951, Folder 5, Box IBI, CCF.

27. "Children's Garden, Hong Kong, dedicated March 22, 1958," 3–4; Verent Mills to K. Keen, Social Welfare Officer, Social Welfare Office, Hong Kong, September 10, 1953, Folder 11, Box IB2, CCF; Edmund W. Janss, *Yankee Si! The Story of Dr. J. Calvitt Clarke and His 36,000 Children* (New York: William Morrow & Company, 1961), 110; "Information Brochure for Visitors" (Hong Kong: Christian Children's Fund, possibly 1962), 2–7; Ernest T. Nash to J. Calvitt Clarke, November 12, 1958, Folder 2, Box IB4, CCF; John C. Caldwell, *Children of Calamity* (New York: John Day Company, 1957), 44.

28. "Information Brochure for Visitors," 8–9; Brooke-Johnson, "Child Care in Hong Kong."

29. Norman Turner to J. Calvitt Clarke, September 29, 1961, Folder 6, Box IB5; James Ming N. Ch'ien, Assistant Superintendent, untitled speech, 1962, and Anna Laukoetter, "Brief Report of the Home Department," 1962, Folder 6, Box IB6; "A Verbal Report Presented to the CCF HK Policy Committee by Mr. J.J. De Ryke at a Regular Meeting Held on July 25, 1963 at the First National City Bank Office," Folder 6, Box IB5, CCF.

30. Caldwell, 56–57; Jessie Ash Arndt, " 'Children's Garden' Outside Manila, a Protestant Home," *Christian Science Monitor,* May 28, 1960, 10; Ethem Yetkiner to Ernest Nash, March 12, 1959, Folder 5, Box IB4, CCF.

31. Incoming Cablegram, International Cooperation Administration, from CINCREP Seoul, Subject: "Opening of Central Social Workers Training Center, Seoul, Korea," November 4, 1957, Folder Welfare Training and Education, Box 15; Child Welfare Section, Ministry of Health and Social Affairs, Republic of Korea, "Summary of Training for Social Work in Korea (as of January 1958)," "Social Welfare Service: Pointing the Way to Happiness for Many Needy Koreans," May 18, 1959, and "Child and Family Welfare in Korea," Folder Central Social Workers Training Institute, Box 2, Records of U.S. Foreign Assistance Agencies, NA.

32. Tieszen and Alvernaz, "Technical Assistance for Child Welfare in Korea," 135–136; Tieszen, "Play Behavior in Deprived Korean Children," 21; Memorandum from Evelyn Peters to Theodore D. Feder, Re: "Final Report on Second Parvareshgah Directors' Seminar December 18–29, 1960," January 8, 1961, File 269, JDC 55/64.

33. Foster Parents' Plan for War Children, Inc., Korea, "Questionnaire for all Children of the Plan," Folder 3, Box IB8, CCF.

34. Mildred Arnold, "Some Impressions of . . . Social Welfare in Asia," *Children* 6, no. 2 (March–April 1959): 66–68.

35. "Diary of a Country Priest: Hard and Soft Hearts Alike Add to Orphanage Problem," *Korea Times,* July 3, 1958, and Ernest Nash, "Reply to 'A Country Priest': The Orphanage Problem," *Korea Times,* July 5, 1958, Folder 4, Box IB10, CCF.

36. Lee, "Social Welfare: East and West," quote at 70.

37. Viviana A. Zelizer, *Pricing the Priceless Child: The Changing Social Value of Children* (New York: Basic Books, 1985); Peter Stearns, "Defining Happy Childhoods:

Assessing a Recent Change," *Journal of the History of Childhood and Youth* 3, no. 2 (Spring 2010): 165–186; Clara Lambert, *Play: A Yardstick of Growth* (New York: Play Schools Association, 1948), i; Clara Lambert, *Play: A Child's Way of Growing Up* (New York: Play Schools Association, 1947), 1. On the emotional importance of play for children, see also E. Rita Davidson, "Play for the Hospitalized Child," *American Journal of Nursing* 49, no. 3 (March 1949): 138–141.

38. Monica B. Owen to Group Leaders, May 1947 (microfilm: file 1885, frame 28), JDC 45/54; "October 1-Wuppertal Nachbarshaftsheim," 1950, Folder American Friends Service Committee, Unitarian Service Committee, Brethren Service Committee—Welfare Branch, Box 15, Record Group 466, Records of the U.S. High Commissioner for Germany, NA; Henrietta Buchman to Playschools Association, July 13, 1948 (microfilm: file 1885, frame 8), and Edward Phillips to Ida Nasatir, August 1, 1947 (microfilm: file 1028, frame 1055), JDC 45/54.

39. Tieszen, "Play Behavior in Deprived Korean Children," 22.

40. Play Schools Association, "Let Them Play," undated (microfilm: file 1885, frame 21), JDC 45/54; Mary Esther McWhirter, *If You Were a Child in Korea,* 1954, and "Let's Get Acquainted with Vietnamese Children and Their Country," July 1966, Box AFSC Serials, Children's Program, AFSC.

41. Margaret Lowenfeld, *Play in Childhood* (New York: Wiley, 1967 [1935]), 323; Lambert, *Play: A Child's Way of Growing Up,* 1; American Joint Distribution Committee, *JDC Handbook for Teachers in Day Care Centers* (Geneva: American Joint Distribution Committee, 1967), 21–23.

42. Wechsberg, "Communism's Child Hostages," 126; Wechsberg, "They're Afraid of Their Own Children," 38, 134; "Indoctrination Begins Early," *Saskatoon Star-Phoenix,* September 27, 1966, 20; "And Now the Children?," *Time* 78, no. 14 (October 6, 1961).

43. On the political salience of children's creative play during the Cold War era, see Amy F. Ogata, *Designing the Creative Child: Playthings and Places in Midcentury America* (Minneapolis: University of Minnesota Press, 2013).

44. Helen Clarke and Jeanne Clarke Wood, *Children's Games around the World as Enjoyed by the Children of the World-Wide "Family" of Christian Children's Fund* (Richmond, VA: Christian Children's Fund, 1963), 38, 33, 36.

45. Elsa Castendyck to Ruth C. Wright, December 22, 1953; and Ruth C. Wright to Elsa Castendyck, March 25, 1954, Folder 5-0-7-2 Foreign, Box 640, Records of the Children's Bureau, NA; "Play Is Our Business," undated (microfilm: file 1885, frames 29–30), JDC 45/54; "Play Is Our Business" Foreign Version, June 10, 1952, Folder Play Is Our Business 1952 English, Box 33, Record Group 306, Records of the U.S. Information Agency, NA.

46. Tieszen and Alvernaz, "Technical Assistance for Child Welfare in Korea," 138; Helen Tieszen to J. Calvitt Clarke, October 31, 1955, Folder 9, Box IB8, CCF; Minette Jee to Henry Kirsch, Re: "Annual Report 1959," March 7, 1960 (microfilm: file 54, frames 428–448), JDC 55/64. Social worker Emily Baca Putnam

observed a similar lack of awareness regarding the importance of the "recreational phase of the child's development" in Japan. See Emilie Baca Putnam, "Japan . . . Its Children's Welfare," *Survey* 88, no. 3 (March 1952): 123.

47. Memorandum from Mary Grist to Abe Loskove, Re: "Report on Day Care Program—October, November, December 1962," January 21, 1963 (microfilm: file 54, frame 292); Dorothy H. Beers, "Summary Report, Day Care Discussions, Morocco," May 23–June 27, 1957 (microfilm: file 54, frame 497); Minette Jee, "Morocco: First Impressions of the Kindergartens," May 22, 1959 (microfilm: file 54, frames 465–469); D. Miller, "Developments in the Nursery School Program— Seventh Week, Tunis," November 25, 1951 (microfilm: file 90, frames 646–651); and Memorandum from Mary Grist to Henry Kirsch, Re: "Report on Day Care Program for La Maternelle, Toledano, and the Nurseries of the South—April, May and June 1962," July 26, 1962 (microfilm: file 54, frame 352), JDC 55/64.

48. Lizabeth Cohen, *A Consumers' Republic: The Politics of Mass Consumption in Postwar America* (New York: Vintage Books, 2003); Ogata, *Designing the Creative Child*.

49. December 1952 mailing, Folder 16, Box 86, FPP; LeRoy Bowman, Benjamin A. Gjenvick, and Eleanor T. M. Harvey, *Children of Tragedy: Church World Service Survey Team Report on Intercountry Orphan Adoption* (New York: National Council of Churches, 1961), 23; Clarke and Wood, *Children's Games around the World*, 76.

50. *Twenty-Third Year of Service to Children, Annual Report of the Save the Children Federation for the Fiscal Year Ending June 30, 1954*, 23; Elma Laurenzi, "Quarterly Report from Italy for the Fourth Quarter 1957," January 13, 1958, Folder 46, Box 33, FPP.

51. Pan Ki to Rod Serling, March 1962, and Pan Ki to Rod Serling, September 1962, Folder 9, Box 5, RS; Memorandum from Elizabeth Whitmore to Director, Foster Parents' Plan, Subject: "Quarterly Report. Period: July 1– September 30, 1956, Supplementary to Report submitted for 2nd Quarter," October 1, 1956, Folder 12, Box 2, FPP; Soon Ok to Casey Miller, August 1966, Folder 4, Box 1, CM.

52. "Foster Parents' Report," December 1952, 20, Folder 16, Box 86, FPP.

53. "Orphans Clothed," *Life*, November 17, 1947, 57–60; "War-Maimed Greek Girls Return Home After Successful Plastic Surgery in U.S.—Two 7-Year-Old Victims of Communist Guerilla Grenades Now Healthy, Happy," Press Release, United States Information Service, September 2, 1952, Folder 284, Box 139, FPP.

54. *Twenty-Third Year of Service to Children, Annual Report of the Save the Children Federation for the Fiscal Year Ending June 30, 1954*, 16; Christina Klein, *Cold War Orientalism: Asia in the Middlebrow Imagination, 1945–1961* (Berkeley: University of California Press, 2003), 158.

55. J. Calvitt Clarke to Reverend Otis Bell, March 27, 1951, Folder 12, Box IB16, and William Asbury to Verent Mills, January 28, 1954, Folder 1, Box IB3,

CCF; Foster Parents' Plan, Inc., "The Children Help the Children," 1956, Folder 35, Box 86, FPP.

56. William H. McCahon, Advisory Committee on Voluntary Foreign Aid, International Cooperation Administration, Advisory Letter Number 5, May 26, 1959 (microfilm: file 1174, frame 844), JDC 55/64; Verbon Kemp to Mrs. Oscar Parrish, November 20, 1968, Folder 5, Box IIB15, CCF.

57. Donald L. Renard to Howard Brooks, March 5, 1952, Folder Home Office—Korea—Education Mission; "UNKRA-USC Teacher Training Program: American Education Mission," Folder Home Office—Korea—miscellaneous—January 1954 (1), Box 21, bMS 16011; Vester M. Mulholland, "Cooperative Attack on Korean Educational Problems," reprinted for the Unitarian Service Committee from the *Virginia Journal of Education,* October 1953 issue, Folder 10, Box 50, bMS 16103, USC.

58. "UNKRA-USC Teacher Training Program: American Education Mission"; James M. Dysart, "Some Impressions from My First Visit to Korean Schools"; and Helen Fogg to Harry D. Gideonse, June 26, 1952, Folder Unitarian Service Committee—Home Office—Korea Project—Harbage, Mary (1); Mulholland, "Cooperative Attack on Korean Educational Problems"; Unitarian Service Committee, Inc., "Teacher Training Program," June 1954, Folder Home Office—Korea—miscellaneous—January 1954 (1), Box 22, bMS 16011, ibid.

59. Elizabeth C. Wilson, "Moral and Social Education," in Harold R. W. Benjamin, Sallie B. Marks, and William P. Lewis, eds., *Curriculum Handbook for the Schools of Korea by the American Education Team, 1954–55, under the Auspices of the United Nations Korean Reconstruction Agency and the American-Korean Foundation and Unitarian Service Committee* (Seoul: Central Education Research Institute, 1955), Folder Home Office—Korea—Education Mission (2), Box 21, bMS 16011, ibid.

60. Unitarian Service Committee, Inc., "Teacher Training Program"; Marcus W. Scherbacher, Cultural Affairs Attache, to Harold Brooks, March 30, 1953, Folder Home Office—Korea—Education Mission, Box 21, bMS 16011; Eun Yong Ki to Helen Fogg, Folder 7, Box 5, bMS 16036, ibid. For an in-depth account of American efforts at educational reconstruction in Korea, see James Sang Chi, "Teaching Korea: Modernization, Model Minorities, and American Internationalism in the Cold War Era" (PhD diss., University of California, Berkeley, 2008).

61. Evelyn Peters, "Summary Report on Day Care Program—Iran," September 1959–June 1960; Evelyn Peters, "Bi-Monthly Report on Day Care Program, Tehran—Iran," March 23, 1961; "Seminar for Alliance Populaire First Grade Teachers," November 13–December 1, 1960; and Memorandum from Evelyn Peters to Theodore Feder, Re: "Alliance First Grade Teachers' Seminar, November 13–December 1, 1960," December 4, 1960, File 269, JDC 55/64.

62. Katya Roberts, "Day Care Department, Report of 2nd Trimestre 1963," August 5, 1963 (microfilm: file 90, frame 574); Evelyn Peters to Mary Palevsky, Re: "Field Trip to Tunis, November 6–14, 1963," November 29, 1963 (microfilm: file 90,

frame 564); and Dorothy H. Beers to Mary Palevsky, Re: "Field Trip to Tunis— November 6–14, 1963," December 2, 1963 (microfilm: file 90, frames 566–567), ibid.

63. William Heard Kilpatrick, *Modern Education: Its Proper Work* (New York: Hinds, Hayden & Eldredge, 1949), 19; Lawrence A. Cremin, *The Transformation of the School: Progressivism in American Education, 1876–1957* (New York: Random House, 1961).

64. For an in-depth discussion of the importance of children's creativity in the postwar era, see Ogata, *Designing the Creative Child.*

65. Helen Fogg, "Report on Survey of Primary Education in Cambodia and Proposal for a Rural Education and Training Center to Foreign Operations Administration," April 1955, Folder 6, Box 68, bMS 16103; "Field Report of Unitarian Service Committee, Inc. in Cambodia, Asia," July 1, 1957, Folder Cambodia Teacher Education Project 1957, Box 3, bMS 16008, USC.

66. William G. Boaz, "Application for Employment," Folder Cambodia Teacher Education 1959—Boaz, Box 6; William G. Boaz, "The Art Program," Folder Cambodian Teacher Education Program 1963—USAID, Box 11; William G. Boaz, "Semi-Annual Report on Art," Folder Cambodia Teacher Education Project 1961—Boaz, Box 8, bMS 16008, ibid.

67. William G. Boaz, "Views on Man, Art and Art Education," September 9, 1959, Folder Cambodia Teacher Education 1959—Boaz, Box 6; William Boaz to Curtice Hitchcock, September 21, 1960, Folder Cambodia Teacher Education Project 1960—Boaz, Box 7; and William Boaz, draft of "Final Report," undated, and Curtice (Peggy) Hitchcock to William G. Boaz, September 11, 1962, Folder Cambodian Teacher Education Project 1962—Boaz, Box 10, ibid.

68. Dorothy Barclay, "Group Conformity Held Risk to Child: Professor Asserts Individuality Is Often Better Than Any Adjustment to Numbers," *New York Times,* March 3, 1953, 24. See also David Riesman, " 'Tootle': A Modern Cautionary Tale," in *Childhood in Contemporary Cultures,* 236–242. Council of National Organizations on Children and Youth, *Focus on Children and Youth; A Report for the 1960 White House Conference on Children and Youth* (Washington, DC: Golden Anniversary White House Conference on Children and Youth, 1960), 18.

69. William H. Kilpatrick, *Modern Education and Better Human Relations* (New York: Anti-Defamation League of America, 1949), 6.

6. TRAINING THE NATIVES OF THE FUTURE

1. David C. McClelland, "Community Development and the Nature of Human Motivation: Some Implications of Recent Research," Background Paper, Conference on Community Development, Sponsored by the Center for International Studies, December 12–13, 1957, 2, 28, Folder Community Development and the Nature of Human Motivation: Some Implications of Recent Research, 1957, Box 20, DM.

2. Malvina Lindsay, "Foreign Aid Test—'N' Achievement," *Washington Post,* May 26, 1958, A14. Members of the American Friends Service Committee working in overseas development studied McClelland's paper. See Jane Bennett to Earl McCoy and William Channel, March 7, 1958, Folder Israel, Social & Technical Assistance, Letters To, 1958, Box Foreign Service, Israel, 1958, AFSC. So, too, did workers serving overseas with the International Cooperation Administration. See memo from Isabel Kelly to John Heilman, June 29, 1959, Folder International Cooperation Admin., [1959–1961], Box 37, DM; David C. McClelland, *The Achieving Society* (Princeton, NJ: D. Van Nostrand Company, 1961), 337.

3. Michael E. Latham, *Modernization as Ideology: American Social Science and "Nation Building" in the Kennedy Era* (Chapel Hill: University of North Carolina Press, 2000), 2; *Children of Developing Countries: A Report by UNICEF* (New York: World Publishing Company, 1963), 2–3.

4. Nick Cullather, "Development? It's History," *Diplomatic History* 24, no. 4 (Fall 2000): 641–653; Nils Gilman, *Mandarins of the Future: Modernization Theory in Cold War America* (Baltimore: Johns Hopkins University Press, 2003), 5.

5. Latham, *Modernization as Ideology,* 1–17; Gilman, *Mandarins of the Future,* 1–19.

6. Michael H. Hunt, *Ideology and U.S. Foreign Policy* (New Haven, CT: Yale University Press, 1987), 159–162; Latham, *Modernization as Ideology;* "Introduction: Modernization, International History and the Cold War World," in David Engerman et al., eds., *Staging Growth: Modernization, Development and the Global Cold War* (Amherst, MA: Amherst University Press, 2003), 1–22. See also Michael Adas, "Modernization Theory and the American Revival of the Scientific and Technological Standards of Social Achievement and Human Worth," in *Staging Growth,* 25–45.

7. On modernity as psychological, see Daniel Lerner, *The Passing of the Traditional Society: Modernizing the Middle East* (New York: Free Press, 1958) and Alex Inkeles and David H. Smith, *Becoming Modern: Individual Change in Six Developing Countries* (Cambridge, MA: Harvard University Press, 1974).

8. On U.S. involvement in infrastructure projects in developing countries, see Nick Cullather, "Damming Afghanistan: Modernization in a Buffer State," *Journal of American History* 89, no. 2 (September 2002): 512–537; David Ekbladh, *The Great American Mission: Modernization and the Construction of an American World Order* (Princeton, NJ: Princeton University Press, 2010). On modernization as a psychological project, see Ellen Herman, *The Romance of American Psychology: Political Culture in the Age of Experts* (Berkeley: University of California Press, 1996), 136–148; Latham, *Modernization as Ideology;* Adas, "Modernization Theory and the American Revival of the Scientific and Technological Standards of Social Achievement and Human Worth," in *Staging Growth.* Historians have yet to explore programs for children as a component of the modernization project.

9. U.S. Children's Bureau, "Cooperation with International Agencies and Representatives of Other Countries in Furthering and Promoting the Well-Being of Children and Young People," June 28, 1957, Folder 0-1-0-7-1, International, 1953–1956, Box 532, Record Group 102, Records of the Children's Bureau, NA. On Point IV consultants in the field of child welfare, see, for example, "Project Description and Justification," Project Number 116–428, January 2, 1951, Folder 0-1-5-4-6, Jan. 1955, India, Box 545; Deborah Pentz, "Report of Activities for the Month of August 1950," September 3, 1950, Folder 0-1-5-4-6, Jan. 1951, India, Box 332; Martha M. Eliot to Paul Cherney, April 18, 1952; and Paul Cherney to Sarah Dietrick and Randolph T. Klemme, "Progress in Reorganization of the Punjab Children's Aid Society," July 1, 1952, Folder 0-1-5-4-16 Pakistan, Box 547, Records of the Children's Bureau, NA. On Point IV, see Ekbladh, *The Great American Mission*, 77–113; Gilbert Rist, *The History of Development: From Western Origins to Global Faith* (New York: Zed Books, 1997), 71–89; Donald W. White, *The American Century: The Rise and Decline of the United States as a World Power* (New Haven, CT: Yale University Press, 1996), 205–209.

10. Quoted in Samuel Hale Butterfield, *U.S. Development Aid—an Historic First: Achievements and Failures in the Twentieth Century* (Westport, CT: Praeger, 2004), 57; Rist, 90–109. On the Alliance for Progress and the Peace Corps, see Latham, *Modernization as Ideology*, 69–150.

11. Lucian W. Pye, "Personal Identity and Political Ideology," *Behavioral Science* 6 (July 1961): 205–221, and *Politics, Personality, and Nation-Building: Burma's Search for Identity* (New Haven, CT: Yale University Press, 1962); Inkeles and Smith, *Becoming Modern;* Lerner, *The Passing of the Traditional Society,* 74–75; David E. Lilienthal, "The Road to Change," *International Development Review* 6 (December 1964): 12–13, quoted in Ekbladh, *The Great American Mission,* 161.

12. Edward W. Said, *Orientalism* (New York: Random House, 1978); Fereidoun Esfandiary, "Is It the Mysterious—or Neurotic—East?," *New York Times Magazine,* March 24, 1957, 217.

13. Oscar Lewis, "The Culture of Poverty," in Daniel Patrick Moynihan, ed., *On Understanding Poverty: Perspectives from the Social Sciences* (New York: Basic Books, 1968), 187–200. For a discussion of the core tenets of "culture of poverty" theories, see John H. Ehrenreich, *The Altruistic Imagination: A History of Social Work and Social Policy in the United States* (Ithaca, NY: Cornell University Press, 1985), 164.

14. Georges Sicault, "The Objectives of a Development Policy," Working Paper, in Herman D. Stein, ed., *Planning for the Needs of Children in Developing Countries; Report of a Round-Table Conference, 1–7 April, 1964, Bellagio, Italy* (New York: United Nations Children's Fund, 1965), 160, 164.

15. Margaret Mead, ed., *Cultural Patterns and Technical Change* (New York: United Nations Educational, Scientific and Cultural Organization, 1955), 287. The

book was originally published in 1953. Conrad M. Arensberg and Arthur H. Niehoff, *Introducing Social Change: A Manual for Americans Overseas* (Chicago: Aldine Publishing Company, 1964), 112.

16. UNICEF Secretariat, "Questions for Discussion about the Content, Method and Organization of Planning for Children and Youth," in *Planning for the Needs of Children in Developing Countries; Report of a Round-Table Conference,* 13; James Riddleberger, Memo from Washington, Subject: "Training for Social Welfare Personnel," July 24, 1959, Folder Welfare Training and Education, Box 15, Record Group 469, Records of U.S. Foreign Assistance Agencies, 1948–1961, NA.

17. Seymour Martin Lipset, *The First New Nation: The United States in Historical and Comparative Perspective* (New York: Basic Books, 1963), 16; Walt Rostow, "Economic Development," speech to the American Chamber of Commerce, Mexico City, August 19, 1963, Folder Speech Materials, 6/63–9/93, Box 11, Teodoro Moscoso Papers, John F. Kennedy Library, Boston, Massachusetts, quoted in Latham, *Modernization as Ideology,* 92; Walt W. Rostow, *The Stages of Economic Growth: A Non-Communist Manifesto* (Cambridge: Cambridge University Press, 1960).

18. On the role of analogies between human and national development, see Naoko Shibusawa, *America's Geisha Ally: Reimagining the Japanese Enemy* (Cambridge, MA: Harvard University Press, 2006), 5–6.

19. Jane Bennett to Earl McCoy and William Channel, March 7, 1958, Folder Israel, Social & Technical Assistance, Letters To, 1958, Box Foreign Service 1958, Israel; Lorraine Cleveland to Joy Ash, May 28, 1959, Folder Country Pakistan Social & Technical Assistance, Dacca—Correspondence—Letters #d To, Box Pakistan 1959, AFSC.

20. David C. McClelland et al., *The Achievement Motive* (New York: Appleton-Century-Crofts, 1953), 275; McClelland, "Community Development and the Nature of Human Motivation: Some Implications of Recent Research," 19; McClelland, *The Achieving Society,* 128.

21. David McClelland to William Channel, April 22, 1958, Folder Israel, Social & Technical Assistance, Reports-Achievement Motivation-McClelland 1958, Box Foreign Service 1958, Israel, AFSC. Emphasis in original.

22. David McClelland to Lorraine Cleveland, April 21, 1959, Folder India Social & Technical Assistance Barpali—Reports, Box India Social and Technical Assistance 1959, ibid.; McClelland, *The Achieving Society,* 401.

23. "Dorothy Beers Boguslawski, 67, an Expert in Day-Care Field," *New York Times,* April 7, 1978, D11; "Mrs. Dorothy Beers Report to JDC Executive Committee Meeting on 9/20/55 (excerpted from verbatim record)" (microfilm: file 50, frames 42–49), JDC 55/64.

24. American Joint Distribution Committee, *JDC Guide for Day Care Centers: A Handbook to Aid Communities in Developing Day Care Center Programs for Pre-School Children* (Geneva: American Jewish Joint Distribution Committee, 1962), foreword.

25. "A Breath of the Twentieth Century on a Lotus Fruit Island," *Canadian Jewish Review,* January 7, 1966, 6.

26. Memorandum from Mary Grist to Abe Loskove, Re: "Report on the Kindergarten of Marrakech, March 4, 1963" (microfilm: file 54, frames 274–275), JDC 55/64.

27. On the JDC's use of surplus commodities available through P.L. 480, the Food for Peace program, see, for example, American Council of Voluntary Agencies for Foreign Service, Inc. Testimony before the House Committee on Agriculture, Draft, February 1964 (microfilm: file 835, frame 484), ibid.; Sally MacDougall, "Child Expert Finds Challenge of Life," *World Telegram,* File 785, ibid.; "Mrs. Dorothy Beers Report to JDC Executive Committee Meeting on 9/20/55 (excerpted from verbatim record)."

28. See, for example, Jacob J. Burghardt to Gloria Matthews, "Quarterly Report, January–March 1960," April 1960, Folder 74, Box 37, FPP; Bernhard R. Klausener, Pamela Klausener, and Mrs. R. Majed Khan, "Friends Center Dacca, Quarterly Report, April through June 1961," July 15, 1961, Folder ISD STA Pakistan Programs Pakistan—E (Dacca)—Reports Quarterly, Box Pakistan 1961; Joy Ash, "Journal Letter No. 3," December 31, 1958; Joy M. Ash, "A Day Nursery in Dacca," *Woman and Health,* 15, Folder Country Pakistan, Social & Technical Assistance, Reports, 1958, Box Pakistan, 1958, AFSC.

29. Dorothy H. Beers, "Report on Field Trip to Morocco, December 19, 1960–March 28, 1961" (microfilm: file 54, frame 398), and Memorandum from Dorothy Beers to Mary Palevsky, Re: "Report on Field Trip to IRAN, April 28 to June 8, 1960," File 269, JDC 55/64; "Mrs. Dorothy Beers Report to JDC Executive Committee Meeting on 9/20/55 (excerpted from verbatim record)."

30. David McClelland to William Channel, April 22, 1958, and Jane Bennett to William Channel, April 18, 1958, Folder Israel, Social & Technical Assistance, Letters from, 1958, Box Foreign Service 1958, Israel, AFSC; McClelland, *The Achieving Society,* 415. For more detailed information on some of the methods used to test *n* Achievement, see McClelland, *The Achieving Society,* 39–46, 124–127, and 211–214.

31. McClelland, *The Achieving Society,* 401, 416.

32. Lorraine Cleveland to William Channel, September 25, 1961, Folder Israel, Social & Technical Assistance, Reports-Achievement Motivation-McClelland 1958, Box Foreign Service 1958, Israel, AFSC.

33. See, for example, Glen Leet, "They Did Not Wait for a Tractor," *Survey* 87, no. 3 (March 1951): 101–105, and Jal F. Bulsara, "Toward Human Welfare . . . The Eastern Way," *Survey* 88, no. 2 (February 1952): 59.

34. Charles G. Chakerian, *From Rescue to Child Welfare* (New York: Immigration Services, Church World Service, 1968), 36–37; James L. Pullman to Gloria Matthews, "Quarterly Report—Korea, January–March 1967," April 11, 1967, Folder 52, Box 34, FPP.

35. For one group of experts' articulation of the preference of family to institutional life, see "The Care of Well Children in Day-Care Centers and Institutions," Report of a Joint UN/WHO Expert Committee Convened with the Participation of FAO, ILO and UNICEF (Geneva: World Health Organization, 1963); Chakerian, *From Rescue to Child Welfare,* 44; "Annual Report of the Japan Office for the Year Ending July 31, 1960," Folder 9, Box IB18, CCF.

36. See, for example, Verbon Kemp to George R. Herbert, October 1, 1968, Folder 9, Box IIB12, CCF; Robert W. Sage to Gloria Matthews, "Quarterly Report—Philippines, April–June 1963," July 3, 1963, Folder 65, Box 36, FPP.

37. James Hostetler, interview by author, Richmond, Virginia, August 30, 2011. As discussed in Chapter 5, the Unitarian Service Committee sponsored three Korean social work students to study at the University of Minnesota in 1954.

38. Robert W. Sage to Gloria Matthews, "Quarterly Report—Philippines, April–June 1965," July 9, 1965, Folder 66, Box 36, FPP; Katharine F. Lenroot, "An Experimental Family Self-Help Program Conducted by the Save the Children Federation: Report of a Review," February 1960, Folder 15, Box 31, KL.

39. Frank W. Ryan to Gloria C. Matthews, "Quarterly Report—Hong Kong, October–December 1968," January 16, 1969, Folder 37, Box 32, and B.L. Weisbart to Gloria Matthews, "Quarterly Report—Peru, October–December 1967," January 3, 1968, Folder 60, Box 35, FPP.

40. Larry E. Tise, *A Book about Children: The World of Christian Children's Fund, 1938–1991* (Falls Church, VA: Hartland Publishing for the Christian Children's Fund, 1993), 72–77; Henry D. Molumphy, *For Common Decency: The History of Foster Parents Plan, 1937–1983* (Warwick, RI: Foster Parents Plan International, 1984), 237–279; Edmund W. Janss, *Yankee Si! The Story of Dr. J. Calvitt Clarke and His 36,000 Children* (New York: William Morrow & Company, 1961); Unpublished History of the Save the Children Federation, 1986, 11, SCF.

41. McClelland, *The Achieving Society,* 400.

42. Riddleberger, Memo from Washington, Subject: "Training for Social Welfare Personnel."

43. Kyung Suk Koh, "Pleasant Home Life," undated, Folder Rural Family Life, Box 13, Records of U.S. Foreign Assistance Agencies, NA.

44. Margaret Mead, "Technological Change and Child Development," *Understanding the Child* 21, no. 4 (October 1952): 110; *Children of Developing Countries: A Report by UNICEF,* 4.

45. Roberta Channel, Draft of "Impressions of a Social Revolution in Tamra," January 5, 1959, Folder Israel, Social & Technical Assistance, Reports 1958, Box Foreign Service 1958, Israel, AFSC; George W. Ross, Untitled, November 4, 1959, Folder 359, Box 147, FPP.

46. William Channel to Corinne Johnson, September 27, 1960, and American Friends Service Committee, "Hong Kong Program," undated [1960], Folder Hong

Kong Refugee Program Letters #d to and from Hong Kong, Box International Service Division 1960, Social and Technical Assistance, Refugee Program Overseas; Grace Wan, "Plan for Parents' Learning Group, Lei Cheng Uk Nursery," April 25, 1967, Folder ISD Refugee Program Overseas Hong Kong Projects Lei Cheng Uk Friendly Centre, Box ISD 1967 Refugee Program Overseas Hong Kong, AFSC.

47. William Channel to Charles Read, April 9, 1960, Folder Hong Kong Refugee Program Letters #d to and from Hong Kong, Box International Service Division 1960, Social and Technical Assistance, Refugee Program Overseas, ibid.

48. "Hong Kong Refugee Program, Quarterly Report, October–December 1961," Folder ISD Refugee Program Overseas Hong Kong Field Directors Reports, Box International Service Division 1961 Refugee Program Overseas, ibid.; Wan, "Plan for Parents' Learning Group, Lei Cheng Uk Nursery."

49. Memorandum from Evelyn Peters to Sidney Engel, Re: "Report of Fourth Parvareshgah Directors' Seminar December 9–20 1962," December 30, 1962, File 268, and Donna Garson, "Narrative Report on AJDC O.H. Day Summer Camp held in Shiraz from 11/6/61 to 24/8/61," File 785, JDC 55/64.

50. Roberta Channel, "Children and Their Mothers in Acre, Israel," August 12, 1958, Folder Israel, Social & Technical Assistance, Reports 1958, Box Foreign Service 1958, Israel; "Friends Centre, Dacca, East Pakistan, Quarterly Report," October–December 1960, Folder ISD STA Pakistan Programs Pakistan—E (Dacca)—Reports Quarterly, Box Foreign Service 1960, Pakistan; Bernhard R. Klausener and Pamela Klausener, "Friends Center, Dacca, East Pakistan, Quarterly Report, January–March 1961," April 15, 1961, Folder ISD STA Pakistan Programs Pakistan—E (Dacca)—Reports Quarterly; Bernhard R. Klausener, "Friends Center Dacca, Some Facts about Our Immediate Neighbours (A Survey Report)," July 1961, Folder ISD STA Pakistan Programs Pakistan—E (Dacca)—Projects Friends Centre Dacca, Box Foreign Service Pakistan 1961, AFSC.

51. George Ross to Gloria Matthews, February 1, 1961, Folder 359, Box 147, FPP. Emphasis in original.

52. American Joint Distribution Committee, *JDC Guide for Day Care Centers,* 1.

53. AJDC Department of Social Services, Geneva Headquarters, Minutes of Day Care Staff Conference (for purpose of formulating basic content for a Teacher's Manual), July 27–31, 1964, File 784, JDC 55/64.

54. *Children and Youth in National Development in Latin America* (New York: United Nations Children's Fund, 1966), 76, 72–73.

55. J. Calvitt Clarke to Lenore Sorin, May 17, 1957, Folder 5, Box IB24; Ernest Nash, "Reply to 'A Country Priest': The Orphanage Problem," *Korea Times,* July 5, 1958, Folder 4, Box IB10; Divine Light School for the Blind–India, "A Brief Case History of Joseph John" and "A Brief Case Sketch of Murthy"; and J. Calvitt Clarke to Beatrice Chu, November 6, 1962, Folder 10, Box IB5, CCF.

56. To Mr. and Mrs. Bruce F., Re: "Moises C., Annual Progress Report," November 1969, Folder 52, Box 49; Kenneth J. Lam to George Ross, April 4, 1961, Folder 371, Box 148; Jacob J. Burghardt to Gloria C. Matthews, "Quarterly Report: Viet Nam, October–December 1959," January 1960, Folder 74, Box 37; Keith R. Turner to Gloria C. Matthews, "Quarterly Report—Colombia, October–December 1963," January 7, 1964; Keith R. Turner to Gloria C. Matthews, "Quarterly Report—Colombia, July–September 1964," October 5, 1964; and Keith R. Turner to Gloria C. Matthews, "Quarterly Report—Colombia, October–December 1965," January 3, 1966, Folder 9, Box 29, FPP.

57. Ernest Nash to Verent Mills, August 13, 1956, and J. Calvitt Clarke to Ernest Nash, August 10, 1956, Folder 5, Box IB9; Ernest Nash to J. Calvitt Clarke and Helen Clarke, July 28, 1958, Folder 6; J. Calvitt Clarke to William H. Henry, Jr., April 30, 1959, Folder 8, Box IB10, CCF.

58. Joy M. Ash, "A Day Nursery in Dacca," *Woman and Health*, 16, Folder Country Pakistan, Social & Technical Assistance, Reports, 1958, Box Pakistan, 1958, AFSC; "Excerpts from the Diary of Edna Blue, International Chairman of Foster Parents' Plan for War Children," April 1951, Folder 16, Box 86, and Elma Laurenzi to Gloria Matthews, "Quarterly Report: July, August, September 1958," October 11, 1958, Folder 365, Box 148, FPP; Evelyn Peters, "Bi-Monthly Report on Day Care Program, Tehran—Iran," November 18, 1959, File 270, and Dorothy Beers, "Report on Field Trip to Iran, May 23–June 22, 1961," File 269, JDC 55/64.

59. Keith R. Turner to Gloria C. Matthews, "Quarterly Report—Colombia, January–March 1963," April 2, 1963, Folder 9, Box 29, FPP; Keith Turner, "Recollection of PLAN's Early Days," Folder 37, Box 304, FPPv1; Verbon Kemp to Peter Cohen, February 22, 1968, Folder 23, Box IIB16, CCF.

60. Dorothy H. Beers, "Summary Report, Day Care Discussions, Morocco, May 23–June 27, 1957" (microfilm: file 54, frame 497), and Memorandum from Mary Grist to Abe Loskove, Re: "Report on the Kindergarten of Marrakech, March 4, 1963" (microfilm: file 54, frames 276–277), JDC 55/64.

61. Lenore Sorin to "Friends," December 1958, Box 86, Folder 27, FPP.

62. Robert H. K. Walter to Gloria Matthews, "Quarterly Report—Peru, January–March 1966," Folder 60, Box 35, ibid.

63. "Foster Parents' Report," December 1952, Folder 16, Box 86 and Robert W. Sage to Gloria Matthews, "Quarterly Report—Philippines, January–March 1965," April 5, 1965, Folder 66, Box 36, ibid.

64. Jerald Huntsinger, "CCF Armchair Traveler: Destination: Dr. Graham's Homes, in the Foothills of the Himalaya Mountains, Kalimpong, West Bengal, India," *CCF World News,* September 1965, Folder 5, Box IIA1; Edmund Janss, "CCF Armchair Traveler: 5 Days in Vietnam," *CCF World News,* July 1966, Folder 1, Box IIA2, CCF.

65. Christina Klein makes the argument about child sponsorship as cultural education in *Cold War Orientalism: Asia in the Middlebrow Imagination, 1945–1961*

(Berkeley: University of California Press, 2003), 158. Stan C. to Anastassia K., October 20, 1960 and July 1960, Anastassia File, Minnesota State Reformatory for Men, Subject Files, MHS.

66. F. Jehangir, India Field Office Annual Report, 1971–1972, May 31, 1972, Folder 1, Box IIIB3, CCF.

67. Eugene Burdick and William J. Lederer, *The Ugly American* (New York: Norton, 1958); "Meet the Beautiful American," *SCF World Reporter,* Spring 1960, 3, Folder 1960s, SCF; Janss, *Yankee Si!,* 7.

68. William Channel to Jane Bennett, March 18, 1958, and David McClelland to William Channel, April 22, 1958, Folder Israel, Social & Technical Assistance, Reports-Achievement Motivation-McClelland 1958, Box Foreign Service 1958, Israel, AFSC.

69. Memorandum from Mary Grist to Abe Loskove, Re: "Report on Day Care Program—October, November, December 1962," January 21, 1963 (microfilm: file 54, frame 292), and "Minutes of the First Parvareshgah Director's Conference," December 13–18, 1959, File 269, JDC 55/64.

70. American Joint Distribution Committee, *JDC Handbook for Teachers in Day Care Centers* (Geneva: American Joint Distribution Committee, 1967), 46.

71. *Cultural Patterns and Technical Change,* 293. On Mead's ideas about technical assistance and cultural integrity, see also Peter Mandler, "One World, Many Cultures: Margaret Mead and the Limits to Cold War Anthropology," *History Workshop Journal* 68, no. 1 (Autumn 2009): 149–172.

72. Helen Tieszen, "Play Behavior in Deprived Korean Children," *Children* 4, no. 1 (January–February 1957): 20–21; Helen Tieszen and Rose Alvernaz, "Technical Assistance for Child Welfare in Korea," *Children* 5, no. 4 (July–August 1958): 138; Evelyn Peters, "Summary Report on Day Care Program: 1956–1963," July 1963, File 268, JDC 55/64.

73. Evelyn Peters, "Report on Day Care Program, Tehran—Iran," November 14, 1962, File 268, JDC 55/64.

74. Elizabeth Brown, "Vietnam—Quarterly Report, October–December 1966," January 13, 1967, Folder 74, Box 37, FPP; Fram Jehangir, "India," *CCF and Our World Today,* October 1968, CCF.

75. "Information Brochure for Visitors" (Hong Kong: Christian Children's Fund, possibly 1962), 17–18; Verbon Kemp to Carla Gray, April 17, 1969, Folder 9, Box IIB13, CCF; Tise, *A Book about Children,* 48; George W. Ross to Gloria C. Matthews, "Quarterly Report—Hong Kong, July–September 1963," October 9, 1963; Frank W. Ryan to Gloria C. Matthews, "Quarterly Report—Hong Kong, July–September 1968," October 1, 1968; and Frank W. Ryan to Gloria C. Matthews, "Quarterly Report—Hong Kong, October–December 1967," January 15, 1968, Folder 37, Box 32, FPP.

76. Tai Ho to Mr. and Mrs. Jose A. Limon, December 1964, Folder 253, JL; Jaime H. to Sponsor, *CCF World News,* September 1965, Folder 5, Box IIA1, CCF.

77. Foster Parents' Plan, Inc., "Lifelines for 100,000 Children, 1937–1962," Folder 33, Box 86, FPP; "Hong Kong Regional Office Annual Report for 1963," September 1963, Folder 3, Box IB6; Ernest Nash to J. Calvitt Clarke, May 4, 1959, Folder 6, Box IB4, CCF. The survey's percentages add up to only 83 percent. However, the survey does provide insight into the fields of employment in which former residents of CCF homes in Hong Kong were active.

78. Frank W. Ryan to Gloria C. Matthews, "Quarterly Report—Hong Kong, October–December 1967," January 15, 1968, Folder 37, Box 32, and Lucile L. Chamberlin to George Ross, Re: "Criteria for Accepting Children and Families," September 15, 1965, Folder 36, Box 12, FPP.

79. Gloria Matthews to Fanny Exarhacos, July 10, 1958, Folder 284, Box 139, ibid. For examples of children cancelled due to "apathy," see Keith R. Turner to Gloria C. Matthews, "Quarterly Report—Colombia, January–March 1965," April 19, 1965, Folder 9, Box 29; Elma Laurenzi to Gloria Matthews, "Quarterly Report—Italy, January–February–March–1961," April 11, 1961, Folder 46, Box 33; and Elizabeth Brown, "Vietnam—Quarterly Report, January–March 1965," April 7, 1965, Folder 74, Box 37, ibid.

80. *22nd Annual Report, Save the Children Annual Report for the Fiscal Year Ending June 30, 1953,* 15; Frank Ryan to Gloria Matthews, "Quarterly Report—Korea, January–March 1965," Folder 51, Box 31, and Gloria Matthews to George Ross, April 14, 1960, Folder 359, Box 147, FPP.

81. Verbon Kemp to Lillian W. Walker, February 11, 1965, Folder 2, Box IIB15; J. Calvitt Clarke to Norman E. Turner, October 22, 1962, Folder 10, Box IB5; and Verbon Kemp to Beatrice Chu, May 11, 1964, Folder 2, Box IIB13, CCF.

82. Lucile Chamberlin to Gloria C. Matthews, "Quarterly Report—Hong Kong, July–September 1966," October 6, 1966, Folder 37, Box 32, FPP; "Jobs First . . . Training Second," Foster Parents' Plan Report, December 1965, Foster Child Scrapbook, Subseries 2.4, Box 1, PG; Frank Ryan to Gloria Matthews, "Quarterly Report—Korea, October–December 1964," Folder 49, Box 34, FPP.

83. "First Quarterly Report for Greece, January–March 1957," Folder 21, Box 302, FPPv1; J. Calvitt Clarke to Norman Turner, May 22, 1962, Folder 8, Box IB5, CCF; Arthur E. C. to Kathryn B. Slevin, February 19, 1957, Folder 30, Box 12, FPP.

84. *Cultural Patterns and Technical Change,* vii.

7. CHALLENGING THE GLOBAL PARENT

1. Unitarian Universalist Service Committee, "Saigon-Vietnam, Six-Month Progress Report," December 1968–July 1969, and "UUSC Program and Review Committee, Vietnam, Recommendations of the Executive Director," October 22, 1969, Folder 1969-Vietnam, Box 12; "On-the-Job Social Work Training Project in Vietnam, Final Summary Report," April 1971, Folder Vietnam Project, Box 20, bMS

16026, USC; Diane [Jones] to Roger Fredrickson and Marty Teitel, September 1, 1970, Folder Letters #d from Saigon, Box ISD RPO 1970, Asia, South Vietnam, AFSC. The Unitarian Service Committee (USC), discussed in previous chapters, merged with the Universalist Service Committee in 1963, becoming the Unitarian Universalist Service Committee (UUSC). The merger of the American Unitarian Association and the Universalist Church of America in 1961 precipitated this move.

2. Ralph Tefferteller to Honorable Mayor of Saigon Colonel Do Kien Nhieu, Subject: "Permission to Use Two Apartments in Ban Co Government Houses to Establish a Multi-Service Community Center for Social Service Activities," March 1, 1969, and Interdenominational Radical Caucus, "Operation Theodore Parker: The IRC Indictment of the Unitarian Universalist Service Committee," Folder 1969-Vietnam, Box 12; Interdenominational Radical Caucus, "Bombard the Headquarters UUSC Liberated," Folder Vietnam-UUSC-Crisis, Box 20, bMS 16026, USC; Ghanda DiFiglia, *Roots and Visions: The First Fifty Years of the Unitarian Universalist Service Committee* (Boston: Unitarian Universalist Service Committee, 1990), 86–87.

3. Unitarian Universalist Service Committee, Inc., "Report of the Ad Hoc Committee to Review the Vietnam (AID) Contract," presented at Corporate Meeting, July 16, 1969, and Richard A. Steckel to Rev. Jack A. Kent, October 31, 1969, Folder 1969-Vietnam, Box 12, bMS 16026; Dennis G. Kuby to Unitarian Universalist Service Committee, May 18, 1967, and F. Allen Wells, Jr. to Donald Sabin, May 24, 1967, Folder 1967 Vietnam, Box 10, bMS 16102, USC.

4. Harry V. F. Edward, "Report for the Quarter Year Ending December 31, 1957," Folder 74, Box 37, FPP; "Foster Home Projects Are Used for Orphans in Viet Nam Zone," unfiled article, CCF; "This Is the Hiet Family in Vietnam," *Coronet,* March 1961, 29.

5. Verent Mills, "Summary Report," Meeting Executive Committee, October 19, 1965, Folder 5, and Verbon Kemp to Members of the Board of Directors, May 13, 1966, Folder 6, Box IIAI; Verbon Kemp to Board of Directors, June 27, 1967, Folder 2, Box IIA2, CCF; Elizabeth Brown, "Vietnam–Quarterly Report, October–December 1965," January 13, 1966, Folder 76, Box 37, FPP. These percentages refer to the increase in requests for Vietnamese children between July and September 1965.

6. Agency for International Development, *The Third Face of War* (Washington, DC: Agency for International Development, 1965), and Agency for International Development Press Release, "Vice President Says Stake in Vietnam Is 'Better Life under Freedom,'" December 3, 1965, Folder Vietnam 1965, Box 5, bMS 16025, USC; Sergeant Bruce O. Gilmore to Verent Mills, July 14, 1965, Folder 14, Box IIB11, CCF.

7. "In Defense of a Youth Program," undated [1968], Folder ODO/NLD Youth Affairs, and Second Lt. William P. Marsik, News Release, Information

Office, Military Assistance Command, Vietnam, Civil Operations and Rural Development Support, "Playground in Dalat," Folder CORDS #251, Box 2, Record Group 472, Records of the United States Forces in Southeast Asia, 1950–1975, NA; Ruth Sheldon Knowles, "The Three-R War in Vietnam," *Reader's Digest,* 1967, Folder 1967 Vietnam, Box 10, bMS 16102, USC; Memorandum from John A. Fasullo to All Youth Affairs Advisors, Subject: "Sports Equipments," October 26, 1968, Folder Youth Affairs—1968, Box 871; Charles A. Corcoran, "Assistance to Vietnamese Youth Organizations," February 7, 1969, Folder Youth Affairs—1969, Box 1170; Department of the Army, 2d Civil Affairs Company, 8th AA Platoon, "Monthly Report of 8th AA Platoon," January 1, 1971, Folder Civil Affairs Platoon 1971, Box 1553; Elmer L. Conrad, Department of the Army, Headquarters I Field Force Vietnam, "Rural Youth Groups," October 25, 1969, Folder Youth Affairs, Box 297, Records of the United States Forces in Southeast Asia, NA. See also Larry Jolidon, "See-Saw Any Way to Win a War? Sure, Says Williamson Man," April 11, 1966, Folder 1967 Vietnam, Box 10, bMS 16102, USC.

8. Verent Mills, "Special Report: Vietnam," *CCF World News,* July 1966, Folder 1, Box IIA2, CCF; "Many Seeking Adoption of Viet Orphans," *Los Angeles Times,* July 29, 1965, 23.

9. Memorandum from Verent Mills to Board of Directors, March 10, 1966, Subject: "Report on Vietnam," Folder Christian Children's Fund A & B FY 1977 (Folder 2 of 2), Container 21, Records of the United States Forces in Southeast Asia, NA; Chandler Brossard, "Vietnam's War-Ravaged Children," reprinted from April 18, 1967, issue of *Look,* Folder Publicity-Brochures, Flyers, Pamphlets, Box ISD RPO 1967, Asia: South Vietnam, AFSC; Elizabeth Brown, "Vietnam—Quarterly Report, January–March 1967," April 10, 1967, Folder 76, Box 37, FPP; William Tuohy, "Unwanted G.I. War Babies Growing Viet Nam Problem," *Boston Globe,* August 29, 1966, 8; Memorandum from Mills to Board of Directors, "Report on Vietnam"; "Child Welfare in Vietnam Fact Sheet," May 22, 1973, Folder 8, Box IIIB12, CCF; Statement of Dr. James Dumpson, U.S. Senate, Committee on the Judiciary, Subcommittee on Refugees and Escapees, *Relief and Rehabilitation of War Victims in Indochina, Part II: Orphans and Child Welfare* (Washington, DC: U.S. Government Printing Office, 1973), 5.

10. Kenneth W. Kindelsperger, "Social Welfare in Vietnam, Training Program and Needs," preliminary draft, March 31, 1966, 5, Folder Vietnam Project, Box 20, bMS 16026, USC.

11. Ibid., 13; Mills, "Special Report: Vietnam"; "UUSC Program and Review Committee, Vietnam, Recommendations of the Executive Director"; Memorandum, "UN Social Welfare Project, Viet Nam," Folder 1967 Vietnam, Box 10, bMS 16102, USC; Elizabeth Brown, "Vietnam—Quarterly Report, January–March 1966," April 8, 1966, Folder 76, Box 37, FPP.

12. Jack Richards to Roger Fredrickson, May 26, 1968, Folder Letters from South Vietnam Jan–June, Box ISD RPO 1968, Asia, South Vietnam, continued;

Jill Richards to Roger Fredrickson, November 1, 1967, Folder Letters from South Vietnam, Oct–Dec, Box ISD RPO 1967, Asia: South Vietnam, AFSC.

13. Jill Richards, "Observations des monitrices sur les enfants," October 24, 1967, and Jill Richards, "Observations des monitrices des enfants, October 27 1967," October 31, 1967, Folder Letters from South Vietnam, Oct–Dec, Box ISD RPO 1967, Asia: South Vietnam, ibid. Translation by author. "Quaker Service—Vietnam," April 14, 1969, Folder Reports General, and Jack Richards, "Home Economics Course," June 30, 1968, Folder Child Day Care Center of Quang Ngai, Box ISD RPO 1969, Asia: South Vietnam, ibid.

14. D. W. Stickney to Roger Fredrickson and Charles Read, December 30, 1968, Folder Field Reports, Box ISD RPO 1968, Asia, South Vietnam, continued, ibid., and Richards, "Home Economics Course."

15. A. Elizabeth Brown to Gloria Matthews, "Quarterly Report Vietnam, January–March 1969," Folder 77, Box 38, and Elizabeth Brown, "Vietnam—Quarterly Report, January–March 1967," April 10, 1967, Folder 76, Box 37, FPP.

16. James L. Pullman to Gloria Matthews, "Quarterly Report—Korea, January–March 1967," April 11, 1967, Folder 52, Box 34, ibid.

17. David Stickney, Draft, "Vietnam Needs an Alternative to Orphanages," October 11, 1966, Folder Reports General, Box ISD RPO 1966, AFSC; Richard Beckett, "South Vietnam's Children of War," *Age,* March 28, 1967, 2.

18. David Stickney, Dedication Address, Child Day Care Center, Quang Ngai, December 18, 1966, Folder Child Day Care Center of Quang Ngai, Box ISD RPO 1966, AFSC; United States Department of Health, Education, and Welfare, "Suggested Principles Governing Care and Protection of Children in War-Torn Countries," December 1966, Folder 7, Box IIB1, CCF; American Council of Voluntary Agencies for Foreign Service, Inc., "Guiding Principles for Child Welfare Concerns in Vietnam," January 12, 1967, Folder Conference, Problems of Children in Vietnam, Box ISD RPO 1966, AFSC; Ministry of Health, Social Welfare and Relief, Notice, Subject: "Limitation on the Establishment of Orphanages throughout the Country," July 25, 1969, Folder 10, Box 10, FPP; Charles G. Chakerian, "Possible Expansion of CCF Services to the Children of Vietnam," July 1973, Folder 2, Box IIIB17, CCF.

19. United States Department of Health, Education, and Welfare, "Suggested Principles Governing Care and Protection of Children in War-Torn Countries."

20. Ed Wright to Bob Gray, Re: "Committee of Responsibility to Save War-Burned Vietnamese Children," January 26, 1967, Folder Committee of Responsibility, Inc., Box ISD RPO 1967, Asia: South Vietnam, and Frank Hunt to Warren Witte, December 30, 1966, Folder Friends Meeting for Sufferings of Vietnamese Children, Box ISD RPO 1966, AFSC.

21. "Report by Jan de Hartog on His Investigation," Summer 1966, Folder Friends Meeting for Sufferings of Vietnamese Children, Box ISD RPO 1966, ibid.; Marjorie de Hartog, "Friends Meeting for Sufferings of Vietnamese Children,"

Folder 7, Box IIB1, CCF; "Summary of Discussion on the Special Needs of Viet-
namese Children, Sponsored by International Social Service, American Branch,"
July 19, 1971, Folder 7, Box IIIB12, CCF. On American legal adoptions of Vietnamese children, see Allison Varzally, "Vietnamese Adoptions and the Politics of
Atonement," *Adoption and Culture* 2 (Spring 2009): 159–202. On American child
welfare experts' recommendations to limit intercountry adoption, see United States
Department of Health, Education, and Welfare, "Suggested Principles Governing
Care and Protection of Children in War-Torn Countries"; Ed Wright for Charles Read
to Robert Gray, November 22, 1966, Subject: "Vietnamese Children and Program
in Vietnam," Folder Correspondence General Vietnamese Children (Adoption of),
Box ISD RPO 1966, AFSC; and American Council of Voluntary Agencies for
Foreign Service, Inc., "Guiding Principles for Child Welfare Concerns in Vietnam."

22. Elizabeth Brown, "Vietnam—Quarterly Report, July–September 1965,"
October 8, 1965, Folder 75, Box 37, FPP; Mills, "Special Report: Vietnam."

23. Elizabeth Brown, "Vietnam—Quarterly Report, January–March 1965,"
April 7, 1965, Folder 75, and "Vietnam—Quarterly Report, April–June 1966,"
Folder 76, Box 37, FPP; Memorandum from Edmund Janss to Board of Directors,
Subject: "Quarterly Report," January 22, 1968, Folder 4, Box IIA2, CCF; A.
Elizabeth Brown to Gloria Matthews, "Quarterly Report Vietnam, April–June
1969," Folder 77, Box 38, FPP; "Agency in Saigon Is Refugee Haven: Foster
Parents' Plan Helps Families Fleeing War," *New York Times,* January 28, 1968, 26;
Marian Guild, "Informal Report to Foster Parents of Vietnamese Children,
August–September 1971," HG; *Save the Children Federation Annual Report for the
Year Ended June 30, 1971,* 12, SCF.

24. John Fitzstevens to Norman Turner, Tet Day, 1968, Folder 15, Box IIB11,
and Edmund Janss to Board of Directors, Subject: "Quarterly Report," September
19, 1968, Folder 5, Box IIA2, CCF; Jack Richards to Roger Fredrickson, April 17,
1968, and Report #16, May 1968, Folder Letters from South Vietnam Jan–June,
Box ISD RPO 1968, Asia, South Vietnam, continued, AFSC; Marian Guild,
"Quarterly Report Vietnam, July–September 1971," Folder 78, Box 38, FPP;
Subcommittee on Children and Youth, Senate Committee on Labor and Public
Welfare, *Children's Charities, 1974, Part 4: Voluntary Foreign Aid Agencies Serving
Children and Youth: Hearings Before the Subcommittee on Children and Youth of the
Committee on Labor and Public Welfare,* 93rd Cong., 2nd sess., October 10, 1974,
1140; A. Elizabeth Brown to Gloria Matthews, written by Frederick Chaffee,
"Quarterly Report Vietnam, January–March 1968," March 5, 1968, Folder 77, Box
38, and A. Elizabeth Brown, "Vietnam—Quarterly Report, October–December
1964," January 12, 1965, Folder 75, Box 37, FPP.

25. Louis Kubicka to Friends, January 9, 1968, Folder Reports General, Box ISD
RPO 1968, Asia, South Vietnam, continued, and David and Mary Stickney to Dave
Elder, June 1, 1967, Folder Letters to South Vietnam, Jan–Sept, Box ISD RPO 1967,
Asia: South Vietnam, AFSC; John Fitzstevens to Verent Mills, "Vietnam Report,"

February 22, 1967, Folder 14, Box IIB11, CCF; David Stickney to Senator Edward Kennedy, December 22, 1967, Folder Visitors to Vietnam, Kennedy Sen Edward, Box ISD RPO 1968, Asia, South Vietnam, continued, AFSC.

26. John Fitzstevens to Norman Turner, Tet Day, 1968, and Edmund Janss to John Fitzstevens, August 20, 1968, Folder 15, Box IIB11, CCF; Brossard, "Vietnam's War-Ravaged Children"; "Quakers in Quang Ngai: A Service of Love in Wartime," Folder Publicity–Brochures, Flyers, Pamphlets, Box ISD RPO 1969, Asia, South Vietnam, continued, AFSC; A. Elizabeth Brown to Gloria Matthews, written by Frederick Chaffee, "Quarterly Report Vietnam, April–June 1968," Folder 77, Box 38, FPP.

27. A. Elizabeth Brown to Gloria Matthews, "Quarterly Report Vietnam, October–December 1969," Folder 77, Box 38, FPP; David McClelland to Robert A. Lyon, October 28, 1969, Folder American Friends Service Committee [1969–1977], Box 26, DM; Memorandum from Allan Brick to MAR Staff and Executive Committee, Subject: "New England Region Minute Asking AFSC Withdrawal from South Vietnam," Folder Regional Offices, New England, Box ISD RPO 1967, Asia, South Vietnam, continued, AFSC.

28. Rachel M. McCleary, *Global Compassion: Private Voluntary Organizations and U.S. Foreign Policy since 1939* (New York: Oxford University Press, 2009), 62–64; Kenneth W. Kindelsperger, Memorandum for File, "UUSC—Appraisal of Conditions in Vietnam and the Need for UUSC Program," October 21, 1967, Folder Vietnam Project, Box 20, bMS 16026, USC; David and Mary Stickney, "Quaker Service in Quang Ngai," reprinted from January 1, 1967, issue of *Friends Journal,* Folder Publicity-Brochures, Flyers, Pamphlets, Box ISD RPO 1967, Asia: South Vietnam, AFSC.

29. Understanding between United States Operations Mission and Christian Children's Fund, February 21, 1966, Folder 14, Box IIB11, CCF; McCleary, *Global Compassion,* 94; Bernard Weinraub, "Volunteer Aides in Saigon Dispute: American Welfare Workers Say U.S. Officials Press Them to Support War," *New York Times,* September 15, 1967, 1.

30. Gloria Matthews to Don D. Roose, December 28, 1970, Folder 6, Box 28, FPP.

31. "Untreated Amputees in Quang Ngai Get Help at Rehabilitation Center," *AFSC Reporter,* Pasadena, California, December 1967, Folder Publicity-Newsclippings, Box ISD RPO 1967, Asia: South Vietnam, AFSC.

32. R. W. Poole to David and Mary Stickney, April 21, 1966, Folder Government United States, Box ISD RPO 1966; Dave Elder to David and Mary Stickney, February 10, 1967, Folder Letters to South Vietnam, Jan–Sept, and "Notes of a meeting of the team with Lou Schneider on 22nd October, 1967," Folder Letters from South Vietnam, Oct–Dec, Box ISD RPO 1967, Asia: South Vietnam; Louis P. Kubicka, February 27, 1968, Folder Reports General, Box ISD RPO 1968, Asia, South Vietnam, continued, emphasis in original; Eric Wright to Major Campbell,

December 9, 1969, Folder Letters from South Vietnam Nov–Dec, Box ISD RPO 1969, Asia, South Vietnam, ibid.

33. "Summary Report of Findings and Recommendations Made by the Independent Study Team to Review the UUSC Saigon Project," October 24, 1969, Folder Vietnam 1971, Box 4, bMS 16102, USC; William D. Lotspeich, "Cambodia-Vietnam Journal," January 17 to February 3, 1967, Folder Visitors to Vietnam—Lotspeich, Wm, Box ISD RPO 1967, Asia, South Vietnam, continued, ibid.

34. Robert W. Sage to Gloria Matthews, "Quarterly Report—Philippines, October–December 1964," January 8, 1965, Folder 65, Box 36 and R. David Elder to Gloria Matthews, "Quarterly Report—Peru, January–March 1969," Folder 61, Box 35, FPP; Evelyn Peters, "Report of Field Trip to Morocco, November 4–15, 1973," File 291; Herbert Katski, HK #6, "Katya Roberts," December 20, 1967, and Theodore Feder to Herbert Katski, Re: "Katya Roberts," December 26, 1967, File 367, JDC 65/74.

35. Albert Sheldon to Louis D. Horwitz, "Annual Report, Tunisia 1967," and Albert Sheldon to Herbert Katski, Re: "Report on Tunisia," July 31, 1967, File 367, JDC 65/74; E. Glenn Rogers to Gloria Matthews, "Quarterly Report—Colombia, April–June 1972," Folder 9, Box 29; Robert L. Jones to Gloria Matthews, "Quarterly Report—Peru, October–December 1972," Folder 61, Box 35; and Gloria Matthews to Members of the Board of Directors, Re: "Executive Director's Visit to Chimbote, January 5–12, 1973," February 5, 1973, Folder 628, Box 177, FPP; Henry F. Harvey, "What's Happening in Korea?," undated, Folder 4, Box IIA2, CCF.

36. Gloria Matthews to John L. Coller, Re: "Sensitivity in Developing Countries," June 6, 1972, Folder 131, Box 23, FPP; Keith Turner, "Recollection of PLAN's Early Days," Folder 37, Box 304, FPPv1; Bill Bray, "Korean Orphan Appeal: How Long?," July 28, 1972, Folder 6, Box IIIB9, CCF.

37. Translation by PLAN staff of article by Enrique Mordoño Aransáenz, *Expresso,* February 25, 1973, Folder 628, Box 177, FPP; Hans Nagpaul, "The Diffusion of American Social Work Education to India: Problems and Issues," *International Social Work* 15, no. 1 (January 1972): 3–17; Rosa Peric Resnick, "Conscientization: An Indigenous Approach to International Social Work," *International Social Work* 19, no. 21 (1976): 21; Jan F. de Jongh, "Western Social Work and the Afro-Asian World," *International Social Work* 12, no. 4 (October 1969): 16–24, quotes at 20 and 21; John H. Ehrenreich, *The Altruistic Imagination: A History of Social Work and Social Policy in the United States* (Ithaca, NY: Cornell University Press, 1985), 199–203.

38. Charles Chakerian, quoted in A. Elizabeth Brown to Gloria Matthews, "Quarterly Report Vietnam, October–December 1969," Folder 77, Box 38, FPP; Lynn Harold Vogel and Betty Vos Vogel, "Social Work in Vietnam: A Western Profession, an Asian Country . . . and a War," *International Social Work* 16, no. 1 (January 1973): 13–19, quote at 17; "Seminar Report: Social Work Professor

Speaks on Foreign Voluntary Agencies," *KAVA News,* no. 2–73, February 7, 1973, 15, Folder 567, Box 171, FPP.

39. Carol Rolloff, "Engaged Couple 'Adopt' 340 Viet Orphans," quoted in "The Needs of the Children of Vietnam," *Congressional Record,* 90th Cong., 1st sess., May 25, 1967, 14008; Verbon E. Kemp, "Why Are We in Vietnam?," *CCF World News,* July 1966, Folder 1, Box IIA2, and Verbon Kemp to Lt. Michael Graham, September 23, 1969, Folder 16, Box IB11, CCF.

40. "Politics Before Children," *New York Times,* May 25, 1974, 28.

41. Jeremi Suri, *Power and Protest: Global Revolution and the Rise of Détente* (Cambridge, MA: Harvard University Press, 2003); Robert W. Sage to Gloria C. Matthews, "Quarterly Report—Philippines, April–June 1969," Folder 66, Box 36, FPP; Richard D. Lyons, "Dr. Spock, Denying 'Permissiveness,' Says Agnew's Gibes Are 'a Compliment,'" *New York Times,* September 27, 1970, 47; "Dr. Peale Hits Spock's Child Advice," *Boston Globe,* February 19, 1968, 28.

42. Evelyn Peters, "Field Trip to Iran, February 1–March 15, 1973," and "Field Trip to Iran, February 13–March 15, 1974," File 113, JDC 65/74. On the complicated relationship between feminism and motherhood, see Lauri Umansky, *Motherhood Reconceived: Feminism and the Legacies of the Sixties* (New York: New York University Press, 1996).

43. Paul R. Ehrlich, *The Population Bomb* (New York: Ballantine Books, 1968); Matthew Connelly, *Fatal Misconception: The Struggle to Control World Population* (Cambridge, MA: Harvard University Press, 2008).

44. Wilbur J. Cohen, "The Developmental Approach to Social Challenges," *Children* 15, no. 6 (November–December 1968): 210–213; Peters, "Field Trip to Iran, February 13–March 15, 1974"; W.H.F. to Foster Parents Plan, March 27, 1972, Folder 50, Box 14, FPP.

45. A. Elizabeth Brown to Gloria Matthews, "Quarterly Report Vietnam, October–December 1969," Folder 77, Box 38, FPP; David McClelland to Bronson P. Clark, November 17, 1969, Folder American Friends Service Committee [1969–1977], Box 26, DM.

46. For a detailed discussion of the decline of modernization theory, see David Ekbladh, *The Great American Mission: Modernization and the Construction of an American World Order* (Princeton, NJ: Princeton University Press, 2010), 226–256, and Nils Gilman, *Mandarins of the Future: Modernization Theory in Cold War America* (Baltimore: Johns Hopkins University Press, 2003), 203–276.

47. David Youmans, "Brazil," 1974, Folder 18, Box 303, FPPv1; Verent Mills to Friend, April 1974, Folder 4, Box IIIB12, CCF.

48. Verent Mills to Richard A. Larson, May 6, 1974, Folder 4, Box IIIB12, CCF.

49. Senate Committee, *Voluntary Foreign Aid Agencies Serving Children and Youth,* 1112–1113; James A. Duff to John L. Ganley, November 21, 1973, Folder 156, Box 26, FPP.

50. By contrast, in 1973, PLAN cared for over 51,000 children and their families in eleven countries, and SCF's work reached 27,000 children and their families in eighteen countries. "GAO Report on Five Children's Charities," in Senate Committee, *Voluntary Foreign Aid Agencies Serving Children and Youth,* 1370, 1419; Verbon Kemp to Mrs. Thomas S. Kandul, Sr., July 31, 1968, Folder 8, Box IIB13, CCF; Senate Committee, *Voluntary Foreign Aid Agencies Serving Children and Youth,* 1057–1060.

51. "GAO Report on Five Children's Charities" in Senate Committee, *Voluntary Foreign Aid Agencies Serving Children and Youth,* 1371, 1375; Senate Committee, *Voluntary Foreign Aid Agencies Serving Children and Youth,* 1184.

52. Robert S. McClusky to JoAnn Robinson, 1974, Folder 172, Box 9, MH.

53. Jack Anderson, "Children's Fund Operation Probed," *Washington Post,* October 1, 1974, B15; John Mathews, "Appeals Sometimes Vary a Bit from the Facts," *Washington Star-News,* October 9, 1974, Folder 159, Box 26, FPP; Verent Mills, "Annual Report of the Executive Director," Annual Reports for FY 1974–1975, Folder 4, Box IIIB3, CCF.

54. National Information Bureau, Inc., "Christian Children's Fund, Inc.," May 19, 1969, Folder 14, Box IIIB4, CCF; National Information Bureau, Inc., "Christian Children's Fund, Inc.," May 1, 1973, Folder 111, Box 20, FPP.

55. Senate Committee, *Voluntary Foreign Aid Agencies Serving Children and Youth,* 1256; Connie Widyatma to David Herrell, January 21, 1974, Folder 8, Box IIIB7, CCF.

56. Verent Mills to Anne Farber, May 21, 1975, Folder 8, Box IIIB14, CCF. Emphasis in original.

57. David Herrell, "The Effects of Sponsorship on Child Welfare," *Child Welfare* 54, no. 10 (December 1975): 684, 686, 687. Many thanks to David Herrell for sharing with me this and other articles in his possession.

58. Ibid., quote at 689.

8. GLOBALIZING A HAPPY CHILDHOOD

1. "Information Brochure for Visitors" (Hong Kong: Christian Children's Fund, possibly 1962) and "Children's Garden, Hong Kong, dedicated March 22, 1958," CCF.

2. Ahti W. Hailuoto, "The Activities of the Christian Children's Fund, Inc.," 1969, Folder 2, Box IIIB17, and Edmund Janss to Board of Directors, Subject: "Quarterly Report," July 24, 1967, Folder 3, Box IIA2, ibid.

3. Verbon Kemp to Robert P. Bagent, April 4, 1968, Folder 11, Box IIB8; Verbon Kemp to Rev. Doan-Van Mieng, January 16, 1969, Folder 16, Box IB11; "Subject: Wu Kwai Sha," Folder 1, Box IIA3, ibid.

4. P.L. 93–189, United States Foreign Assistance Act of 1973; Rachel M. McCleary, *Global Compassion: Private Voluntary Organizations and U.S. Foreign*

Policy since 1939 (New York: Oxford University Press, 2009), 103–107; Rolf H. Sartorius and Vernon W. Ruttan, "The Sources of the Basic Human Needs Mandate," Economic Development Center, University of Minnesota, October 30, 1988, available online at http://ageconsearch.umn.edu/bitstream/7486/1/edc88-04.pdf.

5. Evelyn Peters to Louis D. Horwitz, Subject: "Consultation for the Day Care Program," August 9, 1968, File 113, JDC 65/74; Robert Walter to Gloria Matthews, Re: "FC School Attendance," September 6, 1973, and Gloria Matthews to National Directors and Field Directors, Re: "Directors Conference: Agenda Suggestions," March 1, 1974, Folder 67; David Youmans, "What Kind of Education?," undated [1974], Folder 69, Box 15, FPP.

6. Ahti W. Hailuoto, "Christian Children's Fund, Inc.," 1974, Folder 2, Box IIIB17, and "Study of Non-residential CCF-Supported Projects," October 1975, Folder 6, Box IIIC2, CCF; Frank Ryan to Gloria Matthews, "Quarterly Report, Bali, January–March 1973," Folder 39, Box 32, FPP; "PLAN—Colombia," 1974, Folder 18, Box 303, FPPv1.

7. "CCF Executive Staff Meeting," November 14, 1975, Folder 5, Box IIIB2, CCF; "Narrative Report for Auditors Gaza Programs—1974–75," Folder ISD Middle East Programs Gaza: Reports General, Box ISD 1973 Social Assistance Administration, AFSC; David Youmans to Gloria Matthews, "Quarterly Report—Colombia, July–Sept 1973," Folder 12, Box 29, and Through Mrs. Eler to Robert Sage, Re: "Live-In Camp, April 19–May 1 1976, Camp Manila Makiling Girl Scout Camp, Los Banos, Laguna," April 1, 1976, Folder 681, Box 185, FPP.

8. "Guidelines for Projects Serving Indigenous Communities," May 30, 1980, Folder 8, Box IIIC2, CCF.

9. Subcommittee on Children and Youth, Senate Committee on Labor and Public Welfare, *Children's Charities, 1974, Part 4: Voluntary Foreign Aid Agencies Serving Children and Youth: Hearings before the Subcommittee on Children and Youth of the Committee on Labor and Public Welfare,* 93rd Cong., 2nd sess., October 10, 1974, 1134; Edmund Janss to Verent Mills, October 24, 1970, and Edmund Janss to Verent Mills, Re: "Korean Situation," June 9, 1972, Folder 2, Box IIIB9, CCF.

10. Senate Committee, *Voluntary Foreign Aid Agencies Serving Children and Youth,* 1134; Memorandum from David Herrell to Verent Mills, "Report on Visit to Buenos Aires Field Office," February 9, 1974, Folder 1, and Memorandum from David Herrell to Executive Staff, Subject: "Summary of Staff Review of Dr. David P. Beverly's Consultant's Report," October 9, 1978, Folder 10, Box IIIB14; Memorandum from David Herrell to Verent Mills, "Report on Visit to Philippines Field Office and Program, 8/24–31/74," September 4, 1974, Folder 9, Box IIIB11, CCF; John Anderson to George Ross, "Quarterly Report—Philippines, October–December 1977," Folder 69, Box 36, FPP.

11. Memorandum from David Herrell to Verent Mills and Executive Staff and Mrs. Maria Rosa M. de Cuenc, Subject: "Mexico CCF Program Review," December 14,

1977, Folder 7, Box IIIB13; Sarah Manning to David Herrell, Subject: "Manila Field Office Report—My Visit from October 15 through November 28," November 28, 1979, Folder 2, Box IIIB12; Memorandum from David Herrell to Executive Staff, Subject: "Report on Fortaleza Visit," July 2, 1981, Folder 6, Box IIIB14, CCF.

12. Sandy Sanders to George Ross, "Quarterly Report, Mali, July–September 1976," Folder 57, Box 35, and Asbjorn Osland to George Ross, "Quarterly Report—Upper Volta, July 15, 1977," Folder 73, Box 37, FPP; *Save the Children Federation Annual Report for the Year Ended June 30, 1972,* SCF.

13. George Ross to Members of the International Board, Re: "Benchmark Report on New Countries," December 16, 1974, Folder 29, Box 304, FPPv1; "Macro-Level Criteria for SCF/CDF Normally Favorable Criteria for Site-Selection in Overseas Programs," undated, Folder SCF Philosophy, Goals, Mission Statement, SCF; Belo Horizonte Field Office, "Annual Report May 1, 1972–June 1, 1973," Folder 1, Box IIIB3; Verent Mills to Rev. Hovhannes P. Aharonian, August 12, 1974, Folder 19, Box IIIB16; "Procedural Guidelines for Global Strategy," April 20, 1976, and "Rationale for CCF's Global Strategy," undated [1976], Folder 7, Box IIIB21, CCF; Norman Sibley, Unpublished History of the Save the Children Federation, 1986, chapter 5, SCF.

14. "Ethiopia Jails American for Leaflet Offense," *Modesto Bee,* May 29, 1977, D-10; Leslie Fox to George Ross, "Quarterly Report—Ethiopia, November–December 1976," Folder 25, Box 31, FPP; Henry D. Molumphy, *For Common Decency: The History of Foster Parents Plan, 1937–1983* (Warwick, RI: Foster Parents Plan International, 1984), 281.

15. "Self-Reliance through Sponsorship Assistance-IV," *Newsletter,* CCF New Delhi, January–March 1980, Folder 6, Box IIIB7, and Juana S. Silverio, "Visit with CCF Manila Field Office, 2 thru 14 January; 22–25 January thru 21 March," March 31, 1975, Folder 1, Box IIIB12, CCF; Lloyd J. Feinberg to George Ross, "Quarterly Report, Bali, April–June 1977," Folder 40, Box 33, FPP; Senate Committee, *Voluntary Foreign Aid Agencies Serving Children and Youth,* 1226; *Save the Children Federation Annual Report for the Year Ended 1978,* 11, SCF; John Anderson, "PLAN/ROK Rural Family Program—a Valid Approach for PLAN," undated [1974], Folder 69, Box 15, FPP; "Study of Non-residential CCF-Supported Projects."

16. Proceedings of 1977 Conference of Field Representatives, October 3–15, 1977, 5, Folder 6, Box IIIB17, CCF; Sibley, Unpublished History of the Save the Children Federation, chapter 5; Marion Fennelly Levy, *Bringing Women Into the Community Development Process: A Pragmatic Approach* (Westport, CT: Save the Children Federation, 1981), SCF.

17. William Pierre to Larry Miller, September 18, 1978, Folder ID Middle East Programs Gaza: Reports General, Box ISD 1978 Gaza, AFSC; David Herrell, "Hope and Survival: A Family Affair," *Childworld,* November–December 1979,

Folder 8, Box IIIB13, CCF; Levy, *Bringing Women into the Community Development Process,* 31–32.

18. George Ross to Frank Ryan, Re: "Case Loads . . . and Glenn Rogers (Yours of December 21, 1973 re Nevin Wiley's Final Report)," January 13, 1974, Folder 67, Box 15, and Asbjorn Osland to George Ross, "Quarterly Report—Upper Volta, April–June 1976," Folder 73, Box 37, FPP; David P. Beverly, CCF Field Office, Guatemala, "Report of a Program Review," August 1978, Folder 10, Box IIIB14, CCF; Frank Ryan to Gloria Matthews, "Quarterly Report, Indonesia, October–December 1974," Folder 43, Box 33, and John Anderson to George Ross, "Quarterly Report—Philippines, October–December 1977," Folder 69, Box 36, FPP.

19. Mildred Kane, "In-Service Week at UNWRA's Women's Training College at Tireh," August 21, 1972, Folder Middle East Program Gaza: Correspondence #d Letters from, Box ISD 1972 Social Assistance Administration, and "Learning to Play—Playing to Learn," Folder ID Middle East Programs Gaza: Publicity—Brochures, Flyers, Pamphlets, Box ISD 1978 Gaza, AFSC; Robert Sage to Gloria Matthews, "Quarterly Report—Philippines, April–June 1973," Folder 67, Box 36, and Frank Campbell to Gloria Matthews, "Quarterly Report—Vietnam, July–September 1974," Folder 79, Box 38, FPP.

20. Albrecht Hering to Gloria Matthews, "Quarterly Report, Colombia, April–June 1975," Folder 13, Box 29, and Donald B. Martin to George Ross, "Quarterly Report—Sudan, October–December 1977," Folder 37, Box 72, FPP; Memorandum from Sarah Manning to All Field Offices, Subject: "Revised Standards Recommended by the Participants in the Jalapa Conference," July 30, 1980, Folder 9, Box IIIC2, CCF.

21. Richard M. Cabrera to Gloria Matthews, "Quarterly Report, Ecuador, January–March 1974," Folder 20, Box 30, FPP; Maria Angela Gama, "The Institutionalized Child: Happiness above All Else," *CCF World News,* Summer 1977, Folder 11, Box IIIC4, CCF; Cancellation Memorandum of Foster Child, Teresa B., from Bolivia to the United States, June 1980, and Cancellation Memorandum of Foster Child, Juan P., from Bolivia to the United States, January 1980, Folder 2, Box 41, FPP; "Baiwadis and IYC," *Newsletter,* CCF New Delhi, January–March 1979, Folder 6, Box IIIB7, CCF; Evelyn Peters, "Field Trip to Iran, February 13–March 15, 1974," File 113, JDC 65/74.

22. Edmund Janss, *A Refresher Inservice Training Program for CCF Caseworkers,* January 1973, 63, Folder 1, Box IIIC2, CCF.

23. *CCF World News,* Winter 1977, 7–9, Folder 10, Box IIIC4, and Proceedings of 1977 Conference of Field Representatives, 90–92, Folder 6, Box IIIB17, ibid.

24. George Ross to Gloria Matthews, February 14, 1978, Folder 26, Box 303, FPPv1; "A Discussion of Sponsorship Issues," 1980, Folder Historical Overview 1932–1990s, SCF; Jerry Vink to George Ross, "Quarterly Report—Sierra Leone—Makeni, July–September 1978," Folder 71, Box 36, FPP; Proceedings of South Asia

and Africa Regional Conference held at Anantapur, A.P. and Bangalore, Karnataka, India, March 25–April 6, 1979, 34–42, Folder 7, Box IIB17, and New Delhi Staff, Bangalore Staff and Sarah Manning, "India Think Tank," December 1979, Folder 8, Box IIIC2, CCF.

25. Alton Gould to Ernesto Perez, May 27, 1974, Folder 3, Box IIIB12, CCF.

26. Ester Pangindian to Verent Mills, June 6, 1974, ibid.

27. Children's Garden Club to Christian Children's Fund, June 10, 1974, ibid. Emphasis in original.

28. Verent Mills to Anna Erik-Busser and Theo Erik, July 1, 1974, ibid.

29. "CCF to Intensify World Hunger Related Program," and Edward T. Hurley, "Famine Casts Its Grim Shadow in Wake of East African Drought," *CCF World News,* Summer 1976, Folder 10; Martin Shorter, "CCF's Hope for the Hungry: 'It Works!'" *CCF World News,* Summer 1977, Folder 11, Box IIIC4; Verent Mills, "Executive Report," *Childworld,* November 1978, Folder 12, Box IIIC4, CCF; "History of JDC, 1970: JDC Adapts to a Rapidly Changing World," available online at http://archives.jdc.org/history-of-jdc/history-1970.html, and "History of JDC," available online at www.jdc.org/about-jdc/history.html.

30. Vircher Floyd to George Ross, "Quarterly Report, Colombia, October–December 1976," Folder 14, Box 29, FPP; Molumphy, *For Common Decency,* 271.

31. Report to the President of the United States from the Task Force on International Development, "U.S. Foreign Assistance in the 1970s: A New Approach," March 4, 1970, Folder 3, Box 9; Frank W. Ryan, "Discussion on Program Developments," undated [1977], Folder 110, Box 20; Robert Walter to Gloria Matthews, "Quarterly Report, Brazil, July–September 1970," Folder 5, Box 28; Robert Sage to Gloria Matthews, "Quarterly Report—Philippines, April–June 1973," Folder 67, Box 36; Memorandum from Gloria Matthews to Members of the Board, Re: "Latin American Directors Conference," March 15, 1971, and "A Practical Guide to Combating Malnutrition in the Preschool Child," Folder 83, Box 16, FPP, emphasis in original. PLAN adapted these guidelines from *A Practical Guide to Combating Malnutrition in the Preschool Child: Nutritional Rehabilitation through Maternal Education,* Report of a Working Conference on Nutritional Rehabilitation or Mothercraft Centers, National Institute of Nutrition, Bogota, Colombia, March 1969, sponsored by Research Corporation (New York: Appleton-Century-Crofts, 1970). These lines were lifted directly from the text on page 1 and in the foreword. On the decline of psychoanalysis in the United States, see Nathan G. Hale Jr., *The Rise and Decline of Psychoanalysis in the United States: Freud and the Americans, 1917–1985* (New York: Oxford University Press, 1998). See also John Burnham, ed., *After Freud Left: A Century of Psychoanalysis in America* (Chicago: University of Chicago Press, 2012).

32. Memorandum from John G. Anderson to Gloria Matthews, Re: "Foster Parents Include Canadians, Australians, Europeans, Americans and Now (best of all) Koreans," January 15, 1972, Folder 533, Box 167, FPP; Larry E. Tise, *A Book*

about Children: The World of Christian Children's Fund, 1938–1991 (Falls Church, VA: Hartland Publishing for the Christian Children's Fund, 1993), 108–125.

33. Molumphy, *For Common Decency,* 318–319; Tise, *A Book about Children,* 108–125; Sibley, Unpublished History of the Save the Children Federation, chapter 5.

34. "Report about the Visit to CCF in Brazil," March 5, 1979, Folder 5, Box IIIB14, CCF.

35. William J. Kieffer to George Ross, "Quarterly Report, Indonesia, April–June 1977," Folder 45, Box 33, FPP; Molumphy, *For Common Decency,* 220; Tise, *A Book about Children,* 112.

36. "Mrs. Begin & Mrs. Sadat Get IYC Ideas," *IYC Newsletter,* United States Committee for UNICEF, no. 6 (June 1979): 3, Folder 12, Box IIIB21, CCF; "Message of the Secretary-General for the Mainichi Newspaper Readers," Items in International Year of the Child, Container S-0990-009: United Nations Emergency and Relief Operations, United Nations Archives, available online at http:// archives-trim.un.org/webdrawer/rec/425755/view/Items-in-International%20Year %20of%20the%20Child.PDF; Tara Ali Baig, "Lessons of IYC," *Newsletter,* CCF New Delhi, April–June 1980, Folder 6, Box IIIB7, CCF.

37. Estefania Aldaba-Lim to Shaheda Mahboob, June 1979, Items in International Year of the Child, Container S-0990-009: United Nations Emergency and Relief Operations, United Nations Archives, available online at http://archives-trim .un.org/webdrawer/rec/425755/view/Items-in-International%20Year%20of%20the %20Child.PDF.

EPILOGUE

1. Josephine Brayton, "Cruiser USS *Boston* Carries Foster Parents' Emissaries," *Christian Science Monitor,* August 15, 1962, 13. On the USS *Boston,* see "Boston VI" and "USS *Boston* (CAG-1, previously and later CA-69), 1943–1975," Department of the Navy—Naval Historical Center, Dictionary of American Naval Fighting Ships, available online at www.history.navy.mil/danfs/b8/boston-vi.htm and www.history.navy.mil/photos/sh-usn/usnsh-b/cag1.htm and www.history.navy .mil/photos/sh-usn/usnsh-b/ca69.htm.

2. Ruben Castaneda, "500 March in D.C. to Show Support for First World Summit on Children: Vigil One of 1,200 Worldwide to Focus on Troubles among Young," *Washington Post,* September 24, 1990, D3; "Candle Light Vigil to Aid Children," *Times of India,* September 22, 1990, 18.

3. Paul Lewis, "World's Leaders Gather at U.N. for Summit Meeting on Children," *New York Times,* September 30, 1990, 1.

4. Bruce Wydick, Paul Glewwe, and Laine Rutledge, "Does International Child Sponsorship Work? A Six-Country Study of Impacts on Adult Life Outcomes," *Journal of Political Economy* 121, no. 2 (April 2013): 393–436, quote at

428. The researchers studied the sponsorship program of Compassion International, a U.S.-based organization that in 2013 sponsored over a million children in twenty-six countries.

5. Nicholas D. Kristof, "A Poverty Solution That Starts with a Hug," *New York Times,* January 8, 2012, SR11; Nicholas D. Kristof, "Cuddle Your Kid!" *New York Times,* October 21, 2012, SR11; Nicholas D. Kristof, "Profiting from a Child's Illiteracy," *New York Times,* December 9, 2012, SR1.

Acknowledgments

It takes a village to raise a child—and it has also taken a village to write about it. I owe many people a debt of gratitude for their assistance and support as I worked on this project.

My first thanks go to Brian Distelberg, my editor at Harvard University Press, who offered fantastic suggestions for reorganizing and expanding on my work. Brian's knack for posing just the right questions helped me to push my work to the next level and made this book an infinitely better one.

I have been fortunate to have wonderful teachers and mentors. Joanne Meyerowitz's astute suggestions and insights were instrumental in shaping this project, and her encouragement sustained me throughout my time working on it. Jenifer Van Vleck's guidance challenged and expanded my understanding of the interplay between culture and U.S. foreign affairs, and her support has been invaluable. George Chauncey asked probing questions that pushed my work in new directions. I also thank John Gaddis, who offered useful advice during this book's formative stages.

As an undergraduate student at Barnard College, Rosalind Rosenberg sparked my interest in the study of women's and gender history and introduced me to the joys of historical research. I also thank Laura Roth, a teacher whose belief in me as a writer has resonated for over two decades.

I could not have written this book without the assistance of numerous archivists and librarians. Joan Losen, librarian extraordinaire, interrupted her retirement to return to ChildFund and assist me with my research. Joan not only helped me navigate CCF's records in Richmond but also put me in touch with numerous individuals who offered insights on the organization's past. I really cannot thank Joan enough. At the American Friends Service Committee in Philadelphia, Donald Davis guided me through the organization's extensive collections. At the American Jewish Joint Distribution Committee in New York, Misha Mitsel provided invaluable assistance. At Save the Children in Westport, Connecticut, Andrea Williamson-Hughes kindly provided me with access to the organization's historical documents. My gratitude also goes out to Sarina Wyant at the University of Rhode Island's Special Collections Library, to Fran O'Donnell at the Andover-Harvard Theological Library, and to Yevgeniya Gribov at the Girl Scout National Historic Preservation Center. The archivists and librarians at a number of other institutions—among them Yale, Columbia, Harvard, the National Archives, the New York Public Library, the YIVO Institute, the Schlesinger Library, and Stern College for Women's Hedi Steinberg Library—deserve a hearty thanks as well.

Several former and current voluntary agency officials patiently shared their stories and personal papers with me. I am immensely grateful to David Herrell, James Hostetler, Donna-Jean Rainville, Steven Stirling, and Helen Tieszen.

I have presented portions of this book at workshops and conferences, and I am most grateful for the useful feedback I have received. Particular thanks to Akira Iriye, Kathleen Jones, Jennifer Klein, Paul Kramer, and Naoko Shibusawa. Thank you, also, to the anonymous reviewers at Harvard University Press, *Diplomatic History,* and the *Journal of American History* who took the time to read my work and offer critical feedback.

I thank the Society for Historians of American Foreign Relations (SHAFR), the Mrs. Giles Whiting Foundation, and Yale University for providing funding that assisted with the research and writing of this book.

I have one of the greatest families imaginable. In a work that centers on child rearing, the first thanks must go to those who raised me: my parents, Nina and John Woldin, and my grandparents, Gloria and Daniel Fondiller. My mother and grandmother patiently read multiple drafts of this book and offered invaluable insight. My mother-in-law, sisters, and siblings-in-law have provided encouragement, laughs, and a place to stay on research trips (thank you, Hana and Simon Franzini!). My husband, Brett, is my greatest champion, as well as my best friend and travel partner. And my adorable pug, Charlie Winthrop, warmed my lap through countless days of writing. You all have my deepest love and gratitude.

Index